Winning at New Products

THIRD EDITION

Also by Robert G. Cooper

Product Leadership:
Creating and Launching Superior New Products

Portfolio Management for New Products
(coauthors, Scott J. Edgett and Elko J. Kleinschmidt)

Product Development for the Service Sector
(coauthor, Scott J. Edgett)

Winning at New Products

Accelerating the Process from Idea to Launch

THIRD EDITION

Robert G. Cooper

PERSEUS PUBLISHING
Cambridge, Massachusetts

A CIP record for this book is available from the Library of Congress.

Perseus Publishing is a member of the Perseus Books Group.
Find us on the World Wide Web at http://www.perseuspublishing.com

For more information on the concepts and tools introduced in this book, please visit the Product Development Institute Inc. at www.prod-dev.com

Perseus Publishing books are available at special discounts for bulk purchases in the U.S. by corporations, institutions, and other organizations. For more information, please contact the Special Markets Department at HarperCollins Publishers, 10 East 53rd Street, New York, NY 10022, or call 212-207-7528.

Text design by Jeff Williams
Set in 10.5 pt. New Calidonia

First printing, March 2001
8 9 10—03

*To the three ladies in my life: my wife, Linda,
and my two daughters, Barbara and Heather.*

Contents

Preface

There are two ways to win at new products. One is to do projects right—building in the voice of the customer, doing the necessary up-front homework, using cross-functional teams, and so on. The other way is by doing the right projects—namely, astute project selection and portfolio management. This book is about both routes: doing projects right and doing the right projects!

This book outlines a tried-and-proven process for bringing new products from idea to market launch successfully and quickly. This *Stage-Gate*™ process has been implemented in more than half the firms in the United States involved in product development, according to recent independent surveys. And it works!

This book also focuses on project selection and doing the right projects. This topic, more commonly called "portfolio management," has become an increasingly important one, as more and more senior managers recognize that their portfolios are somewhat lackluster—too many projects and too many low-value ones.

This is the third edition of *Winning at New Products*. The first edition was published in 1986, before we had even begun to use the term "stage-gate." That first book reported the results of a number of research studies that we had undertaken on new product success and failure, and it proposed the use of a systematic new product process for the first time. To my surprise, the book had a profound impact on the way many companies approached product development, and firms such as Procter & Gamble, DuPont, and Nortel Networks embraced the concept of my stage-and-gate process.

But those were the early days of management of the innovation process. More research was undertaken, including some studies that focused on these early adopters of the *Stage-Gate* process. More success factors were uncovered in our NewProd research series, and more experiences were gained with the use of these early *Stage-Gate* methods (I first used the term "*Stage-Gate*" in an article that appeared in the *Journal of Marketing Management* in 1988). And so the second edition was published in 1993. It went on to become the bible for those businesses trying to overhaul their new product process.

This current edition is more than a simple updating of the second edition, however. There is much that is new in it. Some years have passed since I wrote the last edition, and much more has been learned. Since then, our research team has actively probed three vital areas: portfolio management and project selection; benchmarking best practices at the business unit level; and partnering in product development. These new research avenues and their findings have been incorporated into the third edition. Additionally, we now have much more experience and insight into the installation of *Stage-Gate* methods in leading firms worldwide, and these new insights have been built into the current edition.

But there's another reason for this new book, and that is that the *Stage-Gate* process has changed. It has become a constantly evolving process. *Stage-Gate* is now faster and more streamlined. The third-generation *Stage-Gate* process has been implemented by several firms, and portfolio management has been integrated with gating methods. *Stage-Gate* approaches have even been extended to other types of projects, including technology developments.

Four major new themes are dominant in this book and distinguish it from the previous editions. The first is astute project selection. Portfolio management is fundamental to new product success. It is about resource allocation—which new product or development projects you'll invest in, and perhaps more important, which ones you won't. From portfolio management and project selection many other things flow. Picking the right projects and the right number of projects impacts new product success in so many ways: having a steady stream of major breakthroughs; resourcing projects for maximum speed to market; ensuring that new product initiatives support your business's strategy; and maximizing the return from your R&D dollars.

A second new theme is the impact of e-business on product development. Whether you are in the new economy or the old, e-business issues must dominate your thinking about product innovation. An obvious impact is on the market launch of your next new product—using e-channels to direct-sell your product and communicate its benefits to target users. A second impact is the preoccupation with speed and change; nothing is static, markets are fluid, and everything has speeded up. The demand for speed, coupled with fluid markets, requires even faster development cycles and more flexible processes. These e-business themes and impacts are woven throughout this new book.

A third new theme is the need for speed. As mentioned above, this has been partly brought about by the new economy, but it is also a major issue for competitors in traditional businesses. In this book much more attention is given to the topic of cycle time reduction and speeding up the innovation process. The third-generation version of *Stage-Gate*, with its six F's—fluidity, flexibility, fuzzy gates, facilitation, focus, and forever green—introduces new ways to accelerate the process. Also highlighted are fast tracking approaches, the role of cross-functional teams, resource balancing for maximum speed, and the use of overlapping stages.

A final new theme is the front end of the process. Currently, product development is plagued by too many small, mediocre projects and a real lack of major breakthroughs and big hits in most businesses. The problem is not the development process; the problem is at the very front end. In this book, I introduce a new stage called the Discovery Stage. Its purpose is to uncover great new product opportunities. Discovery includes a collection of best-practice techniques—from scenario generation to strategic approaches and the use of voice-of-customer insights—to generate your next breakthrough new product.

A number of people have provided insight, guidance, content, and encouragement in the writing of this new book. Professor Elko J. Kleinschmidt is both a longtime colleague and a friend. He and I have undertaken many research studies over the years, and many are reported in this current edition. For example, the recent benchmarking studies of industry best practices and the new research into portfolio management were conducted with Dr. Kleinschmidt. A second close colleague is Professor Scott Edgett. Dr. Edgett is now also recognized as a leading researcher in the field of innovation management and was a coresearcher and coauthor of the series of research studies, reports, and articles on the topic of portfolio management. He is also a director and the CEO of our consulting firm, Product Development Institute, Inc. (www.prod-dev.com).

Several other people merit special attention. Mr. Jens Arleth, of Copenhagen, Denmark, is managing director of U3-Innovation Management, a consulting firm that specializes in *Stage-Gate* and portfolio management. He has single-handedly introduced these concepts into Scandinavia, where they are now employed at leading firms such as Carlsberg and Lego; he is also the codeveloper of the *ProBE* diagnostic tool (Appendix A). Dr. Angelika Dreher, consultant at SIMMA & Partner in Austria, has taken up the challenge of implementing *Stage-Gate* in German-speaking countries and has provided insights that have found their way into this book. Finally, Mr. Hiroshi Morimoto, formerly of Toray Chemical in Japan, helped us to introduce *Stage-Gate* into Japan. We learned a lot about implementation in a new culture from Morimotosan. He has taken early retirement from Toray but continues to help Japanese companies learn about and implement *Stage-Gate* methods.

Direct assistance was provided by several people. Ms. Andrea Metrick, my research assistant, has been invaluable. She conducted the literature search that provided much of the background material and new research findings needed to update several sections of the book. She did a great job. I would also like to thank my editor, Mr. Nick Philipson of Perseus Books, who provided constant encouragement and adeptly steered the progress of this book from inception to launch. Finally, I thank Mr. Marco Pavia, Senior Project Editor, Perseus Publishing, for doing such a fine job moving the book through production.

—*Robert G. Cooper*

Winning at New Products

Winning Is Everything

In war, there is no second prize for the runner-up.
Omar Bradley, U.S. General

New Products Warfare

Corporations everywhere are engaged in a new products war. The battlefields are the marketplaces around the world for everything from consumer electronics to new engineering resins, from potato chips to electronic chips, from software to hardware, and now e-commerce products.

The combatants are the many companies who vie for a better position, a better share, or new territory on each battlefield or marketplace. They include the large and well-known combatants—the IBMs, GEs, and Intels, as well as an increasing number of foreign players—Siemens, Nokia, and Sony. More recent entrants have gained prominence in the past few decades because of new product victories: Apple with computers, Glaxo with pharmaceuticals, Nortel Networks with telecommunications and networking equipment.

The weapons are the thousands of new products developed every year in the hope of successfully invading chosen marketplaces. Sadly, most new product attempts fail. Increasingly, the quest is for weapon superiority—seeking product differentiation in order to secure a sustainable competitive advantage. Positioning plays a key role too, as combatants deploy their troops to secure an advantageous position on the battlefield. They use tactics such as frontal assaults, outflanking, and even attempts to reposition the enemy.

The combatants have their shock troops who lead the way into battle—the sales teams, advertising people, and promotional experts. The cost of these shock troops is enormous (more is spent *per day* on product innovation in the G5 countries than was spent in the entire Gulf War, beginning to end!). But the battle is often decided by the unsung heroes—the infantry—the many engineers and scientists in R&D labs and engineering departments around the world—less glamorous and less visible, but at the heart of almost every victory.

The combatants have their generals—the senior executives who plan and chart direction and attempt to define a business and technology strategy for their firm. The generals speak in terms of strategic thrusts, strategic arenas, and the need for strategic alignment. Sadly, many generals haven't really grasped the art of new product or technology strategy very well. So, as is often the case with ill-defined strategy, the battle is won or lost tactically in the trenches by the shock troops and infantry.

In the past few decades, the new products war has become a global confrontation. We've seen the advent of global product mandates. There are no longer national borders; domestic markets have become the enemy's international market.

As with recent wars, there are new ingredients for success: advanced technology, superior intelligence, and rapid mobility. Technology makes possible weapon superiority, and those combatants who have wisely invested in technology reap the benefits. Intelligence—market information and competitive intelligence—enables the most effective deployment of weapons and resources and often means the difference between winning and losing. And mobility or speed enables lightning strikes designed to seize windows of opportunity or to catch an enemy off guard.

As in any war, there are winners and losers. The winners are those firms, such as Pfizer, 3M, and Hewlett-Packard, who have an enviable stream of new product successes year after year. There are losers as well: General Motors, who for the past few decades failed to launch new products that captured the consumer's interest (whereas Chrysler, once on the verge of bankruptcy, glowed victoriously with winners such as the Sebring, Chrysler 300M, Concorde, and PT Cruiser and, in earlier years, the Neon and the famous Minivan). Sometimes the defeat is so great that the combatant collapses and simply disappears. Such was the fate of Coleco, the once-giant computer games producer that misfired badly with new products in the home computer market and failed to launch the new generation of computer games, while others, such as the makers of Nintendo and Sega, succeeded.

As the twenty-first century begins, this product innovation war looms as the most important and critical war the companies of the world have ever fought. Winning this war is everything: It is vital to success, prosperity, and even survival of these organizations. Losing the war, or failing to take an active part in it, spells disaster: The annals of business history are replete with examples of companies that simply disappeared because they failed to innovate, failed to keep their product portfolio current and competitive, and were surpassed by more innovative competitors. Forty percent of the major corporations that existed in America in 1975 no longer exist today![1]

Speed and Change

In winning at new products, as in warfare or war games, the goal is victory—a steady stream of profitable and successful new products. On this new product battlefield, the ability to mount lightning attacks—well-planned but swift strikes—is increasingly the key to success. The common denominators across businesses today are *speed* and *change*. Markets and technologies are changing more quickly than ever. Thus *speed is the pivotal competitive weapon:* The ability to accelerate product innovation—to get new products to market ahead of competition and within the window of opportunity—is more than ever central to success. And so this book is about more than success; it's about how to get successful products to market, but in record time.

There are major payoffs to speeding products to market:

- *Speed yields competitive advantage.* The ability to respond to customers' needs and changing markets faster than competition and to beat competitors to market with a new product often is the key to success. But too much haste may result in an ill-conceived product, which has no competitive advantage at all.
- *Speed yields higher profitability.* The revenue from the sale of the product is realized earlier (remember: money has a time value, and deferred revenues are worth less than revenues acquired sooner), and the revenues over the life of the product are higher, given a fixed window of opportunity and hence limited product life.
- *Speed means fewer surprises.* The ability to move quickly to market treats change as an opportunity rather than a threat. For example, the product as originally conceived is more likely to meet market requirements; and the short time frame reduces the odds that market conditions will dramatically change as development proceeds. Contrast this with a seven-year development effort incurred by some U.S. auto companies: market requirements, market conditions, and the competitive situation are likely to change considerably during the project.

So speed to market is a preoccupation throughout this book—but *not at the expense of managing the project properly.* I will never recommend cutting corners or executing in a sloppy fashion in order to save time—it just doesn't pay off. In short, speed is important, but it is only one component of our overarching goal of profitable new products.

Strategy and Tactics

Books about warfare or war games highlight both strategy and tactics. So does this book.

- *Strategy.* The art of determining strategic direction for product innovation is a question of identifying and selecting strategic arenas or battlefields. We will look at how to define the areas of strategic focus or strategic thrust, how to determine what markets, products, and technologies to invest in, and, in light of these decisions, how to devise the best attack plan.
- *Tactics.* Without tactics, strategy is nothing but words; tactics are the tools by which strategy is implemented. This too is a major theme of this book. Having decided on the strategic arena or battlefield, what does one do to win the battle? How does one plan and mount a swift attack? The tactical questions result in a game plan consisting of a set of moves or maneuvers designed to move a new product project from the discovery or idea stage to a successful launch—quickly and effectively.

Although strategy and tactics are military concepts, they are terms increasingly used in sports arenas. Indeed, a sports or game analogy is often the more appropriate one when developing new product strategy and tactics, so terms such as "game plan" and "new product game" are common in this book.

Logically, strategy precedes tactics. But in this book, I reverse the order of presentation: We first tackle the tactical issues—the challenges at the new product project level. And toward the end of the book, we focus on the "big picture"—a product innovation strategy or direction for the firm. Why this sequence? First, most problems lie within the tactical or implementation arena at the project level. Second, tactics, or the game plan, are more concrete, easier to visualize, and certainly more "actionable"—you can see improvements more quickly here.

New Products: The Key to Corporate Prosperity

New product development is one of the riskiest, yet most important, endeavors of the modern corporation. Certainly the risks are high. You and your colleagues have all seen large amounts of money spent on new product disasters in your own firm. But then, so too are the rewards.

New products currently account for *a staggering 33 percent of company sales,* on average[2]. That is, one-third of the revenues of corporations are coming from products they did not sell five years ago. In some dynamic industries, the figure is 100 percent! (Here, a "new product" is defined as new if it has been on the market for five years or less, and includes extensions and significant improvements). The message is simple: Either innovate or die!

Countless corporations owe their meteoric rise and current fortunes to new products. For example:

- JVC, hardly a household word several decades ago, pioneered the VHS format for home VCRs.

- Glaxo, once a mid-sized British pharmaceutical house, rose to number two in the pharmaceutical world on the coattails of a single anti-ulcer drug.
- The development of IBM's DOS operating system helped a start-up company unknown in 1982 to prosper. With one success under its belt, Microsoft struck again with various releases of its popular *Windows* operating system and became the corporate giant it is today. But it's hard to believe that it started with a new product in only 1982.

The Best Really Shine

The percentages cited above are only averages and thus understate the true potential. What CEO wants to be average! A handful of companies do far better than average, according to a recent best practices study,[3] and thus become the benchmark firms. These 22 percent of firms—the Best—are compared to the Rest.

- The Best have 49.2 percent of sales derived from new products (versus 25.2 percent for the Rest).
- The Best see 49.2 percent of profits derived from new products (versus 22.0 percent for the Rest).
- The Best start with 3.5 ideas to achieve one winner (versus 8.4 ideas for the Rest).

The point is that stellar performance is attainable in new products warfare. These firms model the way.

New products are also very profitable, on average. A study of 203 representative new product launches in U.S. businesses reveals that approximately two-thirds are considered to be commercial successes.[4] And these winning products do exceptionally well (see Figure 1.1):

- Return on investment is astounding: The average ROI for successful new products is 96.9 percent.
- New products pay off very quickly: The average payback period is 2.49 years.
- New products achieve an excellent market position: The average market share in their defined target markets is 47.3 percent.

Averages don't tell the entire truth because, as might be expected, a handful of very big winners skew the results. So consider the median values, which are almost as impressive:

- 50 percent of successful new products achieve a 33 percent ROI or better.

FIGURE 1.1   Profitability of New Products: Successes Versus Failures

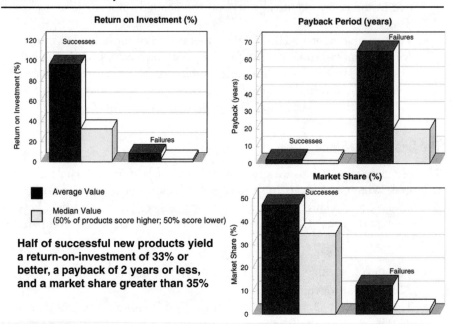

SOURCE: R. G. Cooper and E. J. Kleinschmidt, "Performance topologies of new product projects," *Industrial Marketing Management* 24 (1995): 439–456.

- Half of successful new products have a payback period of two years or less.
- Half of successful new products achieve a market share in excess of 35 percent.

Not all the new ventures studied are winners, however; these exceptional performance results must be tempered with the costs of failure. In the study, about one-third were unsuccessful launches. But even factoring in these losses, product development must be considered a very profitable undertaking overall.

Huge Amounts at Stake

Research and development expenditures are also impressive. In the United States, R&D expenditures in 1999 amounted to $236 billion for the year, or about 2.7 percent of the gross domestic product (GDP). In 1999 alone, U.S. R&D spending grew by a whopping 7 percent! Industrial R&D, now at $157 billion, grew even faster at 9%.[5]

Table 1.1 R&D Spending By Industry (US)

Industry	R&D Spending ($billions)	R&D as a Percent of Sales (%)	R&D as a Percent of Profits (%)
All industry	127.9	4.4	50.7
Aircraft & Aerospace	4.8	3.4	60.9
Automotive (motor vehicles)	18.0	4.2	49.8
Chemicals	5.9	5.8	52.5
Communications Equipment	10.6	12.1	415.4
Computers & Office Equipt.	18.6	6.7	105.4
Computer Services	8.9	11.8	65.6
Electronic Components	8.7	10.3	97.8
Electrical Equipment	3.4	2.1	19.6
Food	1.0	0.7	6.7
Furniture & Wood Products	0.6	1.7	29.0
Glass, Stone & Clay Products	0.5	2.2	50.7
Instruments	7.9	6.8	73.7
Machinery (non-electrical)	5.4	3.2	49.7
Metal Products (fabricated)	0.8	1.6	19.1
Metals – Primary	0.5	0.8	13.5
Paper	1.7	2.0	23.2
Petroleum & Coal	1.8	0.6	12.9
Pharmaceutical	20.3	12.3	56.1
Phone & Telecommunications Services	1.7	2.0	15.4
Polymers & Rubber	0.7	2.4	35.0
Textiles	0.09	1.8	27.7

Used with permission: *Industrial Research and Development Facts with the 1998 Industrial R&D Scorecard*, Industrial Research Institute, Washington, DC. 1999.

Certain industries, noted for their growth and profitability in recent decades, spend heavily on R&D. For example, the pharmaceutical industry spends 12.3 percent of revenues on R&D; communications equipment is next, averaging 12.1 percent of sales on R&D; Computer services and electronic components are close behind at 11.8 percent and 10.3 percent of sales respectively (see Table 1.1 for an industry breakdown). Incredibly, some industries spend more on R&D than the entire annual profit for that industry, for example, communications equipment and computers and office equipment.

Impact on Investment Value

Why is product innovation so central to corporate success? Why is the world speeding up so much when it comes to new products? One factor is the financial market, which seems to dominate corporate behavior so much these days. An annual *Fortune* survey rates top U.S. corporations on a number of criteria, including "value as a long-term investment." Using data supplied by *Fortune,* I studied various predictors of investment value. The results were provocative. *The single strongest predictor of investment value is "degree of innovativeness of the company."*[6] The conclusion is that not only is product innovation important to remain competitive in the firm's marketplace, but it also seems to be important to financial markets—in determining the worth or value of the company as a long-term investment—and hence to the cost of capital to the firm.

The same annual *Fortune* survey lists the top ten most admired companies in America. They are an enviable group: GE, Coca Cola, Microsoft, Dell Computer, Intel, and Merck, to name a few. Their average return on investment is a staggering 45.4 percent over the five years 1993–1998, almost double the average for the S&P 500 firms.[7] Coincidentally, all of the most admired companies are at or near the top of their industry in terms of *innovativeness*. Another *Fortune* article, "Secrets of the Most Admired Companies," explored what distinguishes these most admired companies. Their secret: New ideas and new products are the key. These admired businesses all possess a common quality: "That ingredient is innovation, and all the top companies embrace it passionately."[8]

Drivers of Innovation

New products are clearly the key to corporate prosperity. They drive corporate revenues, market shares, bottom lines, and even share prices. But why is the innovation game speeding up so much, and why is so much more emphasis being placed on product innovation track records? Here are four innovation drivers identified by senior executives.

- *Technology advances.* The world's base of technology and know-how increases at an exponential rate, making possible solutions and products not even dreamed of a decade or so ago. What was science fiction in *Star Trek* in the 1960s—for example, hand-held computers or flip-top portable communicators—is suddenly a technological reality today.
- *Changing customer needs.* Marketplaces are also in turmoil, with market needs and wants and customer preferences changing regularly. The company that seemed omnipotent only a few years ago suddenly falls from favor with the consumer. And witness the flurry of mergers and acquisitions in the communications, entertainment, and Internet sectors in recent years, as major corporations scramble to keep pace with fluid marketplaces. In other markets, customers have come to expect new products with significant improvements. Consumers have become like kids in a candy shop—we see what is possible, and we want it.
- *Shortening product life cycles.* One result of the increasing pace of technological change coupled with changing market demands has been shorter product life cycles. A study done by A. D. Little shows that product life cycles have been cut by a factor of about four over the past fifty years (see Figure 1.2).[9] Your new product no longer has a life of five to ten years; within a few years, sometimes even months, it is superseded by a competitive entry, rendering yours obsolete and necessitating a new product. This has placed a great deal of pressure on businesses. For example, in one leading electronics firm in the United States, as product version number 1 is hitting the market, its replacement, product

version 2, is already in the development phase, and product version 3 is waiting in the wings for a go-to-development decision.

- *Increased world competition.* We now have access to foreign markets like never before, but at the same time, our domestic market has become someone else's international market. This globalization of markets has created significant opportunities for the product innovator: the world product targeted at global markets. It has also intensified competition in every domestic market. Both factors have sped up the pace of product innovation.

A quick review of all four drivers of product innovation reveals that none are likely to disappear in the next decade or two. Technology advances will continue to occur; so will changes in market needs and demands; world trade and globalization of markets marches on; and competition will drive life cycles to become even shorter. Product innovation will be even more critical to corporate prosperity in the years ahead than it has been in the recent past.

☞ **Suggestion**: If you haven't already done so, conduct a review of the strategic role—past, present, and future—of new products in your company. Key questions include:

- What is your historical level of R&D spending as a percentage of sales? Has it been going up or down? How does it compare to your competitors' or industry level (see Table 1.1)? Why is it higher or lower?
- What proportion of your current sales comes from new products introduced by you in the past five years? What is the projection or objective for the future? What will your portfolio of products look like in five years?
- Where will your sales growth come from? What proportion is from new products? From new markets? From growth in existing markets? Or from increased market share?
- Are the answers to the three questions above consistent with each other? Are you investing enough in R&D and new products to yield the results that you want?

In addressing the first question above, some managers ask, *"what is the appropriate level of R&D or technology spending* for my firm?" There are no easy answers here. Remember that technology spending is by no means the sole determinant of new product performance or even sales generated by new products. There are many factors that make a new product effort a success. Indeed, using R&D spending as a measure of new product development activities may be misleading. R&D spending typically accounts for less than 40 percent of a firm's total expenditure for product innovation.

FIGURE 1.2   Decreasing Product Life Cycles

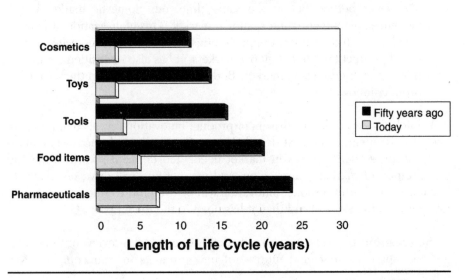

The product life cycle has shrunk by an average of 400% over the last 50 years!

SOURCE: A. D. Little, as cited in C. F. von Braun, *The Innovation War* (Upper Saddle River, N.J.: Prentice Hall PTR, 1997).

More food for thought: In one of our studies on innovation strategies, R&D spending as a percentage of company sales was indeed found to be the strongest predictor of the company's new product sales (also expressed as a percentage of company sales). This comes as no surprise. *But the level of R&D spending explained only 16 percent of this revenue performance!* Many other factors also determined performance. Finally, different strategies or means of introducing new products may not require similar levels of R&D spending. Such low-R&D approaches include acquiring technology from others, purchasing components and materials, and licensing products and technologies.

High Odds of Failure

New products are critical to long-term success. They keep your current product portfolio competitive and healthy and, in many firms, provide you with long-term and sustainable competitive advantage. The dilemma is that product innovation is a crapshoot: Boasting a steady stream of successful new products is no small feat.

The hard realities are that the great majority of new products never make it to market. And those that do face a failure rate somewhere in the order of 25 to 45 percent. For example, the Product Development and Management

Association (PDMA) claims that new products currently have a success rate of only 59 percent at launch, up only 1 percent since 1990.[10] These success rate figures vary from study to study, however, depending on the industry and on how one defines a "new product" and a "failure." Some sources cite the failure rate at launch to be as high as 90 percent. But these figures tend to be unsubstantiated and are likely wildly overstated. According to Crawford, who has undertaken perhaps the most thorough review of these often-quoted figures, the true failure rate is about 35 percent. Our own studies concur: In a review of the new product performances of 122 industrial product firms, the average success rate of fully developed products is 67 percent. But averages often fail to tell the whole story; this success rate varied from a low of zero percent to a high of 100 percent, depending on the firm!

Regardless of whether the success rate is 55 or 65 percent, the odds of a misfire are still substantial. Worse, the figures cited above don't include the majority of new product projects that are killed along the way and long before launch, yet involved considerable expenditures of time and money.

The attrition curve of new products tells the whole story. One study reveals that *for every seven new product ideas, about 4 enter development, 1.5 are launched, and only 1 succeeds.*[11] Another investigation paints an even more dismal picture: For every 11 new product ideas, 3 enter the development phase, 1.3 are launched, and only 1 is a commercial success in the marketplace (see Figure 1.3).[12] The most recent PDMA survey reveals a seven-to-one ratio.[13] The bad news continues. An estimated 46 percent of all the resources allocated to product development and commercialization by U.S. firms are spent on products that are canceled or fail to yield an adequate financial return.[14] This is an astounding statistic when one considers the magnitude of human and financial resources devoted to new products. But a minority of firms (30 percent) do achieve an enviable 80 percent success rate; that is, 80 percent of the resources they spend on innovation go to new product winners. These few firms show that it is possible to outperform the average, and by a considerable margin.

☞ **Suggestion:** How well is your company faring in the new product game? Do you even know? (Most companies cannot provide statistics on success, fail and kill rates, or on resources spent on winners versus losers.)

Keep score in the new product game. Key statistics to track include the following:

- success versus failure rates at launch
- attrition rates: what percent of projects continue at each stage of the process?
- proportion of resources devoted to winners versus losers versus killed projects

FIGURE 1.3   The Attrition Rate of New-Product Projects

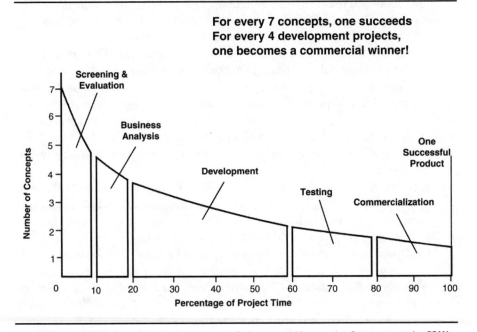

SOURCE: A. L. Page, "PDMA new product development survey: Performance and best practices," paper presented at PDMA Conference, Chicago, Nov. 13, 1991.

Beating the Odds

In many ways, new products are much like a steeplechase horse race: Relatively few new product projects succeed. About ten horses leave the starting gate and must clear various hurdles, hedges, or jumps along the way. And only one horse in ten crosses the finish line as the winner. The racetrack gambler tries to pick the one winning horse but, more often than not, places his or her bet on the wrong one.

But new product management is even more risky than a horse race. True, the odds of picking a winner at the outset are somewhere in the order of ten to one. But the size of the bets is considerably greater—often in the millions of dollars. And unlike the gambler, the new product manager cannot leave the game—he or she must go on placing the bets, year after year, if the company is to succeed. Once into the game, it is difficult to quit!

Faced with these kinds of odds, why would anyone want to play the new product game? Don't forget that there are some important differences between a horse race and new products. First, the payoff from a winning new product can be enormous—enough to more than cover all your losses. Second, and perhaps more subtle, the way the bets are placed is different. At a racetrack, all bets must be placed before the race begins. But in new products, bets are placed as the race proceeds. Imagine the horse race where bets could be placed after the horses clear each hedge or gate! Suddenly the odds are changed dramatically in favor of the shrewd gambler.

The new products race, then, is really more like a game of five-card stud poker than a horse race. In five-card stud, after each card is dealt, the players place their bets. Toward the end of each hand, the outcome—who will be the winner—becomes clearer; at the same time, the betting and the amounts at stake rise exponentially.

Many an amateur poker player has sat down with a professional, assuming that he had equal odds of winning. True, each player has the same odds of being dealt a winning hand; the cards are dealt randomly. But over the long term, the professional will always win—not because she gets better hands, but because of how she bets, knowing when to bet high, when to bet low, and when to fold and walk away. The trick is in the betting!

Unfortunately, too many companies play the new products game like the amateur poker player. They start with an equal chance of winning. But because they don't count cards (that is, don't gather much information about the project, but operate on hunch and speculation instead) and lack solid betting criteria (that is, have poor or nonexistent decision rules for making go/kill decisions), they lose to the professional. And so the odds of losing—especially for the amateur player—are exceptionally high.

The first point of these analogies is to show that new products is a very complex game. It entails high risks, low odds of picking a winner, large amounts at stake, and an incremental betting process, with additional and increasing bets placed as the race proceeds. The second point is that effective betting is one key to winning. We all have the same odds of being dealt a good hand, but it's how we bet—the information we gather and the betting rules or criteria we use—that makes the difference between winning and losing.

What's New About a New Product?

Serious players keep score in the new product game. But in order to keep score, one must have a definition of what counts as a new product. One of the problems with some of the scores cited above is that they include *different types* of new products. For example, the attrition rates for truly innovative new products are much higher than for extensions and modifications of existing company products.

Defining Newness

There are many different types of *new products*. "Newness" can be defined in two senses:

- new to the company, in the sense that the firm has never made or sold this type of product before, but other firms might have
- new to the market or "innovative"; the product is the first of its kind on the market

Categories of New Products

On the two-dimensional map shown in Figure 1.4, six different types or classes of new products are identified.[15]

1. *New-to-the-world products.* These new products are the first of their kind and create an entirely new market. This category represents only 10 percent of all new products. Well-known examples include the Sony Walkman, the first home compact disc player, 3M's Post-It Notes, and more recently the Palm Pilot.
2. *New product lines.* These products, although not new to the market-place, nonetheless are quite new to the particular firm. They allow a company to enter an established market for the first time. For example, Canon was not the first to launch an office version of a laser printer; Hewlett-Packard was, with its LaserJet. When Canon did introduce its version, it was clearly not an innovation, but it did represent a new product line for Canon, with all the investment that entailed. About 20 percent of all new products fit into this category.
3. *Additions to existing product lines.* These are new items to the firm, but they fit within an existing product line that the firm already produces. They may also represent a fairly new product to the marketplace. An example would be Hewlett-Packard's introduction of its LaserJet 7P, a smaller and considerably less expensive version of its laser printers that is suitable for home computers. The printer is a new item within the LaserJet line, and its small size and low cost made it somewhat novel or "new to the market." Such new items are one of the largest categories of new product—about 26 percent of all new product launches.
4. *Improvements and revisions to existing products.* These "not-so-new" products are essentially replacements of existing products in a firm's product line. They offer improved performance or greater perceived value over the "old" product. These "new and improved" products make up 26 percent of new product launches. For example, Kennametal is a world leader in the supply of industrial consumable tools, such as drill bits. Many product development efforts at Kennametal amount to making relatively small changes or improvements to their existing tools that respond to a changing customer requirement or a competitive threat.
5. *Repositionings.* These are essentially new applications for existing products and often involve retargeting an old product to a new market segment or for a different application. For years, aspirin (or ASA, as it is

known in some countries) was the standard headache and fever reliever. Superseded by newer, safer compounds, ASA was in trouble. But new medical evidence suggested that aspirin had other benefits. Now aspirin is positioned not as a headache reliever but as a preventer of blood clots, strokes, and heart attacks. Repositionings account for about 7 percent of all new products.

6. *Cost reductions.* These are the least "new" of all new product categories. They are new products designed to replace existing products in the line, but they yield similar benefits and performance at lower cost. From a marketing standpoint, they are not new products; but from a design and production viewpoint, they could represent significant change to the firm. They represent 11 percent of all new product launches.

Most firms feature a *mixed portfolio* of new products. The two most popular categories, additions to the line and product improvements or revisions, are common to almost all firms.[16] By contrast, the "step-out" new-to-the-world products and the new-to-the-firm product lines constitute only 30 percent of all new product launches, but they represent 60 percent of the products viewed as "most successful."

Sadly, many firms stay clear of these two more innovative categories: 50 percent of firms introduce no new-to-the-world products, and another 25 percent develop no new product lines. This aversion to "step-out" and higher-risk products varies somewhat by industry, with higher technology industries launching proportionately more products that are innovative.

More recent data from industrial product firms in moderate-to-high technology businesses are shown in Figure 1.5 and compared to industry at large (PDMA survey). Note the importance of the two most innovative product categories to the moderate-to-high technology industries; they constitute a total of 58 percent of new products launched, compared to 30 percent in all industry.[17]

☞ **Suggestion:** Review the new products that your business has introduced in the past five years. Make a complete list. Then categorize them according to the six types in Figure 1.4. Questions to consider include the following:

1. What is the split of projects by type (draw a percent breakdown pie chart, as in Figure 1.5)? Does it differ much from the all-industry averages shown in Figure 1.5? Why?
2. What is the breakdown by project type in terms of total resources spent; that is, to which types of projects has your money and effort been devoted?
3. What is the breakdown by sales and profits; that is, which types of products or projects are generating the revenues and profits? What is the success rate by type?

FIGURE 1.4   Categories of New Products

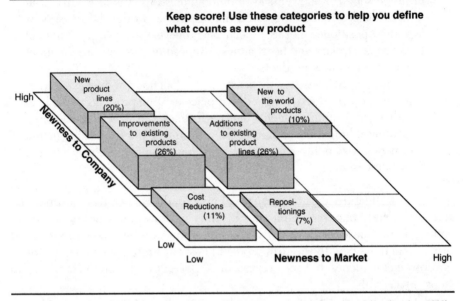

SOURCE: Booz-Allen & Hamilton, *New Product Management for the 1980s* (New York: Booz-Allen & Hamilton, Inc., 1982).

4. Is your current breakdown or split the desirable one? What should be the split of new products by type? (You might use Figure 1.5 as the benchmark.)

Performance and Innovativeness

One of the problems with reading too much into the new product success and performance data cited above or found in your own firm is that *performance depends to a large extent on the types of products and projects undertaken.* As you reviewed your own new product performance by type, were the innovative ones more successful, or was it better to avoid breaking new ground? Two conflicting schools of thought might have emerged. The first is that innovative new products are more successful: They provide more opportunities for sustainable competitive advantage and often open up more significant market opportunities. Although the most innovative categories—new-to-the-world and new product lines—represent only 30 percent of the launches, they account for 60 percent of the most successful products![18]

The other school of thought is the "play it safe" school. The product innovator, because he or she is first into a market, often makes many mistakes. The number two entrant can learn from these mistakes and succeed where the pio-

FIGURE 1.5   How Innovative Are New Product Launches?

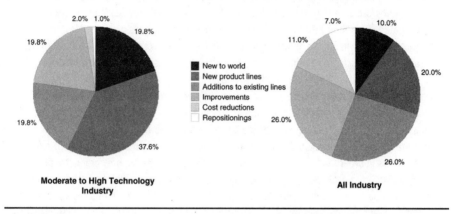

Percentages are "percentages of products launched" - broken down by product type

**In higher tech industries, almost 20% of launches are "new to world" products
For all industry, the figure is only 10% of launches**

Legend:
- New to world
- New product lines
- Additions to existing lines
- Improvements
- Cost reductions
- Repositionings

Moderate to High Technology Industry values: 2.0%, 1.0%, 19.8%, 19.8%, 19.8%, 37.6%

All Industry values: 7.0%, 10.0%, 11.0%, 20.0%, 26.0%, 26.0%

SOURCE: Data from Booz-Allen & Hamilton, *New Product Management for the 1980s* (New York: Booz-Allen & Hamilton, Inc., 1982), and E. J. Kleinschmidt and R. G. Cooper, "The impact of product innovativeness on performance," *Journal of Product Innovation Management* 8 (1991): 240–251.

neer failed. In addition, less innovative products can usually be developed and launched a little faster because the pioneering products show the way.

So what types of new products, in terms of innovativeness, are the most successful? Our own research has pursued this theme of innovativeness and its impact on success rates.[19] To simplify things, consider just three classes of new products in terms of innovativeness:

- *Highly innovative products,* namely, new-to-the-world products and innovative new product lines to the company (these represent 30 percent of the cases we studied).
- *Moderately innovative products,* consisting of new lines to the firm, with products that are not as innovative (that is, not new to the market), and new items in existing product lines for the firm (47 percent of cases).
- *Low innovativeness products,* consisting of all others: modifications to existing products; redesigned products to achieve cost reductions; and repositionings (23 percent of cases).

The impact of product innovativeness on new product success is not nearly as straightforward as expected; failure rates do not necessarily steadily increase (or steadily decrease) with increasing innovativeness. Figure 1.6 shows the results: a U-shaped relationship between product innovativeness and three key meas-

---

FACT-BASED MANAGEMENT: THE RESEARCH UNDERLYING THE BOOK

Military principles are based on facts—facts gathered by military historians and strategists who have studied countless wars and battles since the beginning of time. This book and its prescriptions are also very much fact-based. Since the 1970s, my colleagues and I have investigated more than 2000 new product launches and hundreds of companies. The goal: to uncover what winners do differently from losers, what the common denominators of successful new products and businesses are, and what distinguishes the top performers.

NewProd Studies: Some of our studies have focused on *individual new product projects—more than* 2000 projects, some successes and some failures. Multiple gauges of product performance—profitability, market share, meeting objectives, and so on—were measured. Similarly, characteristics of the project—from the nature of the market to how well the project team executed key activities—were captured. These were then correlated with success in order to identify those factors that distinguish the big new product winners.[20]

Benchmarking Studies: Other studies looked at the business unit or company, rather than individual projects, and asked the broader question, Why are some businesses so much better at new products than others? In the most recent study, business units' new product performances were gauged on ten metrics (for example, percentage of sales from new products, and return on investment for R&D spending), which were then reduced to two key dimensions: *profitability* and *impact.* The drivers of business units' new product performance were then identified.[21]

The success factors uncovered at the project level are somewhat different from those found at the business-unit level. But in both types of studies the fundamental question was the same: What makes a winner?

---

ures of performance—success rate, return on investment (ROI), and market share. Here, success rates, ROIs, and market shares for each of the three innovation categories are shown as horizontal bars.

The results are clear: Innovative products do well; so do non-innovative ones. *The problem lies within the huge middle* category—moderately innovative products—whose performance lags far behind the other two groups.

The success rate (the percentage of products meeting the firms' financial criteria) is greatest for highly innovative products: 78 percent are successful. Success rates are almost as high for low innovativeness products as well (68 percent). But the success rate drops to 51 percent for the middle group—the moderately innovative products.

A similar U–shaped pattern is also evident for ROI—this time, highest for low innovativeness products (124 percent), followed by highly innovative products (75 percent), but dropping to a mean ROI of 31 percent for moderately innovative products.[22]

FIGURE 1.6   Impact of Product Innovativeness on Performance Results

Note how well highly innovative products do.   Non-innovative products - extensions, modifications, improvements - also do very well. The worst performers are "middle of the road" products - the moderately innovative ones

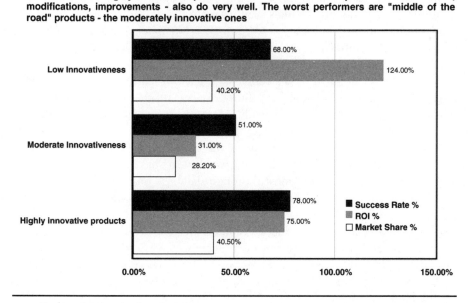

SOURCE: Data from E. J. Kleinschmidt and R. G. Cooper, "The impact of product innovativeness on performance," *Journal of Product Innovation Management* 8 (1991): 240–251.

New product performance can be assessed in other ways as well: for example, obtaining market share, meeting sales and profit objectives, and opening new windows of opportunities for the business. These alternative gauges of performance also show similar and striking U-shaped relationships with innovativeness. This curved pattern is true across the board and not just for one or a few measures of performance.

The message is this: First, *success rates and new product performance do depend on the product type or newness of the product.* So when you keep score, be sure to develop different innovativeness categories of new products. Second, the fact that highly innovative products do so well is a provocative finding; it helps to dispel some myths about what types of projects are more successful and should encourage management to rethink their "short pass" or short-term strategy.

Don't simply make the assumption that highly innovative products are too risky for your company and that they have a negative performance. On average, they do very well! Perhaps it's time to have a hard look again at tackling more innovative projects.

An Introduction to the Game

In this chapter, you have seen that winning at new products plays a critical role in determining company fortunes. You have also witnessed some of the risks in product innovation; developing new products is like a horse race with high odds of failure and significant rates of attrition. The key is on how you place your bets! Keeping score is an important facet of the game, so I have laid out a scheme to help categorize new products so that the scores are more comparable. And finally, you saw some par values or norms for these scores for different types of new products—from the truly innovative to the not-so-new—and witnessed the debunking of some old myths.

In the next chapter, we take a look at the hard evidence. Our research into new product practices over the past twenty-five years has been widely published and has yielded perhaps the most thorough database on new product winners and losers—over 2,000 launches in about 450 companies in Europe and North America. And from observing these many successes and failures, we learn the keys to winning at new products. Additionally our benchmarking studies—where we looked at the best-performing businesses versus the rest—yield many insights into best practices and key success drivers. These investigations—both at the project level and also at the business unit level—provide the foundation for the book's findings.

We begin our voyage in Chapter 2 with a look at the reasons why new products fail, and what goes wrong with product innovation. This is perhaps a negative way to start, but it's the right place; the hope is that we can learn from our past mistakes—that we are not doomed to repeat the same mistakes year after year.

Chapter 3 explores new product successes and pinpoints what separates the winners from the losers. Here we see that there are clear patterns to success and that new product success is both predictable and controllable. Chapter 4 integrates what we have learned into fifteen key lessons for new product success—the *critical success factors,* which we then build into our game plan for winning.

Chapters 5 through 10 deal with tactics or process: the development and implementation of a *Stage-Gate*™ new product process for driving new products to market successfully and quickly.° The newest version of the *Stage-Gate* process—a beginning-to-end product innovation road map—is introduced in Chapter 5, where the critical success factors and best practices are translated into an operational blueprint for action. Chapter 6 deals with Discovery—coming up with breakthrough new product ideas. Chapter 7 lowers the microscope on the "fuzzy front end"—the up-front stages of the process, where success or failure is largely decided. Chapter 8 deals with portfolio management and picking the winners; it focuses on the gates or decision points in the process, where we look at ways to improve your "betting practices"—improving your odds of picking the right projects and also the right balance of projects.

°*Stage-Gate*™ is a trademark of RG Cooper & Associates Consultants, Inc., a member firm of the Product Development Institute, Inc.

Chapters 9 and 10 follow the process as we move through development, testing, and market roll-out.

Chapter 11 looks at implementation issues. First we consider results—specifically, what results businesses achieve that have implemented *Stage-Gate*™ new product processes. Most important, you gain insights into how to handle the difficult job of the design and implementation of *Stage-Gate* within your business.

The final chapter deals with strategy. We stand back and look at how the tactics or new product process fits into the larger picture. This is the master strategy for new products. In which arenas should you play the game? How should you enter each? How should you allocate your resources? What strategic or key initiatives should you undertake?

So read on! First, discover the critical success factors in the next few chapters, and then explore how they can and should be built into your modus operandi in your business so that you, too, can be a big winner at new products.

New Products: Problems and Pitfalls

Those that cannot remember the past are condemned to repeat it.
—George Santayano, American philosopher

We have forty million reasons for failure but not a single excuse.
—Rudyard Kipling, *The Lesson*

Skeletons in Our Closets

Most new product projects fail! An estimated 46 percent of the resources that firms spend on the conception, development, and launch of new products are spent on products that either fail commercially in the marketplace or never make it to market. And for every four projects that enter development, only one becomes a commercial success. Even at launch—after all the tests are complete and plans of action scrutinized—one project in three fails commercially.[1]

Why the high failure rates? A good place to begin our understanding of the keys to success is with analysis of our past failures. This might sound like a negative beginning point, but consider this: One of the inherent weaknesses in books and articles that provide solutions and prescriptions to managers is that they tend to be based on practices identified from observing successful companies. The original *Search of Excellence* and subsequent books by these and other authors follow this pattern. But the approach is flawed—which may explain why many of those so-called excellent companies weren't doing so well several years later.

Consider a fictitious illustration:

Imagine that you and I embark on an investigation of California high-tech companies to study their "secrets to success." We arrange interviews with senior managers in a dozen highly successful firms in Palo Alto. Our approach is to observe what practices these companies share or have in common. When we identify these, we'll then conclude that these are the keys to success.

Sounds like a reasonable approach? Let's continue:

On our first morning visit to a high-tech firm, we note that employees are wearing extremely casual clothes and no shoes—sandals on their feet! We take note of this. Same thing at companies number 2 and 3—a lot of casual clothes and sandals—and so on through the dozen firms.

On our return home, we conclude that the practice that these successful California firms had in common was their dress code. Since this was the common factor, it must be the secret to success. And we publish a best-selling book on dressing for success!

Nonsense, you say, and you're right! The weakness of this type of investigation is that we only looked at one side of the coin—only at successful companies. Had we looked at an equal number of unsuccessful companies in Palo Alto, we might have discovered that their employees also wore casual clothes and sandals. So what have we proven? Only that people on the West Coast like to dress more casually—but this likely has nothing to do with success.

The point is that we have to look at both successful case studies and unsuccessful ones in order to uncover what makes a winner. If we look only at winners, we may end up with some very naive conclusions, as we did with the invented example above.

Analyzing Failure

Let's begin with new product failures. Often a postmortem on new product failures will identify causes of failure, which can then lead to prescriptions for what to avoid. In this way, management can then take corrective action to avoid these pitfalls in the future.

Reasons for New Product Failure

The Conference Board has undertaken perhaps the most comprehensive analysis of new product failures over the past few decades.[2] The failure reasons remain fairly constant over the years—they play like a broken record (see Figure 2.1):

1. *Poor Marketing Research.* Insufficient or faulty marketing research is what managers cite most frequently as the number one cause of new product failure: "A lack of thoroughness in identifying real needs in the marketplace, or in spotting early signs of competitors girding up to take the offensive, is often the finding of a new product postmortem."

The Conference Board report continues: Managers confessed to a serious misreading of customer needs, too little field testing or overly optimistic forecasts of market need and acceptance. Management often fell into the trap described by an executive in one industrial firm: "Simply stated, we decided what our marketplace wanted in this new product without really asking that market what its priorities were."

Another common mistake is to assume that because a product may be adequate in the eyes of the designers or R&D department, the customers will see it the same way. As one manager interviewed in the study put it, "The very important lesson we learned was to determine the requirements of the marketplace through market surveys, and then to interpret that need to our engineers for product development."

2. *Technical Problems.* The second most common cause of new product failure is technical problems in design and production. Difficulties in trying to convert from laboratory or pilot-plant scale to full-scale production are common, while manufacturing glitches and product quality problems frequently arise. In many cases, it is a failure to conduct the earlier phases more thoroughly—technical research, design, engineering—before moving to the commercialization phase. Other times, the technical problems stem from a lack of understanding of the customer's requirements—for example, trying to develop the "perfect product"— one that is simply overengineered (and too costly) compared to what the customer wanted.

3. *Insufficient Marketing Effort.* Here management is guilty of "assuming that the product would sell itself" and simply failed to back the product's launch with sufficient marketing, selling, and promotional resources. Recommendation: Before a project even enters the Development stage, there should be a marketing plan on the table, complete with earmarked resources.

4. *Bad Timing.* Timing issues surface as a key reason for failure, not only in these studies but in countless others. The penalties of moving too slowly, or too fast, stem not only from technical problems but also from flawed planning, organization, or control. Numerous new product failures result from not moving quickly enough, given a limited window of opportunity. In some cases, there is a shift in customer preferences during the development cycle; in others, the competitor moves more quickly with a new product and seizes the market opportunity.

The need to move quickly to market has created yet another set of timing problems: rushing a product through the process and cutting corners to do so. Shortcuts are taken with the best intentions but too often result in disaster. Key steps and stages are often skipped (or handled too quickly), such as market studies, prototype testing, and field trials. This inevitably leads to serious quality

FIGURE 2.1   Main Causes of New Product Failure

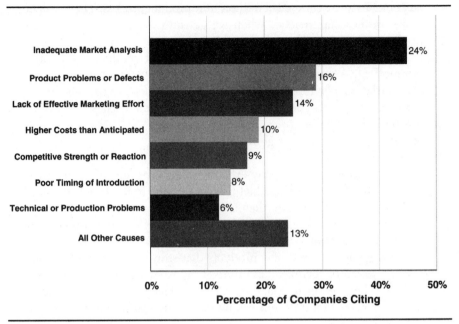

SOURCE: See endnote 3, chapter 2.

problems, the need for product redesign once into production, and marketing and sales weaknesses. There are ways to reduce the cycle time—we'll look at some in later chapters—but doing things in a rush and cutting corners are clearly not the answers.

Product development tends to be dominated by technology and technical issues; yet a review of the first five reasons for product failure in Figure 2.1 reveals that the principal deficiencies are not technological at all; rather, four out of five are directly or indirectly related to marketing deficiencies and problems.

Prescriptions: The Lessons Learned

Some of the prescriptions gleaned from these and other studies are obvious, but apparently not to everyone:

1. *More and better market information, research and analysis.* Note that traditional market research, such as large sample surveys, may not be appropriate for every project. But building in the voice of the customer, seeking customer insights, and getting the right market information before Development proceeds are vital requirements. This need has led

many firms to develop novel ways to include market information and the customer as an integral facet of their new product process. There will be more on these approaches when we get into the details of the "new product process" in Chapters 6 and 7.

2. *Other suggestions.* These include more careful product positioning, more effective concept testing prior to the development phase, better test marketing, sharper evaluation of new product projects (including early screening), and better planning and execution of sales and promotional efforts.

3. *Specific recommendations* go further:

- ✓ Make sure senior company executives are kept informed about the progress of each new product project but aim to limit their personal involvement to no more than is appropriate or necessary.
- ✓ Support a new product with ample selling effort and promotional resources to enable it to achieve its goals.
- ✓ Be wary of proposed new products that stray too far from the company's area of technical and marketing expertise. This is especially true when trying to market a new product through a sales force accustomed to a different selling task or to a different type of customer.
- ✓ Don't discount competitive responses: the launch of a rival "me too" product, price cuts, or heavy promotion of existing entries.
- ✓ Educating customers about the use and value of a new product can be a much longer and harder process than anticipated, especially if the "customer's customer" must be reached.
- ✓ Get the positioning right—price, features, and quality—and not above or below customer expectations.
- ✓ Make a repeat check on expected costs, margins, revenues, and profitability whenever the original product specifications are significantly modified during the course of its development.

Our Projects Studies: Why New Products Fail

Some of our own extensive investigations of new product winners and losers focus on process—what happens during the course of the project. We ask each project team to relate the story of their project from beginning to end—from idea to market launch. A flow of activities, including initial screening, preliminary technical assessment, product development, prototype testing, and so on, is identified. Next, we lower the microscope on each activity to determine quality of execution. In one study, we looked only at product failures. A more recent study validated the results by examining quality of project execution across many new product tasks within hundreds of businesses. The results are provocative (see Figure 2.2).[3]

FIGURE 2.2   Weaknesses in the New Product Process

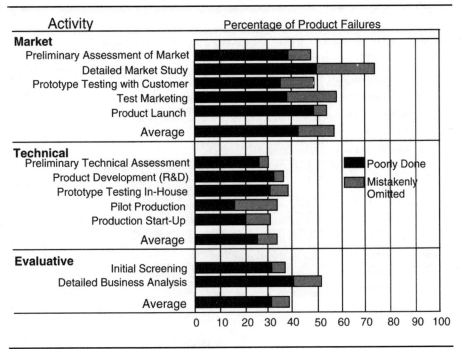

SOURCE: Data from R. G. Cooper, "Why new industrial products fail," *Industrial Marketing Management* 4 (1975): 315–26.

Weaknesses in the New Product Process Lead to Failure

The new product process is broken! In short, quality of execution is found to be sadly lacking in typical projects and businesses, especially failure projects. Here are some details:

The detailed market study is the most deficient activity in the entire new product process. *In 22 percent of the failure projects, no detailed market study was done at all* but in hindsight was considered a critical error of omission. In another 46 percent of projects, it was rated as "poorly done." That is, after adjustment for the few cases where a market study was inappropriate, in 74 percent of projects the detailed market study was scored as "deficient"—either poorly done or not done at all.

Other highly deficient activities (in rank order) include the following: test marketing or trial sell (omitted or poorly done in 58 percent of the projects); product launch (deficient in 54 percent of the cases); and detailed financial/business analysis (omitted or poorly done in 52 percent of projects). Even the customer field trials and the preliminary market assessment were each rated deficient in about half the cases.

FIGURE 2.3   Quality of Execution of Key Tasks in the New Product Process

The most poorly handled activity is the detailed market study - a quality-of-execution rating of only 3.5 out of 10; and it's not even done in more than half the projects (57%)

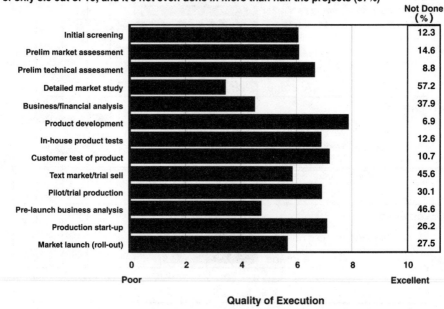

	Not Done (%)
Initial screening	12.3
Prelim market assessment	14.6
Prelim technical assessment	8.8
Detailed market study	57.2
Business/financial analysis	37.9
Product development	6.9
In-house product tests	12.6
Customer test of product	10.7
Text market/trial sell	45.6
Pilot/trial production	30.1
Pre-launch business analysis	46.6
Production start-up	26.2
Market launch (roll-out)	27.5

0   2   4   6   8   10
Poor   Excellent

Quality of Execution

SOURCE: Data from R. G. Cooper and E. J. Kleinschmidt, "Uncovering the keys to new product success," *Engineering Management Review* 21, 4 (Winter 1993): 5-18

Our most recent benchmarking study, in which hundreds of business units (rather than projects) were studied, reveals much the same (see Figure 2.3). The most poorly executed activities or tasks are the detailed market studies. These include user needs studies, building in the voice of the customer, and competitive analyses. These activities are omitted in 57 percent of the companies and given a very poor quality of execution rating (a dismal 3.5 on a scale of 10).

Also rated as "poorly executed" are the following tasks:

✓ business and financial analysis leading to "go to development" decisions (building the business case)
✓ test market or trial sell—selling the product to a limited number of customers
✓ prelaunch business analysis—the final business analysis prior to commercialization
✓ market launch—the actual commercial roll-out of the product

By contrast, the technologically oriented activities—preliminary technical assessment, product development, in-house product tests, pilot production, and production start-up—while not perfect, receive much better ratings.

Rethinking Your Game Plan

Imagine that you are a coach of a North American football team. You've identified twelve key plays that make up a march to a touchdown. Think of the twelve activities in Figure 2.2 as these plays. You review the last several hundred touchdown attempts by your team and sadly discover two things:

- On Play #1, the team fumbled the ball 48 percent of the time; Play #2 was worse—a fumble or missed pass 74 percent of the time; on Play #3, they dropped the ball 49 percent of the time; and so on. These are very discouraging statistics indeed.
- Closer scrutiny reveals that the fumbles and missed passes mostly happen on one side of the field; there's a consistent pattern as to where the deficiencies lie.

As a coach, you would be distraught. How do we ever score a touchdown! Yet these are the statistics in a play-by-play analysis of the new product game. And if your company is typical, these statistics are likely not far from the truth for you!

One more point: These play-by-play statistics reported for the new product game are taken from a biased sample of projects. Every one of these products, reported in Figure 2.2, was expected to be a winner; every one went to market; and every one failed! What we have here is the profile of a loser. If losing is your objective, then here are the rules:

- ✓ Don't do a detailed market study, or at best, do a fairly superficial one.
- ✓ Forget the test market or trial sell (no time or money), and make a feeble attempt at a launch.
- ✓ At all costs, avoid doing a detailed financial and business analysis.

Follow these and a few more patterns from Figures 2.2 and 2.3, and I can almost guarantee that you'll have a steady stream of failures. If your play-by-play statistics look like those in Figures 2.2 or 2.3, perhaps it's time to rethink your game plan! A typical first reaction is that these results simply couldn't be valid for my company. We're not that bad! The point is that you don't know unless you've measured them.

☞ **Suggestion:** Undertake a postmortem or "retrospective analysis" of past new product projects in your business. These should include both winners and losers, as well as aborted or killed projects, that were well into or past development. Undertake a strengths-and-weaknesses analysis on each, focusing on what was done well and what poorly. Go through each project from idea to launch and search for good practices as well as areas that need improvement.

Marketing: The Culprit

One recurring theme in these studies is that many marketing activities are seriously deficient, and in particular, the lack of good market information hurts many new product projects. This is not a new theme—it was first pointed out in the 1960s—but it's a persistent one.

One facet of the problem is this: In the early stages of a new product project, we make many assumptions in order to justify the project. We make technological assumptions: We assume that the product is technically feasible; we map out a probable route to the technical solution; manufacturability at a certain cost is assumed; and so on.

There are also marketing assumptions: We make estimates of market size, growth, and need; we expect that the product's features or performance are superior to competing products and that "the world will beat a path to our door"; and we make competitive assumptions—for example, the competitive response will be minimal.

Based on these assumptions, the project is given a go decision. And then what happens? Considerable effort is devoted to verifying and validating the technological assumptions: A team of technical people undertake lab or engineering work, alpha tests or lab tests of prototypes, and trial or pilot product runs. But where is marketing? Unfortunately, remarkably little marketing work gets done until the project is nearing completion.

There is a decided imbalance in how firms allocate resources to the technology and the marketing aspects in an "average" new product project. Our study of 203 new product projects in 123 companies—this time both product winners and losers—reveals that *78 percent of the total effort (person-days) goes to technological and/or production activities, whereas only 16 percent is devoted to marketing activities,* and much of that goes to the launch![4] If launch is not counted, then marketing's share of effort drops to less than 10 percent of the project. This picture of where the time, money, and effort are spent provides strong evidence that marketing activities receive relatively little attention and are badly underresourced in the new product processes of many firms.

This evidence is strong: In most projects, precious little effort (in terms of people and time) is devoted to confirming the marketing assumptions until the product is actually in the launch phase. And only then do we learn the truth: The market isn't quite as large as expected; the product's features are a little off what the customer values; and competitors *do* respond. Some of the original marketing assumptions or expectations are invariably wrong, and we failed to check them out. But by then it's too late—the damage is done.

Very often, this failure to undertake the needed marketing activities and the inability to obtain good market information stem simply from inappropriate resource allocation—the 78/16 percent split we saw above. The resources aren't in place! In our new product failure study, further questioning revealed that the most damaging resource deficiency was a lack of marketing research skills, capabilities, and people. Other areas that contributed to these product failures included a lack of general management skills and a lack of selling resources or skills. A lack of engineering, R&D, and production resources were rated much further down the list in terms of contributors to the failure.

What Really Happens in Typical New Product Projects?

Can new product development really be this badly flawed? In a nutshell, yes! In countless firms, horror stories abound about mistakes made during new product ventures. But perhaps these miscues are restricted to only a handful of highly visible projects—bad product failures. To check this, the specific problems, pitfalls, and misfires were pinpointed in our extensive new product study of 203 projects, one of the NewProd research series.[5] Here we looked in detail at both winners and losers—what happened in 123 commercial successes and 80 failure products. This is a 61 percent success rate, which is fairly typical. Managers related the story of each project—a "blow-by-blow" description of what happened from idea to launch. In particular, we focused on thirteen key activities that are often found as part of a new product project. These activities are listed and defined in Table 2.1.

Holes and Omissions

Our study shows that what the literature prescribes and what most firms do are miles apart when it comes to the new product process! This was one provocative finding of the study. The literature features numerous process models or game plans that describe how one should develop new products. Reality is much different! Reviews of what actually happened in the 203 projects reveal that many commonly recommended stages, activities, and practices are omitted altogether from the process. Figure 2.4 shows the frequency results, that is, in what proportion of the projects a given stage or activity is carried out. Some highlights from our findings include the following:

- Many key activities are simply left out altogether. Commonly prescribed activities such as a market research study, a trial sell, and a detailed business and financial analysis were each undertaken in less than half the projects studied.
- The weakest activities (those most often omitted) are two of the market-related tasks, namely, test market or trial sell and a detailed market study or marketing research. Three-quarters of project leaders chose

TABLE 2.1   Thirteen Key Activities in the New Product Process

Initial screen	The idea screen – the first decision to go ahead with the project; the initial commitment of resources (people and money).
Preliminary market assessment	The initial market study: a "quick and dirty" assessment of the marketplace, customer requirements, possible market acceptance, and competitive situation; largely nonscientific and relying principally on in-house sources.
Preliminary technical assessment	An initial technical appraisal, addressing questions such as "can the product be developed? how? can it be manufactured? etc."; based largely on discussions, in-house sources, and some literature search.
Detailed market study	Marketing research: detailed market studies such as user needs-and-wants studies, concept tests, positioning studies and competitive analyses; involves considerable field work and in-depth interviews with customers.
Predevelopment business and financial analysis	The decision to go to a full development program; involves, for example, a financial analysis, risk assessment, and a qualitative business assessment, looking at market attractiveness, competitive advantage, etc.
Product development	The actual development of the physical product.
In-house product tests	Testing the product in-house under controlled or laboratory conditions; alpha tests.
Customer product tests	Testing the product with the customer; field trials, beta tests, or preference tests: giving the product to customers and letting them try it under live field conditions.
Trial sell	A trial sell or test market of the product: an attempt to sell the product to a limited number of customers or in a limited geographical area; a "soft launch".
Precommercialization business analysis	The decision to commercialize: a final business and financial analysis prior to launch.
Production/operations start-up	Start-up of full-scale or commercial production or operations.
Market launch	The full market launch of the product: the implementation of the marketing plan.

not to do a detailed market study in their project, in spite of the fact that a lack of market information remains the number one cause of product failure! A test market or trial sell was undertaken in even fewer projects: Only 23 percent of projects featured such a market test of the product.

FIGURE 2.4   How Consistently Are Key Activities Undertaken in Projects?

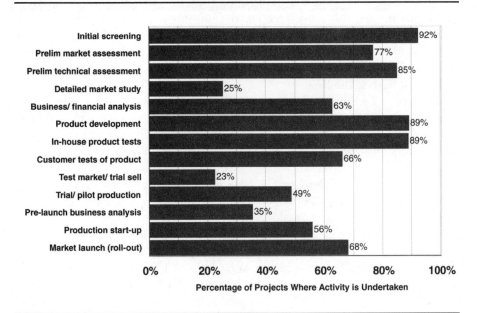

Percentage of Projects Where Activity is Undertaken

SOURCE: Data from R. G. Cooper and E. J. Kleinschmidt, "An investigation into the new product process: Steps, deficiencies, and impact," Journal of Product Innovation Management 3, 2 (1986): 71–85

- Other overlooked activities—undertaken in less than half of the projects studied—are precommercialization business analysis and trial production.

The picture is bleak—a process full of holes and serious errors of omission. When one stands back and looks at the new product process, very few projects—only 1.9 percent—featured all thirteen activities listed in Table 2.1. Indeed, in the majority of the projects studied, less than nine of the thirteen possible activities are carried out—a very limited and truncated process. Further, in almost one-third of the projects, seven activities or fewer were undertaken; that is, approximately half the new product process is left out! Could it be that what ails product innovation is that we're simply taking too many shortcuts—that we're leaving too many things out along the way?

Lame Excuses for No Action

No doubt there are good and valid reasons for omitting certain commonly recommended actions. Not every project needs a test market or trial sell, for example. But the frequency of omission of too many activities was substantial, certainly more than one might have expected from the occasional skipping over a step in the process. Moreover, the excuses for omission were often fairly lame. Below are some examples, along with our rebuttals:

Excuse #1 (from marketing): "We had a limited window of opportunity, so we had to move fast. And that meant cutting a few corners . . . things we might normally do if we had the time."

My reply: This is probably the most popular of all lame excuses. More often than not, it results in disaster. Cutting corners, doing things in haste, and leaving out important steps mean, at best, having to cycle back to do them again and, at worst, a significant product failure, the result of poor quality of execution.

Excuse #2 (from the R&D team): "We didn't do a user study (market study) because we didn't have the budget. Besides there was nobody to do it . . . the marketing folks were too busy doing other things."

My reply: But can you afford not to do it? Can you afford to assume that you really do understand customer needs and wants? And what will it cost you if you're wrong? Finally, if marketing won't help, maybe it's so important that, working with marketing, you should do some of the customer contact work yourself!

Excuse #3 (from a project team): "We don't usually do a detailed financial or business case analysis prior to development. The numbers really aren't too reliable."

My reply: True. But maybe you should focus on getting better estimates of expected revenues, costs, and so on. And even if the analysis is not very reliable, at least some insight is gained into the financial viability of the project. The analysis acts as a "sanity check."

Excuse #4 (from the product manager): "We did alpha tests (in-house product tests) but no beta tests (field trials). We didn't want competitors to find out about the new product, which might have happened if we had tested in the field."

My reply: Confidentiality is always a concern, but so is the fact that the product really does perform under field conditions and in a way acceptable to the customer. Moreover, you can preserve confidentiality in a field trial through tighter test controls, the selection of trusted customer partners, and a signed agreement with the customer.

A Step-by-Step Description

Let's now conduct a step-by-step review of the new product process (a look at the 203 projects and the thirteen activities outlined in Table 2.1) with a particular view to uncovering what can go wrong.

Initial Screening

Initial screening, although said to be undertaken in over 90 percent of the projects, is rated as the weakest activity overall, scoring lowest on the proficiency scale, and is cited as an activity greatly in need of improvement. Consider some of the ways that firms undertook screening:

- Sixty percent of firms indicated that screening was conducted by a multidisciplinary group of decision makers from R&D, marketing, and other functions. However, no formal criteria were used to make the decision. This first commitment to the project boils down to an informal discussion.
- In 24 percent of the projects, a single individual made the initial go/kill decision, again using no formal criteria. The assumption here is that one person in the company knows everything about technology, markets, production, and strategy and that this person is so proficient at decision making that criteria are not needed!
- In only 12 percent of the projects did initial screening come even close to what it should have been: a multidisciplinary decision making group (in order to provide different inputs to the decision) armed with go/kill criteria upon which to base the decision.

Given these practices, it is little wonder that initial screening is singled out as one activity where improvement is sorely needed. Forty percent of managers sought better inputs at this decision point (for example, from marketing); another 23 percent wanted more consistent and formal procedures (for example, decision criteria or go/kill screening rules).

Preliminary Market Assessment

Preliminary market assessment—the first attempt to determine market potential and expected market penetration—is also rated as a weak activity. It was omitted altogether in almost one-quarter of projects; that is, the project charged ahead without even a cursory look at the marketplace. And when it was done, it was rated weakly.

What does a preliminary market assessment entail? Direct contact with customers was made in fewer than half the cases! Other actions included discussions with the sales force, a review of competitors' products, a library search, and an "internal discussion among colleagues."

Like initial screening, preliminary market assessment is an activity singled out for improvement. Suggestions for improvement included a sharper, more focused definition of the market, more customer contacts, and the devotion of more time and effort to the activity.

Preliminary Technical Assessment

Preliminary technical assessment—the first technical appraisal of the new product project—is rated more positively; it was undertaken in the great majority of projects (85 percent) and was rated as proficiently executed.

Detailed Market Study

The detailed market study is among the weakest of the thirteen activities studied in the new product process. It was omitted in three-quarters of the 203 projects! And when it was undertaken, it was rated as "very poorly handled" on average.

The types of market investigations undertaken include the following:

- ✓ a study of competitive products and prices (26 percent);
- ✓ a study of what customers needed or wanted in the new product, to generate product specifications (19 percent);
- ✓ a study to determine market size (19 percent).

Managers may not understand what is meant by the term "detailed market study"; it certainly entails more than a study of competitive products and prices. Studies of customers to determine their needs (a user needs-and-wants study) and concept tests (a study of customer reactions to the proposed new product to gauge expected acceptance), though rarely conducted, should be integral facets of this market study.

Suggestions for improvement were varied but included better focus (better definition of the market or segment to be investigated), greater effort (more customer contacts and interviews, more depth), better definition of the product and technology before a customer survey is undertaken, and sharper market research objectives.

Predevelopment Business and Financial Analysis

Many firms (63 percent) conducted a business or financial analysis of the project prior to moving into full-scale development. Generally, this analysis was rated as moderately proficiently handled, and there was not a strong call for improvements here. Suggestions included more multidepartmental inputs, more market information and inputs from customers, more time and effort spent on the business analysis, and more formal and consistent procedures.

Product Development

The product development phase—the actual design and development of the product—was perceived by managers as a well-executed activity, on average. There were some requests for improvement, however:

✓ a more formally laid out process, with better coordination among people and departments;

✓ more depth and detail regarding technical issues, problems, and questions during development;

✓ more resources, more and better experienced people, and better facilities; and

✓ more time and effort devoted to this phase.

In-house Product Testing

Following the development phase, the product is typically subjected to a set of in-house tests (89 percent of projects). This stage was rated as the strongest one, on average. Requested improvements included more time and effort spent on testing, and a more detailed, rigorous, and formal testing procedure.

Customer Tests of the Product

The conducting of customer tests of the product is a fairly well-rated activity and one that was undertaken in the majority of projects studied (66 percent of cases). Most often, the customer test involved giving a sample or prototype of the product to the customer at no charge and letting the customer try the product (78 percent of cases). In a minority of cases (14 percent), there was a rigorously designed customer test, complete with written testing procedures. In a few cases (7 percent), the customer was brought to the company's premises for an on-site user test of the product.

Requested improvements included a more thorough testing program (more tests undertaken and at more test sites) and better control over the customer tests.

Trial Sell

The test market was undertaken the least frequently of all thirteen activities in the process. Less than one-quarter of projects attempted to gauge market acceptance based on a limited sell (for example, in one geographic area, or to a limited set of customers) prior to full commercialization. When undertaken, the activity was rated as proficiently executed, but recommended improvements included sharper definition of test market customers and more objective and better measures of test market results.

Trial/Pilot Production or Operation

Trial production/operation was carried out in less than half the projects, but when it was undertaken, it was rated positively. Trial production focused on either a test of the production system (54 percent of projects) or a test of the integrity of the product that the production system yielded (42 percent of projects). There were few improvements deemed necessary here.

Prelaunch Business Analysis

Managers were queried about whether a detailed business analysis was undertaken after product development, but before the full launch. Only a minority of projects (35 percent) conducted such an analysis, even though most experts recommend a full prelaunch business review.

Typically, if carried out, this prelaunch business analysis was executed in a quality fashion. Typical methods included a detailed financial analysis, a detailed market information review (sales forecasting, marketing costs), and a detailed cost review. Suggestions for making this final go/kill decision more effective included a total "start from scratch" review; revision and update of all data; and better market information, including input from a market acceptance or test market study.

Production or Operations Start-up

In the majority of cases, production start-up was a relatively straightforward activity, and it tends to be rated proficiently. It involved either no changes to the existing production facilities (13 percent of cases) or few changes (35 percent).

Market Launch

The market launch stage was rated moderately positively on average. Surprisingly, in more than 30 percent of the projects, *the launch stage was not recognized as a formal, distinct, or identifiable stage* or activity. Suggested improvements included the following:

- ✓ the allocation of more resources and efforts to the advertising and promotion effort for the new product;
- ✓ a clearer definition of marketing objectives;
- ✓ better in-house communication among the sales, advertising, service, and production departments at launch, and better training and preparation of the sales force.

Quality Is Missing

Many of the new product projects we studied ran into serious trouble. They took too long; they fell below sales and profit targets; and in some cases, they performed so badly that they were eventually removed from the market. Why did they encounter so many difficulties?

What we observed throughout this study is the lack of a quality process. Too many key activities were omitted; in the activities that were conducted, it seems that often the team just went through the motions; in still others, corners were cut or important tasks were overly rushed. In many cases, management or the project leader and team knew what had to be done but simply failed to do it (or did it poorly). As one manager said, "We all know how to dance; but once on the dance floor, we don't dance so well." *Quality of execution is the missing ingredient* in the great majority of new product projects.

☞ **Suggestion:** In undertaking your postmortem or "retrospective analysis" of past new product projects, pay special attention to the various activities, actions, and tasks in the process (our *ProBE* methodology outlined in Appendix A provides help here). Measure quality of execution, and identify "good practices" and deficient actions throughout. If your company is typical, you'll be shocked at how many deficiencies there are. After the audit is complete, try to pinpoint where and why quality of execution is lacking and what must be built into a new product game plan to ensure quality of execution.

Where the Resources Are Spent

One of the recurring themes throughout this study is the call for more time, money, and effort to be spent on various activities and actions. Managers constantly indicated that they had done a rushed or sloppy job on too many critical activities and that there was a need for more time, care, and effort. These comments beg the question: Just how are the resources allocated? Where is the time and effort spent in projects?

The allocation of resources has rarely been the topic of detailed investigation. Figure 2.5 provides the approximate breakdown of total company expenditures by major stage in the innovation process and the proportion spent on successes versus failures, based on a study by Booz-Allen & Hamilton.[6] The results are provocative. (Note that Figure 2.5 shows a breakdown of total company spending, not a per-project analysis; there are far more projects at the beginning stages than at the end.) This chart indicates that for every $1 million a firm spends on product innovation, roughly $150,000 is spent on exploration and screening—on exploratory research, idea generation, and on initial attempts to qualify the idea. Most of this goes to losers. This is no surprise: One must shovel a lot of earth to find a few diamonds! Remember the attrition curve in Figure 1.3 in Chapter 1.

Next comes business analysis, where the concept is defined and the project justified. Here's where the detailed market, technical, and operations studies are done in order to build a business case and to weed out the bad projects. Relatively little is spent here: only 5 percent of the total.

FIGURE 2.5   Effectiveness of New Product Expenditures

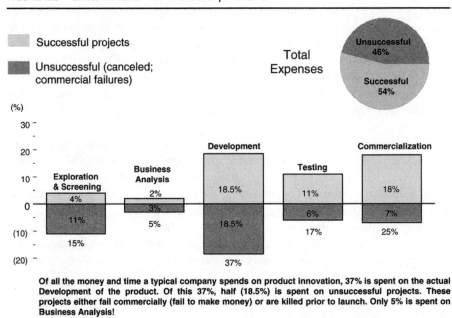

Of all the money and time a typical company spends on product innovation, 37% is spent on the actual Development of the product. Of this 37%, half (18.5%) is spent on unsuccessful projects. These projects either fail commercially (fail to make money) or are killed prior to launch. Only 5% is spent on Business Analysis!

SOURCE: Adapted with permission from Booz-Allen & Hamilton, *New Product Management for the 1980s* (New York: Booz-Allen & Hamilton, Inc., 1982).

Development takes the biggest piece of the pie, representing 37 percent of total spending or $370,000 of our $1 million. But here, *half the resources still go to unsuccessful projects.* One might have hoped that by the time development began, the "bad" projects would have been largely culled out. Not so. Even at this very expensive stage, and after all the up-front screening and business analysis work has been done, half the resources are still misspent! This apparent misallocation of resources raises serious questions about the accuracy of the analyses in the steps that precede the development phase. For example, just how good a business analysis is being done? And is a 5 percent allocation really enough for the business analysis stage?

Testing follows and takes about 17 percent of the total. This includes field trials, trial production runs, and test markets designed to validate the product and project. The final stage is commercialization, which entails production start-up and market launch and accounts for about 25 percent of the total, or $250,000 of our $1 million total spending. At this last stage, note that the majority of resources are devoted to successful projects—finally! By this final stage, many of the poor projects have been culled out, and the majority of resources are at last going to the good ones. But this is a bit late in the game to be figuring out which are the good projects—most of the money has already been spent!

FIGURE 2.6   Money Spent on Each Key Task in a Typical New Product Project

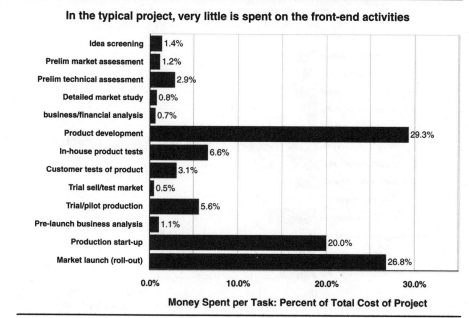

In the typical project, very little is spent on the front-end activities

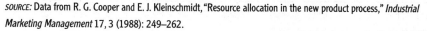

Money Spent per Task: Percent of Total Cost of Project

SOURCE: Data from R. G. Cooper and E. J. Kleinschmidt, "Resource allocation in the new product process," *Industrial Marketing Management* 17, 3 (1988): 249–262.

This study provides some rough benchmarks that are useful as a comparison to your company's spending patterns. It also raises serious questions. Spending or resource allocation is not as it should be; something is very wrong with the product innovation process. Why do half of development expenditures go to unsuccessful ventures? Why are the correct project priorities determined so late in the process? Is business analysis adequately funded? This phase is critical, but its 5 percent allocation appears pitifully small.

By observing these spending patterns, one gains valuable insights into problems in product innovation. But the Booz-Allen & Hamilton study and others on spending do not yield the level of detail needed to diagnose the problems and pitfalls in the innovation process. For example, the stages considered in this study are rather broad, and there is no breakdown of spending by specific activity, such as the market research study. Second, results are reported only in terms of dollars. This is obviously one important measure, but as many new project leaders will attest, often the issue is more one of time and people and not so much a lack of money.

Our study of 203 actual new product projects also dissected spending and resource allocation. Figures 2.6 and 2.7 show the percentage breakdown (for dollars and person-days, respectively) spent on the thirteen activities outlined in Table 2.1.

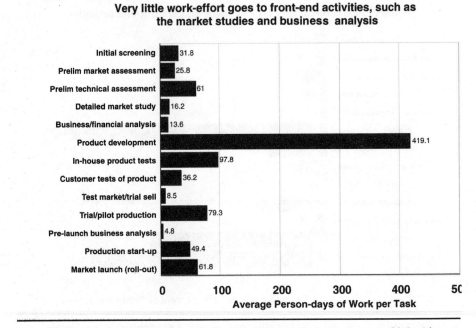

**Very little work-effort goes to front-end activities, such as
the market studies and business analysis**

Task	Average Person-days of Work per Task
Initial screening	31.8
Prelim market assessment	25.8
Prelim technical assessment	61
Detailed market study	16.2
Business/financial analysis	13.6
Product development	419.1
In-house product tests	97.8
Customer tests of product	36.2
Test market/trial sell	8.5
Trial/pilot production	79.3
Pre-launch business analysis	4.8
Production start-up	49.4
Market launch (roll-out)	61.8

SOURCE: Data from R. G. Cooper and E. J. Kleinschmidt, "Resource allocation in the new product process," *Industrial Marketing Management* 17, 3 (1988): 249–262.

The typical new product project is characterized by a *very concentrated expenditure pattern*. Of the thirteen activities, three account for more than three-quarters of the dollar expenditures. Not surprisingly, these activities include the following:

- Product development: the actual design and development of the product (29.3 percent of total dollars)
- Market launch: the formal launch of the product into the marketplace (26.8 percent)
- Production or operations start-up: the acquisition of production equipment and production start-up (20.0 percent)

In contrast to these high expenditure areas, activities such as the predevelopment business analysis and the detailed market study have little in the way of allocated resources—less than 1 percent of total project costs for each! Indeed, of the thirteen activities studied, a total of six add up to only 5 percent of total project costs. Not surprisingly, these six underfunded activities correspond quite closely to the "poorly executed activities" identified in Figure 2.4. Quality of execution and resources spent are closely linked.

The market-oriented activities (with the exception of launch) are noticeable for their lack of expenditure. On average, only 1.2 percent of project costs are devoted to a preliminary market assessment; even less (0.8 percent) is spent on the detailed market study (partly a reflection of the fact that most project leaders did not do one at all!); only 3.1 percent is allocated to customer tests or field trials; and 0.5 percent is spent on a test market or trial sell. These results provide strong evidence that the new product process is a relatively unbalanced one, that it remains largely dominated by technological activities, and that many critical marketing actions receive little attention and even fewer funds.

When person-days rather than dollars are used as the measure of resources spent, the picture remains almost the same. Figure 2.7 displays the results. Again, the product development function dominates, accounting for 46 percent of the person-days effort. Note that although the dollars spent on market launch and production start-up are high, the person-days spent here are considerably less: Expenditures are not for people but for out-of-pocket items such as equipment, plant, advertising, and promotion. Other actions, such as in-house tests and trial production, account for a relatively higher proportion of manpower.

In contrast, very little effort is devoted to activities such as the trial sell or test market (0.5 percent of the total person-days) or the detailed market study (1.8 percent of the total).

When the dollars and people expenditures are collapsed into three categories, the picture becomes even clearer (see Table 2.2).

Note that of the 32 percent of total dollars spent on marketing activities, 83 percent goes to the launch.

If how people spend their time and money is any indication of the importance accorded different activities, then *clearly marketing activities remain a distant second in the new product process* for many firms. And most of the marketing effort boils down to one activity, namely, market launch—sales force, advertising, and promotion—with little going to earlier marketing activities, such as market assessments, detailed market studies, and customer tests and trials. These results are frightening, especially when one recognizes that almost every study of new product failure has identified a lack of a market orientation and inadequate marketing inputs as the major culprit in new product failure!

Yet another way of looking at these resource allocation results is to consider various major stages of the new product process. For this analysis, the new product process was broken into three major stages:

- *Predevelopment:* those actions from the idea stage up to (but not including) the product development phase—the "front end" of the process
- *Development and testing:* the middle of the process, including product development, as well as in-house and customer tests of the product
- *Commercialization:* the "back end" of the process, including market launch, production or operation start-up, trial sell, and trial production

ditures by Activity

Type of Activity	(% of total project)	
	% of Dollars	% of Person-days
Technological and production	65%	78%
Marketing (including launch)	32%	16%
Evaluation (screening, business analysis, project approvals	3%	6%

Figure 2.8 shows the breakdown in expenditures for both dollars and person-days for the average project. What stands out in here is how much the typical new product project is loaded toward the middle and the back end. Only 7 percent of the dollars and 16 percent of effort (person-days) are expended on the front end of the process. Some of this imbalance is inevitable, especially in projects where there is major capital spending. But dollars aside, notice how little effort goes "up front"!

Yet it is the front end that houses so many critical and decisive activities central to new product success. The critical nature of these front end activities was highlighted in the Booz-Allen & Hamilton study, which showed that successful U.S. firms devote more effort to the predevelopment activities and that the Japanese spend even more in the predevelopment stage.[7] And it is in the up-front activities where the seeds of so many new product disasters are sown—inadequate market analysis, poor screening and evaluation, and a failure to understand customers' needs.

The importance of getting the first few steps of the project right is obvious. But apparently the lesson hasn't been learned in the majority of firms. Simply stated, *companies allocate very little effort and even fewer dollars to the front end or "homework" phases* of most new product projects! And the results are predictable.

☞ **Suggestion:** Undertake a resource allocation appraisal for your new product efforts. Determine how many person-days and how much money is spent by people in various functions or departments on product innovation. Determine where and how it is spent. Get breakdowns by activity and by project. Then develop some of the charts that you've seen in this chapter. The results will be provocative!

FIGURE 2.8   Resources Spent on Each Major Phase of the Typical Project

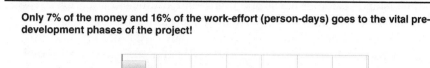

Only 7% of the money and 16% of the work-effort (person-days) goes to the vital pre-development phases of the project!

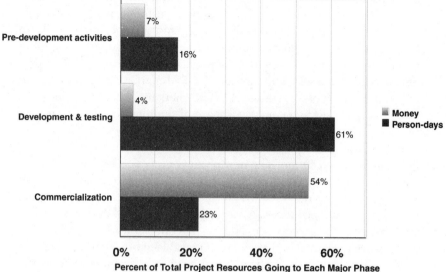

SOURCE: Data from R. G. Cooper and E. J. Kleinschmidt, "Resource allocation in the new product process," *Industrial Marketing Management* 17, 3 (1988): 249–262.

1. *Determine the total spending allocations* (dollars and person-days) by major stage, and what proportion is spent on winners versus losers at each stage (as in Figure 2.5).
2. *Perform the breakdown on a per-project basis.* That is, determine where the resources go (by major stage and by specific activity) for the average project, and also for successes versus failures (as in Figures 2.6, 2.7, and 2.8).
3. Using the same data, *report the breakdown of resources per project by function* (in both person-days and dollars), that is, by R&D, engineering, marketing, operations, and so on, to determine if you have a skewed distribution of effort, much like we saw in the results presented above.

Problems and Pitfalls

This chapter has identified some of the problems and pitfalls that result in new product failures and mediocre new product efforts. There are others as well. Let's review the important deficiencies as a first step to taking corrective actions:

1. *A lack of a market orientation.* Inadequate market analysis, a failure to understand customer needs and wants, and insufficient attention to the marketplace are consistently cited as major reasons for new product failure. Simply stated, firms tend to omit many of the critical marketing tasks, particularly those in the early phases of a project. Activities such as the detailed market study (to determine customer needs and wants and to assess likely market acceptance) and test markets or trial sells (to test the launch plan and determine market penetration) are most often omitted—in about three-quarters of projects. And activities such as preliminary market assessment and the detailed market study are plagued by poor quality of execution. Finally, marketing actions appear to receive a disproportionately small share of the total resources spent on projects: 32 percent of funding (most of which goes to the market launch), and only 16 percent of the effort (measured in person-days).

2. *Poor quality of execution.* The new product process is replete with deficiencies; errors of omission and errors of commission abound. Key actions, often considered central to success, are arbitrarily omitted; the typical new product process is very much a truncated one, with only a small minority of projects—less than 2 percent—considered to be complete. Certain pivotal activities are noticeable more for their absence than their presence in the typical firm's process; activities such as the detailed market study, the test market, and the precommercialization business analysis are undertaken in a minority of cases. When they are undertaken, the quality of execution is most often poor. Quality of execution was rated as "mediocre" across a broad spectrum of actions, with some of the weakest areas being initial screening, detailed market study, precommercialization business analysis, production start-up, and market launch. *It is clear that the new product process is broken!*

3. *Moving too quickly.* Many of these errors—the failure to do certain key tasks and short-cutting others—are made in the interest of saving time. But these efforts are false economy; invariably, they come back to haunt the perpetrators. What little time may be gained by moving quickly is usually lost several times over later in the project. When corners are cut, mistakes are made, the project moves off target, and activities have to be repeated, all at great time and money expense. Sometimes time-saving measures are fatal: Bypassing a needed market study or cutting short the field trials often leads to a product disaster.

4. *Not enough up-front homework.* The three themes above—inadequate market analysis, poor quality of execution, and moving too quickly—all converge on the homework phase or fuzzy front-end of the innovation process. For a multitude of reasons, the homework simply doesn't get done. The project moves from idea through a rather superficial "definitional and homework" phase right into a full-scale development.

Management has adopted a cavalier or macho "ready, fire, then aim" approach when it comes to new products. Doing homework may not be exciting, but it's got to be done! Sadly, the evidence indicates otherwise. The predevelopment activities receive a relatively small proportion of the total resources: 7 percent of the dollars and 16 percent of the effort. And these homework phases are the same ones that are plagued with errors of omission and commission. Yet these homework phases are central to success. It is here that the market and product are defined, the obvious losers should be weeded out, and the key decisions to commit significant resources are made.

5. *A lack of product value for the customer.* Moving ahead into product development with only a vague understanding of customer requirements leads to too many ill-defined products that provide little significant benefit or value for the customer. And too many new products are reactive efforts—a "me too" product that meets a competitive brick wall. The failure to do one's homework, a lack of willingness to seek customer input, and the desire to move quickly often lead to a reactive, unimaginative, and undifferentiated product. Product advantage—differentiated products offering unique customer benefits and real value for money—is essential to winning, as we shall see in the next chapter.

6. *No focus, too many projects, and a lack of resources.* A lack of resources, from certain departments in the company (for example, marketing) and for specific activities in a project (for example, the up-front or predevelopment stages), plagues too many new product projects. This lack of time, money, and people is the root cause of many errors of omission and poor quality of execution, which in turn have such serious consequences for product performance. Why does this lack of resources exist? In some firms, senior management has simply starved product innovation; the resource requirements for an effective new product program are grossly underestimated. In most firms, however, it boils down to not enough focus and hence too many projects for the available resources. The result is that scarce resources are dissipated across many fronts and that the truly deserving projects are underresourced.

7. *The lack of a systemic new product process with discipline.* Many companies complain that their new product process is not working. Key tasks don't happen when they should or as well as they should. And many companies that have installed such a process often complain that they lack the discipline to follow it. Sometimes it's simply a lack of discipline; but other times it's because the process is flawed—too cumbersome, too bureaucratic.

These problems and deficiencies are interlinked (see Figure 2.9). For example, the lack of focus—doing too many projects for the limited resources avail-

FIGURE 2.9   How the Problems Feed Each Other—A Downward Spiral

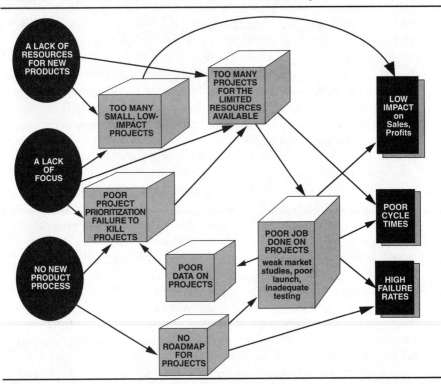

SOURCE: Adapted from R. G. Cooper, S. J. Edgett, and E. J. Kleinschmidt, "New problems, new solutions: Making portfolio management more effective," Research-Technology Management 43, 2 (2000): 18–33.

able (item 6 above)—results in poor quality of execution (item 2), a lack of a market orientation and poor market information (item 1), and insufficient up-front homework (item 4). The desire to move quickly—cutting too many corners (item 3)—has a similar impact. The lack of a new product process with discipline (item 7) means there is no road map and there are no tough go/kill decision points. When go/kill decisions are lacking, too many projects are approved and none are killed—projects develop a life of their own. And so the pipeline suffers from gridlock—too many projects, not enough resources (item 6). And with no road map in place, it's not surprising to find key activities overlooked or not addressed until it's too late. And so the new product problems continue, feeding one another in an endless downward spiral.

From Losers to Winners

This chapter has begun our quest for the ideal new product game plan—a blueprint for new product success. We started with an understanding of our weaknesses: the problems, pitfalls, and deficiencies that beset new product projects.

Seven key weaknesses have been pinpointed. Correcting these weaknesses is the first step. But a word of caution: If we correct these deficiencies, does it stand to reason that success will be the result? If a football team fixes everything it does wrong, it doesn't necessarily win the game! The next chapter looks at winners. More specifically, we explore what makes a winner and what separates winners from losers in the new product game.

What Separates the Winners from the Losers?

The game is done! I've won, I've won.
—Samuel Taylor Coleridge, *The Ancient Mariner*

Winning isn't everything . . . it's the only thing.
—Vince Lombardi, Green Bay Packers football coach

The Right Products Right

What makes a new product a success? And what can be done to improve the odds of winning at new products? These questions have plagued senior executives for decades. But today more than ever, the answers are critical. The ability to develop and launch new products successfully and quickly is the key to business success.

There are two fundamental ways to win at product innovation, according to studies on innovation success. The first is *doing projects right;* the second is *doing the right projects.*[1] Here's what I mean:

1. *Doing projects right.* Research over the past twenty-five years has uncovered many success factors—common denominators of successful new product projects.[2] For example, employing true cross-functional teams, doing the up-front homework prior to the development stage, building in the voice of the customer, getting a sharp, early, and stable product definition, and so on, have all been found to positively impact new product outcomes.

2. *Doing the right projects.* Equally important, but often missed in traditional research, is the issue of doing the right projects. As one executive put it, "Even a blind man can get rich in a gold mine by swinging a pickaxe; it's not so much how you mine—the trick is picking the *right* mine!" Thus project selection decisions and portfolio management techniques become critical facets of a successful new product effort.

Much of the recent emphasis in new product management has been on doing projects right—on the *process of innovation.* Research has revealed about ten to fifteen major success factors that capture the things the project team does (or too often doesn't do). As a result, many companies have turned to new product processes as the answer. According to the latest best practices study by the Product Development and Management Association (PDMA), "nearly 60 percent of the firms surveyed use some form of *Stage-Gate*™ process."[3] The company's rationale is that by defining a road map from idea to launch, project teams will build in these success factors by design rather than by chance. We will learn more about *Stage-Gate* and its latest versions in Chapter 5.

Results from new product processes, although impressive in many companies such as 3M, Dow Chemical, and Microsoft, have not always been 100 percent positive. Why? Because the focus has been only on the first success factor—on doing projects right—rather than on doing the right projects. In short, companies have focused on the wrong projects and often on too many projects. In fact, our benchmarking studies (discussed later in this chapter) reveal that *project selection and project prioritization are the weakest area* of new product management. So now it's time to turn to project selection and portfolio management as areas to improve new product performance.

In order to understand the why's and how's of both types of success drivers—doing projects right and doing the right projects—it is important to drill down into some of the research that underlies these principles. In short, let's lower the microscope on the studies that have probed what separates successful new products, winning product innovation projects, and high-performing business units from the unsuccessful ones. In other words, what distinguishes the best from the rest?

The Keys to New Product Success

In Chapter 2, we looked at why new products fail and what goes wrong in product innovation. But identifying what makes a new product a winner is considerably more difficult than merely pinpointing reasons for failure.

In one of my early investigations of three significant high-technology new industrial products—a new milk packaging system by DuPont of Canada, a new telephone handset by Nortel Networks, and a new turbojet engine by United Technologies—much was learned about what went into successful product development.[4] The one common thread in these three developments was a *strong commitment and orientation to the marketplace.* In all three cases, there was extensive and careful analysis of the market; in fact, in two of the cases, eleven separate market studies were undertaken—from user needs-and-wants studies to concept tests, field trials, and test markets. These market studies, particularly those early in the project, dealt not only with the more obvious issues, such as market potential and size, but also with the nature of customer needs, the benefits they sought in a new product, and the design requirements that would achieve meaningful product differentiation. All three project teams had built in the voice of the customer before the term was even popular!

The three cases dramatically demonstrate the importance of marrying *technological prowess* to a *strong market orientation* and the need to undertake one's *homework before product development begins.* The result in all three cases was the development and launch of a new product that was not only technologically superior, but one that met customer needs and delivered unique benefits to end users far better than anything else on the market.

A second common facet of these three winning products was the *logical and stepwise flow of activities* as the projects moved from idea to launch. None of the firms at that time had a formal new product process in place; yet when we laid the flow charts that captured what happened in each of the three projects on top of one another, they were almost identical. It was almost as though the three firms, each in a different industry, had adopted the same road map or process: similar steps and activities; similar sequencing and timing; and similar allocations of effort to each stage or step.

A final discovery was the extent of *interaction between people from different functional groups* within each firm. The project, from idea to launch, passed back and forth among marketing, technical, and manufacturing groups. It was much like watching a rugby match. Although there was a project leader in each case, the effort was by no means a one-person or one-department show. A multidisciplinary approach, with strong interaction between players from different functions, was prevalent in all three cases.

☞ **Suggestion:** We need to learn from history. Identify some recent new product successes in your company and undertake a *retrospective analysis:* chart the chronology of events and actions from idea to launch. Then, let the project team analyze what happened, why the project was successful, and what we can learn about what it takes to win. Build these case illustrations and lessons into your management training programs and into your company practices.

Success Versus Failure

We can learn much from observing successful new products. Equally, there is much to be gained from doing postmortems on failures. But as pointed out in the previous chapter, the fundamental flaw with both research directions is that they look at only one side of the coin: They report what successes have in common or why products fail, but they do not look at both types of projects—successes and failures—in the same study. Simply because a number of successes have one factor in common does not mean that this factor leads to success. Perhaps failures also share the same characteristic! In order to uncover the keys to success, one must identify those factors that separate winners from losers—the discriminating variables—and hence a comparison of both types of projects is needed.

The First NewProd™ Study

My original Project NewProd[5] was an exploratory study into success versus failure, which sought to identify those characteristics that separated 102 new product successes from 93 failures in 102 companies.[6] Three important factors were uncovered that distinguished successes from failures:

1. A unique, superior product *in the eyes of the customer* that offers the customer *unique benefits and superior value for money*
2. A strong market orientation that builds in solid market knowledge and sound market inputs and undertakes the market research and marketing launch tasks well.
3. Technological leverage (the company leveraged its core competencies in terms of both development and production technology) and quality execution of the technological tasks in the project

Secondary factors that also have an impact on success include marketing and managerial leverage (a good fit between the needs of the project and the firm's marketing and managerial competencies); dynamic market situations (customer needs in a state of flux, and a market characterized by many new product launches); large, high-need growth markets; a strong marketing communications, sales force, and launch effort; and finally, weak competitors (whose customers were dissatisfied with them).

The Stanford Innovation Project

A major success/failure study, the Stanford Innovation Project, looked at high-tech electronics firms and new products.[7] In this comparison of successes and failures, winning products were found to have the following factors in common:

- Winning products have a high performance-to-cost ratio (the result of an in-depth understanding of the customers and the marketplace).
- The market launch is proficient and backed by strong resources.
- The product yields a high contribution margin.
- The R&D process is well planned and executed.

- The create, make, and sell functions are well interfaced and coordinated.
- The product is introduced into the market early, that is, ahead of competition.
- There exists marketing and technological synergy (a good fit between the project needs and company capabilities).
- Top management support exists for the project, from development to launch.

More recent studies by the Stanford Innovation Project researchers on the U.S. electronics industry (86 successes and 86 failures) identified these main factors separating winners from losers:

- Successes have a quality R&D effort, based on strong interfaces with both manufacturing and the customer. Here, "interfaces with the customer" means a detailed understanding of the customer's problems and a sound visualization of how the new product will solve the customer's problems.
- Winning products are technically superior and feature strong product uniqueness.
- Successful products have a positive market environment; they are first in the market and enjoy a large and growing market.
- Winning products provide significant value to the customer.
- Successes build upon the firm's existing technological and organizational competencies (but strengths in the marketing and manufacturing departments did not contribute to success in this study of the electronics industry).

The Booz-Allen & Hamilton Investigation

An investigation of new product practices in 700 firms by Booz-Allen & Hamilton identified the existence of common characteristics in companies that were successful at product innovation:[8]

1. *Operating philosophy.* Successful companies are more committed to growth through new products developed internally. They are more likely to have had a formal new product process in place for a longer period of time than unsuccessful companies. They are more likely to have a strategic plan that includes a certain portion of company growth from new products. They are also likely to prescreen new product ideas more thoroughly, considering almost ten times fewer new product ideas per successful new product as unsuccessful companies.
2. *Organizational structure.* Successful companies are more likely to house the new product organization in R&D or engineering and are

more likely to allow the marketing and R&D functions to have greater influence on the new product process. They also keep the senior new product executive in place for a longer period of time than unsuccessful companies.

3. *The experience effect.* Experience in introducing new products enables companies to improve new product performance. New product development costs conform to the experience curve: The more you do something, the more efficient you become at doing it. For the 13,000 new product introductions studied in these 700 firms over a five-year period, the experience effect yields a 29 percent cost curve: At each doubling of the number of new product introductions, the cost of each introduction declines by 29 percent. This experience advantage stems from the acquisition of a knowledge of the market and of the steps required to develop a new product.

4. *Management styles.* Successful companies appear not only to select a management style appropriate to immediate new product development needs but also to revise and tailor that approach to changing new product opportunities. Three styles were identified:

✓ an entrepreneurial approach, associated primarily with new-to-the-world products
✓ a collegial approach, associated with entering new businesses and adding new items to existing lines
✓ a managerial approach, most often associated with developing new products that are closely linked to existing businesses

The study concludes with a list of "best practice prescriptions" for new product management:

- *Commitment.* Firms must make a long-term commitment to new products. They must look inward for their future product opportunities and must be committed to internal product development as the major source of growth. They must be willing to mount well-defined new product efforts that are driven by corporate objectives and strategies. They must support these efforts with consistent commitments of the necessary funds, as well as management and technical skills.
- *Strategy.* At the core of a company-specific approach to a sound new product program is a well-defined new product strategy. A new product strategy links the new product process to company objectives and provides focus for idea/concept generation and guidelines for establishing appropriate screening criteria. The outcome of new product strategic planning is a set of strategic roles used not to generate specific new product ideas but to help identify markets for which new products will be developed.

- *Process.* The multistep new product process is an essential ingredient in successful new product development. And there is a new step in this process, namely, strategy formulation. This revised new product process focuses the search for ideas, reduces the attrition rate of ideas, and contributes to a higher success rate. The net result of the improved process is better expenditure allocations: Companies are able to increase the portion of total new product expenditures going to products that are ultimately successful.

The Hewlett-Packard Studies

An internal study undertaken at Hewlett-Packard using the NewProd methodology identified ten distinguishing factors of successful new product projects:[9]

1. *Understanding user needs.* The product's potential users and customers and the product's contribution to the customer are totally understood by the project team.
2. *Strategic alignment.* There is alignment of the project with the strategy of the business unit, clear identification of the specific target segment, and a consistent charter in the development organization.
3. *Competitive analysis and product superiority.* The competitors' solutions for customer problems are well understood, and every effort is made to create a product plan that ensures that the new product will be better than the competitors' at the time of market launch.
4. *Regulation compliance.* All regulatory issues in the product's arena are identified and addressed: patent infringement issues; industry standards and approval body regulations; and environmental, health, ergonomic, and globalization issues.
5. *Priority decision criteria list.* Priority decision criteria are defined before development begins in order to make sound trade-off decisions during development. These decision criteria include the manufacturing cost target, the target time to market, key product features, the strategy for extending the technological platform, the reliability goals, and the design for manufacturability goals.
6. *Risk assessment.* The priority decision criteria list (above) also identifies high-risk areas including piece-parts, processes, and marketing plans, so that they can be addressed early in the development phase.
7. *Product positioning.* The product is positioned correctly, based on an in-depth understanding of users' needs and purchase motivations, in order to provide higher value to the user than competitive products.
8. *Product channel and support.* Successful products have the right channel of distribution and support plan for the product.

9. *Project endorsement by upper management.* Upper management is well aware of the development project and provides support.
10. *Total organizational support.* Management provides adequate financial and human resources from all functions to complete the project according to plan.

One finding is that successful projects studied within Hewlett-Packard, with very few exceptions, have *no "holes" or deficiencies in the ten practices* listed above, whereas unsuccessful projects have numerous inadequacies in these ten areas.

Organizational Structure

Many of the studies above probed characteristics of the projects—the way the project was undertaken and the nature of the project, product, and market. But what about organizational structure—the way the project is organized and the roles of key players? The organizational design question was addressed in a major study of 300 firms by Song, Montoya-Weiss, and Schmidt.[10] The research underscores the importance of incorporating *multiple functional perspectives* in product development teams and projects. The authors note that "all critical organizational functions should take part in the NPD [new product development] process from the *beginning of the process.*" The study went on to look at the role of top management as well: "Management plays a dual role in the NPD process. Top management must actively champion the project and provide strategic direction, as well as create policies and procedures (e.g., reward and evaluation systems) that foster an internal culture of cross-functional cooperation."

But what type of cross-functional approach works best? The relative effectiveness of different *project management structures* for product development was assessed in a large empirical success/failure study by Larson and Gobeli.[11] The researchers identified five types of structures on a continuum from single-function segments to the multifunctional project team:

1. *Functional.* The project is divided into segments, which are assigned to relevant functional areas or groups. The project is coordinated by functional and upper levels of management.
2. *Functional matrix.* A project manager with *limited authority* is designated to coordinate the project across different functional areas. The functional managers retain responsibility and authority for their specific segments of the project.
3. *Balanced matrix.* A project manager is assigned to oversee the project and *shares the responsibility and authority* for completing the project with the functional managers; there is joint approval and direction.

4. *Project matrix.* A project manager is assigned to oversee the project and has *primary responsibility and authority* for the project. Functional managers assign personnel as needed and provide technical expertise.

5. *Project team.* A project manager is put in charge of a project team composed of a core group of personnel from several functional areas. The functional managers have *no formal involvement.* Project teams are also referred to as tiger teams or venture teams.

The results of the study indicate that there is no one best way to organize a new product project but that some are better than others. The three multifunctional team approaches (structure types 3, 4, and 5 listed above) yield the best performance: Project team, project matrix, and balanced matrix structures all have roughly the same high success rates. By contrast, the two functional approaches (structure types 1 and 2 above) fare much more poorly: Success rates drop dramatically in the case of both functional matrix and functional organization. Projects using either of these two management structures lag behind the others in terms of schedule, cost, and technical performance.

Project teams (type 5) appear to be best suited to very complex projects but are not as appropriate for less complex projects. By contrast, project matrix structures (type 4) work equally well for both complex and simple projects and as well as project teams for complex projects. Functional structures (types 1 and 2) fare poorly for both complex and simple projects.

Finally, there is a decided preference among managers in the study for structures that provide *strong project leadership.* Although the project manager may be able to rely on informal sources of influence to manage the project, the results of the study indicate that these informal sources need to be bolstered by formal designations of authority.

Winners Versus Losers: More Recent NewProd Studies

Is there really a pattern to new product success? And if so, what separates successful new product projects from unsuccessful ones? The answers have been sought in our more recent Project NewProd investigations.[12] To date, more than 2,000 new product projects—about two-thirds successes and one-third failures—have been studied, and they provide the basis for insights into what makes a winner.

Eight Key Factors Underlying Success

There is a pattern to success. Indeed, significant differences emerge between successful and unsuccessful new products projects with new product success most strongly decided by eight key factors. The impacts of these factors are described below. Figures 3.1, 3.2, and 3.3 show the magnitude of some of the most important factors graphically, and Table 3.1 summarizes the eight factors

Table 3.1: Effect of Success Factors on
Various New Product Performance Metrics

Success Drivers	Correlations (0-1)[3]	
	Effect on Profitability	Effect on Timeliness
A unique, superior & differentiated product with good value-for-money for the customer	0.534	None
A strong market orientation – voice of customer built in	0.444	0.406
Sharp, early, fact-based product definition before development begins	0.393	0.242
Solid up-front homework – doing the front-end activities well	0.369	0.408
True cross-functional teams: empowered, resourced, accountable, dedicated leader	0.328	0.483
Leverage – where the project builds on business's technology & marketing competencies	0.316	None
Market attractiveness – size, growth, margins	0.312	0.215
Quality of the launch effort: well planned, properly resourced	0.286	0.205
Technological competencies & quality-of-execution of technological activities	0.265	0.316

Notes:
"Profitability" captures how profitable the product was relative to the business's acceptable profit level, however the firm measures profits.

"Timeliness" includes both "time efficiency" (how fast the project was executed) and "on time performance" (was the product launched when promised?)

Source of table data: NewProd studies, endnotes 2 & 5; also endnote 20 in Chapter 1.

and their impacts. In each figure, the hundreds of projects studied are divided into three categories: the top 20 percent, the middle 60 percent, and the bottom 20 percent of projects when rated on each factor.

Here, then, are the eight key factors that distinguish winning projects from the losers (in descending order of importance).

1. A superior product that delivers unique benefits to the user. Superior products that *deliver real and unique advantages to users* tend to be far more successful than "me too" products with few positive elements of differentiation (see Figure 3.1). When we contrast the high-advantage products (the top 20 percent) with those with the least degree of differentiation (the bottom 20 percent), we find that the superior products share the following characteristics:

FIGURE 3.1   Impact of Product Superiority on Performance

Superior, differentiated products have five times the success rate and market share as "me too" efforts; they are also much more profitable!

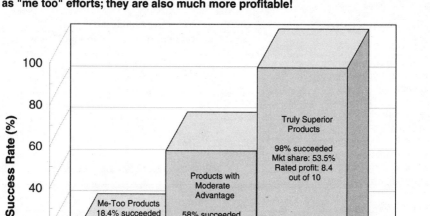

SOURCE: Cooper and Kleinschmidt, endnote 12.

✓ Superior products have an exceptional commercial success rate of 98.0 percent, versus only 18.4 percent for undifferentiated ones.

✓ Superior products have a market share of 53.5 percent of the defined target market, versus only 11.6 percent for "me too" new products.

✓ Superior products have a rated profitability of 8.4 out of 10 (versus only 2.6 out of 10 for undifferentiated products—here 10 = exceptional profits, far exceeding the company's minimum hurdle).

✓ Superior products meet company sales and profit objectives to a greater degree than do undifferentiated products.

What do these superior products with real customer benefits have in common? These winning products offer unique features not available in competitive products; they meet customer needs better than competitive products; they have higher relative product quality; they solve a problem the customer has with a competitive product; they reduce the customer's total costs—high value in use; and they are innovative—the first of their kind on the market.

These six ingredients of a superior product provide a useful checklist in assessing the odds of success of a proposed new product project. In short, the six items above logically help you select winning new product projects—they become the key questions in a project screening or prioritizing checklist.

FIGURE 3.2   Impact of Having Sharp, Early Product Definition on Performance

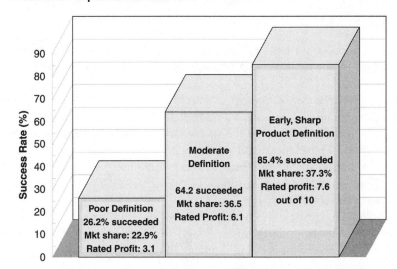

Getting sharp, fact-based product definition before development begins is key to success—triple the success rate!

Success Rate (%)

Poor Definition
26.2% succeeded
Mkt share: 22.9%
Rated Profit: 3.1

Moderate Definition
64.2 succeeded
Mkt share: 36.5
Rated Profit: 6.1

Early, Sharp Product Definition
85.4% succeeded
Mkt share: 37.3%
Rated profit: 7.6 out of 10

SOURCE: Cooper and Kleinschmidt, endnote 12.

The central role of product superiority also provides prescriptions for the management of the new product process. The development of a new product with real advantages and customer benefits becomes paramount. Simply being "equal to the competition" or "having good product/market fit" is not enough; the goal throughout the process must be product superiority and advantage.

2. A well-defined product prior to the development phase.   Successful products have *much sharper definition prior to development.* Projects that have these sharp definitions are 3.3 times as likely to be successful, have higher market shares (by 38 share points on average), are rated 7.6 out of 10 in terms of profitability (versus 3.1 out of 10 for poorly defined products), and do better at meeting company sales and profit objectives (see Figure 3.2).

What type of definition do these winners have? Before the project is allowed to proceed to development, winning products have a clear and agreed-upon definition of items such as the target market; customer needs, wants, and preferences; the product concept—what the product will be and do; and the product's specifications and requirements.

The role of sharp product definition prior to the commencement of a development program cannot be understated:

✓ Build in this *definitional step and checkpoint* into your new product process.

    ✓ This definitional step should occur before the door to development is opened—a "must have" before development can proceed.
    ✓ This definition must be based on solid evidence gathered through *voice-of-the-customer* research; it should force discipline into the preceding steps.

Make it a rule: No project proceeds to development unless this product definition is pinned down, fact-based, and signed off by the entire project team.

3. Quality of execution of technological activities. Projects where the *technical activities are carried out in a quality fashion* are considerably more successful. For example, they have 2.5 times the success rate and a higher market share, by 21 share points. These successful products have particularly high ratings for quality of execution for actions such as the preliminary technical assessment, product development, in-house product or prototype testing, trial or pilot production, and production start-up.

The implications are clear: Quality of execution is critical. How well these technological tasks are undertaken is strongly tied to new product success. The challenge for management is to build quality of execution into the new product process by design rather than as an afterthought.

4. Technological leverage. Successful projects feature a strong fit between the needs of the project and the firm's R&D or product development and engineering competencies and resources, and its production or operations resources and skills. Such products have 2.8 times the success rate and are rated higher in terms of profitability and in meeting company sales and profit objectives.

The message here is attack from a position of technological strength. The ability to leverage in-house technological competencies and resources is a key success factor. These elements of technological leverage are critical screening criteria in the evaluation and prioritization of projects.

5. Quality of execution of the front end of the project (predevelopment activities). Products that feature a high quality of execution of activities that precede the development phase—the *fuzzy front end*—are more successful. Figure 3.3 shows that these products have the following characteristics:

    ✓ a success rate of 75.0 percent (versus only 31.3 percent for projects where the predevelopment activities are found lacking)
    ✓ a higher rated profitability (7.2 out of 10 versus only 3.7 for projects where predevelopment activities are poorly undertaken)
    ✓ a market share of 45.7 percent (versus 20.8 percent)

These predevelopment activities that are found to be so pivotal to new product success include initial screening, preliminary market and technical assessments, detailed market studies, and business or financial analysis.

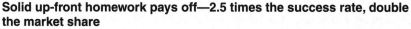

FIGURE 3.3   Impact of Doing Solid Up-front Homework

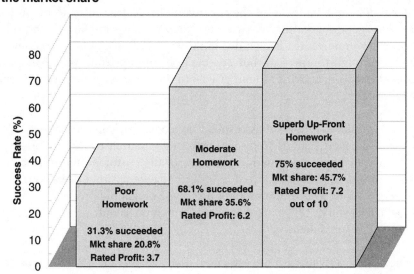

Solid up-front homework pays off—2.5 times the success rate, double the market share

Success Rate (%)

Poor Homework
31.3% succeeded
Mkt share 20.8%
Rated Profit: 3.7

Moderate Homework
68.1% succeeded
Mkt share 35.6%
Rated Profit: 6.2

Superb Up-Front Homework
75% succeeded
Mkt share: 45.7%
Rated Profit: 7.2
out of 10

SOURCE: Cooper and Kleinschmidt, endnote 12.

These five key front-end activities must be built into the new product process as a matter of routine rather than by exception. In too many projects, we observed a new product idea that moved directly into development with very little in the way of up-front homework to define the product and justify the project—a "ready, fire, aim" approach. These front-end activities are also closely linked to the product definition (item 2 above). If these predevelopment or "up-front homework" actions are not well executed, then product definition is likely to be weak, vague, or, at best, based on hearsay evidence.

6. *Marketing leverage.* Successful products feature a strong fit between the needs of the project and the firm's sales force and distribution system, its advertising resources and skills, its marketing research and intelligence resources, and its customer service capabilities. Where marketing leverage exists, the success rate is 2.3 times as great; the rated profitability is higher (a rating of 6.6 versus 3.7 out of 10); and market share is 14 share points higher than for products where marketing leverage is lacking.

When selecting and prioritizing projects, remember the critical importance of marketing leverage. These descriptors of marketing leverage (above), along with items that characterize technological leverage (item 4 above), are key criteria to build into your model for screening, selecting, and prioritizing projects.

7. *Quality of execution of marketing activities.* Many companies were particularly deficient in the way they handled the marketing side of projects. Note that "good marketing" means more than just a strong launch and selling effort; most importantly, it includes building in the voice of the customer all the way through the project, but especially in the up-front, predevelopment phases. Marketing activities found crucial to the success of the project include the following:

- ✓ a preliminary market assessment done very early in the project
- ✓ a detailed market study or marketing research to determine customer needs and build in the voice of the customer and to test the proposed product concept in order to gauge customer reaction
- ✓ customer tests of the product prototype or sample product
- ✓ a trial sell or test market to ensure purchase intent
- ✓ a market launch

When these activities are well executed, the success rate is 2.2 times as great, and market share rises 18.5 share points.

A dedication to *building in marketing activities* is central to new product success. Too often these actions are not an integral facet of the project, and when done, they are often included as an afterthought or are poorly resourced. The message is that a strong market orientation, coupled with quality of execution of these vital actions, is essential.

8. *Market attractiveness.* Products targeted at more attractive markets are more successful. In this study, attractive markets are defined as large markets with a high growth rate and markets in which the customer has a high need for the product and considers the purchase to be an important one. The success rate of products targeted at more attractive markets is 1.7 times higher, and they are rated much higher in terms of profitability and meeting sales and profit objectives.

The key drivers of new product performance at the project level, along with their impacts, are summarized in Table 3.1.

Quality of Execution

Our NewProd studies also looked at the quality of execution of key activities typically found in a new product project. Here we contrasted successes with failures in order to uncover which activities are pivotal. Where are the greatest quality differences between winners and losers? Figure 3.4 shows the results.

FIGURE 3.4   Quality of Execution

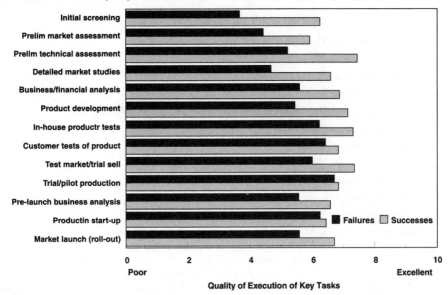

Successes have better quality-of-execution across the board; but execution quality overall is mediocre.

SOURCE: Cooper and Kleinschmidt, endnote 12.

The conclusions are provocative and raise many concerns about the way teams execute new product projects.

The greatest differences lie in the *first few steps of the new product process*— the up-front or predevelopment steps. Simply stated, the first few plays of the game seem to decide the outcome!

The dilemma is this: These up-front actions are critical and make all the difference between winning and losing. Yet management continues to "back-end load" projects, throwing resources at projects at the middle and later stages. Little time and energy are devoted to these vital predevelopment steps—only 7 percent of the dollars and 16 percent of the effort!

We saw in Chapter 2 that quality of execution was lacking in the new product process. But does it really make a difference? Does high quality of execution truly lead to success? Our NewProd results are convincing: *Successful products feature better quality of execution across the board.* (In Figure 3.4, the black bars show quality of execution for failures; the lighter bars denote successes).

Regardless of the activity, the pattern is consistent. For almost every activity in Figure 3.4, successful project teams execute the play consistently better— often not by huge differences, but consistently. It's this steady attention to executing every play better than the opposition that seems to make winners!

FIGURE 3.5   Effort Spent

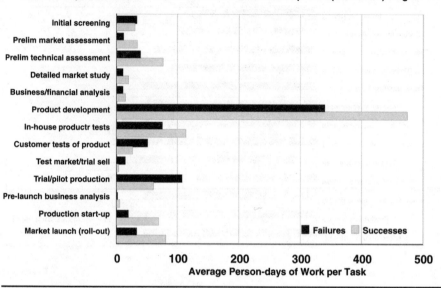

Successful products feature much more work-effort in the up-front (homework) stages.

SOURCE: Chapter 2, endnote 4.

One key to success, then, is ensuring that *every step of the new product process is executed in a quality fashion;* quality consistency is key! That's why so many companies have adopted systematic new product processes—an attempt to ensure quality and consistency of execution.

The allocation of resources within projects helps to explain why some steps and activities closely tied to success and failure are so poorly handled. Figure 3.5 provides an analysis of the number of person-days spent on a typical project, broken down across the various activities. (A similar breakdown for dollars spent was also developed but is not shown here.) This figure is similar to Figure 2.8 in the last chapter, except that this time, expenditures are broken down for successes versus failures.

What stands out in an analysis of these spending patterns is how little is spent on product failures on some of the up-front or predevelopment activities. For example, for the typical failure, the detailed market study represents only 1 percent of the total project effort, yet deficiencies here remain the number one cause of new product failure. Successes fare somewhat better with more than 2 percent devoted to this pivotal market-oriented activity, but still the effort is small. Similar patterns emerge for other predevelopment activities.

Another conclusion is that successes generally have more time and money spent on them. This is particularly true in the early stages of the process.

FIGURE 3.6   Impact of an International Orientation on New Product Success

The best place to operate is upper right, with an international product design (Global product or "Glocal" product) targeted at a world or nearest neighbor (regional) market—higher success rates and higher profits!

	Domestic Product Design	International Product Design (Global or "Glocal" Product)
World Target Market	Too few cases	84.9% successful (17.2% of cases)
Nearest=Neighbor (Regional) Target Market	45.5% successful (6.7% of cases)	78.1% successful (18.3% od cases)
Demestic Target Market	43.1% successful (31.1% of cases)	61.5% successful (23.7% ofd cases)

SOURCE: Cooper and Kleinschmidt, endnote 12.

Overall, successful products have about 75 percent more person-days devoted to the predevelopment activities than do failures.

The only steps where failures receive more effort are in the activities immediately following development: customer tests, trial sell, and trial production. By this point in the process, troubles had already appeared in the project. People resources were allocated in a desperate attempt to "fix the project," but the effort was in vain. The product still failed. Had some of this energy been applied much earlier in the project, the evidence suggests that the results would have been more positive.

The Role of an International Orientation

The globalization of markets has an obvious impact on product innovation. Two dimensions of an international orientation were investigated—markets and products:

1. *Target market.* Was the principal target market for the new product a domestic one or international? And if international, was this for "nearest neighbor" countries (for example, only within a trading region) or for the world?

2. *Product design.* Was the product principally a domestic product that was later modified to be sold abroad? Or was the product developed with international requirements in mind from the outset?

These two strategy dimensions together yield six possible strategic scenarios, as shown in Figure 3.6.

New product success rates are profoundly affected by the particular strategic scenario elected. For example, those project leaders who opted for a product with international design aimed at world markets achieved an enviable 85 percent success rate (see Figure 3.6). Unfortunately, only 17 percent of projects fit this scenario.

The most popular scenario, not surprisingly, is a domestic product strategy aimed at a domestic market. About one-third of all cases are classified in this scenario. Here, the success rate falls to a low of 43 percent.

The message is this: On all performance measures, products that are designed to meet international requirements (versus only domestic) and that are targeted at international markets—either world or nearest-neighbor export markets—are the top performers, and by a considerable margin. As expected, such products do better in foreign markets; *they also do better at home!* And most important, they perform better overall—in both profitability and in meeting sales and profit targets.

These results make a strong case for adopting an international orientation in one's product design and development efforts. The results also point to defining the world, or at minimum, your trading zone's export markets, as one's target market in product innovation.

NewProd in the Chemical Industry

The chemical industry in four countries provided the setting for yet another of our success/failure studies.[13] This NewProd investigation uncovered many of the same success factors as previous studies. But some new insights were gained:

- *Source of the idea.* Supplier-derived new product ideas, although representing only a handful of projects, have the highest success rate (86 percent). Next are customer-derived ideas (77 percent success rate). The worst source of ideas is competitors—products developed in response to a competitive introduction—only 59 percent successful. (Note: The average success rate is 66 percent.)
- *Order of entry.* The strategies of "first in" versus "be a follower" are just about equal. Products that are first into the market have a marginally higher success rate: 71 percent. Success rates drop off with later orders of entry: down to 57 percent for third into the market or later.
- *Product life cycle.* The stage of the product life cycle (PLC) of the new product's market has some impact on performance. Products aimed at

markets or product categories in the introductory PLC stage yield high failure rates: 58 percent. By contrast, new products in early growth phase categories fare well (81 percent successful), with a gradual falling off of success rates with successive stages (down to 58 percent successful for new products aimed at mature markets or categories).

- *Product advantage.* As in virtually every new product study, competitive or product advantage proves critical to success. Elements of product advantage are decisive: relative product quality, good value for money, superior to competing products in meeting customers' needs, and superior price/performance characteristics. By contrast, nonproduct elements of competitive advantage—for example, brand name, company image, aggressive sales force or advertising effort—have relatively little impact on new product financial performance (the one exception is customer service, which has a fairly strong positive impact).

- *Benefits delivered.* The exact nature of the benefit delivered does not decide success or failure. There are two exceptions:

  ✓ Lower price as a benefit strategy is not effective; the success rate drops to 29 percent!
  ✓ Improved customer service level pays off! This was the principal benefit in a small minority of cases, but the success rate was an impressive 88 percent.

- *Organization.* Projects undertaken by cross-functional teams are far more successful than projects undertaken without teams or by single-department teams. Success rates are also higher for projects where the team is responsible and accountable for the project from beginning to end (no handoffs to another group partway through the project). And where team leaders are strong, empowered, and dedicated to the project, projects have a higher success rate.

☞ **Suggestion:** Why not do what Hewlett-Packard tried? Undertake a NewProd study in your own company. Take a sample of new product projects in your firm—known successes and failures. Then characterize each, using the descriptors, factors, and variables outlined in this chapter. Take a close look at what was done in each project (and how it was done) and at the way the project was organized—team and leader. Examine other aspects of each project—the marketplace, competitive situation, leverage, and product advantage. Then try to determine what your successes shared in common that distinguished them from the failures. Finally, make up a list of prescriptions—lessons that can be learned from your own winners and losers.

Benchmarking Studies of Best Practices

The quest for the drivers of new product success has been a popular research topic for the past twenty-five years.[14] Note that most of the studies reported above focused on specific new product projects as the unit of analysis, and they contrast the characteristics of winning and losing projects. But this type of research does have its limitations. Perhaps the most fundamental flaw is the fact that research done at the project level often fails to identify company practices that decide success. There are three reasons:

1. First, success at the company level may be somewhat different than success at the project level. For example, a business may have a string of "successful" projects—measured by the return on investment of each project; but overall, these projects have relatively little impact on the firm, and so the business's total new product effort is judged to be mediocre.
2. Often important practices—for example, having an innovative climate and culture—are not readily apparent or measurable at the project level, so they are missed in such success/failure studies.
3. A final and more subtle reason for omissions is the way the research is designed. When pairs of successes and failures are selected from each firm, company characteristics that may have a strong impact on success will be common to both projects. And so these company characteristics do not emerge in an analysis of factors that distinguish the successes.

In recent years, benchmarking studies of companies' practices have become popular and have, in part, overcome some of the deficiencies listed above. But benchmarking, as practiced by most investigators, has its problems. First, there's the problem of getting the cooperation and the truth from participating firms. Second, there are methodological problems. Those doing the benchmarking are often not professional researchers, aren't sure what to measure, talk to the wrong people, interpret the "data" incorrectly, and so on—all the classic errors made by the amateur investigator. Finally, relationships typically are not studied. Best practices are noted, but the link between practices and improved performance remains largely speculative. Thus, there always remains the concern that an observed practice did not really have much impact on performance.

The Cooper-Kleinschmidt benchmarking studies sought to overcome these problems. First, by focusing on the business or business unit as the unit of analysis (rather than individual new product projects), we identified a number of company characteristics or practices often missed. Second, the research was rigorously designed, employed a large sample of firms, and utilized sophisticated data analyses methods. Finally, the link between practice and performance was investigated, so that one could conclude that certain practices really did discriminate the top performers from the rest.

FIGURE 3.7   The Three Key Drivers of a Business's New Product Performance—the Cornerstone of Performance.

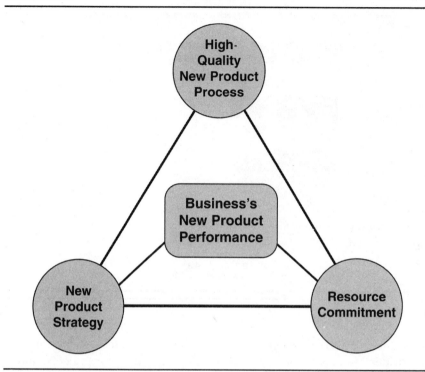

SOURCE: Cooper & Kleinschmidt, *Engineering Management Review*, endnote 3 in chapter 2.

The Cornerstones of Performance

Three critical success factors were found to be the drivers of new product performance at the business-unit level (see Figure 3.7). This is the central finding of our benchmarking of 161 businesses. The study probed ten different measures of the business's new product performance, including percentage of sales by new products, success rates, impact on the business, and overall profitability of the business's total new product efforts.

The top three drivers of performance—what really separates the best performers from the rest—in order, are the following:

1. A *high-quality new product process*—one that demands up-front homework, sharp and early product definition, tough go/kill decision points, and quality of execution and thoroughness, yet provides flexibility
2. A *defined new product strategy for the business*—one where there are new product goals for the business, where areas of focus are delineated, where the role of new products is clearly communicated, and where there is a longer-term thrust

FIGURE 3.8   Benchmarking Results: Impacts and Profit

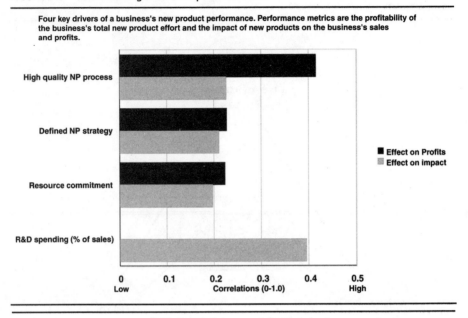

Four key drivers of a business's new product performance. Performance metrics are the profitability of the business's total new product effort and the impact of new products on the business's sales and profits.

High quality NP process

Defined NP strategy

Resource commitment

R&D spending (% of sales)

■ Effect on Profits
▨ Effect on impact

| 0 | 0.1 | 0.2 | 0.3 | 0.4 | 0.5 |
| Low | | | Correlations (0-1.0) | | High |

SOURCE: Endnote 14 in Chapter 3.

3. *Adequate resources (people and money)*—where senior management provides the needed people (and frees up their time for projects) and supports the effort with adequate R&D funding

A fourth driver follows from #3 and is also quite important:

4. *A commitment to R&D spending* for new product development (as a percentage of sales)

The other success factors, with a more modest effect on performance, include the following:

5. The use of high-quality cross-functional project teams
6. Senior management commitment to and involvement in new products
7. An innovative climate and culture
8. Senior management accountability for new product results for the business

Two composite performance metrics are highlighted in Figure 3.8: new product profitability (how profitable the business's new products efforts are overall), and the impact that new products have on the business. Consider now the top four success drivers in more detail.

1. A high-quality new product process.   A high-quality new product process is the strongest common denominator among the best-performing businesses.

Here the term "new product process" means those steps, activities, and decision points that new product projects follow from idea to launch and beyond.

A word of caution is in order here. The mere existence of a formal product development process has absolutely no effect on performance. Those companies who mistakenly believe they can "go through the motions" and reengineer their new product processes (usually amounting to documenting what they're already doing) are in for a big disappointment. Having a process didn't seem to matter; rather it was *the quality and nature of that process*—building in best practices—that really drove performance.[15]

Here now are the ingredients of such a quality process, uncovered in the benchmarking study.

There is an emphasis on up-front homework—both market and technical assessments—before projects move into the development phase.

Too many projects move from the idea stage right into development with little or no assessment. The results of this "ready, fire, aim" approach are usually disastrous. Inadequate up-front homework has been found to be a major reason for failure in product development. In the best processes observed, management has deliberately built in one or two homework stages before the "go to development" decision point, comprising vital "must do" actions.

The process includes sharp, early product definition, before development work begins.

A failure to define the product—its target market, the concept, benefits, and positioning, and its requirements, features, and specs—before development begins is a major cause of both new product failure and serious delays in the development cycle. Some companies have placed major emphasis in their new product process on getting the product definition pinned down before a formal development project is approved. This definition is based on facts, rather than hearsay and speculation, hence the need for a solid up-front homework phase.

There are tough go/kill decision points in the process, where projects really do get killed.

Projects tend to get a life of their own! In many companies we investigated, projects moved too far down the process without serious scrutiny. And it was only as the project approached commercialization that the hard truths were recognized . . . that the market wasn't quite as large as expected, or that manufacturing costs were higher than anticipated, and so on. The lack of tough go/kill decision points means too many product failures, resources wasted on the wrong projects, and a lack of focus. The result is too many marginal projects in the pipeline, while the truly deserving projects are starved. In the better processes we observed, companies had designed a *funneling or culling process* in the form of tough review points or gates where mediocre projects really did get killed.

There is a focus on quality of execution, where activities in new product projects are carried out in a quality fashion.

An emphasis on quality of execution in many firms came about after internal studies revealed that too many projects suffered from weak, inconsistent work—some of the most deficient areas being the market-related ones. Top-performing firms worked at improving quality of execution of key tasks and activities throughout the process from idea generation right through to launch. By specifying the key deliverables at each gate or decision point, and by conducting a thorough review at the gate (where the quality of work done in the previous stage or phase is rigorously scrutinized), the quality of work significantly improved. Project teams and leaders know that rigor is expected of them and, hence, set their own quality or action standards higher.

The new process is complete or thorough, and every needed activity is carried out.

Many companies discovered that not only was the quality of work lacking but, in some cases, the *work was lacking altogether*. That is, key tasks, such as market analysis, business assessment, and customer research, were simply not done (or left until far too late in the process). This deficiency caused some companies to redesign their processes, building in these tasks at the appropriate location in the process. In many companies' processes, *deliverables* are defined for each decision point or gate review; these deliverables specify what is required at a given point in the project and, hence, determine what work or tasks must be undertaken within a given stage.

The new product process is flexible; stages and decision points can be collapsed, combined, or overlapped, as dictated by the nature and risk of the project.

One pitfall some firms encounter when they do reengineer their product development process is the failure to build in flexibility. Instead of being a template or road map, the "formal process" becomes a straitjacket beset with bureaucracy. By contrast, flexible processes recognize different project risk levels. For example, for low-risk projects, the process can be fast-tracked; stages can be collapsed and decision points combined; long lead-time items can be moved forward; and detours can be allowed where risk permits.

A high-quality new product process clearly pays off. Companies that boast proficient new product processes—ones that incorporate the six ingredients listed above—are rewarded with superior performance: higher profitability and higher impact efforts. Once again, note that merely having a formal process yields no performance improvements; it is the quality of that process that makes the difference!

2. *A defined new product strategy for the business.* Having a product innovation strategy for the business—a clear and visible one—is the #2 driver of businesses' new product performance. Strategy is linked to both performance dimensions (see Figure 3.8 and Table 3.1).

There are *four main ingredients* of a positive new product strategy, which, when taken together, add up to positive performance.

There are goals or objectives for the business's total new product effort (for example, what sales, profits, etc., new products will contribute to the business).

What surprised us in our study was how many businesses lacked defined, clear, and written goals for their total new product effort. And the lack of this rather basic ingredient of strategy has negative consequences for the business. By contrast, the best performers make new product goals, such as "30 percent of our division's sales will come from new products introduced over the next three years," an explicit part of every division's business goals. Other commonly cited goals, besides percentage of sales, were "dollars sales to be generated from new products"; "percentage of profits"; and "numbers of major and minor launches per year."

The role of new products in achieving business goals is clearly communicated to all.

The reason for having goals is so that everyone involved in new products has a common purpose—something to work toward. Yet, far too often, the people who worked on new product projects were not aware of their business's new product objectives or the role that new products played in the total business objectives.

There are clearly defined areas of strategic focus to give direction to the business's total new product effort.

The new product strategy specifies the arenas where you'll play the game, or perhaps more important, where you won't play . . . what's *inbounds* and *out-of-bounds*. These strategic arenas are often defined in terms of the types of products, markets, or technologies the business will focus on. Without defined arenas, the search for specific new product ideas or opportunities is unfocused, and over time, the portfolio of new product projects will likely contain a lot of unrelated projects, in many different markets, technologies, or product types—a shotgun effort.

The business's new product effort has a long-term thrust and focus, including some longer-term projects (as opposed to short-term, incremental projects).

The short time horizon of firms has been a criticism widely voiced. This ingredient is the most important of the four strategy ingredients and is significantly linked to a number of specific performance metrics.

A sound new product strategy lies at the heart of a business's new product effort. Those businesses that lack goals for their total new product efforts, where arenas or areas of strategic thrust have not been defined, where the strategy and projects are short term in nature, and where the strategy is not well communicated are at a decided performance disadvantage on both performance dimensions.

3. *Adequate resources—people and money.*   The best performers had in place the needed resources to undertake new products; that is, senior management had made the *necessary resource commitment and kept it.* Resource commitment drives both the profitability of the business's total new product efforts and the impact that this effort has on the business (see Figure 3.8).

There are three main ingredients that lead to resource adequacy and, in turn, positive performance for the business.

The necessary resources are devoted by senior management to achieve the business's new product objectives.

In an effort to overcome weak new product performance, some managements had undertaken a reengineering or a strategic planning exercise. The problem was that the resulting strategy, goals, and process were not backed up with the needed resources, and so the initiative floundered. A lack of resources continues to plague new product projects and is often the culprit underlying poor quality of execution; there simply are not the necessary people in place or the time available to do a quality job. The result is that corners are cut, activities are done in haste, tasks are left out . . . and the results are predictable. The point is that *the resource commitment must be aligned with the business's new product objectives and processes* for positive results.

R&D budgets are adequate to achieve the stated objectives.

This is just another facet of the resource question, but with a specific focus on technical budgets. Later, we look specifically at R&D spending as a percentage of sales and its effect on new product performance.

The necessary people are in place, and release time is given for specific new product projects.

Projects are approved, and people are assigned to them. The problem is that the assigned people are often expected to work on six other projects as well or in the case of marketing and operations people, to do "their real job" in addition to the new product project. Some enlightened firms, however, are taking steps to overcome this deficiency. Some businesses "ring fence" resources—set aside dedicated resources for solely product innovation work. Other companies ensure that when projects are approved, people are assigned to projects; assignments are made realistically and in full awareness of other duties and obligations.

Creating a solid new product process (success driver #1) and articulating a new product strategy (success driver #2) are only parts of the solution. Unless the process and the strategy are properly resourced with people, time, and money, don't expect stellar performance.

4. *R&D spending.*   R&D spending going to product development, measured as a percentage of sales, is by far the strongest determinant of the *impact* of the product development effort (see Figure 3.8). But R&D spending has *no effect* whatsoever on the other performance dimension, namely, profitability of the total new

product effort. Thus, metrics that capture performance magnitude or impact, such as the popular measure "percentage of sales by new products," are driven by the magnitude of spending. The message is clear: If your performance goal is to have a high-impact new product effort—for example, to achieve a high percentage of your business's sales from new products—then increased R&D spending is the most obvious lever to pull. The relationship isn't one to one, but it is strong!

Four additional drivers of new product performance were also identified.

5. High-quality cross-functional project team. The people side of the equation—how the business organizes for product innovation—is vital to success. High-quality and effective cross-functional teams are at the heart of any well-executed project. Here's what we found made for an effective team:

- ✓ The project has an *assigned team of players*—players are clearly identified.
- ✓ These assigned players are *a cross-functional team*—from R&D, marketing, operations or manufacturing, engineering, and so on.
- ✓ The project has a *defined and accountable team leader*—a person who is ultimately responsible for the project.
- ✓ The project leader and team are *responsible* for the project *from beginning to end* (as opposed to being responsible for only one phase of a project or having project leadership change many times during a project's life).
- ✓ The team leader is *dedicated to this one project* (as opposed to leading many projects or having many other assignments). Unfortunately, in many businesses we studied, team leaders were spread too thinly across too many projects or had too many other duties to run projects effectively.
- ✓ The team interacts and communicates well and often, with *frequent project update meetings*, progress reviews, and problem resolution sessions. The best teams we observed had short weekly meetings to ensure that the entire team was up to speed.

Businesses that boast good-quality project teams, as defined above, have positive results on both performance dimensions (see Figure 3.8).

6. Senior management commitment. Businesses with greater senior management commitment to and involvement in new products produce more profitable total new product efforts.

- ✓ Management commits the *necessary resources* to achieve the firm's new product goals.
- ✓ Senior management has a central role in the new product project review process; they are *closely involved in the project go/kill* and in new product spending decisions.

7. *Innovative climate and culture.* The climate for innovation within the firm is a success factor, but it is not as strong as one might expect. Nevertheless, the average scores on this particular success factor are among the lowest of the factor scores. Here, positive climates are characterized by the following:

- ✓ There is *a new product idea scheme* within the firm that solicits ideas from all employees.
- ✓ Technical people are given *free time, scouting time,* or time off to work on projects of their own choice. Typically this constitutes 10–20 percent of the work week. Although some firms made this option available to their technical employees, we found that relatively few employees took advantage of it.
- ✓ *Resources are made available* to employees so that they can informally pursue their own projects or undertake creative work of their own choice. Such resources often include seed money for technical research and bootstrapping accounts to fund unapproved projects.
- ✓ Skunk works or *teams working on unofficial projects* are encouraged.

8. *Senior management accountability.* This final driver has the least effect overall on performance, but it does help to drive the profitability that the business achieves from new products. Management accountability captures the degree to which new product performance is measured, and senior management is held accountable for the program results. However, most businesses perform very poorly on all metrics of senior management accountability. Consider each success ingredient:

- ✓ New product performance is a part of senior management's personal *performance objectives.* The best performers do this; most businesses do not!
- ✓ Senior *management's compensation* or bonus scheme is tied to the business's new product performance. Very few businesses employ this practice.
- ✓ The *performance results* of the business's new product effort are *measured* (for example, percentage of annual sales generated by new products; or success, fail, and kill rates). Surprisingly, this practice is rare. Firms simply fail to keep score!

The evidence suggests that not only are new product performance results not closely tied to senior management's compensation scheme, or even an integral facet of senior management's annual performance objectives, but that new product performance results are rarely even measured at all in a great many firms. This may explain why the impact of this factor is so small.

The PDMA Benchmarking Study

The Product Development and Management Association (PDMA) conducts numerous studies on product development practices. One major investigation by Griffin begins with a comprehensive review of a number of noteworthy industrial benchmarking studies.[16] Her conclusion is that these studies repeat similar themes.

New product processes are vital.   Although new product development processes are a relatively recent phenomenon, they are seen as necessary for effective new product development (NPD). Over the years, the focus has moved from defining the process to assuring implementation, to better managing the up-front portion, to better measuring the process, and to continually improving the process.

Cross-functional teams are essential, but there is no magic organizational design.   Organizationally there are two consistent themes, according to Griffin. First, virtually every study claims that effectively implementing multifunctional teams is crucial to NPD success. Second, the studies consistently relate that NPD is melded into the firm's organization through multiple structures within each firm; there is no one best structure or organizational design that supports effective cross-functional teams.

Support is needed from top management.   Another consistent finding is the need for tangible and visible top management support of NPD, especially in terms of providing adequate funding and resources and explicit and consistent strategies. This includes having a rational process for allocating resources across projects and a well thought-out strategy for NPD both at the firm level and for the particular project under way.

Here are some specific findings from the PDMA review of various benchmarking studies:

✓ A Mercer study recommends formulating product strategy early in the project, involving potential customers directly in product development, consistently following the project execution process from project to project, having top management visibly and tangibly committing to NPD, and explicitly formulating and communicating the firm's NPD strategy.[17]

✓ Another study finds that marketers and engineers in best-in-class firms carefully distinguish between customer requirements (needs) and product features (solutions to customer needs) and have explicit documents that describe each separately.[18]

✓ Another study concludes that at the project level, best practices include using cross-functional teams, a structured development process with action-oriented stage reviews, and an integrated set of development tools (such as quality function deployment, rapid prototyping, and simulation).[19]

✓ In a survey by Fact Finders, Inc., about 57 percent of the respondents used a formal NPD process, with 52 percent including test marketing as part of that process prior to launch.[20]

The PDMA Best Practices Survey

The PDMA study led by Griffin conducted a major survey of 383 member firms in the United States—a hard look at both NPD performance as well as practices employed. Best companies are contrasted with the rest in terms of their new product practices. Here are some key findings of this study.[21]

NPD Process.   The best companies are more likely to use some type of formal NPD process than the rest (68 percent versus 44 percent). Griffin notes, however, that "nearly 60 percent of the firms surveyed use some form of *Stage-Gate*™ process for NPD. They are more likely to have moved from simpler *Stage-Gate* processes to more sophisticated facilitated or third-generation processes and are more likely to have had processes in place for a longer period of time."

Activities in the Process.   Processes that include more activities are associated with increased success. The best firms are more likely to include the following activities in their process:

✓ product-line planning
✓ strategy development
✓ concept generation
✓ concept screening

For example, the best companies start each project with a strategy-setting exercise that outlines the goals and activities of the project, and they are more likely to have a more comprehensive set of front-end activities completed before the development phase.

An NPD Strategy.   The best base their new product efforts on a new product strategy for the business. Because the best initiate only projects that are more closely aligned with strategy, their projects have a much higher likelihood of success. They undertake "the right projects" rather than large numbers of projects.

Teams.   The best are more likely to use multifunctional teams. Despite the fact that multifunctional teams are more difficult to manage, the best find that their benefits outweigh the drawbacks. And the best reward project teams in many ways. These rewards tend to be based on recognition rather than remuneration.

Tools and Techniques. The best do significantly more qualitative market research than the rest. They use four different types of research:

- ✓ voice of customer: one-on-one in-depth situation-based customer interviews to uncover needs
- ✓ customer site visits: in-depth interviews conducted at the customer's place of work or residence
- ✓ concept testing: potential users provide either qualitative or quantitative reactions to concepts prior to development
- ✓ beta site testing: evaluation of the product prototype and precommercial product's performance in actual use conditions

The best also make more use of advanced engineering design tools, including the following:

- ✓ value analysis for determining the relative cost/benefit ratio for differing feature sets
- ✓ rapid prototyping
- ✓ concurrent engineering

The PDMA's study concludes with this summary:

The Best do not succeed by using just one NPD practice more extensively or better, but by using a number of them more effectively. They expect more, and get more by

- ✓ measuring NPD performance and expecting more out of NPD efforts. Best firms expect 45 percent of their sales to come from new products commercialized in the last three years.
- ✓ focusing on doing NPD right to achieve higher results. Best practice firms achieve significantly better outcomes than other firms. On average 49 percent of their sales came from products commercialized in the last five years, about twice the rate of the Rest of the firms; and over 80 percent of the projects commercialized are successful.
- ✓ implementing *Stage-Gate*™ processes and progressing to more advanced forms as quickly as possible
- ✓ starting NPD projects with a strategy activity and including more activities in their processes
- ✓ driving product development efforts through specific NPD strategies at both the program and project level

✓ rewarding teams nonfinancially both publicly and privately, in multiple ways. Best-practice firms currently do not use team-based financial rewards for NPD.

✓ quickly implementing new market research and engineering design tools, especially those that help them more efficiently deliver products that solve problems for consumers.[22]

The checked items above are logical recommendations for you and your company. After all, they're based on what the best do.

☞ **Suggestion:** Take a closer look at the benchmarking studies of best practices outlined above. For example, take the eight success drivers uncovered in the Cooper-Kleinschmidt benchmarking study, along with some of the ingredients of each factor, and evaluate your company. Ask, "How well are we doing on each success driver?" Better yet, use our *ProBE* analysis, a detailed questionnaire-based benchmarking and diagnostic tool based on the same study (Appendix A).[23] Next consider some of the best practices uncovered in the PDMA and other studies. Make a list of the ones that are relevant to your business. Be sure to consider the dominant themes that Griffin uncovered: a systematic NPD process; an articulated NPD strategy; and effective cross-functional teams. And again rate yourself. And be sure to review the checklist of activities and practices (above) that the best rely on in order to achieve superior performance.

What Makes a Winner?

What emerges from a review of the many studies of new product performance—both at the project level and at the business-unit level—is a clear pattern. New product success is not a matter of luck. Rather, it is fairly predictable and, in many cases, quite controllable. At the project level, factors that describe the way the project is organized and undertaken—actions, process, and players—dominate the list of success factors. And specific business practices—having a new product process, an articulated product innovation strategy, adequate resources, and effective cross-functional teams—characterize the top-performing businesses. In the next chapter, I take these many findings and conclusions and fashion them into a concise set of fifteen critical success factors for stellar product innovation.

4

Lessons for Success:
The Critical Success Factors

I am the master of my fate; I am the captain of my soul.
—W. E. Henley, *Invictus*

Fifteen Critical Success Factors

The challenge is to design a blueprint or process for successful product innovation—a process by which new product projects can move quickly and effectively from the idea stage to a successful launch and beyond. Before charging into this process, reflect for a moment on what we have learned from the many investigations into new product performance. A number of underlying themes and recurring messages emerge as one examines the experiences of various companies. Consider now the more evident lessons—the critical success factors that make the difference between winning and losing; reflect on how you can benefit from each and how you can translate each into an operational facet of your new product process. See Table 4.1 for a summary of the fifteen critical success factors (CSF).[1]

1. The number one success factor is a unique superior product: a differentiated product that delivers unique benefits and superior value to the customer.

Product superiority—delivering unique benefits and product value to users—separates winners from losers more often than any other single factor. Such superior products have five times the success rate, over four times the market share, and four times the profitability as products lacking this ingredient, according to

---

Table 4.1: Fifteen Critical Success Factors in Product Innovation

1. The number one success factor is a unique superior product: a differentiated product that delivers unique benefits and superior value to the customer.

2. A strong market orientation – a market-driven and customer-focused new product process – is critical to success.

3. Look to the world product: An international orientation in product design, development, and target marketing provides the edge in product innovation.

4. More predevelopment work – the homework – must be done before product development gets under way.

5. Sharp and early product and project definition is one of the key differences between winning and losing at new products.

6. A well-conceived, properly executed launch is central to new product success. And a solid marketing plan is at the heart of the launch.

7. The right organizational structure, design, and climate are key factors in success.

8. Top management support doesn't guarantee success, but it sure helps. But many senior managers get it wrong.

9. Leveraging core competencies is vital to success – "step-out" projects tend to fail.

10. Products aimed at attractive markets do better: market attractiveness is a key project-selection criterion.

11. Successful businesses build tough Go/Kill decision points into their new product process, where projects really do get killed: better focus is the result.

12. New product success is controllable: More emphasis is needed on completeness, consistency, and quality of execution of key tasks from beginning to end of project.

13. The resources must be in place – there is no free lunch in product innovation.

14. Speed is everything! But not at the expense of quality of execution.

15. Companies that follow a multistage, disciplined new product process – a Stage-Gate™ process – fare much better.

---

our research. Product advantage, superiority, or differentiation as the key determinant of success is a recurring theme in many new product studies.

This result should come as no surprise to product innovators. Apparently it isn't obvious to everyone, however. Indeed, most firms miss the mark here: A number of studies point out that "tired products" and "me too" offerings are the rule rather than the exception in many firms' new product efforts. The NewProd investigations revealed that much time and energy are devoted to projects that yield "copycat," undifferentiated products; and 82 percent of such efforts fail! A second very popular scenario, which also yields poor results, is the technical solution in search of a market.

Very few firms can point to specific facets of their new product methodology that emphasize this one vital success ingredient. Often product superiority is absent as a project selection criterion, and rarely are steps deliberately built into the process that encourage the design of such superior products. Indeed, quite the reverse is true: The preoccupation with cycle time reduction and the tendency to favor simple, inexpensive initiatives actually penalize projects that lead to product superiority.

Consider a new product project that is currently under way at your company. How high does your new project score on each of the following ingredients of a unique, superior product?

- ✓ has unique features for the customer
- ✓ meets customer needs better than competitors' products
- ✓ has high relative product quality
- ✓ solves customers' problems with competitive products
- ✓ reduces customers' costs
- ✓ is innovative or novel

If it scores high on each, then your new product project has a good chance of success, and it should be prioritized accordingly. These ingredients are useful *screening criteria* for rating and ranking new product projects—a checklist. But if your project is like many and scores low on these product superiority items, then take care! Its odds of becoming a big winner are low.

The challenge the product developer faces is to ensure that the elements of product superiority are built into each and every new product. In short, the list of these six ingredients of product advantage should become personal objectives of the project leader and team and must be molded into the game plan.

But how does one invent or build in product superiority? Note that superiority is derived from design, features, functionality, attributes, specifications, and even positioning. The important point here is that "superiority" is defined from the customer's standpoint, not in the eyes of the R&D, technical, or design departments. More than unique features are required to make a product superior, however. Remember: Features are those things that cost you, the supplier, money. By contrast, benefits are what customers pay money for! Often the two—features and benefits—are not the same. In defining "unique benefits," think of the product as a "bundle of benefits for the user" and a benefit as something the customer views as having value to him or her.

☞ **Suggestion:** The definitions of "unique and superior" and "benefit" are constructed from the customer's perspective—so they *must be based on an in-depth understanding of customer needs, wants, problems, likes, and dislikes.*

1. *Determine customer needs at the outset—build in voice-of-customer research early in your projects.* The goal here is to identify customer needs, not just their wants. *Wants* are usually fairly obvious and easy for the customer to talk about. But spotting *needs,* particularly *unmet and unarticulated needs,* is more of a challenge but often yields your break-

through new product. So start with a user needs-and-wants study—market research and customer insights—to probe customer needs, wants, problems, preferences, likes, and dislikes. Determine the customer's "hot buttons"—the order-winning criteria, the customer's problems, and what the customer is *really seeking* in a much-improved or superior product. Let the customer help design the product for you.

2. *Do a competitive product analysis.* There is no such thing as a perfect competitive product. If you can understand the competitor's product weaknesses, then you're halfway to beating him or her. Remember: The goal is product superiority, and that means superiority over the current or future competitive offering. Take the competitor's product apart in your lab or design department; and when you do the voice-of-customer research, be sure to ask your customers for their opinions about the strengths and weaknesses of the competitor's product. One more point: Anticipate what the competitor's product might be in the foreseeable future. Never assume his or her current product will be the competitive benchmark by the time you hit the market! Once these two investigations are complete, the project team translates the information into a product definition, paying special attention to the benefits and the *value proposition* that the product will offer to the customer (see CSF #5).

3. *Build in multiple test iterations to test and verify your assumptions about your winning product design.* Once the product concept and specifications are defined (based on user inputs), test the concept with users and make sure they respond favorably. That is, even before serious development work begins, start testing the product—even though you don't yet have a product!—through concept, virtual prototype, or protocept tests.

Once into development, continue to test through a series of rapid prototypes—an *iterative* or "back and forth" process. That is, build or develop a facet of the product and take it to the customer for reaction. Involve the customer in this iterative process of build-and-test, even as the product takes shape: Let the customer react to working models, rapid prototypes, and final prototypes as the development progresses. Finally, after development, build in field trials or beta tests to gauge product acceptance, and even consider a test market or trial sell.

This disciplined approach to discovering product superiority is decidedly customer-focused, which leads to CSF #2, the need for a strong market orientation.

2. A strong market orientation—a market-driven and customer-focused new product process—is critical to success.

A thorough understanding of customers' needs and wants, the competitive situation, and the nature of the market is an essential component of new product success. This finding is supported in virtually every study of product success factors. Recurring themes include the following:

- ✓ need recognition
- ✓ understanding user needs
- ✓ constant customer contact
- ✓ strong market knowledge and market research
- ✓ quality of execution of marketing activities
- ✓ more spending on the up-front marketing activities

Conversely, a failure to adopt a strong market orientation in product innovation, an unwillingness to undertake the needed market assessments and to build in the voice of the customer, and neglecting to include the customer in product development lead to disaster. Poor market research, inadequate market analysis, weak market studies, test markets, and market launch, and inadequate resources devoted to marketing activities are common weaknesses found in virtually every study of new product failure.

Unfortunately, a strong market orientation is missing in the majority of businesses' new product projects. Marketing activities tend to be the weakest-rated activities of the entire new product process. And relatively few resources and little money are spent on marketing actions—particularly those that occur in the early stages of the project.

To be successful, a market orientation must prevail throughout the entire new product project. It begins with *idea generation:* Companies must devote more resources to market-oriented idea generation activities, such as focus groups with customers; in-depth, one-on-one interviews with customers; customer site visits, especially by technical people; the active solicitation of ideas from customers by the sales force; and the development of relationships with lead users.

A market orientation also has a vital role in the actual design of the product— when the product's requirements and specs are being defined. Too often market research, when it is conducted, is misused in the new product process. It tends to be done as an afterthought, after the product design has been decided and to verify that the proposed product indeed has market acceptance. If the results of the market study are negative, most often they are conveniently ignored, and the project is pushed ahead regardless.

The mistake is clear: Market research, seeking customer insights, and building in the voice of the customer must be used as an *input to the design decisions* and not solely as an after-the-fact check. Investigations to determine users' needs, wants, and preferences and to identify competitive product strategies, strengths, and weaknesses provide insights that are invaluable guides to the design team *before* they charge into the design of the new product.

Make sure that you understand the customer's problem before you jump to a solution! Build in the voice of the customer early in the project through

✓ in-depth, one-on-one personal interviews
✓ customer site visits (done by the entire project team)
✓ "fly-on-the wall" or "day-in-the-life-of" research
✓ "camping out" with the customer (extended site visits, similar to anthropological research)
✓ customer panels
✓ larger sample quantitative market research

Even in the case of technology-push new products (where the product emanates from the lab or technical group, perhaps the result of a technological breakthrough or a technical possibility), there still should be considerable marketing input as the technology is shaped into a final product design. That is, following the technical discovery, but before full-fledged development gets underway, there is ample opportunity to research and interact with the customer to determine needs and wants, to shape the final product the way the customer wants it, and to gauge likely product acceptance.

Before pushing ahead into development, be sure to test the product concept with the customer. This you can do by presenting a representation of the product–models, mock-ups, protocepts, drawings, and even virtual products created on a computer–and gauging the customer's interest, liking, and purchase intent. It's much cheaper to test and learn before development begins than to develop the product first and then begin customer testing!

Customer inputs shouldn't cease at the completion of the up-front market studies. Testing concepts or designs with the customer is very much an interactive or "back and forth" process. During the actual development phase of the project, and after the market research is done, *constant and continuing customer contact* remains essential. Keep bringing the customer into the process to view facets of the product as the prototype or final product takes shape. Develop rapid prototypes, working models, or facsimiles of the product as early as possible to show to the customer in order to seek feedback regarding market acceptance and needed design changes. Don't wait until the very end of the development phase—the field trials—to unveil the product to the customer. There could be some very unpleasant surprises!

3. Look to the world product: An international orientation in product design, development, and target marketing provides the edge in product innovation.

Here the evidence is clear. International products targeted at world and nearest-neighbor export markets are the top performers, according to the NewProd studies described in Chapter 3. By contrast, products designed with only the domestic market in mind and sold to domestic and nearest-neighbor export markets fare less well. The magnitude of the differences between these international and exported new products and domestic products are striking: International products perform two to three times higher on various new product gauges. And the fact that international new products aimed at foreign markets also do better in the home market—almost double the domestic market share as domestic products—is a provocative finding.

The comfortable strategy of "design the product for domestic requirements, capture the home market, and then export a modified version of the product sometime in the future" is myopic. It leads to inferior results today; and with increasing globalization of markets, it will certainly lead to even poorer results in the years ahead. The threat is that your domestic market will become someone else's international market. To define the new product market as "domestic" and perhaps a few other "convenient countries" severely limits your market opportunities. For maximum success in product innovation, the objective must be to design for the world and market to the world. Unfortunately, this international dimension is an often overlooked facet of new product game plans, or if it is included, it is often handled late in the process or as a side issue.

An international orientation means defining the market as an international one and designing products to meet international requirements, not just domestic. The result is either a *global* product (one version for the entire world) or a *glocal* product (one development effort, one product concept, but perhaps several product variants to satisfy different international markets).

One implication of this need to adopt a global orientation is the design and implementation of a *transnational new product process.* The global requirement increases the complexity of product development considerably; it means that, more than ever, firms must adopt a systematic and consistent new product process. This transnational new product process is one that both domestic and international units utilize and that integrates the following activities across country borders.

- ✓ Ideas for new products are solicited from many countries and are screened and prioritized through a global project prioritization (or portfolio management) group.
- ✓ Global gatekeeping or go/kill decision-making groups are established where senior managements from multiple countries make the decision to move ahead together and jointly fund the project.
- ✓ Global criteria for go/kill and project prioritization decisions replace the traditional domestic ones.
- ✓ Projects are executed by international project teams; team members reside in different countries and different tasks are undertaken in various countries.
- ✓ International customer contact and input is the rule; for example, market studies and field trials in a variety of countries are built into the process.

4. More predevelopment work—the up-front homework—must be done before product development gets under way.

We all learned in school how distasteful homework was. Many of us haven't forgotten: We hate homework! But then, as now, homework or due diligence is critical to winning. The NewProd and other studies reveal that the steps that precede the actual design and development of the product—screening, market studies, technical feasibility assessment, and building the business case—are key factors separating winners from losers. Errors and omissions in these vital activities can and often do spell disaster later in the project.

Studies of new product failures show that weaknesses in the up-front activities seriously compromise the projects. The *fuzzy front end* of the project is too often the culprit! Inadequate market analysis and a lack of market research, moving directly from an idea into a full-fledged development effort, and a failure to spend time and money on the up-front steps are familiar themes in product failures. Most firms confess to serious weaknesses in the up-front or predevelopment steps of their new product process. The evidence from the data on resources spent in the NewProd studies shows pitifully small amounts of time and money devoted to these critical steps: 7 percent of the dollars and 16 percent of the effort.

More homework prior to the initiation of product design and development has been consistently found to be a key factor in success. The quality of execution of the predevelopment steps—initial screening, preliminary market and technical studies, market research, and business analysis—is closely tied to the product's financial performance. And successful projects have more than 1.75 times as many person-days spent on predevelopment steps as do failures. The emphasis that the Japanese devote to the planning stage of the new product process is described by Havelock and Elder:

> Japanese developers make a clear distinction between the "planning" and the "implementation" phases of a new technology initiative. . . . The objective of planning is complete understanding of the problem and the related technology before a "go" decision is made. It is reported to be an unrushed process, which might look agonizingly drawn out to Western eyes.[2]

The predevelopment activities are important because they qualify and define the project. They answer these key success questions:[3]

- Is the project an economically attractive one? Will the product sell at sufficient volumes and margins to justify investment in development and commercialization?
- Who exactly is the target customer? How should the product be positioned?

- What exactly should the product be to make it a winner? What features, attributes, and performance characteristics should be built into it to yield a unique superior product?
- Can the product be developed and at the right cost? What is the likely technical solution?
- What about source of supply? By us or by others? And at what cost and investment?
- Do we need a partner? Who and with what capabilities?

"More homework means longer development times" is a frequently voiced complaint. This is a valid concern, but studies have shown that homework pays for itself in reduced development times as well as improved success rates.

- First, all the evidence points to a much higher likelihood of product failure if the homework is omitted. The choice is between a slightly longer project or greatly increased odds of failure.
- Second, better project definition—the result of sound homework— actually *speeds up the development process.*[4] Many projects are poorly defined when they enter the development phase: vague targets and moving goalposts. This is usually the result of weak predevelopment activities. The target user is not well understood, user needs and wants are vaguely defined, and desired product features and performance requirements are clouded. With a poorly defined product and project, R&D, engineering, and design people waste considerable time seeking definition, often recycling back several times as the project parameters change.
- Third, rarely does a product concept remain the same from beginning to end of the project. The original idea that triggered the project is seldom the same as the product that eventually goes to market. Given this inevitable product design evolution, the time to make the majority of these design improvements or changes is *not* as the product is moving out of development and into launch. More homework up-front anticipates these changes and encourages them to occur earlier in the process rather than later, when they are more costly. The result is considerable savings in time and money at the back end of the project and a more efficient new product process overall.

The message is that more time and resources must be devoted to the activities that precede the design and development of the product. These initial screening, analysis, and definitional stages are critical to success. Managers must resist the temptation to skip over the up-front stages of a project and move an ill-defined and poorly investigated project into the development phase.[5]

5. Sharp and early product and project definition is one of the key differences between winning and losing at new products.

How well the project is defined prior to entering the development phase is increasingly cited as a key success factor.[6] Crawford implores managers to include a *product definition step* just prior to the development phase, where the requirements of the product are clearly spelled out and agreed to by all parties involved in the project.[7] Getting the product definition right was also uncovered as the key to success in an internal study undertaken by Hewlett-Packard.[8] And the NewProd studies find that sharpness of product definition prior to development is the number two factor in new product success, right after product advantage. Sharply defined products have over three times the success rates of less-defined products!

By contrast, a failure to define the product and project scope before development begins is a major cause of both new product failure and serious delays in time to market. In spite of the fact that early and stable product definition is consistently cited as a key to success, businesses continue to perform poorly here. Terms such as "unstable products specs" and "project scope creep" describe far too many new product projects in our studies.[9]

☞**Suggestion:** Build in a product and project definition step or checkpoint before the door is opened to a full development program. This definition should include the following:

- ✓ the project scope: What are the bounds of the development effort? Is it a single new product? A family of products or series of releases? Or a platform development?
- ✓ the target market definition: Who precisely is the product aimed at?
- ✓ the product concept: What will the product be and do (written in the language of the customer)?
- ✓ the benefits to be delivered: What is the value proposition for the customer?
- ✓ the positioning strategy: How will the product be perceived by potential customers? What is the price point?
- ✓ the product features, attributes, performance requirements, and high-level specs.

This definition must be fact-based: It is developed with inputs and agreement from the functional areas involved: marketing, R&D, engineering, and production. It must be signed off by the entire project team, and senior management should also commit to the definition. This is the essential "buy in."[10]

Projects that have sharp product and project definition prior to development are considerably more successful. Here's why:

1. Building a definition step into the new product process forces more attention to the up-front or predevelopment activities. If the homework hasn't been done, then arriving at a sharp definition that all parties will buy into is next to impossible.

2. The definition serves as a communication tool and guide. All-party agreement or "buy in" means that each functional area involved in the project has a clear and consistent definition of what the product and project are—and is committed to it. How often have you left a meeting, thinking that agreement was achieved, only to find out later that there are many different versions of what was agreed to, depending on whom you speak to! This product definition is the agreement in black and white.

3. This definition also provides a clear set of objectives for the development phase of the project and for the development team members. With clear product objectives, development typically proceeds more efficiently and quickly: no moving goalposts and no fuzzy targets!

The one exception I make to demanding sharp, firm product definition is in the case of very fast-paced markets and technologies. Some high-tech and information technology (IT) industries are typical. Here it may be difficult to pin down all the details of the product requirements at the outset, simply because the market is so fluid; requirements and competitive products are changing quickly. But throwing up one's hands and saying "nothing can be defined—the definition is 100 percent fluid" is also wrong. Another common error in such projects occurs when, in the desire to get to market quickly in order to beat competition, one skips over the up-front homework. This makes fact-based product definition almost impossible.

Both arguments—fluid markets and the desire for speed—are very lame excuses for not getting the product definition nailed down early in the project. The arguments for moving in haste would be compelling if it weren't for the heavy evidence against them! Recognize that a *disproportionate number of high-tech and software projects fail commercially:*

   ✓ Only 20 percent of software projects are commercial winners, according to a survey by Kleinschmidt.[11] One study he cites notes that companies scrap almost one-third of new projects for a loss of $80 billion annually and that 50 percent of projects run more than 180 percent over budget.

   ✓ "Only around one-quarter of IT projects are completed on time, on budget, and with all the functions originally specified," according to the U.S. research organization, the Standish Group.[12]

Recommendations for high-tech and IT industries include the following:

✓ Build in the necessary up-front homework. A fast-paced market is no excuse for taking costly shortcuts. The choice is between fast failures or thoughtful successes.

✓ Pin down the product definition as best you can before development begins, using the list of items outlined above.

✓ Specify which parts of the product requirements and specs are fixed and which are fluid or variable before development begins (ideally more than 50 percent should be fixed on entering development).

✓ Build steps into the development process to gather data so that the variable parts of your product definition can be pinned down as development proceeds.

The approach is not ideal, but it's a reasonable solution to the problem of designing products in very fluid markets.

6. A well-conceived, properly executed launch is central to new product success, and a solid marketing plan is at the heart of the launch.

Whoever said "Build a better mousetrap and the world will beat a path to your door" was a poet, not a businessman. This old adage may never have been true, and it certainly hasn't been true for the past several decades. Not only must the product be superior, but its benefits must be communicated and marketed aggressively for it to succeed.

The best products in the world won't sell themselves! A strong marketing effort, a well-targeted selling approach, and effective after-sales service are central to the successful launch of the new product. But a well-integrated and properly targeted launch does not occur by accident; it is the result of a *fine-tuned marketing plan*, properly backed and resourced, and proficiently executed.

Marketing planning—moving from marketing objectives to strategy and marketing programs—is a complex process. Entire books have been devoted to the subject. But this complex marketing planning process must be woven into your new product process. For example, defining the target market and the development of a positioning strategy, one of the core steps in developing a marketing plan, is logically part of the product definition step just before development begins (success factor #5 above). And answers to many key questions—How do customers buy? Through what channels of distribution do they buy? What are their sources of information? What servicing do they require?—are central to developing the nuts and bolts of marketing programs. Answers to these questions must come from market research investigations that are built into the new product process or game plan.

☞ **Suggestion:** There are three important points regarding new product launch and the marketing plan:

1. The development of a marketing plan is an *integral part of the new product process;* it is as central to the new product process as the development of the physical product. Thus the marketing planning process must be integrated into the new product process.
2. The development of a marketing plan *must begin early* in the new product project. It should not be left as an afterthought to be undertaken as the product nears commercialization, as one manager admitted: "When the product's rolling down the production line, that's when our sales and marketing people become involved." Critical facets of the marketing plan must already be in place before the product's design and development phase even begins. Some of these facets will be concrete, such as target market definition, positioning strategy, and product design requirements; others will be more tentative, such as the pricing strategy and promotional approach.
3. A marketing plan is only as good as the *market intelligence* upon which it is based. Market studies designed to yield information crucial to marketing planning must be built into the new product game plan.

7. The right organizational structure, design, and climate are key factors in success.

Design your organization for product innovation. Product innovation is not a one-department show! It is very much a multidisciplinary, cross-functional effort. Organizational design—how you organize for new products—is critical. Except for the simplest of products and projects—line extensions and product updates—product innovation must cut across traditional functional boundaries and barriers.

The evidence is compelling: Investigations into new product success consistently cite interfaces between R&D and marketing, coordination among key internal groups, multidisciplinary inputs to the new product project, and the role of teams and the team leader. Successful new product projects feature a balanced process consisting of critical activities that fall into many different functional areas within the firm: marketing and marketing research, engineering, R&D, production, purchasing, and finance, to name a few. The Stanford Innovation Project study of new product launches in high-technology firms reveals that a critical distinguishing factor between success and failure is the "simultaneous involvement of the create, make, and market functions." Our NewProd studies show that projects undertaken by empowered multifunctional teams are more successful. Similarly, analyses of Japanese successes emphasize their attention to manufacturability from the start of development efforts, the location in one place of engineers, designers, and manufacturers, and the conception of management unconstrained by traditional American functionalism.[13] Finally, Griffin's review of multiple benchmarking studies, along with her own PDMA best-practices study, reveals that effective cross-functional teams are fundamental to success.[14]

How does one design a process that integrates these many activities and multifunctional inputs? And how does one ensure quality of execution of these varied tasks, which are spread throughout the organization? One answer is to develop a systematic approach to product innovation—a blueprint or road map—that cuts across functional boundaries and forces the active participation of people from different functions. Make every step or stage a multifunctional one. That is, the new product process builds in different tasks and provides checks and balances that require the input and involvement of these various functions.

For example: A project cannot proceed into a full-scale development effort until a detailed market assessment has been completed and a manufacturing or operations appraisal is complete. Without the active participation of both operations and marketing people, the project does not get released to development—it goes nowhere!

A second and equally important answer lies in *organizational design.* What type of organization structure will bring many players from different walks of life in the company together in an integrated effort? In short, how do we take a diverse group of players and turn them into a team?

It's clear that the traditional functional organizational structure does not suit many of the needs of product innovation. Indeed, functional and functional matrix approaches led to the lowest new product performance, according to one study reported in Chapter 3. Companies must move to team approaches that cut across functional lines. There are three approaches that appear to work best:

- *Balanced matrix:* A project manager is assigned to oversee the project and *shares the responsibility and authority* for completing the project with the functional managers. There is joint approval and direction.
- *Project matrix:* A project manager is assigned to oversee the project and has *primary responsibility and authority* for the project. Functional managers assign personnel as needed and provide technical expertise.
- *Project team:* A project manager is put in charge of a project team composed of a core group of personnel from several functional areas. The functional managers have *no formal involvement or authority.*

Tom Peters argues strongly in favor of project teams: "The single most important reason for delays in development activities is the absence of multifunction (and outsider) representation on development projects from the start."[15] Peters continues: "The answer is to co-mingle members of all key functions, co-opt each function's traditional feudal authority, and use teams." Project teams appear to be best suited for large, complex projects, whereas a project matrix approach works best for both complex and simpler projects.

Regardless of which of the three structures is elected, strong project *leadership*—a dedicated and empowered project leader—appears to be essential for timely, successful projects. The leader must have formal authority (this means co-opting authority from functional heads); the leader and team must be empowered to make project decisions and must not be second-guessed, over-ruled, or micromanaged by the functional heads or senior management.

To work well, team members should be located close to each other. "Physical proximity is one of the keys to good teamwork" is the conclusion of studies done in a number of firms. 3M reports that physical distances beyond 100 yards thwarts team interaction severely. Co-location is one solution—team members from different functions in the company are relocated in one area or depart-ment. A team office is another solution. Although many people may work on a project during its life, the core team should number no more than eight people, according to studies done at AT&T; the ideal number is five to seven. And core team members should be dedicated to the project 100 percent of their time!

The final organizational ingredient essential to making this multifunctional team work is *climate and culture.* The climate must reward and encourage cre-ativity and innovation. One 3M executive was asked at a recent conference why 3M is so innovative, in spite of the many traditional industries it embraces. She replied simply, "We *pay* people to be innovative; and we give them *the time* to be innovative!" For example, 3M provides cash awards to about 10 percent of its employees annually for doing innovative and creative things. Milliken has a hall of fame, whereby individuals and teams are publicly recognized for their contributions to innovative projects. And the best companies in the PDMA best-practices study emphasize employee recognition for new product performance.

At the same time, the climate must avoid punishment for failure. The only way to ensure no failures is to take no chances. So if failures are punished, expect little in the way of risk-taking and entrepreneurial behavior. The next time you have a product failure, throw a party—not to reward incompetence, but to celebrate all you have learned. Of course, the real reason is to send out a message to would-be intrapreneurs that it's okay to fail!

Additionally, the resources must be available to enable people to do creative and innovative work. Some companies have a deliberate policy to make resources available to innovators. 3M provides its technical people with about one day per week to work on their own pet projects, and many a successful new product project has been initiated as a "boot-strapped" project—using spare time and spare money. Both Rohm & Haas and Bayer-U.S. allow 10 percent time off for scouting work.

8. Top management support doesn't guarantee success, but it sure helps. But many senior managers get it wrong.

Top management support is a necessary ingredient for product innovation. But it must be the right kind of support. Many managers get it wrong! The Stanford Innovation Project and the Hewlett-Packard study both found top management support to be directly linked to new product success. But one of our NewProd studies found a different twist. Top managers supported failures with almost equal frequency as successes. Those projects in which top management is committed, is involved directly in the management of the project, and provides considerable guidance and direction for the project are only marginally more successful.

Where top management support is critical, however, is in getting the product to market. When killed projects were compared to launched products in the NewProd studies, top management support emerged as an important variable. Top management can muster the resources, cut through the red tape, and push the right buttons to get the project done.

The message is that top management's main role in product innovation is to *set the stage* for product innovation to occur, to be a "behind-the-scenes" facilitator, and not so much to be an actor front and center.

This stage-setting role is vital: Management must make the long-term commitment to internal product development as a source of growth. It must develop a vision and a strategy for product innovation that are driven by corporate objectives and strategies. It must make available the necessary resources and ensure that these resources aren't diverted to more immediate needs in times of shortage. It must commit to a disciplined process to drive products to market. And most important, senior management must empower project teams and support committed champions by acting as mentors, facilitators, or executive sponsors to project leaders and teams—acting as "executive champions," as Peters calls them.[16]

Senior management's role is not to get involved in projects on a day-to-day basis, or to be constantly meddling and interfering in the project, or to micromanage projects. This meddling behavior is unproductive for two reasons: It usurps the empowerment of the team (and hence defeats the empowered team concept); and frankly, senior management doesn't do such a great job at either picking winners or managing projects!

9. Leveraging core competencies is vital to success; "step-out" projects tend to fail.

Leverage and synergy are the common threads that bind the new business to the old. When translated into product innovation, the ability to leverage existing and in-house strengths, competencies, resources, and capabilities increases the odds of success of the new product project. By contrast, "step-out" projects take the firm into territory that lies beyond the experience and resource base of the company and increase the odds of failure.

If at all possible, "attack from a position of strength" when it comes to new products. That is, leverage your in-house resources and skills, seeking synergies in product development programs. This has been the message from a number of studies into new product success and failure. The reasons for the impact of leverage are clear:

1. *Resources are available and at marginal cost.* In short, if the product can be developed using existing and in-house technical skills, this is usually less expensive (and less risky) than seeking outside technology and skills. Similarly, if the product can be sold to existing customers through an already-established sales force or distribution channel system, then this, too, is less expensive, less risky, and less time-consuming than seeking new distribution channels, building a new sales force, and targeting unfamiliar customers.

2. *Knowledge.* Operating within one's field of expertise—either markets or technology—provides considerable "domain knowledge," which is available to the project team. By contrast, moving into new fields for the business often yields unpleasant surprises. When faced with a recent major product failure where domain knowledge was lacking, one executive declared, "We didn't even know what questions to ask—we didn't know what we didn't know!"

3. *Experience.* The more often one does something, the better one becomes at doing it. If new product projects are closely related to (leveraged from) current businesses, chances are that there has been considerable experience with such projects in the past. The result is that it costs less (29 percent less at each doubling of the number of new introductions, according to Booz-Allen & Hamilton).

Two types of leverage are important to product innovation:

- *Technological leverage:* the project's ability to build on in-house development technology, utilize inside engineering skills, and use existing manufacturing or operations resources and competencies.
- *Marketing leverage:* the project/company fit in terms of customer base, sales force, distribution channels, customer service resources, advertising and promotion, and market-intelligence skills, knowledge, and resources.

The impact of these two dimensions of leverage operating together is shown in Figure 4.1, based on the NewProd study results. Note that "step-out" projects that lack both marketing and technological leverage—those in the upper-right cell—suffer a failure rate of 77 percent. By contrast, better-leveraged projects have much higher success rates. (Note that some cells in the figure have too few cases to draw meaningful conclusions.) Ironically, the most successful projects seem to be those with medium-to-high technological leverage coupled with moderate marketing leverage—a 71 to 82 percent success rate! Indeed, those projects that feature extremely high leverage in both technology and marketing dimensions (lower-left cell) are few in number (8.6 percent of cases) and have about average success rates (53 percent successful), raising questions about staying "too close to home."[17]

FIGURE 4.1   Impact of Marketing and Technological Synergy on New Product Success Rates

The best place to operate is the middle-upper right: strong technology leverage; and moderate-to-strong marketing leverage—where the check-marks are. The result: higher success rates, high profits!

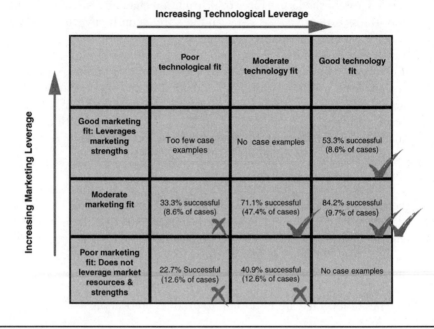

SOURCE: Chapter 3, endnote 12.

In designing new product strategies and selecting which new products to develop, never underestimate the role of leverage. Arenas and projects that lack any leverage from the base business invariably cost the firm more to exploit. Furthermore, projects where leverage is missing usually take the firm into new and uncharted markets and technologies, often with unexpected pitfalls and barriers. There are simply too many unpleasant surprises in arenas that are new to the firm.

These two dimensions of leverage—technological and marketing, and their ingredients—become obvious checklist items in a scoring or rating model to help prioritize new product projects. If your leverage score is low, then there must be other compelling reasons to proceed with the project. Leverage is not essential, but it certainly improves the odds of winning.

If leverage is low, yet the project is attractive for other reasons, then steps must be taken to bolster the internal resources and competencies. Low leverage scores signal the need for outside resources—partnering or outsourcing. But neither solution is a panacea. There are risks and costs to both routes to securing the needed resources and competencies.[18]

10. Projects aimed at attractive markets do better; market attractiveness is a key project-selection criterion.

Market attractiveness is an important strategic variable. Porter's "five forces" model considers various elements of market attractiveness as a determinant of industry profitability.[19] Similarly, various strategic planning models—for example, portfolio models used to allocate resources among various existing business units—employ market attractiveness as a key dimension in the two-dimensional map or portfolio grid.[20]

In the case of new products, market attractiveness is also important. Clearly, products targeted at more attractive markets are more successful. There are two dimensions of market attractiveness:

1. *Market potential:* positive market environments, namely, large and growing markets, markets where a strong customer need exists for products, and where the purchase is an important one for the customer. Products aimed at such markets are more successful.
2. *Competitive situation:* negative markets characterized by intense competition, competition on the basis of price, high quality, and strong competitive products and by competitors whose sales force, channel system, and support service are strongly rated. Products aimed at such negative markets are less successful, according to both NewProd and the Stanford Innovation Project.

The message is this: Both elements of market attractiveness—market potential and competitive situation—impact the new product's fortunes. And both should be considered as criteria in your model or scoring scheme for project selection and prioritization.

11. Successful businesses build tough go/kill decision points into their new product process, where projects really do get killed. Better focus is the result.

Tough go/kill decision points are a critical but often missing success ingredient. Having tough go/kill decision points is strongly correlated with profitabilities of businesses' new product efforts, according to our benchmarking study in Chapter 3. But tough go/kill decision points are *the weakest ingredient* of all process factors we have studied![21]

Many firms confess that their portfolio of projects contains too many low-value, mediocre projects. Often they are simply "bad" ideas—products with an insignificant market, no fit with the company, or no competitive advantage. But new product resources are too valuable and too limited to allocate to the wrong projects, especially these days when companies are tying to maximize shareholder value. The desire to weed out bad projects, coupled with the need to focus limited resources on the best projects, means that tough go/kill and prioritization decisions must be made.

Unfortunately, in many firms, project evaluations are weak, deficient, or non-existent. In the NewProd studies, many managers confessed to weak evaluation and prioritization decisions. For example, initial screening was one of the most poorly handled activities of the entire new product process. In 88 percent of the projects studied, screening was judged as deficient; the decision involved only one decision-maker, and/or there were no criteria used to screen projects. Furthermore, 37 percent of projects did not undergo a business or financial analysis prior to the development phase, and 65 percent did not include a pre-commercialization business analysis.

Another critical problem is too many projects for the limited resources available. This stems from the reluctance to kill projects—there are no project priorities. As one frustrated executive put it, "We never kill projects; we just wound them." He was referring to the fact that resources are removed from projects a little at a time (rather than making a tough kill decision) and end up being spread so thinly that all projects are set up for failure. In several cases, managers confessed that projects simply aren't killed once they're into development: "Projects get a life of their own" and become like "express trains, slowing down at the stations, but never with the intention of stopping until they reach their final destination, market launch."

What management must learn to do is to *drown some puppies*. No one likes to drown puppies—they're so cuddly and cute. But for the good of the litter, some must go. And so it is with new product projects in your portfolio. You aren't doing anyone any favors by saying "yes" to all the projects. Resources get thinly spread; quality of execution suffers; cycle time and time to market increase; and there are too many ho-hum projects in the portfolio.

Often the problem of poor project prioritization boils down to *a lack of a mechanism or system* for ranking, rating, prioritizing or even killing projects. There are no specified decision points or gates; it's not clear who the right decision-makers are because the locus of decision-making is ill-defined; and finally, there are no formal criteria against which to judge or evaluate projects.

The many studies into success and failure provide insights into what prioritization criteria to use. Indeed, new product success is *fairly predictable*. Certain project characteristics consistently separate winners from losers, and in a strong way. These characteristics can and should be used as criteria for project selection and prioritization.

☞ **Suggestion**: Build gates or decision points into your new product process, complete with go/kill criteria. Important characteristics that discriminate successful, profitable projects and products from the losers, and that make ideal screening or project prioritization criteria, include the following:

✓ strategic alignment and strategic importance (the role of a new product strategy to guide project selection is highlighted in numerous studies)

✓ product superiority—unique superior products, offering unique benefits and superior value to the customer (critical success factor #1 above)

✓ market attractiveness—market potential and a positive competitive situation (CSF #10 above)

✓ leverage, both technological and marketing (CSF # 9 above)

✓ technical feasibility—can it be done? does the company have the necessary technology competency to undertake the project? (CSF #9)

✓ return versus risk (the ultimate goal, of course, is profitability for a given risk level)

These six factors should be an integral part of businesses' screening and project prioritization decision model. A checklist of questions that capture strategic alignment, product superiority, market attractiveness, leverage, technical feasibility, and profitability can be used as a tool to make more effective go/kill and prioritization decisions. (A computer-based new product screening-and-diagnostic model, the NewProd Model, has been constructed from the NewProd results;[22] see Appendix B).

12. New product success is controllable; more emphasis is needed on completeness, consistency, and quality of execution of key tasks from beginning to end of project.

New product success is very much within the hands of the men and women leading and working on the project. Certain key activities—how well they are executed, and whether they are done at all—are strongly tied to success. These activities include undertaking preliminary market and technical assessments early in the project, carrying out a detailed market study or marketing research prior to product design, performing a detailed business and financial analysis, and executing the test market and market launch in a quality fashion. These activities are all within control of the project leader and team. Conversely, omitting some or all of these activities (or poor quality of execution) is strongly linked to failure. In short, success is not so much a matter of technology, market, or product, but how well the project is undertaken.

Quality of execution of the project is the key to success. Note the major impact of factors that capture quality of execution of technological, marketing, and pre-development activities in the NewProd studies. Similarly, the completeness of the process—what activities and how many activities are actually undertaken—

is an important success determinant. Finally, the expenditures on different activities—of person-days and dollars—for successes versus failures reveal the impact of resource commitment, and by inference, quality of execution.

The message is this: *There is a quality crisis in product innovation.* No, not the usual product quality problems, but rather serious weaknesses in quality of execution. The best way to double the success rate of new products in your company is to strive for significant improvements in the way the innovation process unfolds. Management and project teams must develop a more disciplined approach to product innovation that emphasizes quality of execution—doing every task in a quality fashion! The way to save time and money is *not* to cut corners, execute in a hurried and sloppy fashion, or cut out steps. This is false economy. It results in more time and effort spent later in the project and in a higher failure rate.

Why does poor quality of execution plague so many projects (recall the dismal quality scores in Figure 3.4 in the last chapter)? It's not that project teams deliberately set out to do a poor job! Rather, they are simply set up for failure. Here are *six causes of poor quality of execution* that I have observed, along with possible solutions.[23]

Cause #1. *Plain simple ignorance.* Sometimes project team members and even management don't comprehend what should be done in a well-executed project. That is, they lack a complete understanding of the key steps and tasks in the process—of what a well-run project looks like. As an example, technical people often do not know what marketing studies, market research, and industry analysis are appropriate; sometimes marketing people don't either! And so projects proceed with the technical activities well executed, but with big holes in the marketing and market research actions.

Solution: Processes! That's what the 1990s were all about—re-engineering business processes. Processes have become instant cookbooks and have created adequate chefs out of even the worst of us! Thus many companies adopted a new product process as a solution. A well-designed process is a road map or blueprint that lays out the key steps and activities expected in a properly executed project, stage by stage. It defines the end points of stages or deliverables and builds in best practices.

Cause #2. *A lack of skills.* Many project team members simply don't know how to do the key tasks, and they underestimate what's involved in these tasks.

Solution: Again, processes are a partial answer, certainly an enabler. A world-class new product process should define *standards of performance expected,* or at minimum, an understanding of *what constitutes best practices.* These are built into the new product process through defined stages, with explicit deliverables for each gate review, complete with performance expectations (often in the form of deliverables templates).

Education and training are next. Train team members for the various tasks in the process (how to do a decent market study; how to properly define product specs; and so on) along with project management training. Next, ensure that there are effective cross-functional teams (CSF #7), with appropriate representation from the various skill areas needed on the project, and some dedicated resources (players with appropriate release times to spend on the project). Finally, groom project team leaders; a good project leader is rare and makes all the difference between an effective team and one that falters.

Cause #3. *A faulty new product process.* Some companies have implemented new product processes, but they're too cumbersome or miss very important activities.

Solution: Time for an overhaul! Review the fifteen critical success factors in this chapter, and see if your process measures up. Does it build in each factor by design? And if your new product process is more than two years old, it needs updating. Get rid of the time wasters, speed bumps, and unneeded bureaucracy—work that adds no value. Recall that our research reveals that merely having a new product process makes no difference to business performance; rather it's the *nature of that process*—and whether or not it builds in the key success factors—along with its effective implementation that makes the difference.

Cause #4. *Overconfidence.* You already know the answers, so why bother with all that extra work!

Solution: Apply a little common sense. Look at the evidence—at why new products fail! Most failures are built on assumptions of managers who thought that they already knew the answers! A retrospective analysis of your past projects usually reveals two truths:

✓ Many activities aren't done well or don't occur at all.
✓ Success hinges on these key tasks.

So before you skip over key activities, take heed: Some of your project assumptions are certain to be wrong, based more on opinion and guesswork than on facts. And those "simple, obvious" projects are often far more complex than originally thought.

Cause #5. *You're in a big hurry, so you cut corners!*

Solution: Recognize the need for cycle time reduction. There is a strong positive correlation between time efficiency and profitability (CSF #14, later in this chapter). But note that some things done in the interest of saving time have exactly the opposite effect. There is a also a dark side to accelerated product development. Indeed, quality of execution or "doing it right the first time" actually saves time! It's false economy to cut corners.

Cause #6. *Pipeline gridlock.* There are too many projects and not enough resources to get the job done right. The failure to make tough choices results in a lack of focus and resources that are spread too thinly. Projects end up in a queue, pipeline gridlock occurs, cycle time starts to increase, and quality of execution suffers. The end result is that projects are late to market and success rates drop.

Solution: Take another look at CSF #11, where I suggested several solutions to a lack of focus, namely:

- ✓ Learn to drown some puppies—get rid of some projects!
- ✓ Build in tough go/kill gates into your process and use a checklist of criteria for prioritizing projects.

☞ **Suggestion**: Review the six causes of poor quality of execution above. Take a hard look at the various solutions proposed. The solution to many of the causes is to *treat product innovation as a process;* design and implement a systemic product innovation process or road map that *builds in quality assurance approaches.* For example, your process should map out the stages, activities and best practices within stages, the deliverables or end points of stages, and even performance expectations or standards. Introduce checkpoints in the process—the gates—that emphasize both doing the right projects and doing projects right. Gates should focus on quality of execution, ensuring that every play is executed in a quality fashion, and on getting rid of some mediocre projects and freeing up resources for the deserving projects.

13. The resources must be in place; there is no free lunch in product innovation.

Having a sound game plan does not guarantee success. There must be players on the field as well—not just part-time or Saturday afternoon players—but full-time dedicated resources. Too many projects simply suffer from a lack of time and money commitment. The results are predictable: much higher failure rates.

This success factor, at first glance, seems to be a trivial one. Unfortunately, too many managers don't get the message. As the competitive situation has toughened, companies have responded with restructuring (downsizing) and doing more with less. The result is that product innovation, rather than being treated as an investment, is viewed as a cost that must be reduced, and so resources are limited or cut back. This short-term focus takes its toll. Certain vital activities, such as market-oriented actions and predevelopment homework are highly underresourced, particularly in the case of product failures.[24]

A strong market orientation is missing in the typical new product project. And much of this deficiency is directly linked to a lack of marketing resources available for the project. Only 16 percent of the project's total dollar costs and 32 percent of the person-days go to marketing actions, and most of these are applied at the back end or launch phase of the project. The conclusion is that new product marketing activities are typically underfunded.

By contrast, successful projects have far more dollars and person-days committed to marketing activities than failures. Overall, success projects spend more than twice as much money on marketing activities (other than the launch) than failures. Moreover, these trends are consistent across marketing activities: double-to-triple the spending on each marketing action for successes as opposed to failures. The message to managers is this:

- Consider how much (or how little) you now devote to these new product marketing activities—preliminary market assessment, marketing research, customer tests, trial sell, and market launch.
- Next, consider the fact that managers who take winning products to market spend considerably more on these activities than managers who are responsible for failures.
- Armed with this evidence, rededicate the company to more spending and resources for these critical marketing actions.

Another serious pitfall is that the homework doesn't get done. Again much of this deficiency can be directly attributed to a lack of resources: not enough money, people, and time to do the work. Only 7 percent of the dollars and 16 percent of the effort spent on new product projects go to these vital up-front actions.

Again the evidence is clear: Successful projects have considerably more spent on the front-end stages of the new product process. More than twice as much money and 1.75 times as many person-days are spent on the up-front activities for successes as opposed to failures. Management must recognize the importance of the first few steps of the new product process and realize that money spent here appears to have a major positive impact on product performance.

☞ **Suggestion**: Are you suffering from a *resource crunch* in your new product pipeline? The problem of too many projects and too few resources can be partly resolved by undertaking a *resource capacity analysis*.[25] This analysis quantifies your projects' demand for resources (usually people, expressed as person-days of work) versus the availability of these resources. You can do this analysis in one of two ways:[26]

1. *Do you have enough of the right resources to handle projects currently in your pipeline?* Begin with your current list of active projects. Determine the resources required to complete them according to their timelines. Then look at the availability of resources. You'll usually find major gaps and hence potential bottlenecks. Finally, identify the key resource constraints—the departments, people, or capabilities that you run out of first (see Figure 4.2 for details).
2. *Do you have enough resources to achieve your new product goals?* Begin with your new product goals. What percentage of your business's

FIGURE 4.2   Two Ways to Undertake a Resource Capacity-Versus-Demand Analysis

Resource Demand Vs. Capacity Chart - Example

Project	Product Mgmt		Marketing		Research Group A		Research Group B	
	Persondays	Cumulative	Persondays	Cumulative	Persondays	Cumulative	Persondays	Cumulative
Alpha	3	3	2	2	10	10	5	5
Beta	4	7	2	4	10	20	5	10
Gamma	3	10	2	6	15	35	5	15
Delta	5	15	3	9	15	50	8	23
Epsilon	6	21	3	12	5	55	8	31
Foxtrot	6	27	2	14	5	60	5	36
Available Persondays		20		10		60		40
% Utilization		135.00%		140.00%		100.00%		90.00%

sales will come from new products? Now, determine the resources required to achieve this goal. Again you'll likely find a major gap between demand, based on your goals, and available capacity. It's time to make some tough decisions about the reality of your goals and whether more resources are required (again, see Figure 4.2 for details).

This resource capacity analysis is not a total solution. But it does provide information necessary to begin work on a solution. Most companies find that this resource capacity analysis

✓ detects far too many projects in the pipeline, resulting in an immediate prioritization and pruning effort; the result often is that half the
projects are killed or put on hold!
✓ causes senior management to rethink their goals; often new product
goals, such as percentage of sales by new products, are based on
wishful thinking or on an unrealistic corporate dictum.
✓ identifies departments or groups that are major bottlenecks in the
innovation process; this leads to decisions to increase or shift personnel.

Resource capacity analysis is a fairly tactical move, but it is relatively straight-forward to undertake and provides real insights into the nature and magnitude of the resource constraint problem. When looking at resources and resource allocation, this is a good place to begin.

14. Speed is everything! But not at the expense of quality of execution.

Speed is a vital competitive weapon. Speed yields competitive advantage; it means less likelihood that the market or competitive situation has changed by the time you launch, and it means a quicker realization of profits. Therefore, the goal of reducing the development cycle time is admirable.[27] Most firms have reduced product development cycle times over the past five years, with the average reduction being about one-third.[28]

But a word of caution is in order here: *Speed is only an interim objective . . .* a means to an end. The ultimate goal, of course, is profitability. A better metric than time to market is *time to profit:* How long from the beginning of the project does it take to recover costs and show profits? But many of the practices naively employed to reduce time to market ultimately cost the company money; they achieve the interim objective—bringing the product quickly to market— but fail at the ultimate objective—profitability. An example is moving a product to market quickly by shortening the customer-test phase, only to face serious quality problems after launch.

Be careful in your quest for cycle-time reduction. Too often the methods used to reduce development time yield precisely the opposite effect, and in many cases, are very costly; they are at odds with sound management practice. Shortcuts are taken with the best intentions, but far too frequently they result in disaster. They lead to serious errors of omission and commission, which not only add delays to the project, but often lead to higher incurred costs and even product failure. For example, the PDMA's best practices study found that the best firms actually took a little longer to develop new products than the average performer, which might be a reflection of both the more challenging projects undertaken and the desire to do a high-quality job.

There is a dark side to accelerated product development, according to Crawford:[29]

- Shortcutting key activities, such as

  - ✓ moving in haste through the early phases of a new product project— the up-front-homework and the market studies—only to discover later that the product design does not meet customer needs and that the project itself is an ill-conceived one;
  - ✓ moving a product to market quickly by shortening the customer-test phase, only to incur product reliability problems after launch, result- ing in lost customer confidence and substantial warranty and servic- ing costs.

- Focusing only on easy, quick hits—the "low-hanging fruit," such as line extensions and minor modifications—but paying the price later through a lack of significant new products and loss of long-term competitive advantage.
- Setting an unrealistic time line to achieve a launch deadline, only to cre- ate frustration and tension among project team members when mile- stones are invariably missed. Ultimately, attempting to operate under an unrealistic time line destroys the effectiveness of cross-functional teams,

as team members start blaming each other for the failure to meet deadlines.

Here are five sensible ways to reduce cycle time that are totally consistent with sound management practice, derived from our critical success factors outlined above. Not only will *these five methods increase the odds of winning, but they also reduce the time to market.* In short, they reduce the overall *time to profit:*

1. *Do it right the first time.* Build in quality of execution at every stage of the project. The best way to save time is by avoiding having to recycle back and do it a second time. Quality of execution pays off not only in terms of better results, but also by reducing delays (see CSF #12).
2. *Homework and definition.* Doing the up-front homework and getting clear product and project definition, based on fact rather than hearsay and speculation, saves time downstream: Sharper technical targets result in less recycling back to get the facts or redefine the product requirements (see CSFs #4 and #5).
3. *Organize around a true cross-functional team with empowerment.* Multifunctional teams are essential for timely development. "Rip apart a badly developed project and you will unfailingly find 75 percent of slippage attributable to (1) 'siloing,' or sending memos up and down vertical organizational 'silos' or 'stovepipes' for decisions; and (2) sequential problem solving," according to Peters.[30] Unfortunately, the typical project resembles a relay race, with each function or department carrying the baton for its portion of the race and then handing off to the next runner or department (see CSF #7).
4. *Parallel processing.* The relay race, or sequential, or series approach to product development is antiquated and inappropriate for today's fast-paced projects. Given the time pressures of projects, coupled with the need for a complete and quality process, a more appropriate model is a rugby game or parallel processing. With parallel processing, activities are undertaken concurrently (rather than sequentially), and thus more activities are undertaken in an elapsed period of time. The new product process must be multidisciplinary with each part of the team—marketing, R&D, operations, engineering—working together and undertaking its parallel or concurrent activity. Note that the play is a lot more complex using a parallel play or rugby scheme (versus a series approach), hence the need for a disciplined game plan (see CSF #15 below).
5. *Prioritize and focus.* The best way to slow projects down is to dissipate your limited resources and people across too many projects. By concentrating resources on the truly deserving projects, not only will the work be done better, but it will be done faster. But focus means tough choices: It means killing other and perhaps worthwhile projects. And that

requires good decision making and the right criteria for making go/kill decisions (see CSF #11).

15. Companies that follow a multistage, disciplined new product process—a *Stage-Gate*™ process—fare much better.

The product innovation process in many companies is broken. It is a process plagued by errors of omission and commission—things don't happen when they should, how they should, or as well as they should! It lacks consistency and quality of execution. And it is a process very much in need of repair. These are the findings of study after study. They reveal that many businesses' new product processes are deficient or nonexistent and point to the need for a complete and a quality process.

A systematic product innovation process is the solution to which many firms have turned. Recall from the PDMA best practices study in the last chapter that the majority if U.S. product developers have adopted a *Stage-Gate*™ process. The best firms have embraced such a process even more so, and the best have even moved to more sophisticated versions or *third-generation Stage-Gate processes.*

Managing a new products program without a process in place is like putting a dozen players on a football field without huddles or preplanned plays and expecting them to score. It works once in a while, but over the long run, the better-disciplined competitor will win.

The term "new product process" means a conceptual and operational model for moving new product projects from idea to launch and beyond. It is a blueprint for managing the new product project, improving its efficiency and effectiveness. The model outlines the key plays and huddles necessary to score a goal, hence the analogy with rugby or North American football.

Operationally, game plans break the new product process into a series of multifunctional stages or plays composed of multiple, parallel activities; each stage is preceded by a gate, decision point, scrum or huddle. The stage and gate format leads to terms such as "gating," "gateways," "stage-gate," and "toll-gate" systems.

The evidence in support of a new product game plan or process is strong. Booz-Allen & Hamilton found that companies that had implemented new product processes were more successful and that those firms with the longest experience with the process were even more successful.[31] As one vice president put it, "The multistep new product process is an essential ingredient in successful new product development." And the PDMA best practices study provides more recent evidence of the pervasiveness of stage-and-gate processes among the top performing companies.[32]

Later in this book, we'll look at what happened to a sample of firms that have implemented such game plans. The results have been dramatic: faster new product introductions, less recycling to redo steps, and a higher success rate of launched products.

If your firm does not have an effective new product process in place, its design and implementation should become a top-priority task. The next chapter outlines a skeleton of a typical or generic process—a step-by-step procedure for turning a new product idea into a winning new product in the marketplace.

Toward a *Stage-Gate*™ New Product Process

This chapter has given us fifteen critical success factors for product innovation. They are success factors based not on hearsay and wishful thinking but on facts—on the many research studies that have probed new product performance, both successes and failures. Now the challenge of translating these success factors into operational reality begins. In the next chapter, we'll fashion these fifteen success factors into a game plan that is designed to drive new product projects from idea to launch—successfully and in a time-efficient manner.

The New Product Process:
The *Stage-Gate*™ Game Plan

A process is a methodology that is developed to replace the old ways and to guide corporate activity year after year. It is not a special guest. It is not temporary. It is not to be tolerated for a while and then abandoned.
—Thomas H. Berry, *Managing the Total Quality Transformation*

Stage-Gate™ Systems

A world-class process for product innovation is one solution to what ails so many firms' new product efforts.[1] Facing increased pressure to reduce the cycle time and yet improve their new product success rates, companies look to new product processes, or *Stage-Gate*™ systems, to manage, direct, and accelerate their product-innovation efforts. That is, they have developed a systematic process—a blueprint or road map—for moving a new product project through the various stages and steps from idea to launch. But most important, they have built into their road map the many *critical success factors* and *best practices* in order to heighten the effectiveness of their programs. Consider these examples:

> 3M has traditionally had an enviable new product track record. An innovative corporate culture and climate are often cited as 3M's secret to success. But for years 3M has also had in place various stage-gate systems in different businesses for managing the innovation process. Thus creativity and discipline are blended to yield a successful new product effort.

Corning Glass has always been a world-leading innovator, beginning generations ago with Pyrex glass and Corningware, and in more recent years, with fiber optics. Corning's successes continue. What drives new products to market at Corning is their version of a stage-gate process, designed and installed in the early 1990s. The process has been refined and streamlined over the years, and also broadened in scope, so that today, virtually every resource-intensive project—from new or improved products to new manufacturing processes—is stage-gated.

Guinness, the Irish-U.K. brewer, is not exactly renowned as the world's greatest innovator; the company has been making essentially the same product since before the American Revolution. But all that's changing, as drinking habits and tastes change everywhere. A noted innovation by Guinness is the widget—a nitrogen capsule in the beer can that releases nitrogen when the can is opened, thus putting a perfect head on a can of beer! More recently, Project Genie was created to do the same thing, but in bottled beer. Today, Guinness's new product efforts around the world are driven by their *NaviGate* process—a stage-gate new product process that builds in best practices and helps to focus resources on the best projects.

Exxon Chemical began piloting a stage-gate process in its polymers business unit a decade ago. So successful was the process that Exxon Chemical has adopted the method throughout its entire chemical business. According to the father of Exxon's Product Innovation Process, "The implementation of the PIP has probably had more impact on the way we do business than any other initiative at Exxon Chemical undertaken in the last decade."

Lego, the successful Danish toy manufacturer, replaces about one-third of its product line every year with new items—new castles, new towns, and so on. In order to accomplish this rapid introduction of new products consistently, successfully, and year after year, a process was needed. Today, Lego relies on a stage-gate new product process to ensure that everything comes together for these many rapid launches each year.

Hewlett-Packard continues to grow, largely because of a steady stream of brilliant new products. How? Some say it is because of the passion for innovation that was established right from the beginning by the company's two founders. Others say it is because of the dynamic nature of the industries that HP elects to target. Both reasons are right. But underlying successful new products at HP is a stage-and-gate process—their Phased Review process—which has been in place since the 1960s (although their current Life Cycle version is quite different from the original model).

The adopters of new product processes or *Stage-Gate* methods include leading firms around the world, such as Polaroid and Kodak; many firms in the chemical business, such as Exxon Chemical, Rohm and Haas, ICI, Mobil Chemical, Dow Chemical, Air Products, Asahi Chemical, Toray Chemical, and various divisions at DuPont, Bayer, and B. F. Goodrich; high-technology companies such as Hewlett-Packard, Nortel Networks, IBM, Lucent, Microsoft, Corning Glass, GE-Honeywell, and Emerson Electric; consumer goods firms, such as Procter & Gamble, SC Johnson Wax, Reckitt-Benckiser, Carlsberg, Pillsbury, General Mills, Hillshire Farm, Unilever, and Guinness; and numerous service providers, such as NYNEX, American Express, VISA, and Royal Bank of Canada.

Stage-Gate methods work! According to the PDMA best practices study, "the Best [companies] are more likely to use some type of formal NPD [new product development] process than the Rest. They are more likely to have moved from simpler *Stage-Gate™* processes to more sophisticated facilitated or third-generation processes."[2] The challenge in this chapter is this: Given the fifteen critical success factors gleaned from new product success-and-failure experiences and the various benchmarking studies (reviewed in the last chapter), how can we translate these into an operational and effective new product game plan? For example, how does one build in quality of execution, or a strong market orientation, or better predevelopment homework? Let us begin the design of this process with a quick look at what this new product process must achieve.

Seven Goals of a New Product Process

Goal #1: Quality of Execution

The argument that the proponents of total quality management make goes something like this: "The definition of quality is precise; it means meeting all the requirements all the time. It is based on the principle that all work is a process. It focuses on improving business processes to eliminate errors." The concept is perfectly logical and essentially simple. Most smart things are. And the same logic can be applied to new product development.

Product innovation is a process. It begins with an idea—even earlier—and culminates in a successful product launch. But processes aren't new to the business environment. There are many examples of well-run processes in business, for example, manufacturing processes, information processes, and so on.

A quality-of-execution crisis exists in the product innovation process, however. We saw in the last two chapters clear evidence that the activities of the new product process—their quality of execution and whether these activities are carried out at all—have a dramatic impact on product success or failure. Further, there are serious gaps—omissions of steps and poor quality of execution—in the new product process. These serious gaps are the rule rather than the exception. And they are strongly tied to product failures.

This quality-of-execution crisis in the product innovation process provides strong evidence in support of the need for a more *systematic and quality approach* to the way firms conceive, develop, and launch new products. The way to deal with the quality problem is to visualize product innovation as a process and to apply *process management* and *quality management techniques* to this process. Note that any process in business can be managed, and thus it can be managed with a view to quality. Get the details of your processes right, and the result will be a high-quality end product or output. For example, there has been a great deal of focus on quality in manufacturing processes over the past few decades.

Quality of execution is the goal of the new product process. More specifically, the ideal game plan should

1. *focus on completeness:* Ensure that the key activities that are central to the success of a new product project are indeed carried out—no gaps, no omissions, a complete process.
2. *focus on quality:* Ensure that the execution of these activities is first class; that is, treat innovation as a process, emphasize DIRTFooT (doing it right the first time), and build in quality controls and checks.
3. *focus on the important:* Devote attention and resources to the pivotal and particularly weak steps in the new product process, notably the up-front and market-oriented activities.

The new product process or *Stage-Gate* system is simply a *process management tool.* We build quality of execution into this process, in much the same way that quality programs have been successfully implemented on the factory floor.

Goal #2: Sharper Focus, Better Prioritization

Most companies' new product efforts suffer from a lack of focus: too many projects and not enough resources. Earlier, adequate resources was identified as a principal driver of companies' new product performance; but a lack of resources plagues too many firms' development efforts. Sometimes management hasn't devoted the needed people and money to the business's new product effort. But often this resource problem stems from a lack of focus, the result of inadequate project evaluations and the failure to set priorities and make tough go/kill decisions. In short, the "gates" are weak. Indeed, most of the critical evaluation points—from initial screening to prelaunch business analysis—are characterized by serious weaknesses: little or no real prioritization, poor information inputs, no criteria for decisions, and inconsistent or haphazard decision making.

The need is for a *new product funnel,* rather than *tunnel.* A "new product funnel" builds in tough go/kill decision points throughout the process; the poor projects are weeded out; scarce resources are redirected toward the truly deserving projects—the high-value ones; and more focus is the result. One funneling method is to build the new product process around a set of gates or go/kill decision points. These gates are the bail-out points where we ask, "Are we still in the game?"

Gates are analogous to the *quality-control checkpoints* on a manufacturing assembly line. They serve to check the quality, merit, and progress of the project. Like a production line, gates are preset at different points throughout the new product process. Each gate has its own set of *metrics and criteria* for passing, much like a quality-control check in production. These criteria and questions deal with various facets of the project, including the following:

1. *Quality of execution:* Is the project being executed in a quality fashion? Is the project unfolding as it should? Specifically:

   ✓ Are the data reliable?
   ✓ Are the key deliverables in place?
   ✓ Have the essential steps necessary to pass through the gate been completed?
   ✓ Is the quality of execution of these activities first rate?
   ✓ Is the project on time and on budget?
   ✓ Have the milestones since the last gate been hit?

2. *Business rationale:* Does the project continue to make economic and business sense?

   ✓ Does it continue to meet or exceed the business and financial criteria?
   ✓ Is it strategically aligned with the business?
   ✓ Does the product boast competitive advantage, that is, unique product benefits and superior value for the customer?
   ✓ Is the market attractive, that is, large, growing, a positive competitive scene?
   ✓ Is the project technically feasible with the given resources?
   ✓ Does it leverage your core competencies, capabilities, and strengths?
   ✓ Can the product generate profits? Is the risk level satisfactory in light of the return?

3. *The path forward:* Is the proposed action plan through to launch a good one?

   ✓ Is the plan of action—the action items and time line—sound?
   ✓ Are the resources requested reasonable?
   ✓ Are the resources available?

These gates, like quality-control checkpoints in manufacturing, serve to map and guide the new product process. They signal a "kill" decision when a project's economics and business rationale become negative, where the barriers to completion become insurmountable, or where the project is far over budget or behind schedule. Gates prevent projects from moving too far ahead into the next stage until the critical activities have been completed in a quality fashion. And gates chart the path forward: They determine what tasks and milestones lie ahead and the budgets and time frames for these tasks.

Goal #3: Fast-Paced Parallel Processing

New product managers face a dilemma. On the one hand, they are urged by senior management to compress the cycle time—to shorten the elapsed time from idea to launch. On the other hand, the manager is urged to improve the effectiveness of product development: Cut down the failure rate! Do it right! This desire to "do it right" suggests a more thorough, longer process.

Parallel processing is one solution to the need for a complete and quality process that also meets the time pressures of today's fast-paced business world. Traditionally, new product projects have been managed through a series approach—one task strung out after another, in a series. The analogy is that of a relay race, with each department running with the project for its 100 yards. Phrases such as "hand off," "passing the project on," "dropping the ball," and "throwing it over the wall" are common in this relay approach to new products.

In marked contrast to the relay or sequential approach, with parallel processing many activities are undertaken *concurrently* rather than in a series. The appropriate analogy is that of a rugby football match rather than a relay race.[3] A team (not a single runner) appears on the field. A scrum or huddle ensues, after which the ball emerges. Players run down the field with much interaction, constantly passing the ball laterally. After 25 yards or so, the players converge for another scrum, huddle, or gate review, and another stage of activities takes place.

With parallel processing, the game is far more intense than a relay race, and more work gets done in an elapsed time period; three or four activities are done simultaneously and by different members on the project team. Second, there is less chance of an activity or task being overlooked or handled poorly because of lack of time; the activities are done in parallel, not in a series, and hence the total elapsed project time is reduced. Moreover, the activities are designed to feed each other; the ball is passed back and forth across the field. And finally, the entire new product process becomes cross-functional and multidisciplinary; the whole team—marketing, R&D, engineering, operations—is on the field together, participates actively in each play, and takes part in each gate review or scrum.

Goal #4: A *True* Cross-functional Team Approach

The new product process is multifunctional: It requires the inputs and active participation of players from many different functions in the organization. The multifunctional nature of innovation coupled with the desire for parallel processing means that a *true cross-functional team approach is mandatory* in order to win at new products.

I emphasize the word "true" in describing a cross-functional team, as opposed to the many "fake" or "pretend" teams one sees in business. Telltale signs of a fake team include the following:

- ✓ So-called team members show up at meetings, but they aren't really committed to the team; they're there as functional representatives at a meeting.
- ✓ Team members aren't given release time from their "day job"; this team activity is just piled on top of an already hectic schedule.
- ✓ Team members promise to get things done by the next team meeting, but invariably their "real jobs" get in the way and their functional boss puts them onto some other assignment.
- ✓ Team members are given lots of responsibility and very little authority; the functional bosses are still making the decisions about the project, often micromanaging from afar.
- ✓ Team members receive no merit points or variable pay based on the results achieved by the team.

Does this sound familiar? If so, it's time to have a hard look at the way you're organized for new products.

The *Stage-Gate* process demands that every significant new product project has a true cross-functional project team. Essential characteristics of this team include the following:

- The project team is cross-functional, with committed team players from the various functions and departments—marketing, engineering, R&D, and operations. Release time from their normal jobs to spend on the project is provided to team members.
- The project team has a clearly defined team captain or leader. This leader is dedicated to the project (not spread across numerous other duties or projects) and is accountable from beginning to end of the project—not just for one phase.
- The leader has formal authority; this means co-opting authority from the functional heads. When senior management approves the team's action plan at gate meetings, they also commit the resources—money, people, and release time—to the project leader and team. At the same time, senior management *transfers decision-making power* to the team. Expectations and the scope of this authority are made very clear to the team at the gate.
- Some of these resources are "ring-fenced"; that is, people working on the project are 100 percent dedicated to new product efforts—to this one project and perhaps one other. New product development is their full-time job!

- The team structure is fluid, with new members joining the team (or leaving it) as work requirements demand. But *a small core group of responsible, committed, and accountable team players should be present from beginning to end of the project.*
- Senior management holds the entire team—all team members, not just the team leader—accountable for results. And rewards, such as merit increases, bonuses or variable salary, are tied to the team's performance and results.

Goal #5: A Strong Market Orientation with Voice of the Customer Built In

A market orientation is the missing ingredient in too many new product projects. A lack of a market orientation and inadequate market assessment are consistently cited as reasons for new product failure. Moreover, the market-related activities tend to be the weakest in the new product process, yet they are strongly linked to success. Although many managers profess a market orientation, the evidence—where the time and money are spent—proves otherwise.

If superb new product success rates are the goal, then a market orientation—executing the key marketing activities in a quality fashion—must be built into the new product process as a matter of routine, rather than by exception. Marketing inputs must play a decisive role from beginning to end of the project. The following nine marketing actions are *integral and mandatory plays* in the new product game plan (but they rarely are):

1. *Customer-based idea generation:* working with lead users and key customers to identify problems, gaps, and emerging opportunities for new solutions
2. *Preliminary market assessment:* an early, relatively inexpensive step designed to assess market attractiveness and to test market acceptance for the proposed new product
3. *Market research to determine user needs and wants:* in-depth, face-to-face, and on-site interviews with customers to determine customer needs, wants, preferences, likes, dislikes, and buying criteria, as inputs to the design of the new product
4. *Competitive analysis:* an assessment of competitors—their products and product deficiencies, prices, costs, technologies, production capacities, and marketing strategies
5. *Concept testing:* a test of the proposed product—perhaps as a virtual product or protocept—to determine likely market acceptance
6. *Customer reaction during development:* continuing concept and product testing throughout the development phase, using rapid prototypes,

models, and partially completed products to gauge customer reaction and seek feedback

7. *User tests:* field trials or beta tests using the finished product (or commercial prototype) with users to verify the performance of the product under customer conditions and to confirm intent to purchase and market acceptance

8. *Test market or trial sell:* a mini-launch or "soft launch" of the product in a limited geographic area or single sales territory as a test of all elements of the marketing mix, including the product itself[4]

9. *Market launch:* a proficient launch, based on a solid marketing plan, and backed by sufficient resources

Goal #6: Better Homework Up-Front

New product success or failure is largely decided in the first few plays of the game—in those crucial steps and tasks that precede the actual development of the product. Solid up-front homework and sharp early product definition are key ingredients in a successful new product process, according to our benchmarking studies, and result in higher success rates and profitability in studies of project performance. The up-front homework helps to define the product and to build the business case for development. Ironically, most of the money and time spent on projects is devoted to the middle and back-end stages of the process, while the up-front actions suffer from errors of omission, poor quality of execution, and underresourcing.

The ideal new product process ensures that these early stages are carried out before the project is allowed to proceed—before the project enters full-fledged Development. Activities essential to building the business case become mandatory plays before the project is given formal approval for development.

What are these essential up-front activities in a well-designed game plan? They include the following:

- *initial screening:* the initial decision to spend time and money on the project
- *preliminary technical assessment:* an initial attempt to assess technical feasibility, outline manufacturing/operations implications, and identify technical risks and issues
- *preliminary marketing assessment:* the first-pass market study
- *detailed technical assessment:* detailed technical work (not development) to prove technical feasibility and address technical risks
- *manufacturing or operations assessment:* technical work to determine manufacturing, operations or source of supply implications, capital expenditures, and probable manufacturing or delivered costs

- *detailed market studies:* the user needs-and-wants study, competitive analysis, and concept tests
- *resource and capabilities assessment:* identification of the need for a partner or outsourcing
- *financial and business analysis:* probes the expected financial consequences and risks of the project
- *product definition and business case:* integrates the results of the technical, operations, marketing, and financial analyses into a product definition, project justification, and project plan
- *decision on business case:* a thorough project evaluation and decision to go to full development

Goal #7: Products with Competitive Advantage

Don't forget to build in product superiority–differentiated products, unique benefits, and superior value for the customer—at every opportunity. This is perhaps the most important driver of new product success, yet all too often, when redesigning their new product processes, firms fall into the trap of repeating current, often faulty, practices. There is no attempt to seek truly superior products. And so the results are predicable—more ho-hum, tired products. Here's how to drive the quest for product advantage:

- Ensure that at least some of the criteria at every gate focus on product superiority. Questions such as, "Does the product have at least one element of competitive advantage?" "Does it offer the user new or different benefits?" and "Is it providing excellent value for money for the user?" are vital for rating and ranking would-be projects.
- Require that certain key actions designed to deliver product superiority be included in each stage of the process. Some of these have been highlighted above (Goals #5 and #6) and include customer-focused ideation; user needs-and-wants market research studies; competitive product analysis; concept and protocept tests, preference tests and trial sells; and constant iterations with customers during the development stage through rapid prototypes and tests.
- Demand that project teams deliver evidence of product superiority to project go/kill reviews; make product superiority an important deliverable and issue at such meetings (rather than just dwelling on the financial projections).
- Ensure that the product definition, so critical to new product success, not only includes performance requirements and specs but also is very clear about the *value proposition* for the customer.

☞ **Suggestion**: Take a close look at the new product process within your firm. Does the process ensure quality of execution? Is it built around a set of gates, or evaluation and decision points, to get rid of bad projects and focus resources on the truly deserving ones? Does it emphasize parallel processing—a rugby match—or does it resemble a relay race? Does it use the project matrix or project team approach—an empowered, cross-functional team headed by a leader with authority? Or are you still largely functionally based? Does it emphasize a market orientation? What proportion of project expenditures goes to marketing actions? And how many of the nine marketing actions do you routinely undertake in your new product project? Do you devote enough resources to the upfront or homework phases of the process? And do you build in activities and criteria designed to yield unique, superior products with real competitive advantage (or does your process favor small, simple me-too efforts)?

If some of the answers are no, then the time is ripe to rethink your new product process or game plan. Look to a *Stage-Gate* new product process, with best practices built in, to provide you with some needed solutions.

Managing Risk

The management of new products is the management of risk. So the game plan must also be designed to manage risk. Indeed, if you look closely, you see that most of the fifteen critical success factors outlined in the last chapter deal with ways of reducing risk. Total risk avoidance in new product development is impossible, unless a company decides to avoid all innovation—and face a slow death.

Most of us know what is meant by the phrase "a risky situation." From a new product manager's perspective, a high-risk situation is one in which much is at stake (for example, the project involves a lot of money or is strategically critical to the business), and where the outcome is uncertain (for example, it is not certain that the product is technically feasible or will do well in the marketplace). There are two components of risk: amounts at stake and uncertainties (see Figure 5.1).

A Life-or-Death Gamble

Imagine for a moment that you are facing the gamble of your life. You've been invited to a millionaire's ranch for a weekend. Last night, you played poker and lost more money than you can afford—around $100,000. All of the other players are enormously wealthy cattle and oil barons. Tonight they've given you the opportunity to get even. Each of the other ten players antes $1 million into the pot. That's $10 million in thousand-dollar bills—more money than you are ever likely to see again stacked in front of you.

FIGURE 5.1 The Components of Risk in a New Product Process

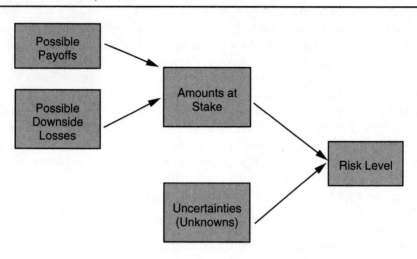

Risk is a combination of how much is at stake and the uncertainties of the outcome

SOURCE: Adapted with permission from R. G. Cooper and R. A. More, "Modular risk management: An applied example," *R&D Management* 9 (February 1979): 93–99.

Here is the gamble. One of the players takes out a six-shooter pistol, removes all the bullets, and, in full view of everyone, places one live bullet in the gun. He then spins the chamber. For $10 million, you are asked to point the gun at your head and pull the trigger. Will you take the gamble?

Most people would say no! But the situation exhibits the key elements of risk: a great deal at stake (the $10 million or your life) and a high degree of uncertainty—the bullet could be in any location.

Reducing the Stakes

This hypothetical gamble represents an unacceptable risk level. Yet this is precisely the way many managers play the new product game: huge amounts at stake coupled with high levels of uncertainty. How can the risk be reduced? One route is to *lessen the amounts at stake.* For example, use blank bullets along with earmuffs to deaden the noise, and point the gun not at your head but at your foot. The potential downside loss, if the gun were to fire, is now merely being laughed at by a group of poker players.

But upside gains are inevitably tied to downside losses. So instead of anteing in $1 million, every player now puts in one dollar. Will you still take the gamble? Most would reply, "Who cares?" There is no longer enough at stake to make the gamble worthwhile or even interesting. The risk is now so low that the decision becomes trivial.

Some Gambling Rules

Rule number one in risk management is: If the uncertainties are high, keep the amounts at stake low. Rule number two is: As the uncertainties decrease, the amounts at stake can be increased. These two rules keep risk under control.

There is another way in which risk can be managed in our hypothetical example. The pot remains at $10 million, a live bullet is used, and the gun must be aimed at your head. But this time, your opponent, in plain view, marks the exact location of the bullet on the chamber. He spins the chamber and asks you to reach into your pocket and give him $20,000 in return for a look at the gun to see where the live bullet has ended up. Then you decide whether or not you still wish to proceed with the gamble.

Most of us would consider this a "good gamble" (assuming we had the $20,000)—one with an acceptable risk level. A relatively small amount of cash buys a look at the gun and the location of the bullet. Having paid for the look and determined the bullet's location, you then make your second decision: Are you still in the game? It's much like buying options in the stock market.

The risk has been reduced by converting an all-or-nothing decision into a two-stage decision: two steps and two decision points. Your ability to purchase information was also instrumental in minimizing risk: Information has reduced the uncertainty of the situation. Finally, the ability to withdraw from the game—to bail out—also reduced risk.

Three more gambling rules designed to manage risk evolve from this second gambling situation. Rule number three is: Incrementalize the decision process; break the all-or-nothing decision into a series of stages and decisions. Purchase options on the project, stage by stage. Rule number four is: Be prepared to pay for relevant information to reduce risk. And rule number five is: Provide for bail-out points—decision points that provide the opportunity to fold, walk away, or get out of the game.

Risks in New Product Management

These five rules of risk management apply directly to the new product game. Near the beginning of a project, the amounts at stake usually are low, and the uncertainty of the outcome is very high. As the project progresses, the amounts at stake begin to increase (see Figure 5.2). If risk is to be managed successfully, the uncertainties of outcomes must be deliberately driven down as the stakes increase. Furthermore, the stakes must not be allowed to increase unless the uncertainties do come down. Uncertainties and amounts at stake must be kept in balance.

Unfortunately, in many new product projects, the amounts at stake increase as the project progresses, while the uncertainties remain fairly high (see Figure

FIGURE 5.2   Relationship Between Uncertainties and Amounts at Stake

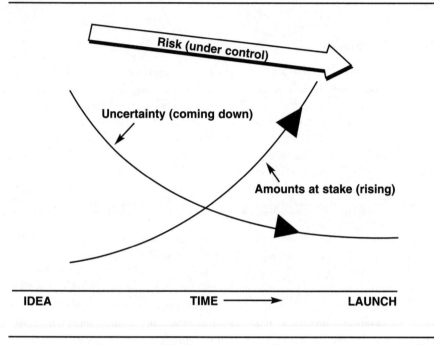

SOURCE: Adapted from R. G. Cooper and B. Little, "Reducing the risk of industrial new product development," *Canadian Marketer* 7 (Fall 1974): 7–12.

5.3). Additional spending fails to reduce the uncertainties! By the end of the project, as launch nears, management is no more sure about the commercial outcome of the venture than it was on day one of the project. The amounts at stake have increased, uncertainty remains high, and the risk level is unacceptably high.

For every thousand-dollar increase in the amounts at stake, the uncertainty curve in Figure 5.2 must be reduced by an equivalent amount. To do otherwise is to let risk get out of hand. In short, every expenditure in the new product process—every notch up on the amounts-at-stake curve in Figure 5.2—must bring a corresponding reduction in the uncertainty curve. The entire new product process, from idea to launch, can be viewed as an uncertainty-reduction process. Remember the five gambling rules:

1. When the uncertainties of the new product project are high (that is, when the prospects of success are fuzzy), keep the amounts at stake low. When you don't know where you're going, take small steps.
2. As the uncertainties decrease, let the amounts at stake increase. As you learn more about where you're going, take bigger and bigger steps.

FIGURE 5.3   Risk out of Control in the New Product Process

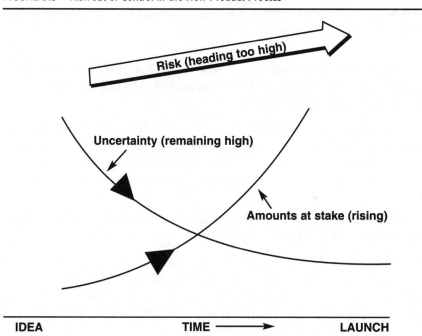

SOURCE: Adapted from R. G. Cooper and B. Little, "Reducing the risk of industrial new product development," *Canadian Marketer* 7 (Fall 1974): 7–12.

3. Incrementalize the new product process into a series of steps or stages. Treat it as a series of *options purchases.* Each step should be more costly than the one before.
4. View each stage as a means of reducing uncertainty. Remember that information is the key to uncertainty reduction. Each step in the process that creates an expenditure must reduce uncertainty by an equivalent amount. "Buy a series of looks" at the project's outcome.
5. Provide for timely evaluation, decision, and bail-out points. These decision points pull together all the new information from the previous stage and pose the questions, "Are you still in the game? Should you proceed to the next stage, or kill the project now?"

☞ **Suggestion:** The five decision rules outlined above apply to almost any high-risk situation. Does your company follow them in its day-to-day management practices? Review your firm's new product practices, perhaps using an actual case, and assess whether your management group is handling risk appropriately.

A Systematic New Product Process

I have made eight points so far in this chapter:

1. The new product process must be a *quality process.* There is a clear need for a systematic new product process to guide and facilitate the new product project from idea to launch.

A new product process or *Stage-Gate*™ system is one solution to correct the serious deficiencies and the quality-of-execution crises that are common to many firms' new product efforts. These deficiencies and holes are glaring and pervasive, and unfortunately, they impact strongly and negatively on performance.

2. The process or game plan must be designed to *manage* risk; a multistage and gate framework is most appropriate.

Build the five gambling rules into the process. The innovation process is broken into a series of stages, each stage more costly than the one before. Expenditures for early stages are kept low but allowed to increase as uncertainty is reduced. Each stage is viewed as an information acquisition stage. And timely bail-out points (in the form of gates) are provided.

3. *Gates are central* to the new product process.

These gates serve several functions; they provide the quality-control mechanism in the process. Before a project is allowed to proceed to the next stage, essential tasks and deliverables must be complete. Gates also provide for bail-out points—go/kill decision points—to weed out bad projects and focus resources on the high-value ones. And gates help chart the path forward, determining the tasks and deliverables for the next stage.

4. *Parallel processing* balances the need for a complete and quality process with the desire for a speedier process.

The process is designed much like a rugby match (rather than a relay race). Activities and tasks are undertaken concurrently rather than sequentially. The result is a faster, more intense process. There are fewer temptations to delete key activities due to lack of time, and a multifunctional process is the outcome.

5. The process requires a *cross-functional, empowered team* headed by a team leader with authority.

The cross-functional team approach is one critical ingredient, and it is essential to the success of the *Stage-Gate* game plan. The team is a *true* cross-functional one with active involvement and commitment by players from different functions in the firm. It must be empowered by senior management, but it is also accountable for results, with rewards tied to results. And the leader is given formal authority over the resources (people) on the team.

6. The process is *market-driven* and *customer-focused*.

Customer inputs and constant customer focus throughout the process are paramount. Nine key marketing actions—from customer-focused idea generation to market launch—have been identified and are a central feature of the innovation process.

7. Up-front or *predevelopment homework is* crucial to success, and these activities must be built into the game plan in a consistent and systematic way.

The seeds of success and failure are sown in the first few steps of the new product process. Like the marketing actions, those steps that precede the development of the project are typically weak, yet they make all the difference between winning and losing. Nine key up-front actions have been pinpointed—from initial screening up to the business case—and these too are built into the game plan.

8. The quest must be for *superior differentiated products* that offer *value to the user*.

Build in activities throughout your new product process that focus on gaining insights into what the customer sees as a unique, superior product with an excellent value proposition for the user. And utilize go/kill and project prioritization criteria that favor such projects.

The *Stage-Gate™* Process

These eight key goals, together with the fifteen critical success factors from the last chapter, have been fashioned into a *Stage-Gate* new product process—a *conceptual and operational model* for moving a new product project from idea to launch.[5] This *Stage-Gate* process is a blueprint for managing the product innovation process to improve effectiveness and efficiency. I first begin with the simplest view of *Stage-Gate*–the second-generation process, and then later in the chapter, move to its more sophisticated version, the third-generation process.[6]

Stage-Gate breaks the innovation process into a predetermined set of stages, each stage consisting of a set of prescribed, cross-functional, and parallel activities (see Figure 5.4). The entrance to each stage is a gate. These gates control

FIGURE 5.4   The Typical *Stage-Gate*™ Model—From Discovery to Launch

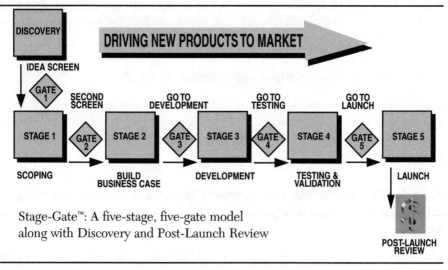

Stage-Gate™: A five-stage, five-gate model
along with Discovery and Post-Launch Review

SOURCE: Taken from various sources; See endnote 5.

the process and serve as the quality control and go/kill checkpoints. This stage-and-gate format leads to the name *"Stage-Gate* process."

The Stages

The *Stage-Gate* process breaks the new product project into discrete and identifiable stages, typically four, five, or six in number. Each stage is designed to gather information needed to progress the project to the next gate or decision point. Each stage is cross-functional: There is no "R&D stage" or "marketing stage"!

Each stage consists of a set of parallel activities undertaken by people from different functional areas within the firm. These activities build in the following:

- best practices—for example, the nine vital marketing actions of Goal #5 above
- the fifteen success factors—for example, quality of execution and sharp, early product definition
- the eight goals—for example, the unrelenting quest for a superior, differentiated product

These activities are also designed to gather information and drive uncertainties down. Each stage costs more than the preceding one: The process is an incremental commitment process.

The general flow of the typical *Stage-Gate* process is shown pictorially in Figure 5.4. The key stages consist of the following:

- *Discovery:* pre-work designed to discover and uncover opportunities and generate ideas
- *Scoping:* a quick, preliminary investigation of the project—largely desk research
- *Building the Business Case:* a much more detailed investigation involving primary research—both market and technical—leading to a business case, including product and project definition, project justification, and a project plan
- *Development:* the actual detailed design and development of the new product, and the design of the operations or production process
- *Testing and Validation:* tests or trials in the marketplace, lab, and plant to verify and validate the proposed new product and its marketing and production/operations
- *Launch:* commercialization—beginning of full operations or production, marketing, and selling

There is one additional stage: *strategy formulation,* an essential activity. This strategy formulation stage is left out of the game plan model for now, not because it's unimportant, but because it is all encompassing in nature—strategically oriented as opposed to process or tactics. Thus, strategy formulation is best superimposed over (or atop) the model in Figure 5.4; it is a prerequisite to an effective *Stage-Gate* process and is the topic of Chapter 12.

The Gates

Preceding each stage is a gate or a go/kill decision point. The gates are the scrums or huddles on the rugby or football field. They are the points during the game where the team converges and where all new information is brought together. Gates serve as quality-control checkpoints, as go/kill and prioritization decisions points, and as points where the path forward to the next play or stage of the process is decided.

The structure of each gate is similar. Gates consist of the following:

1. A set of required *deliverables:* This is what the project leader and team must bring to the decision point (for example, the results of a set of completed activities). These deliverables are visible, are based on a standard menu for each gate, and are decided at the output of the previous gate. Management's expectations for project teams are thus made very clear.
2. *Criteria* against which the project is judged: These include "must-meet" or "knock-out" questions (a checklist) designed to weed out misfit projects quickly. For example:

Gates have a common format:

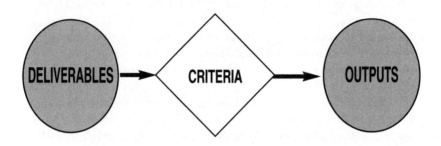

    ✓ Does the proposed project fit our business's strategy?
    ✓ Does it meet our environmental, health and safety policies?

There are also "should-meet" criteria or desirable factors, which are scored (a point count) and used to prioritize projects. For example:

    ✓ the degree of product advantage—the strength of the value proposition
    ✓ the ability to leverage core competencies
    ✓ the market attractiveness

3. Defined *outputs*: These include a decision (go/kill/hold/recycle), an approved action plan for the next stage (complete with people required, money and person-days committed, and an agreed time line), and a list of deliverables and date for the next gate.

Gates are usually tended by senior managers from different functions, who control the resources required by the project leader and team for the next stage.

An Overview of the *Stage-Gate*™ Process

Now for a bird's-eye look at the *Stage-Gate*™ process—an overview of what's involved at each stage and gate. In the next chapter, we'll lower the microscope on the Discovery Stage or how to generate breakthrough ideas. We then focus on the up-front or predevelopment stages and gates in Chapter 8. Chapter 8 also takes a close look at how to design and operate gates or decision points. Chapter 9 focuses on the middle and back-end stages of the process. But for now, let's just have a quick walk-through of the model, which you can follow stage by stage in Figure 5.4.

Begin Stage: Discovery

Ideas are the feedstock or trigger to the new product process, and they make or break the process. Don't expect a superb new product process to overcome a deficiency in good new product ideas. The need for great ideas coupled with high attrition rate of ideas means that the idea generation stage is pivotal: You need great ideas and lots of them.

Many companies consider ideation so important that they handle this as a formal stage in the process, which we call the Discovery Stage. They build in a *defined, proactive idea generation and capture system.* Activities in the Discovery Stage include undertaking directed but fundamental technical research, seeking new technological possibilities; working with lead users to uncover unarticulated needs; and conducting strategic planning exercises to uncover disruptions in the marketplace leading to identification of gaps and significant opportunities. The Discovery Stage is a vital phase, and I devote Chapter 6 to the topic.

Gate 1: Idea Screen

Idea screening is the first decision to commit resources to the project: The project is born at this point. If the decision is go, the project moves into pre-

Idea Screen

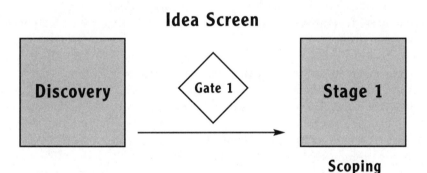

Scoping

liminary investigation or the Scoping Stage. Thus, Gate 1 signals a preliminary but tentative commitment to the project—a flickering green light.

Gate 1 is a "gentle screen" and amounts to subjecting the project to a handful of key "must-meet" and "should-meet" criteria. These criteria often deal with strategic alignment, project feasibility, magnitude of opportunity and market attractiveness, product advantage, ability to leverage the firm's resources, and fit with company policies. Financial criteria are typically not part of this first screen. A checklist for the must-meet criteria and a scoring model (point rating scales) for the should-meet criteria can be used to help focus the discussion and rank projects in this early screen.

Exxon Chemical has implemented its Product Innovation Process (PIP), whose initial gate has a handful of key yes/no criteria:

- Strategic fit: Does the proposal fit within a market or technology area defined by the business as an area of strategic focus?
- Market attractiveness: Are the market size, growth, and opportunities attractive?
- Technical feasibility: Is there a reasonable likelihood that the product can be developed and produced?
- Killer variables: Are there any known killer variables (for example, obsolescence, environmental issues, legislative actions)?

At Exxon Chemical, the gatekeepers include both technical and business (marketing) people. At this "Start Gate" meeting, project ideas are reviewed against these four criteria using a paper-and-pencil approach. This list of must-meet criteria is scored (yes/no), and the answers to all questions must be yes; a single no kills the project.

Stage 1: Scoping

This first and inexpensive homework stage has the objective of determining the project's technical and marketplace merits. Stage 1 is a quick scoping of the project, involving desk research or detective work; little or no primary research is done here. It is often done in less than one month's time with 10–20 person-days work effort.

A *preliminary market assessment* is one facet of Stage 1, and it involves a variety of relatively inexpensive activities: an Internet search, a library search, contacts with key users, focus groups, and even a quick concept test with a handful of potential users. The purpose is to determine market size, market potential, and likely market acceptance and also to begin to sculpt the product concept.

Concurrently a *preliminary technical assessment* is carried out, involving a quick and preliminary in-house appraisal of the proposed product. The purpose is to assess development and manufacturing (or source of supply) routes, technical and manufacturing/operations feasibility, possible times and costs to execute, and technical, legal, and regulatory risks and roadblocks.

Stage 1 thus provides for the gathering of both market and technical information—at low costs and in a short time—to enable a cursory and first-pass financial and business analysis as input to Gate 2. Because of the limited effort, and depending on the size of the project, very often Stage 1 can be handled by a team of just several people—perhaps from marketing and from a technical group.

Consider this example of a preliminary technical and market assessment:

OMNOVA Solutions (formerly GenCorp) of Akron, Ohio, had the good fortune of stumbling across a new technology through fundamental research, which has become the platform for a number of new product projects. The new technology enables traditional polymers to have an extremely slippery surface; yet unlike other slippery materials, the resulting polymer retains its usual positive physical properties (for example, abrasion resistance and toughness).

The first product to be launched was vinyl wall covering with a difference—it's a relatively low-cost, dry-erase whiteboard. Imagine having walls in meeting rooms, or walls in your child's room, that everyone can write on!

Before embarking on extensive development work for this project, a preliminary assessment or scoping was undertaken. The company was already in the wall covering business, so ample in-house data on markets, sizes, and trends were available. Additionally, the project leader sought and found published data—trade publications, reports, and so forth—on the existing whiteboard market. Informal chats with some distributors revealed the pricing structure. Technical work was relatively limited at Stage 1, as fundamental research had already uncovered the technical possibility. Nonetheless a core group of scientists got together with manufacturing people to discuss technical and manufacturing feasibility (note how early manufacturing was involved in the project). Finally, a first-cut financial analysis was developed—based largely on guestimates—but this sanity check revealed a huge opportunity.

As this book is being written, the product is in the launch phase, and initial sales and customer reaction are very positive. The company has already launched colored and patterned versions of Memerase™, and innovative new products based on the concept and technology are still coming down OMNOVA's stage-gate pipeline!

Gate 2: Second Screen

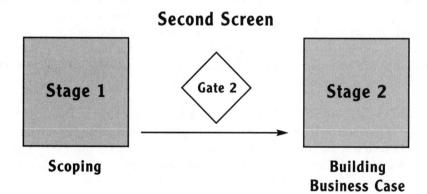

The project is subjected to a second and somewhat more rigorous screen at Gate 2. This gate is essentially a repeat of Gate 1; the project is reevaluated in the light of the new information obtained in Stage 1. If the decision is go at this point, the project moves into a heavier spending stage.

At Gate 2, the project is again subjected to the original set of must-meet and should-meet criteria used at Gate 1. Here additional should-meet criteria may be considered, dealing with sales force and customer reaction to the proposed product and potential legal, technical, and regulatory "killer variables," all the result of new data gathered during Stage 1. Again, a checklist and scoring model facilitate this gate decision. The financial return is assessed at Gate 2, but only by a quick and simple financial calculation (for example, the payback period). Another example:

> Reckitt & Colman, now Reckitt-Benckiser, makers of such well-known consumer brands as Lysol, Easy-Off, and Air Wick, uses a well-crafted four-stage, four-gate product development process. Gate 2 follows the preliminary investigation, called the "Concept Stage," and opens the door to a more detailed investigation, the "Feasibility Stage." The spirit of Gate 2 is: "Does the initial evidence suggest that the concept can win in the marketplace?" Gate 2 features a combination of must-meet and should-meet criteria. The must-meet items must yield positive answers; the should-meet items are rated on scales.

Stage 2: Building the Business Case

Stage 2, Building the Business Case, opens the door to product development. Stage 2 is where the business case is constructed. This stage is a detailed investigation stage that clearly defines the product and verifies the attractiveness of the project prior to heavy spending. It is also the *critical homework* stage—the one so often found to be weakly handled.

The definition of the winning new product is a major facet of Stage 2. The elements of this definition include target market definition; delineation of the product concept; specification of a product positioning strategy, the product benefits to be delivered, and the value proposition; and the spelling out of essential and desired product features, attributes, requirements, and specifications.

Stage 2 sees *market investigations and market research studies* undertaken to determine the customer's needs, wants, and preferences, that is, to help define the "winning" new product. Here's an example:

> Fluke Corporation of Seattle is well noted for its innovative products in the field of hand-held electrical measurement instruments. A strategic decision to diversify into new markets led to the creation of the Phoenix team—a project team whose mandate was to deliver a superior product or two in a market outside of the firm's normal scope, namely, in the chemical industry.
>
> Facing a totally new market, the project team had no one in the company to turn to, so they began their voyage of discovery with some pre-work, beginning with project planning, Synectics (innovative team process training), and a review of the trade literature. The first team visit was to a chemical industry trade show in Chicago, followed by a few field visits to nearby chemical plants. The plant field visits were not based on sophisticated market research methodology; it was sim-

ply spending an afternoon in the control room, chatting with and observing the customer, the plant instrument engineers. The project leader calls this "fly-on-the-wall research"; others call it "anthropological research" or "camping out."[7]

After some twenty-five site visits, the project team acquired a good understanding of the instrument engineer's problems and needs. One fact that was observed was the amount of equipment the engineers needed to carry out to the plant merely to calibrate common instruments, such as pressure or temperature gauges. Every gauge and brand, it seemed, needed a different calibration instrument. Second, observation revealed that after the engineer had calibrated the gauge, he spent several minutes taking readings and recording them on a clipboard. After calibrating a number of gauges, the engineer returned to the control room and typed into his computer all the hand-recorded readings from the field—a time-consuming process.

You've probably guessed what the Phoenix team came up with for a new product project: a hand-held universal calibration instrument that utilized software (rather than hardware) to record readings in the field, which could then be down-loaded directly into the control room computer. The Documenting Process Calibrator product line went on to become a great success, another testimony to really understanding customer needs and to designing a superior product in response to these needs.

Competitive analysis is also a part of this stage. Another market activity is concept testing: A representation of the proposed new product is presented to potential customers, their reactions are gauged, and the likely customer acceptance of the new product is determined.[8]

A detailed *technical appraisal* focuses on the "do-ability" of the project at Stage 2. That is, customer needs and "wish lists" are translated into a technically and economically feasible solution. This translation might even involve some preliminary design or laboratory work, but it should not be construed as a full-fledged development project. A manufacturing (or operations) appraisal is often a part of Building the Business Case, where issues of manufacturability, source of supply, costs to manufacture, and investment required are investigated. If appropriate, detailed legal, patent, and regulatory assessment work is undertaken in order to remove risks and to map out the required actions.

Finally, a detailed *business and financial analysis* is conducted as part of the justification facet of the business case. The financial analysis typically involves a discounted cash flow approach, complete with sensitivity analysis to look at possible downside risks.

The result of Stage 2 is a *business case* for the project: The *product definition*—a key to success—is agreed on, and a thorough *project justification* and *detailed project plan* are developed.

Stage 2 involves considerably more effort than Stage 1 and requires input from a variety of sources. Stage 2 is best handled by a team consisting of cross-functional members—the core group of the eventual project team.

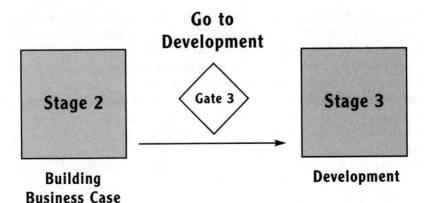

Gate 3: Go to Development

This is the final gate prior to the Development Stage, the last point at which the project can be killed before entering heavy spending. Once past Gate 3, financial commitments are substantial. In effect, Gate 3 means "go to a heavy spend." Gate 3 also yields a "sign off" of the product and project definition.

The qualitative side of this evaluation involves a review of each of the activities in Stage 2, checking that the activities were undertaken, the quality of execution was sound, and the results were positive. Next, Gate 3 subjects the project once again to the set of must-meet and should-meet criteria used at Gate 2. Finally, because a heavy spending commitment is the result of a go decision at Gate 3, the results of the financial analysis are an important part of this screen.

If the decision is go, Gate 3 ensures commitment to the product definition and agreement on the project plan that charts the path forward. The development plan and the preliminary operations and marketing plans are reviewed and approved at this gate. The full project team—an empowered cross-functional team headed by a leader with authority—is designated.

Stage 3: Development

Stage 3, Development, witnesses the implementation of the development plan and the physical development of the product. Lab tests, in-house tests, or alpha tests ensure that the product meets requirements under controlled conditions. For lengthy projects, numerous milestones and periodic project reviews are built into the development plan. These are not gates per se; go/kill decisions are not made here. Rather these checkpoints provide for project control and management. The "deliverable" at the end of Stage 3 is a lab-tested prototype of the product.

The emphasis in Stage 3 is on technical work, but parallel marketing and operations activities are also undertaken. For example, market-analysis and customer-feedback work continue concurrently with the technical development, with customer opinion sought on the product as it takes shape during development. These activities are back-and-forth or iterative, with each development result—for example, rapid prototype, working model, or first prototype—taken to the customer for assessment and feedback. Meanwhile, detailed test plans, market launch plans, and production or operations plans, including production facilities requirements, are developed. An updated financial analysis is prepared, while regulatory, legal, and patent issues are resolved.

Go to Testing

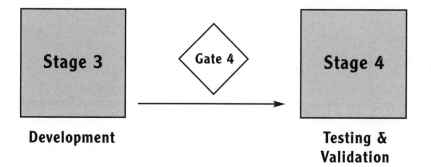

Gate 4: Go to Testing

This post-development review is a check on the progress and the continued attractiveness of the product and project. Development work is reviewed and checked, ensuring that the work has been completed in a quality fashion and that the developed product is indeed consistent with the original definition specified at Gate 3.

This gate also revisits the economic question through a revised financial analysis based on new and more accurate data. The test or validation plans for the next stage are approved for immediate implementation, and the detailed marketing and operations plans are reviewed for probable future execution.

Stage 4: Testing and Validation

This stage tests and validates the entire viability of the project: the product itself, the production process, customer acceptance, and the economics of the project. It also begins extensive external validation of the product and project. A number of activities are undertaken at Stage 4:

- *In-house product tests:* extended lab tests or alpha tests to check on product quality and product performance under controlled or lab conditions
- *User or field trials of the product:* to verify that the product functions under actual use conditions, to gauge potential customers' reactions to the product, and to establish purchase intent
- *Trial, limited, or pilot production:* to test, debug, and improve the production process and to determine more precise production costs and throughputs
- *Pretest market, test market, or trial sell:* to gauge customer reaction, measure the effectiveness of the launch plan, and determine expected market share and revenues
- *Revised business and financial analysis:* to check on the continued business and economic viability of the project, based on new and more accurate revenue and cost data

Sometimes Stage 4 yields negative results, and it's back to Stage 3. Here's an example:

All was proceeding well for the OMNOVA dry-erase wall covering. A successful trial production run in Stage 4 yielded sufficient semi-commercial product to permit customer trials in several test buildings. The product had been extensively tested in the lab on all known performance metrics—temperature, humidity, scuff resistance, and so forth. But one small factor was overlooked—as it often is. Some customers used a certain brand of dry-erase markers with a unique solvent. The result: When left on the whiteboard for several days, writing from this one brand of marker proved difficult to erase. And so "ghosts" appeared. This ghosting problem had not been identified until real customers started using the product. But OMNOVA was alert and acted on the field trial results. The problem was rectified, and now the commercial product meets all customer requirements.

Gate 5: Go to Launch

Go to Launch

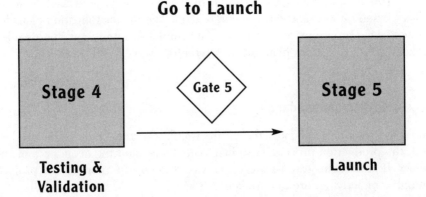

This final gate opens the door to full commercialization—market launch and full production or operations start-up. It is the final point at which the project can still be killed. This gate focuses on the quality of the activities in the Testing and Validation Stage and their results. Criteria for passing the gate focus largely on expected financial return and appropriateness of the launch and operations start-up plans. The operations and marketing plans are reviewed and approved for implementation in Stage 5.

Go to Launch

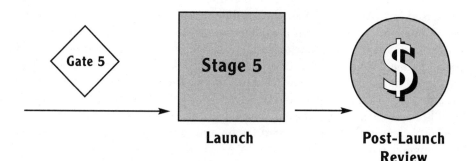

Gate 5 → **Stage 5** → **$**

Launch   **Post-Launch Review**

Stage 5: Launch

This final stage involves implementation of both the marketing launch plan and the production or operations plan. Given a well thought-out plan of action and backed by appropriate resources, and of course, barring any unforeseen events, it should be clear sailing for the new product—another new product success!

Post-Launch Review

At some point following commercialization (often 6–19 months), the new product project must be terminated. The team is disbanded, and the product becomes a "regular product" in the firm's product line. This is also the point where the project and product's performance is reviewed. The latest data on revenues, costs, expenditures, profits, and timing are compared to projections to gauge performance. Finally, a post-audit is carried out; this involves a critical assessment of the project's strengths and weaknesses and a discussion of what was learned from this project and how the next project can be done better. This review marks the end of the project. Note that the project team and leader remain responsible for the success of the project through this post-launch period, including the Post-Launch Review.

What the *Stage-Gate* Process Is Not!

With this overview of the new product game plan fresh in our minds, and before we get into its details in the next few chapters, let's deal with some potential misconceptions. The *Stage-Gate* process is designed to facilitate and speed products to market. Here are some of the things the system *is not*.

1. Not a Functional, Phased Review System

Don't confuse this game plan of the new millennium with the traditional "phased review" process of the 1960s–1990s. This phased review process, endorsed by NASA and others, broke the innovation process into stages, each stage reporting to a function or a department. Implemented with the best of intentions, the process managed to almost double the length of new product development. Why? The process was designed like a relay race—activities in sequence rather than in parallel. There were hand-offs throughout the process, as one team or function passed the project on to the next department (and with hand-offs, there arise the inevitable fumbles!), and there was no commitment to the project from beginning to end by any one group or team—accountability was missing.

By contrast, today's *Stage-Gate* process is built for speed. The stages are multifunctional; they are not dominated by a single functional area (for example, the notion of an "R&D stage" followed by a "manufacturing stage" and then a "marketing stage" is obsolete). The play is rapid, with activities occurring in parallel rather than in series, and with defined gates and criteria for efficient, timely decision making. And the game plan is executed from idea to post-launch by a dedicated and empowered team of players drawn from the functional areas, headed by a leader.

2. Not a Rigid System

The game plan or new product process outlined in Figure 5.4 is fairly typical. But remember, this is a road map or template; as in any road map, when the situation merits, detours can be taken. For example, most companies tailor the model to their own circumstances and build lots of flexibility into their game plans:

- Not all projects pass through every stage or gate of the model.
- In any one project, activities and deliverables can be omitted or bypassed.
- Similarly, activities can be moved from one stage to another—for example, moving an activity ahead one stage in the event of long lead times.

3. Not a Bureaucratic System

Properly implemented, the *Stage-Gate* system fosters all the attributes of a timely, successful development effort: a clearly visible road map with defined deliverables and objectives; a cross-functional team approach with empowerment; and defined decision points with spelled-out criteria. Unfortunately, some managers see *any system* as an opportunity to impose more paperwork, lots of forms, unending meetings and committees, and needless red tape. Remember: The objective here is a systematic, streamlined process, not a bogged-down bureaucratic one!

4. Not the Same as Project Management

Stage-Gate is a *macro* process—an overarching process. By contrast, *project management* is a *micro* process. *Stage-Gate* is not a substitute for sound project management methods. Rather, *Stage-Gate* and project management are used together. Specifically, project management methods are applied *within the stages* of the *Stage-Gate* process. For example, there is an expectation that during the larger, more complex stages (Stages 3, 4, and 5: Development, Testing and Validation, and Launch), project management methods must be applied:

- ✓ A team initiation task to define the mission and goals of the project
- ✓ Team-building exercises
- ✓ Computer-generated time lines
- ✓ Parallel processing (undertaking activities concurrently rather than sequentially)
- ✓ Milestone review points (built into the action plans approved at each gate)
- ✓ Regular project reviews

Built-in Success Factors

The logic of a well-designed game plan, such as the *Stage-Gate* system in Figure 5.4, is appealing because it incorporates many of the factors and lessons vital to success that I highlighted in the previous chapters. For example:

1. The process places much more emphasis on the homework or predevelopment activities. Stages 1 and 2—Scoping and Building the Business Case—are essential steps before the door to Development is opened at Gate 3.
2. The process is multidisciplinary and cross-functional. It is built around an empowered, cross-functional team. Each stage consists of technical,

marketing, operations/production, and even financial activities, necessitating the active involvement of people from all of these areas. The gates are also cross-functional: Gates are tended by gatekeepers from different functions or departments in the firm—the managers who own the resources needed for the next stage.

3. Parallel processing speeds up the process. Activities in each stage are undertaken concurrently, rather than sequentially, with much interaction between players within each stage.

4. A strong market orientation is a feature of the game plan. Marketing inputs begin at the Discovery Stage and remain an important facet of every stage from beginning to end of the process. Projects cannot pass the gates until the marketing actions have been completed in a quality way.

5. There is more focus. The game plan builds in decision points in the form of gates. These gates weed out poor projects early in the process and help focus scarce resources on the truly deserving projects.

6. A product-definition step is built into the process at Stage 2, Building the Business Case. It is here that the project and product are both defined and justified. This product definition is a key deliverable to Gate 3; without it, the project cannot proceed to Development.

7. There is a strong focus on quality of execution throughout. The stages and recommended activities within each stage lay out a road map for the project leader and team, so that there is less chance of critical errors of omission. The gates provide the critical quality-control checks in the process; unless the project meets certain quality standards, it fails to pass the gate.

☞ **Suggestion:** As soon as you finish this chapter, take a hard look at your own new product process. First, do you have a process? If yes, lay it out in front of you. Go through the seven success factors listed just above, and ask yourself: "Does my new product process build in each of these items?" If not, read on— it's time to rethink your process.

Speeding Up the Process: The Third-Generation Process

What's beyond the new product process I described above? Those companies that have successfully installed this process (what I call a "second-generation process") are now moving toward my *third-generation version* of the process, according to the latest PDMA survey of best practices.[9] Here's the evolution:

First-generation processes were the phased review processes that appeared in the 1960s. They were largely engineering driven and featured laborious check-offs at each review point to ensure the successful completion of a number of key tasks. Thus the method was more a *measurement and control* methodology, designed to ensure that the project was proceeding as it should and that every facet of it was completed and on time. Waterfall processes, often found in software development companies, were typical. But this first-generation process was very technically focused. It applied strictly to the physical design and technical development of the product (for example, it was not cross-functional and excluded marketing and operations/manufacturing people). It did not specify what actions should be taken in each stage, nor were best practices a part of the process. And the process was accused by some of being very time-consuming, with very laborious check-offs.

Today's second-generation *Stage-Gate™* process, as described so far in the chapter, is a step change from the phased review process of the 1960s. *Stage-Gate* also consists of identifiable and discrete stages preceded by review points or gates. But that is where the similarities end. *Stage-Gate* overcomes many of the objections found with first-generation processes. *Stage-Gate* is cross-functional, with no department owning any stage—marketing and operations are now integral parts of the process. The gates are also cross-functional, so that there is alignment of senior people on project priorities. The process is more holistic. There is greater emphasis on the front end (up-front homework and a stronger customer input). It specifies stage activities and best practices. And it builds in parallel processing.

Stage-Gate processes are *evergreen processes*, that is, constantly evolving and improving. Experienced stage-gaters have improved their processes to emphasize *efficiency,* speeding up an already effective second-generation process and *more efficiently allocating development resources.* According to the latest PDMA survey, almost one-half of the companies that have adopted *Stage-Gate* processes have redesigned it to include some of the elements of my third-generation process.[10]

The third-generation process is a natural evolution, once the second-generation *Stage-Gate* process has been successfully installed in your business. It features six fundamental F's:[11]

1. Flexibility
2. Fuzzy (conditional) gates
3. Fluidity
4. Focus (project prioritization and portfolio management)
5. Facilitation
6. Forever green—always regenerating and improving

1. Flexibility

The process is not a straitjacket or a hard-and-fast set of rules. Rather, each project can be routed through the process according to its specific risk level and needs. Stages can be omitted and gates combined, provided the decisions are made consciously and with a full understanding of the risks involved. The new product process is essentially a *risk-management process,* and thus the risk level, the uncertainty, and the need for information dictate what steps and stages need to be done and which can be left out. Typically, lower-risk projects omit some stages, activities, and gates, with this routing decision made at the previous gate.

In the Royal Bank of Canada, one of North America's largest banks, the Business Banking unit uses a five-stage, five-gate new product process called RPR (right projects right), not unlike the process shown in Figure 5.4. Senior management uses a *triage approach* and has defined three categories of projects, based on project scope, investment, and risk level:

- *system change requests*, which are relatively minor product changes and improvements, often in response to a request from a major corporate client. These go through a two-stage, two-gate version of the model.
- *fast-track projects*, which are medium-cost projects and feature some risk (less than $500,000 development cost, but impact multiple customers). These moderate-risk projects are tracked through a four-stage version of the model, which collapses the two homework stages into a single stage.
- *major projects*, over $500,000, are considered higher-risk projects. These pass through the full five-stage model.

I recommend an abbreviated process for lower-risk projects, as portrayed in the three-stage, three-gate process in Figure 5.5. But this short-cut process should be reserved for low risk projects only–extensions, fixes, improvements and product renewals.

2. Fuzzy Gates

Here I mean "fuzzy" in the sense of fuzzy logic—a newer form of mathematics—where instead of just being binary (open or closed), gates can have various states in between. Thus, go decisions can be *conditional on some future event occurring;* the decision is made in the absence of perfect information, conditional on positive results delivered later.

Consider the AtoFina's acrylics business (formerly Ato-Haas at Rohm and Haas). If a project is reviewed at a gate and found to be missing one key deliverable (for example, the results of a legal or regulatory investigation), with the second-generation process, the decision is to *hold the project* until the results of this study are known. In the faster-paced third-generation *Stage-Gate* process, the gate decision becomes a "conditional go." The team moves ahead to the next stage, but it is required to report back to the head gatekeeper the results of the missing study. If he is comfortable with the results,

FIGURE 5.5   A Three-Stage Version of *Stage-Gate™* Model for Lower-Risk Projects

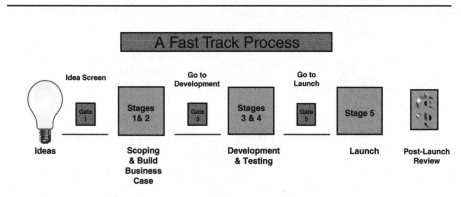

Stage-GateTM is flexible. This 3-stage fast-track version
is for lower risk, smaller projects: line extensions,
product improvements, modifications, etc. - where costs
and times are less

the conditional go decision becomes a *full go;* if not, the head gatekeeper calls for a full gate meeting and the project is reviewed again, possibly to be killed or reconsidered. The point is that the project moves ahead and is not held up awaiting one piece of information, but there is also a check to ensure that the future information is forthcoming and that results are positive.

Another fuzzy gate concept involves the project team acting as its own gatekeeper. Nortel Networks has introduced the notion of self-managed gates—an attempt to reduce bureaucracy and speed up the process. The jury is still out on this approach!

3. Fluidity

The third-generation new product process is fluid and adaptable. Activities are not married to specific stages, but rather there is an overlapping of stages. Some activities, normally done in the next stage, will begin before the previous stage is completed; long lead-time activities can be brought forward from one stage to an earlier one; and the demarcation between stages is more fluid. For example, in the case of overlapping stages, a project can be starting the next stage before the preceding one is complete, as shown in Figure 5.6.

Where stages are allowed to overlap, there are still gates that mark the ramping up of the next stage, complete with the approval of additional funding and resources for the next stage. Before the gate can occur, however, most of the activities of the previous stage must be complete, and the pivotal deliverables are in place. Fluidity, namely, overlapping stages, goes hand in hand with the

FIGURE 5.6   The Third-Generation *Stage-Gate*™ Process for Greater Speed

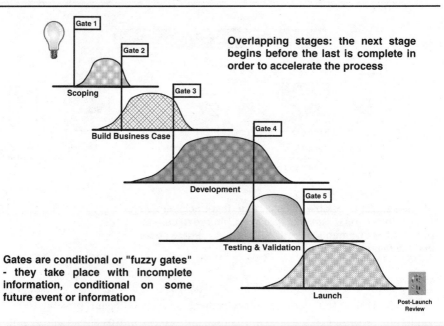

idea of fuzzy or conditional gates—approvals for the next stage made in the absence of complete information.

Here's the rule at GTE's Network System Division in Boston:

> Long lead-time activities can be brought forward from one stage to a previous one. For example, ordering materials or equipment with very long lead times may best be done in an earlier stage even though the project may yet be canceled. The risks of placing the order earlier must be weighed against the extra cost of postponement of the launch (a quantitative assessment).

4. Focus

The third-generation new product process is focused, much like a funnel, where poor projects are weeded out at each gate and resources are reallocated to the best projects. But this means more than just tough go/kill decision points or gates; it means moving to effective *portfolio management,* where one manages an entire portfolio of projects rather than considering just the merits of the one project under review. Because focus, gates, and portfolio management are such vital concepts, I devote an entire chapter, Chapter 8, to these important topics.

5. Facilitation

The next F is facilitation, a new element I have added since the original article on third-generation processes was written. To my knowledge, there has never been a successful installation of a *Stage-Gate* process without a process manager or facilitator in place! And for larger companies, this is a full-time position. The role of this process facilitator—often called the key master, process manager, gate meister or process keeper—is to make sure that the *Stage-Gate* process works efficiently and effectively. The process keeper facilitates every important gate meeting, acting as a referee, ensuring that gatekeepers follow the rules of the game, and ensures that a decision is made. She coaches the project teams, helping them overcome difficulties and roadblocks, making sure that all the key deliverables are in place. The process keeper updates the process and provides for continual process improvement; she trains new employees on how to use the system, and most important, she is the scorekeeper in the game.

No complex process, no matter how good, ever implemented itself. Experienced stage-gaters readily admit that the key to success here is not just in the design of the process but in its implementation and that if *Stage-Gate* processes fail, it is because of faulty implementation rather than faulty design. So provide for facilitation: Install a full-time "keeper of the process" in your business.

6. Forever Green

Stage-Gate™ processes are evergreen. They are being constantly renewed, redesigned, and improved as user-companies gain experience with this approach. Some of the general improvements that businesses have made include the five F's listed above. Other companies have adjusted their *Stage-Gate* processes to suit their specific needs. Some examples:

- International Paper has a number of major projects that cut across many business units within the huge corporation. Getting project sponsors (gatekeepers) together was proving almost impossible, so IP has replaced traditional gate meetings with *web-based gates*. Sponsors can review the deliverables (these are available through e-delivery) and then score the project remotely.
- The Thomson Corporation, in the financial, medical, and legal information business, has added an extensive Discovery Stage to the front end of their *Thomson Solutions Process*. This stage focuses on generating major opportunities for new solutions development; it is based on identifying industry, market, and technology disruptions or step changes.

- One major financial institution has adjusted the front end of their *Right Products Right™* (a *Stage-Gate* process) to provide a funnel to "suck in" and deal with third-party new products (products developed by other banks and/or software that might be available for license, joint venture, or sale).
- Guinness has replaced the traditional idea phase or "lightbulb" in its *NaviGate* process with a stage designed to identify unmet consumer needs and to define major new opportunities.

The point is that you should be constantly reviewing and re-energizing your new product process. And if you haven't updated your current process in the last two years, chances are it's out of date . . . time for an audit and an overhaul!

Before moving too quickly to a six-F third-generation process, a word of caution is in order: Knowledgeable stage-gaters argue strongly that you should strive first for a basic and effective new product process, perhaps initially incorporating *only some* of the elements of my third-generation process (for example, facilitation, focus, and some facets of flexibility). Once this process is up and running well, then seek the full-fledged, fast-paced third-generation process. As one executive put it: "It's much like learning to drive an automobile. After taking a rigorous driver instruction course, the inexperienced driver needs rules and rigidly follows them—he signals at every turn or lane change, and stays exactly within the speed limit. With experience, the professional driver does some things automatically; and he learns when certain rules can be broken without additional risk in order to speed up the driving—for example, speeding or sliding through a stop sign." Advancing immediately to a full six-F process has its downside unless your process is in good shape to begin with; you should walk before you run.

There is a seventh F, namely, fallibility. The six F's of the third-generation highlighted above are all positive. The last F is a possible negative consequence. This flexible, fluid process with fuzzy gates introduces much more freedom and discretion to project leaders, teams, and senior managers (the gatekeepers or decision makers). With freedom and discretion, of course, comes risk; the odds of making mistakes go up. This new process is more delicate, sophisticated, and sensitive, and thus it requires a more experienced, professional management approach. Some of the possible fail points have been noted in the discussion above. Using the automobile driver analogy, with more discretion over the rules and with increased speed, comes an increased risk of disaster.

What About Fundamental Research Projects or Platform Developments?

An obvious question is: Can the *Stage-Gate* process be applied to research projects, fundamental science projects, or to platform developments? The answer is: generally no—at least not as I've described *Stage-Gate* above. But wait . . .

First, here are some definitions to make sure we're all speaking about the same kinds of projects:

Platform projects build a capability. The analogy is the construction of an oil-well drilling platform in the ocean, at great cost. Once the platform is in place, many holes can be drilled from it, each at much less cost than the first. In new products, the platform establishes the capability, and this capability spawns many new product projects—much more quickly and cost effectively than starting from scratch each time. Examples include a deposit software platform in a bank, from which many different end-user deposit products can be developed, and a new catalyst in the chemical industry, which might spawn an entire new family of polymers— many new products. More on platform developments in Chapter 12.

Fundamental research projects are those where the deliverable is new knowledge. When the project begins, there may be no specific new product (or new manufacturing process) defined or even in mind. Rather, the scientist initiates some experiments with the hope of finding some technical possibilities and discoveries that might yield ideas for commercial products or processes. I also call these "science projects" and "technology developments."

The main difference between these projects and a new product project—for which *Stage-Gate* was designed—is that science projects and platform developments are often more loosely defined at the outset than is the typical new product project. Although a fundamental research or science project may ultimately yield a new product, often the new product cannot be well defined at the beginning. Indeed, it may take months of technical research before it's even clear what might be technically possible. So undertaking market analysis in Stage 1 and detailed market studies in Stage 2 makes little sense. And the criteria for project selection are clearly different than for a very tangible, well-defined new product project (see Chapter 6).

Similarly, platform projects are often visionary in scope, with little concretely defined in the way of tangible products. Rather, management is building a capability that they hope will lead to multiple new product projects. Again, it is difficult to undertake detailed market analyses and full financial projection when only the first or second product from the platform is even envisioned—the rest are "yet to be defined." Thus, the decision to move ahead must be largely a strategic one that looks at what this platform *might yield* in terms of multiple new products, most of which are unknown.

Both types of projects are important, and a certain percentage of your resources should be devoted to each type. But the *Stage-Gate* process described above may be inappropriate for both types.

However, some companies have *adapted and adjusted Stage-Gate* to handle these types of projects. The stage-and-gate approach seems to work, but clearly the spirit of the stages and the specific criteria used at gates are quite different from those described above and in Figure 5.4. Some examples include the following:

- Corning Glass now stage-gates just about every discretionary expenditure—from technology developments to plant expansions. That is, they have taken their original gating system far beyond new products.
- Rohm and Haas has expanded their *Stage-Gate* process to accommodate science and exploratory research projects.
- Mobil Chemical has a custom-tailored *Stage-Gate* process to cope with the development of technology platforms.
- Exxon has published a synopsis of its *Stage-Gate* process to handle research projects.[12]

☞ **Suggestion:** If some of your development projects are science (fundamental research) or platform developments, get your *Stage-Gate* process working for new product projects first. It is easier to design a process for new products–at least conceptually. Don't try to ram science projects or platform projects through this new product process; this will create nothing but frustration and may even damage the credibility of your well-designed new product process.

Once your new product process is working, then turn to your more visionary projects—science projects and platform developments—and design a parallel process for them as well. The processes for platform developments or fundamental research projects should look a lot like your new product *Stage-Gate* process; for example, they should have stages and gates. Even the names of some of the stages and gates may be the same. But the details of the stages and the specific gate criteria you use will be quite unique to these types of projects. In Chapter 6, I outline a stage-and-gate process designed to handle fundamental research projects.

Toward a Winning New Product Process

Many investigations, including our NewProd studies, have provided insights into how to mount a successful product innovation effort. This chapter has translated these insights into a carefully crafted new product process—a plan that focuses on quality of execution, builds in the up-front homework, is strongly market-oriented, and is backed by appropriate resources.

The benefits of the *Stage-Gate*™ process are evident. The model puts discipline into a process that, in many firms, is seriously deficient. The process is visible, relatively simple, and easy to understand and communicate. As one manager exclaimed, "At least we're all reading from the same page of the same book." The requirements are clear; what is expected of a project team at each stage and gate is spelled out. The process provides a road map to facilitate the project, and it better defines the project leader's objectives and tasks.

But the design and implementation of a *Stage-Gate* new product process is more complex than simply photocopying Figure 5.4 of this book and displaying it on the office bulletin board. The next four chapters provide a much more detailed examination of the elements of this *Stage-Gate* model. We begin in Chapter 6 by focusing on the Discovery Stage—seeking breakthrough new product opportunities.

CHAPTER

Discovery:
The Quest for Breakthrough Ideas

History is in essence a history of ideas.
—H. G. Wells, *The Outline of History*

The Discovery Stage: Ideation

After a decade of development focused on extensions and quick hits, the quest for the super-idea—the "home run," breakthrough idea, or major innovation—is quickly becoming a key management issue. The trigger for the *Stage-Gate*™ process is a new product idea: when technological possibilities are matched with market needs and expected market demand. A good new product idea can make or break the project: Ideas are the feedstock of the new product process. But don't expect a well-oiled new product process to make up for a shortage of quality ideas. If the idea was mundane to start with, don't count on your *Stage-Gate* process to turn it into a star!

So important is idea generation that I now treat this as a separate stage. In previous editions of this book, the idea stage was treated as a given; it was always assumed that there are lots of ideas sitting around waiting to be worked on. Perhaps this is true, but the quality of these ideas is lacking in too many firms, and so the development pipeline is filled with mediocre, low-value projects. Thus a vital facet of a successful new product effort is the development of an idea-generating system. I call this the "Discovery Stage." And there are some specific actions that you can build into your Discovery Stage to generate some breakthrough ideas for new products.

A Product Innovation and Technology Strategy in Place

One prerequisite to effective idea generation is having a new product strategy for your business in place. This strategy, among other things, defines the *arenas of strategic focus*—in short, where you want to hunt. This is important for idea and opportunity identification, because it specifies what's in bounds, and perhaps more important, what's out of bounds. This specification makes the quest for great new product ideas much more directed and hence more effective; you avoid the scattergun approach often found in traditional idea search. I devote an entire chapter to this topic of innovation strategy—Chapter 12.

Bottom-Up or Top-Down?

An important point is that idea generation can be both top-down and purposeful, as well as bottom-up and serendipitous. Both routes have their place:

- An example of bottom-up, serendipitous idea generation is where a scientist, perhaps using her free time, uncovers a technological possibility, does a few experiments, and then realizes that a new product might be the outcome. Or perhaps a salesperson, walking through a customer facility, notices a problem, and after some thought, sees a potential solution. Even better, both ideas are in arenas deemed strategic by senior management, so the scientist and the salesperson submit their ideas, and two new product projects are born.
- Top-down is usually more directed. An example is where a strategic exercise defines a particular market segment as a key area of focus. Market research reveals that there are some significant customer problems waiting to be solved in this arena, and these problems ultimately result in a product road map or in envisioning a set of new products to be developed over the next few years.

The point is that both approaches have their place. In too many companies I visit, it's all one or the other. One major communications company develops a rolling three-year new product strategy and plan. Included in it are the key areas of strategic focus and a product road map with all the new products—even their launch dates—mapped out for the next three years. It's a totally top-down process with not a lot of room for originality or creativity. No wonder most of the company's new products are fairly predicable and bland. At the other end of the spectrum is the company that relies strictly on employee suggestions—bottom-up. Some come from scientists, but most are from the sales force. And the results are as one might expect: Many of the submissions are quite short term, and the few creative ones are typically way off strategy. There's not much vision or direction to the entire ideation effort.

My point is that if you're only relying on one of these as a route to getting ideas, you're missing half the best bets. Of course, you need a new product strategy for the business, and from this strategy should evolve significant opportunities and new products. Equally, don't shut out the serendipitous, creative, or bottom-up approach. Some businesses at 3M claim that their best new products emerge from bottom-up, free-time work on the part of technical people.

☞ **Suggestion:** Review your new product pipeline. Is there a shortage of really great projects—products that promise major revenues or that will have a high impact on your business? If so, maybe it's because you're neglecting the Discovery Stage of the process. Ask yourself some questions: Where do new product ideas come from? Where should they be coming from? Are the ideas good ones? Do you have enough of them? How does your company actively solicit new product ideas? Do you have a new product idea generating system in your business? If the answers to these questions make you uneasy, don't worry; this chapter suggests some concrete actions that can be taken to improve idea generation.

A Strategic Outlook—
Look for Disruptions in Your Customer's Industry

Let's now develop a map for the Discovery Stage designed to generate significant new product opportunities and ideas.

Big ideas solve big problems! And big problems often come from major shifts or disruptions in an industry. Strategic approaches can be used to identify shifts, dislocations, or disruptions in the industry or marketplace, which often signal an emerging market or a major new product opportunity.

Begin by assessing your customer's industry or your marketplace. Unmet or unarticulated needs are often the result of changes and shifts in a user industry. Thus, an understanding of your customer's industry is essential to determine where to focus, what changes are taking place, and what new needs may be emerging, all of which help you identify possible product opportunities. This philosophy is built into the *Thomson Solutions Process*, a stage-gate process with an extensive front end designed to uncover major opportunities. (Recall from Chapter 5 that Thomson is a major firm in the financial, medical, and legal information business.) Here are the questions that Thomson asks in its Discovery Stage:[1]

- What arenas in the customer industry—segment, value chain, activities—are the most attractive for us?
- What changes are occurring in customer needs or value chains? How will they affect the industry and its key players?

FIGURE 6.1   Market Maps: Custody, Trust, and Settlements (Financial Institutions)

Reveals the distribution of an industry's profits along 2 dimensions—activities and type of player

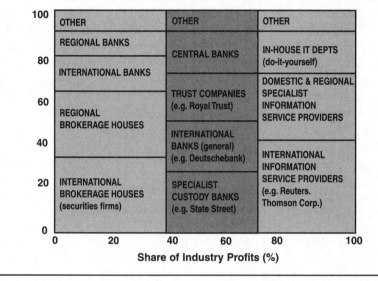

SOURCE: Adapted from O. Gadiesh and J. L. Gilbert, "How to map your industry's profit pool," *Harvard Business Review* (May-June 1998): 3–11.

- What new opportunities could emerge from these changes—from new value chains and work flows to help make our customers more successful?
- Are there opportunities to better meet customer needs and/or capitalize on a changing environment?

These are good questions, but they involve legwork to get the answers; it's not just a desk exercise! Start by developing a map of the value chain, identifying the various types of players. Next, assess their futures: changing roles, who will gain, and who might be dis-intermediated (cut out).

Next, identify the customer's industry drivers and potential shifts in these drivers. That is, try to assess what factors make them (or their competitors) profitable and successful. Is it costs of materials or low-cost production or response time to customer requests? And how are these changing in a way that might open up opportunities for you? And finally, can *you* provide solutions here to help your customers?

Then analyze historical trends and estimate future trends; spell out a scenario (or alternate scenarios) of where your customer's industry—your marketplace—is heading. Use Porter's Five Forces model to assess the industry and changes in it.[2]

The Thomson Discovery Stage also uses some new tools. For example, they prepare market maps. This is simply a chart that shows which types of players have what piece of the revenue in the industry (see Figure 6.1). A similar and useful tool is the profit pool map; this map identifies the activities in an industry, percentage of revenue by each, and profit margins in each (see Figure 6.2).[3]

The result of this assessment of your customer's industry should be the identification of the most attractive arenas (segments or parts of their industry where you should focus your development efforts). Assessing your customer's industry, when coupled with voice-of-the-customer research (below) and working with lead users (later in the chapter), is a powerful technique; it leads to the identification of emerging or unmet customer needs and new opportunities for new products and solutions.

In parallel, conduct an internal assessment on your own business—an analysis of strengths, weaknesses, and core competencies (see Strategic Analysis in Chapter 12). This assessment establishes a baseline of performance (how well your business is doing). It also identifies your competitive position. This gives senior management a place to start when discussing a strategic vision and in deciding which arenas they wish to focus on for innovative new products and solutions.

Imagine that your are in the competitive world of airline reservations systems. You currently sell a reservation system aimed at travel agents. You conduct an industry analysis, as described above, and the results are provocative. Increasingly, travelers are using the Internet to book their flights, especially with major carriers that have easy-to-use web pages. A profit pool map reveals that for airline travel, the travel agent's margins have been squeezed by the major carriers. The travel agent, your principal customer, is in danger of becoming dis-intermediated, and is quickly becoming the least profitable link in the value chain. This disruption threatens your business but also opens up new possibilities. A core competency assessment reveals that you have world-class technical skills in information technology (IT) and also in the operations and development of travel reservations systems.

End-user market research reveals that not all travelers are satisfied with booking flights on the web. They must search through the home pages of multiple airlines to get the best schedule, and often they end up with a fare higher than an experienced travel agent could obtain. This voice-of-the-customer research reveals new opportunities for an IT product, but one aimed directly at the end user: a single booking system that includes all airlines and finds the best deal. And so you conceive, develop, and launch your new product.

Travelocity is the travel-booking service that promises best prices and best schedules across multiple carriers. The company was launched by Saber, one of the largest airline reservations systems, aimed at travel agents.

FIGURE 6.2   Profit Pool Maps: U.S. Auto Industry

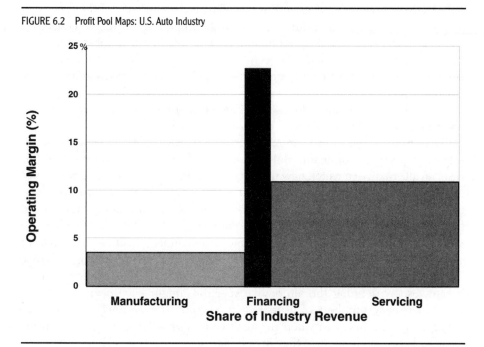

SOURCE: Adapted from O. Gadiesh and J. L. Gilbert, "How to map your industry's profit pool," *Harvard Business Review* (May-June 1998): 3–11.

☞**Suggestion:** Define a product innovation and technology strategy for your business (more on this in Chapter 12). Prepare profit pool maps and market maps and use Porter's Five Forces Model to assess where you want to operate in this industry. Take a close look at your own strengths and core competencies to determine where you have strategic leverage. Next, let this strategy guide your search for opportunities in your marketplace. Analyze the value chain; identify the industry drivers; and review historical trends and develop scenarios of the future. Look for gaps, emerging needs, and disruptions in your market or your customer's industry. These gaps and problems may signal your next major new product opportunity.

The Value of Scenarios

One of the most significant strategic decisions in recent years was made when AT&T turned down a free offer to take control of the Internet.[4] In the late 1980s, the National Science Foundation (an agency of the U.S. government) wanted to withdraw from its role of administering the Internet and offered

AT&T a free monopoly position. But AT&T had a mental map of the future—a scenario or picture of the future—in which their centrally switched technology would remain dominant. The notion of a packet-switched technology (what the Internet uses) was discarded. The technical experts at AT&T concluded that the Internet was insignificant for telephony and had no commercial significance in any other context.

What AT&T should have done—and indeed what your company should do— is develop *alternate scenarios of the future*. Yes, develop the scenario of the "official" or expected future—in AT&T's case, one with centrally switched architecture remaining dominant. But develop an alternate scenario too—in this case, an alternative in which new markets for Internet services and new kinds of telephony challenge the dominant AT&T architecture. Such a scenario at a minimum would have given decision makers a sense of the Internet's potential and may have led them to consider alternate courses of action. Developing alternate scenarios helps decision makers become much more *sensitive to signals of change*. As Schwartz, who advocates the use of scenarios in planning, declares, "What has not been foreseen is unlikely to be seen in time." For example, AT&T executives, by defining the alternative scenario, might have been more alert when increasing numbers of users began to go on the web, when web pages began to mushroom, and when personal computer (PC) sales to home users grew by leaps and bounds in the early 1990s.

Developing alternate scenarios of the future usually involves senior people taking part in extensive discussions and work sessions. Since your purpose is to arrive at new product opportunities, restrict the discussion to scenarios that are relevant to the business, and deal with the external (or extended market) environment. For a bank, this might entail describing the future of financial and related markets, and the financial industry as a whole.

Questions to work on include:

1. What is the best future scenario? Try to describe in as great detail as possible what your (company's) world will look like, given the best case external environment assumptions.
2. What is the worst possible scenario of the future for your company's external environment?
3. What are some relevant dimensions that characterize these scenarios? For example, in AT&T's case, a relevant dimension was "centralized versus decentralized switching." The best scenario was at one end—centralized; the worst case was at the other—decentralized or packet-switching dominant.

Then identify the *primary decisions* that managers face. In order to identify new product opportunities from scenarios analysis, ask the following questions: Should you launch a new business or new product? Should you invest in a new technology or technology platform? What types of new products should you be seriously looking at? Scenarios are utilized by imagining that one or another "future scenario" will be true and assessing the consequences of making each decision, assuming each alternate future.

Finally, markers or signals of each scenario should be identified so that managers can spot the telltale signs over the next months or years that indicate which way the world is moving. For example, one banking scenario is that there will be no bank branches in the future—that bricks and mortar will be history. Telltale signals over the next decade might include the number of new e-banks launched, the proportion of users in various age groups moving to e-banking, and the development of new Internet devices that make the Internet more portable (for example, wireless devices linked to the Internet that can handle financial transactions). If such trends or devices gain rapid momentum, then look for 100 percent branchless banking around the corner.

The failure to generate alternate scenarios led to the greatest business mistake in history:

In 1980, IBM developed its view of the future of the PC. IBM studied the potential market and predicted that 275,000 PCs would be in use by 1990. As a result, very generous contracts were signed with Intel and Microsoft to build and design key components for PCs. By 1990, the installed base had reached 60 million PCs, and it became apparent that the study foresaw only one future, causing IBM to transfer an enormous amount of wealth to two new companies that eventually became formidable competitors.

The point is that if alternate scenarios of the future had been generated—the official future, and another future that saw PCs in every home—and if a tiny probability had been allowed for this alternate future, then IBM would have altered its decisions to better protect its interests. And as PCs increased in popularity in the early 1980s, IBM management would have been tipped off that the alternate future, and not the official future, was indeed coming true and would have been better prepared for it.

☞ **Suggestion:** When developing your product innovation and technology strategy, be sure to develop scenarios of the future. But do more that just develop the most likely scenario or your "official scenario." Develop *alternate scenarios*—best case and worse cases. Imagine that each alternate scenario actually occurs. How would it alter your strategy and new product decisions? And what would be the financial consequences of making decisions assuming the official scenario, if one of the alternate scenarios were to come true (as happened with IBM and AT&T)? Assign just a small probability to these alternate scenarios occurring, and reconsider your new product selection decisions! And move ahead with techniques to uncover imaginative ideas, with the assumption that each scenario—official and alternate—may occur (these techniques are outlined in the rest of the chapter).

Use Voice-of-Customer Research to Uncover New Opportunities

Your customer probably has your next new product idea! In the last chapter, you read about the calibrating instrument produced by Fluke Corporation, where voice-of-customer research was employed to define a winning new product design. Similar research can be used to uncover new opportunities as well. Having analyzed the customer's industry and undertaken some scenario planning, your company is now ready to move from this 50,000-foot macro-view to a much closer look—focus specifically on your customer, trying to identify his or her problems, unmet needs, and even unarticulated needs. There is no set methodology here, but the research usually involves working closely with the customer, listening to their problems, and understanding their business or operation and its workflow.

> One Hewlett-Packard division in the medical field produces cardiac measurement devices for hospital use. Because the failure of such a cardiac device can be life-threatening, when field trials are done, members of the design team must camp out in the hospital to baby-sit the new device, often for months at a time. At first, this 24-hour vigil was considered a necessary expense of the field trial. But it proved otherwise. After weeks at the hospital, the design engineers became so familiar and integrated into the hospital routine that they almost *became hospital staff*. They were in a superb position to observe and listen, as hospital staff used and sometimes abused cardiac equipment. The camping-out experience provided the design team with great customer insight, which in turn yielded numerous ideas for new products, so much so that other HP businesses have copied the camping-out procedure.

This anthropological style of research has been used by many companies to uncover unmet needs and new product opportunities. It's called "camping out," "fly-on-the-wall," or "day-in-the-life-of" research. The point is, if you want to study gorillas, a couple of focus groups, an e-mail survey, and a few interviews probably won't be enough. You must buy a tent and move into their site—camp out with them.

Camping out is obviously expensive. There are times when one does not have to camp out in order to gain insights. In-depth, on-site interviews and visits with customers can often point to unmet, even unarticulated, needs that yield your next new product breakthrough. If you're in business-to-business marketing, focus on the customer's workflow—how she does her work and uses your product. Look for ways to offer entire solutions to improving effectiveness and efficiency of their workflow, rather than just another product upgrade. And focus on the customer's problems; find out what's irking them about the current solution. An example:

The West Group had for years produced a legal directory, listing all lawyers in the United States. It was not a very profitable business, because the market leader, Company M-H, had the lion's share of the business. By the early 1990s, profits had become negative, and it was time for action.

The company undertook a strategic assessment of the legal directory business. Why did law firms list themselves in a directory? Focus groups with lawyers revealed the answer: to get referral business from other law firms. So how do lawyers promote themselves to potential clients directly? In-depth, on-site interviews along with secondary research showed where and how the promotional dollar is spent. For example, the assessment showed that law firms spend a huge amount of money in the yellow pages. In Minneapolis alone (where the business is located), there are one hundred yellow pages listing law firms! A technological assessment revealed that most lawyers were on the Internet (although many lacked web pages), as were the great majority of their business clients. Thus, the concept of an Internet-based directory of lawyers with a package of associated services was born. The directory would be targeted at both other law firms as well as business clients; it would be interactive and would offer much more information (for example, case information and articles written) than the traditional directory or the yellow pages. Banner ads would be sold to law firms. And West even provided standard web-page formats to help lawyers develop their own web pages.

The product, called Lawoffice.com (when targeted at businesses) and Westlaw.com (when targeted at law firms) was launched in 1997 and has become a huge success. In 1999 alone, sales increased by 400 percent.

Another voice-of-customer method is Product Value Analysis™, as pioneered by Ron Sears. In this experiential method, customers have interactions with facets of your product and then express their views, concerns, and difficulties.[5] A good example is the major redesign of vacation travel trailers. Users were invited to a site where a number of travel trailers were parked. They then undertook a tour of each vehicle, accompanied by a guide taking notes. The users were encouraged to express their views about what they liked and did not like, how they used it, and what annoyed them about each and every part of the vehicle. By interfacing with the product, the customer is able to respond in a much more creative and expressive fashion than if they had merely been asked what they were looking for in a new travel trailer. Traditional focus groups are rather sterile by comparison. Some findings included the following:

- A minor but consistent complaint was with the shower stall. Most people did not use it because it was too small and because they usually stayed at trailer parks with excellent showers. Therefore, many users had converted the stall to a clothes closet. In response to this information, the company redesigned the shower stall to make it easily convertible to a closet.

- A more significant set of expressed views led to development of an innovative trailer design, whereby the entire side of the vehicle in the kitchen area could be moved out several feet, thereby increasing kitchen space dramatically.

A final voice-of-customer approach is to identify market trends and needs by conducting customer surveys or focus groups and then to convene a group of experts to discuss the problem and possible breakthrough solutions. Viactiv™ nutritional products for women provides an example:[6]

The idea for the new product started with a group of women at Mead Johnson Nutritionals, who knew they all shared the struggle to do it all in life, while still being able to appreciate it all.[7] This Women's Health Team conducted extensive market research, which concluded that women are in need of more stamina to make it through the day—and that their situation is quite serious. A nationwide survey conducted by the company (942 respondents) revealed that 60 percent of women felt that the condition of their declining vitality levels was very serious or extremely serious, with 80 percent of women feeling the negative impact of tiredness on their relationships with family and friends. A follow-up summit meeting, with dozens of the most prominent women's health experts in the country, helped to further define the problem and brainstormed potential solutions.

One area of focus was nutrition, with experts noting that key nutrients not sufficiently met include calcium, antioxidants, B vitamins, zinc, folic acid, and iron. A second conclusion was that women should indulge themselves more, taking greater care of their personal needs. Another conclusion was that snacking should be taken "out of the closet"; health experts said that women should eat less food, but more frequently, especially snack foods that are nutritious and rich in vital but lacking nutrients. Yet another conclusion was that women found nutritional information to be confusing and contradictory; they wanted clarity and simplification.

Thus was born Viactiv™, a new product line of women's nutritional products. The new product line combines the need for a healthy and indulgent snack food with vital but lacking nutrients in female diets. The first release was Viactiv Soft Calcium Chews, a chocolate snack product with a tailored combination of nutrients specific to women's needs, including calcium and 100 percent of the recommended daily values for B vitamins, folic acid, and antioxidants, launched in 1999. The Viactiv line now includes eight new items, such as Hearty Energy Bars and Energy Fruit Spritzers. This simple solution to a confusing problem has been a hit with the target audience; sales have been stunning and have exceeded management's expectations. As a result, *Business Week* voted Viactiv one of the top thirty new products for 1999.

☞ **Suggestion:** Voice-of-customer research is a powerful tool for uncovering great new product opportunities, as illustrated by the examples above. But it takes considerable effort and extraordinary insight to uncover these customer-generated opportunities. Use some of the techniques outlined above: camping out or anthropological research as practiced by Hewlett-Packard and Fluke; experiential research (Product Value Analysis) where the customer interacts with products to reveal unmet needs; and focus groups and large sample surveys to identify and quantify customer problems.

Work with Lead or Innovative Customers

If you work with an average customer, you'll get average ideas. But if you identify a select group of *innovative or lead users,* and work closely with them, then expect much more innovative new products. It's an approach that Eric Von Hippel of MIT pioneered years ago, and it has recently gained prominence at 3M as a key tool for uncovering innovative new product ideas.[8]

Research by Von Hippel reveals that many commercially important products are initially thought of and even prototyped by users rather than manufacturers. He also found that such products tend to be developed by "lead users"—companies, organizations, or individuals that are well ahead of market trends and have needs that go far beyond the average user. The trick is to track down lead users, who are, by definition, rare—the right tail of the distribution curve.

The lead-user process has four main steps:[9]

1. Laying the foundation: Identify the target market and company goals for innovations in this market (seeking buy-in of the stakeholders).
2. Determining the trends: Talk to people in the field who have a broad view of emerging technologies and leading-edge applications.
3. Identifying lead users: Use a networking process in which project team members explain their quest to people with apparent expertise on the subject, for example, research professionals or people who have written about the topic. Then ask for a referral to someone who has even more relevant knowledge. According to Von Hippel, it's usually not long before the team reaches the lead users of the target market. Based on what they learn, teams begin to shape preliminary product ideas and to assess their business potential.
4. Developing the breakthroughs: Host a workshop with lead users and key in-house technical and marketing people. Participants work in small groups, then as a whole, to define final product concepts.

The Viactiv example at Mead Johnson described above comes close to Von Hippel's approach of working with lead users. 3M has also adopted the approach and has used the lead-user process to develop innovations in fields from new medical products to telecom systems, as have other firms:

At Hilti, the leading European company in the demolition and fastening equipment and materials business, lead-user analysis is extensively used. First, innovative customers in the construction or demolition field are identified. Hilti's direct sales force provides guidance here. Hilti's Innovation Management Department then invites a group of these lead users for a weekend retreat; they watch and they listen, attempting to understand lead users' problems. Suggestions and possible solutions from lead users are fashioned into tentative new product concepts. Hilti management claims that this lead–user technique has been used with great success across a wide variety of product groups within in the company.

Fundamental Research Breakthroughs— Changing the Basis of Competition

The past decade or so has witnessed the dismantling of the corporate central research laboratory. In many businesses, fundamental research is no longer fashionable, as corporate scientists have been parceled out to the business units. The results are predictable: The research has shifted to a much shorter-term focus, and now industry leaders complain that that there is nothing great coming down the pipe. Could it be that we've killed the goose that lays the golden egg?

If your corporation still does fundamental research, be sure to engage this unit in the Discovery Stage of your new product process. Fundamental research will often plant the seed for a great new product or product family. The success rates may not be as high as for smaller, less venturesome projects undertaken within business units, but the payoffs can be enormous.

The trouble is that much fundamental research is undirected, unfocused, and unproductive, which is why so many CEOs have terminated it. If fundamental research is not yielding the breakthrough projects it should, then consider introducing a little stage-gate discipline here as well. Some scientists may scream their disapproval, but remind them that this is not a university where curiosity-based research is the rule; this is a business. Other scientists will welcome the opportunity to become more engaged in value-producing research for the corporation.

Here's how to provide more direction and focus to your fundamental research lab: Introduce the concept of a *stage-and-gate process for science projects.* For example, Exxon Chemical has modified its excellent Product Innovation Process to accommodate industrial fundamental research projects.[10]

The nature of a *Stage-Gate* process for technology developments or science projects is quite different from the standard product-oriented process outlined in the last chapter; it allows much more experimentation. We call the process

FIGURE 6.3   A Two-Stage Model Directs Technology Developments: *StageGate-TD*

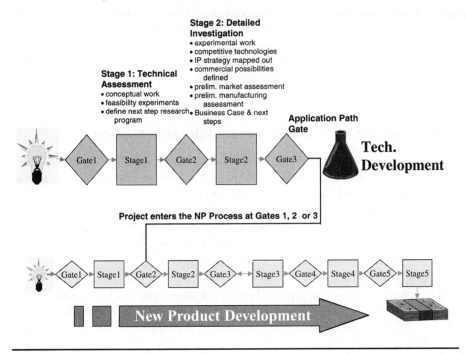

StageGate-TD, for *technology developments:* projects where the immediate deliverable is *not* a new product or new manufacturing process but new knowledge or a capability that may spawn new products or processes. The model in Figure 6.3 is a composite example of a technology development process for science projects (taken from a number of leading firms). Note that there are only two stages and three gates. And Gate 3—Application Path—may be combined with Gates 1 or 2 in the standard new product process of Figure 5.4. In effect, the two processes are merged or overlapped.

The gate criteria in *StageGate-TD* are much less financial and more strategic in nature than for the standard new product model. For example, Toray Chemical in Japan (developers of breakthroughs such as microfiber and ultrasuede fabrics) uses the following rating criteria for judging their technology development projects:

✓ degree of strategic fit and strategic importance to the corporation
✓ ability to achieve strategic leverage (for example, platform for growth, impact on multiple business units)
✓ potential for reward (value to the company, if successful)
✓ likelihood of technical feasibility
✓ likelihood of commercial success (for example, competitive advantage, existence of in-house competencies)

☞**Suggestion:** If fundamental research, science projects, or technology developments are undertaken in your business, try introducing a stage-and-gate process similar to that in Figure 6.3 in order to provide a little more direction and focus. But note that the process—its stages, gates, activities, and gate criteria—will differ substantially from your new product process. Don't try to force these science projects through your normal *Stage-Gate* process!

Harness the Creative Ability of Your Entire Organization

MRG means *major revenue generator*. And an MRG event is an off-site company event designed to produce or scope out at least several MRGs at the end of a few days of tough work. It's fun and it works!

The principle is that your own people, including senior people, often have the seeds of great new products within them. By harnessing the creative energy of the entire group, unexpected outcomes are often the result. An MRG event is a way to stimulate creativity but in a structured fashion.

Here's how to proceed:

An annual off-site company conference of senior and middle people is the venue. We've all been to these—two or three days of assorted speakers, some from inside the company, others from outside. A nice event, but not much happens as a result of these.

This year, make the event yield a different result. Invite fewer speakers, and build in a series of MRG exercises. Let's assume a three-day meeting.

Morning of Day 1: After the usual opening speech, split the audience into break-out teams. Here's the assignment:

"You have 90 minutes to identify the major trends, shifts, changing customer needs, and potential disruptions that are taking place in our marketplace." Be sure to challenge teams to answer the money question: "So what? Do these shifts suggest any major new opportunities?" After the break-out session, teams report back. Pick some teams at random to present their conclusions.

Afternoon of Day 1: The same break-out teams meet again but with a new assignment: "Identify the major technology shifts in your and your customers' industry that will impact the market and change the way you do business." Again pick teams at random to report back.

Other break-out sessions over the first two days deal with similar topics, including an assessment of internal company strengths and core competencies that might be leveraged to advantage and shifts in the industry and value chain structure. What new players and competition are emerging? Which old ones may disappear? The challenge to all break-out teams in all sessions is: "What opportunities do these changes suggest to you?"

By the end of Day 2, shift the challenge from assessment to *opportunity mapping*. That is, have the teams map out some of the opportunities that their assessments have suggested; this usually results in a clustering of the many new opportunity suggestions around major opportunity themes. At the end of Day 2, ask each team to present their list of major opportunity themes.

Overnight, the event organizers work feverishly to cluster and collapse these many opportunity themes into a manageable subset of major opportunities. In one service company, we even used "concept generators"—professional artists who translated the verbiage into drawings, sketches, and even prototype brochures. Display these major opportunities on large placards or posters around the conference room, providing as much detail and description on each. There can be as many as a dozen major opportunity themes. The next morning, as coffee is served, invite everyone to wander around the conference room, visiting each display.

Now for the hard work: Translate some of these major themes into actionable new product ideas. We usually hold an open discussion here to get any comment regarding which are simply "bad idea themes" or "science fiction." These are removed. Then attendees vote with their feet; they are asked to go to the cluster that they wish to work on. These self-selected teams are the work groups of Day 3.

The rest of Day 3 is spent in a series of team meetings where each opportunity team fleshes the opportunity out further, starts to shape the product, product family, or solution, and then begins to think about the path forward.

It's a great exercise. Sure, it costs money and some time to plan and execute, but the rewards are worth it. The result is usually four to five major opportunities identified and partially defined, a core of enthused people willing to work on each, and the beginnings of an action plan. OMNOVA's "slippery polymer"—the wall covering that is also a whiteboard, discussed in the last chapter—was the outcome of such an MRG event. During one of the team break-outs, a scientist surfaced an obscure research program, funded by the U.S. Navy, that had yielded this interesting polymer. Nobody knew what to do with it . . . until the MRG event!

☞ **Suggestion:** If you seek breakthrough new products, try rethinking your idea stage using the proven discovery approaches discussed above. Figure 6.4 shows the activities that flow and converge to generate great new product ideas. Begin with a strategic approach, where you undertake a thorough analysis of your external environmental, looking for shifts and disruptions that signal new opportunities (top part of Figure 6.4). Concurrently undertake an internal core competencies assessment. Try to pinpoint arenas of strategic focus where you can concentrate your idea-hunting activities (more on this in Chapter 12). Develop alternate scenarios of your future, and identify the opportunities for new products (left side of Figure 6.4)—but don't get caught in the "official futures trap" like AT&T did!

Next, lower the microscope on your customers or potential customers in this arena (right side of Figure 6.4). Employ voice-of-the-customer research, with a

FIGURE 6.4   The Discovery Stage: Multiple Activities Converge to Generate Great New Product Opportunities

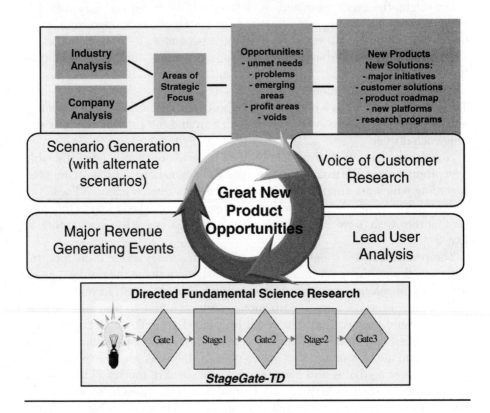

particular emphasis on understanding customer problems. Then seek solutions leading to great new products. Working with lead users, as practiced at 3M or Hilti, may be right for you—it's voice-of-the-customer research, but with a different twist. And fundamental technical research is a source. But harness your technical talent by engaging them in your Discovery Stage; introduce *StageGate-TD* to your corporate labs (bottom of Figure 6.4). Finally, hold a major revenue generating event, as described above, instead of your annual management conference—time much better spent!

An effective Discovery Stage, as shown in Figure 6.4, is fundamental to coming up with great ideas to feed your new product process. Seeking extraordinary ideas sometimes means doing some extraordinary things!

One Dozen More Ways to Get Great New Product Ideas

1. Establish a proactive idea focal point—an "on ramp"— and work the idea sources.

Table 6.1: Primary Sources of New Product Ideas
(40 companies)

Sources of ideas	Numbers of Companies
Internal Sources:	
Research & Engineering	33
Sales, Marketing & Planning	30
Production	12
Other company executives	10
External Sources:	
Customers & prospects	16
Contract research organizations & consultants	7
Technical publications	4
Competitors	4
Universities	3
Inventors	3
Unsolicited sources	3

Idea generation is everyone's job and no one's responsibility. There's no one in the company or business unit charged specifically with the responsibility of idea generation. And often when ideas do surface, there's no one to send it to for action.

The first step in setting up an idea-generating system is to assign one person the responsibility of stimulating, generating, and receiving new product ideas— a focal point for ideas. This person identifies the sources of ideas both inside and outside the company and then sets about establishing flow lines or mechanisms to generate or solicit ideas from these sources. The focal point also is the person that employees phone or e-mail about a new product idea.

Implicit in this role is action. The focal person moves the idea to the next step in the process—Gate 1 or the initial screen. The commitment here is that if an idea is submitted, then it gets a hearing and a decision. In addition, the focal person is responsible for providing feedback from Gate 1 to the idea submitter; a timely answer is essential in order to encourage further submissions.

One role of the focal person is to *work the sources of ideas*. Where do new product ideas come from in your company? Where should they be coming from? The second step is to make a list of possible sources of ideas. Table 6.1 provides a starting point. Note that although ideas from inside the company are the obvious place to begin, the majority of good new product ideas in many industries are derived from the customer.[11]

Step 3 is to establish flow lines or mechanisms to solicit ideas (or stimulate idea generation) from each source. Some examples include a customer problem form for the sales force, an idea contest open to all, and a customer visitation program, where technical people get to see customers and their problems first hand.

2. Set up an idea bank.

Not all new product ideas get acted upon. For some, the timing is wrong; others aren't sufficiently developed—they need a little more work; for still others, there simply aren't the resources available, or they don't mesh with the company's current priorities. One danger is that some potentially good ideas may be lost forever. Consider setting up an "idea bank"—a holding tank for inactive ideas. In this bank are ideas that need more work, ideas that have been rejected at Gate 1 (or simply haven't been moved ahead), and ideas that no one has taken to Gate 1.

Some companies make this idea bank an open file; the inventory of ideas is publicly displayed on their internal network. The hope here is that some creative person in the company will add to an existing idea, or figure out a solution to a barrier, or perhaps even arrive at original ideas as a result of reading the idea list.

Combining items 1 and 2—establishing a focal person, working the sources, and setting up an interactive idea bank—is a sound way to begin managing the capture and handling of new product ideas. Figure 6.5 shows a schematic of an effective front end used in a number of firms. Make it your model, too!

3. Try immersion—then harvest the ideas.

A novel approach, employed by Procter & Gamble and others, is immersion. The company selects a product area where it currently has no presence but that it wants to attack. This selection is based on strategic assessment.

Next, a dedicated, cross-functional team is assembled. Their challenge is to immerse themselves in this area for the next eight to twelve months. After the immersion period, the team harvests the many ideas uncovered during this period. An example:

Suppose the selected area is "dry cleaning of fabrics." A dry cleaning immersion team is dedicated to the topic full time. They live, eat, breath, sleep, and drink dry cleaning. They read every article, magazine, report, and book on the topic; they attend every dry cleaning trade show, seminar, and convention; they surf the web looking for information; they speak to every guru in the world on dry cleaning; they interview dry cleaners, their customers, their suppliers, and their competitors. And by the end of the year, they have become *the* worldwide experts on dry cleaning. It's almost like doing a Ph.D. dissertation: You immerse yourself in a narrow topic, so that by the end of the period, you *are* the expert!

FIGURE 6.5   Move to a Systematic Idea Capture and Handling Process

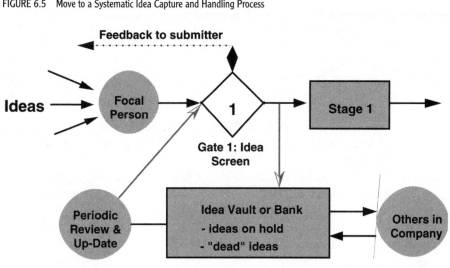

Now it's time to harvest the ideas. The immersion team sits down with others in the company, and through a series of meetings, discussion groups, and creativity sessions, a list of product opportunities and solutions is developed.

4. Amplify your thin ideas through plussing.

Plussing is a clever technique that Hallmark, the greeting card and gift company, and others have employed. Very often, an idea that is conceived in one business unit has potential much beyond the one business. But because businesses tend to be inwardly focused, the idea never grows to its full potential.

Plussing aims at overcoming this. In Stage 2 of Hallmark's new product process (the same as my Stage 2, Building the Business Case), there is a mandatory plussing activity. Here the project leader invites people from the other business units. The challenge: What could this idea become if all the business units in the room worked on it? Here is a hypothetical example:

The idea is for a line of everyday cards with a "bears" theme—a Winnie the Pooh look-alike. At a plussing session, all businesses brainstorm as to how the idea could be plussed. Maybe it could grow into a line of gift items—teddy bears of all sizes and in different costumes. How about wrapping paper or ribbons with a bears motif? Or crayons suitable for marketing through Hallmark's Crayola brand name? Or what about a bears television show to be produced by Hallmark Productions? The list is endless.

The point is to put together a group of fairly creative people (Hallmark people are!), give them a skinny new product idea, and ask how it can be amplified and grown by employing the strengths of each of their business units. The result is a very exciting and magnified set of new product possibilities.

What happens to all these plussed ideas? The project leader of the mother project—in this case, everyday cards with a bears theme—is required to submit *two* product definitions to Gate 3:

1. the "traditional" production definition: the product and project she is seeking funding for (in this case, it might be the everyday card concept with the bears theme)
2. the plussed product definition: what the broader product could become if management had the courage to invest more generously, for example, a gift line, wrapping paper, and ribbons and bows

Then it's up to management to make the choice!

5. Competitors trigger ideas.

Competitors represent another valuable source of new product ideas. The objective is not to copy your competitors—copycat products have a much lower chance of success—but to gain ideas for new and improved products from competitors. Often the knowledge of a competitive product will stimulate your team in creating an even better product idea.

Routinely survey your competition. Periodically perform a complete review of competitive products, particularly new ones. Obtain a sample of your competitor's new product. Once obtained, undertake a thorough evaluation of the product from a technical standpoint. Arrange an internal brainstorming session aimed at improving on your competitor's product. Better yet, rip your competitor's product apart using reverse brainstorming—identify everything that's wrong with it! Be sure to determine how well the product is doing in the marketplace from published data or from your sales force and customers. Finally, obtain copies of the advertising and literature for the product; knowing what the competitor is emphasizing or how it is positioning the product can yield new insights for your own new products.

6. Trade shows are an excellent source of ideas.

Trade shows present the perfect opportunity to uncover dozens of ideas at relatively little expense. Where else can you find all that's new in your field displayed for public consumption? And where else can you find customers ready to give their opinions on new products presented at the show?

Organize a trade show visitation program. Get a list of the relevant trade shows in your industry. Arrange to have at least one person visit each show, even if your firm is not displaying, for the sole purpose of getting new product ideas. This should not be a social event but a serious intelligence mission. Arm your intelligence officer with a sketch pad, a notebook, and a list of key exhibitors. His or her task is to visit each of the key exhibit booths and to itemize and describe new products on display. Sketches and brochures add detail to this description. At the end of the trip, your intelligence officer's task is make a formal presentation to the rest of the new products group: "Here's what I found that was new at the show, and here are some product ideas that we might build on."

7. Trade publications provide ideas from around the world.

As most intelligence officers will attest, the majority of "intelligence information" is in the public domain; it's just a matter of gaining access to it in a regular and coordinated fashion.

Trade publications report new product introductions through advertisements and new product announcement sections. Like a trade show, these publications provide the stimulus for your group to conceive an even better idea. Don't ignore foreign publications: In certain countries, new products may be years or months ahead of yours, and foreign publications may feature unfamiliar competitors who offer products that you've never seen before. So hire an outside clipping service or search company, domestically and abroad, to clip relevant ads, articles, and announcements in selected journals. Alternately, set up an internal search group, assigning different publications to each person in your group.

8. Review patents—the universal clearinghouse.

The files in the U.S. patent office contain millions of American and foreign patents, and thousands more are added each year. To keep abreast of developments and to stimulate their new product ideas, some firms keep a close eye on the weekly *Official Gazette*, which provides a precise record of the recent patents issued. It's also available on-line.

9. Suppliers are an untapped source of ideas.

Suppliers are often a good source of new product ideas and help. This is particularly so when the supplier is a large firm with well-funded R&D and customer applications or technical service facilities. Suppliers, too, are looking for new applications for their products and often come up with ideas for their customers. Have your technical and marketing people regularly visit your supplier's lab and technical service facilities and stay in close touch with your supplier's technical people. Chances are they're working on a development that could lead to your next new product winner.

10. Universities are a brain trust in your backyard.

University professors and researchers are an excellent source of ideas. Scholars working in science, engineering, or medicine can offer a wealth of information on developments in their fields. They may lack an appreciation of the commercial potential of their work or the ability to commercialize it, however. To exploit this source, consider establishing contact with key researchers in your field at various universities. Innovation centers or technology transfer centers have been set up at a number of schools to help professors commercialize their inventions. Survey the universities to locate these innovation centers and make contact with them.

11. Implement an in-house suggestion scheme.

Probably the least expensive way to solicit new product ideas is to implement an in-house suggestion scheme. Most companies have cost-savings suggestion schemes. Posters are mounted on bulletin boards throughout the office and factory urging employees to submit their cost-saving ideas. Often employees share in some of the cost-savings dividends. But new product suggestion schemes are much rarer. Does management assume that employees are quite creative in generating cost-saving ideas, but real dullards when it comes to money-making ideas? Experiences in many firms prove this assumption quite wrong!

Here are some tips and hints for setting up such a scheme:

- ✓ Focus the scheme strictly on new product ideas (don't combine it with other suggestion schemes in the company).
- ✓ Publicize the scheme widely; use in-company promotion.
- ✓ Make it easy to submit ideas on either hard copy or electronically.
- ✓ Offer some guidance; provide a pamphlet or web page that defines what a good idea is and what areas are in bounds and out of bounds, and create an idea submission sheet or template.
- ✓ Provide fast and fair feedback to submitters (for example, ideas should be rated on the Gate 1 scorecard).
- ✓ Provide recognition or rewards for successful submitters.

12. Provide scouting time to promote creativity.

One reason why 3M is so innovative is that the company *pays people to be innovative* and it *gives them the time to be innovative* (see Chapter 4). One cannot expect employees to suddenly turn on the creative juices at 4:45 P.M. on Friday afternoon. A handful of progressive firms encourage select groups of employees to be creative by providing free time—"scouting time"—and some financial help for personal projects. Some divisions at 3M have a day-a-week rule for technical employees: R&D people are encouraged to work on their own "discovery" projects with the hope that some useful idea—for example, another *Post-It Notes* product—will result. Rohm and Haas and Bayer-U.S. both devote about 10 percent of a technical person's time to scouting work and personal projects. And money can usually be found "under the table" or from some other research account to cover out-of-pocket costs (for example, equipment needs). Not every employee takes part in these free-time projects, of course, but the hope is that a handful of creative and passionate people will and that innovative ideas will be the result.

Using this scouting time, it is often possible to "progress" a project well down the pipeline before asking for formal approval and funding. "Isn't this danger-ous?" ask some people. Yes and no—it depends on how far down the pipeline the project progresses. Some companies that have implemented formal new product processes are happy to see these scouting projects arrive as late as Gate 2 or even Gate 3 (that is, Stage 1 and 2 have been undertaken "outside the sys-tem" using scouting time). I agree. My argument is that highly innovative, embryonic ideas are fragile things; perhaps a select few should be handled in a special way. But the majority won't follow this route, nor should they. Otherwise you truly would have chaos!

☞ **Suggestion:** I've identified a number of potential outside sources of ideas and have suggested ways to tap into them. Similarly, internal techniques—from establishing a focal point to idea submission schemes—have been outlined. And don't forget the approaches for generating breakthrough and blockbuster ideas outlined earlier in the chapter. Pick the sources and approaches that are most appropriate for your firm, and then design your own proactive idea generation system. If you do, you'll be blessed with a plethora of good ideas, ready for an initial screen and to move into Stage 1 of the new product process.

The Early Game:
From Discovery to Development

Ideas won't keep. Something must be done about them. When the idea is new, its custodians have fervor, live for it, and if need be, die for it.
—Alfred North Whitehead, English philosopher and mathematician

The game is won or lost in its first few plays. In Chapter 2, we saw that the seeds of disaster were often sown in the early phases of a new product project—poor homework, a lack of a customer orientation, and poor quality of execution. In Chapters 3 and 4, we saw that the keys to new product success often lie in the up-front or predevelopment activities. Unfortunately, these early stages receive little time, effort, and attention.

The steps from when an idea is born to the time it is miraculously transformed to a winning product concept and solid product definition—one ready for development—are the topic of Chapter 7. Here we focus on the critical up-front actions that precede the actual physical development of the product, which are so crucial to the product's ultimate success—the so called "fuzzy front end." These steps are laid out in the flow model in Figure 7.1, which takes us from the project's inception—the Discovery Stage—through Stages 1 and 2 and up to Gate 3, the door to the Development Stage.

On to Stage 1: Scoping

Assume that you've done a good job of idea generation. You've got lots of good ideas. Now the task is to sift and sort through these ideas to see which ones are worthy of more time and money. That's the role of the Idea Screen, Gate 1.

FIGURE 7.1   The First Few Stages in the *Stage-Gate*™ Process

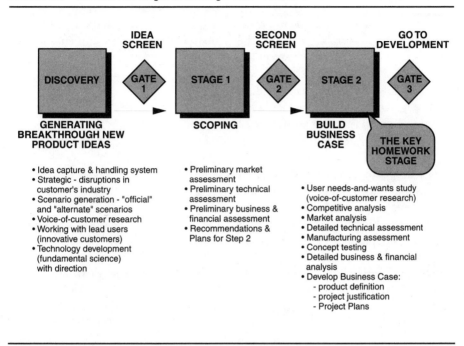

Designing these gates, screens, or decision points is no easy task, so I devote Chapter 8 to this task. But for now, let's walk the idea through the first two stages of the new product process: Let the idea pass Gate 1 and give it a green light for Stage 1, Scoping.

The spirit of Stage 1 is to "spend a little money, gather some information, so that the project can be re-evaluated at Gate 2 in the light of the better information." Therefore, this first stage is a quick and inexpensive assessment of the technical merits of the project and its market prospects. Preliminary market, technical, and financial assessments make up Stage 1.

Expenditures at this preliminary stage are quite small. Although Stage 1 is the first stage where resources are formally allocated to a new product project, note that Gate 1, the Initial Screen, was a fairly tentative commitment—a flickering green light. Indeed, some firms place a tight limit or ceiling on Stage 1 spending and time. In short, the output of a go decision from Gate 1 can be expressed thus: "On the basis of the very limited information available, this idea or proposal has merit. Spend no more than $10,000 and 10 person-days, and report back in one month at Gate 2, armed with much better information for a more definitive review."

Below are some of the actions in Stage 1, Scoping.

Preliminary Market Assessment

Preliminary market assessment involves a quick-and-dirty market study. The purpose is to determine whether the proposed product has any commercial prospects. The preliminary market assessment

- ✓ assesses market attractiveness and potential;
- ✓ gauges possible product acceptance;
- ✓ sizes up the competitive situation; and
- ✓ sculpts the product (shapes the idea into a tentative product design).

The task is to find out quickly (usually less than one month) and for minimal cost as much as possible about market size, growth, segments, customer needs and interest, and competition.

Given the limited cost and the short time duration of the study, this type of market assessment is clearly not a professional and scientific piece of market research. Rather it's detective work and desk research: gathering available in-house information (for example, talking with the sales force, distributors, and technical service people); examining secondary sources (for example, reports and articles published by trade magazines, associations, government agencies, and research and consulting firms); contacting potential users (for example, through a phone blitz or focus groups); and canvassing outside sources (for example, industry experts, magazine editors, or consultants). It's tough work, much like playing detective and following up on leads, but it's surprising how much information about a product's market prospects can be gleaned from several days of solid sleuthing.

Here are some sources of market information that can be accessed relatively inexpensively for Stage 1:

- *Internet searches.* There's a wealth of information out there, and most of it's available on the Internet. But you need someone who knows how to do an Internet-based market analysis. Hunt through trade magazines, journals, reports, and other published items looking for information on your market, the product type, and your competitors.
- *Your own library.* Your reference librarian may be worth his or her weight in gold in conducting a preliminary market assessment. If your company doesn't have its own library, try a major public library or a library at the local university's business school.
- *Internal reports.* In larger firms, there are often numerous reports and surveys undertaken annually. Often the information you need is buried somewhere in one of these many studies, so start with your own library or market research department.
- *Key customers.* Stage 1 is premature for a detailed, large-sample customer survey or even multiple on-site and in-depth interviews. But

insights from a limited number of leading, key, or trusted customers can prove very useful at this early stage. Have direct, face-to-face discussions with a few customers. These need not be based on a detailed questionnaire but can be unstructured and exploratory. For industrial goods, try to pick trusted yet representative or leading users. Talk to several people within each firm. If budgets are tight and time is pressing, try telephone interviews.

- *Focus groups.* In spite of their limitations, focus groups, made up of a handful of customers, either consumers or industrial users, remain a cost-effective and relatively fast way to gain insights into customer needs, wants, and preferences.

- *Advertisements.* Get your hands on your competitors' advertisements and trade literature. Find out what they are saying about their products—features and performance characteristics, as well as how competitors are trying to position their products.

- *Your own people.* Interview your own sales force and service representatives. These people are your frontline troops—the eyes and ears of the company. Often they can provide you with superb information on customer habits, likes, and dislikes and the order-winning criteria, on product preferences, and on the competitive situation and pricing practices.

- *Consulting and research firms.* Some consulting and research firms publish multiclient or standardized reports that provide an overview of an industry. Although they may not be specific to your new product, these reports or studies are a cost-effective way to gain information on market size, trends, and competition.

- *Financial houses.* Stockbrokers can even be a help. Many keep up-to-date files or can provide an overview of companies listed on the stock market. Annual reports are a help, as are the 10K reports that publicly listed firms must submit to the stock exchange.

- *Government agencies.* Governments collect a myriad of data. Finding it is the problem. But don't give up before you begin. Often a phone call to a state, provincial, or federal government office will identify the right department, and that department just happens to have the report or statistics that you were looking for.

- *Industry experts.* Hire an industry expert or guru for a day or two and pick his or her brain. Although the per diem fee may be high, the knowledge gained may save you weeks of work.

- *Editors:* Editors of trade magazines are not the normal source of market information, but on occasion they have proven very useful in tracking down reports, studies, and even informed individuals. A good editor usually has a good breadth of knowledge about what's going on in an industry.

- *Trade associations.* Some industries have excellent trade associations that provide valuable market data. Contact these associations. And while you're on the telephone, be sure to talk to the association secretary or president to seek advice about where to go for the other information you're looking for.

When undertaking your preliminary market assessment, do not neglect the international dimension (recall success factor #3 in Chapter 4). Gather market information for multiple international markets, not just your domestic one. And engage international business units, too; for example, Guinness, the brewer, builds in an international alert into Stage 1 of their *Navigate* new product process where brand managers around the world are contacted to see if they are interested in participating in the project.

Here's a real-life illustration of a market assessment for Stage 1:

A small firm, Isofab Inc., makes insulation products. The firm wanted to develop a new product, a sound-absorbing brick. The idea came about as a result of some lab work on ceramic sponge-like materials. The product would be used chiefly in highway sound barriers. Management had no idea of market size, pricing structure, or market acceptance for the proposed premium-priced product. Development costs were estimated at about $500,000—a sizable amount for this small firm.

The owner-manager contacted a nearby business school and acquired the services of a graduate student. The student's instructions were to phone every highway department in every state and province in the United States and Canada, to talk to the sound abatement engineer, and to ask ten minutes' worth of questions. The questions related to the number of miles of past and future installations of sound barriers, types of barriers used, cost per square or linear foot, problems with current products, and the engineer's reactions to the new product idea. The budget for the study was $5,000.

The phone blitz was finished in less than two weeks, the student was $1,500 richer, and the owner-manager saved himself a half-million-dollar disaster. It was discovered that the market was shrinking; current barrier products, although they only reflected rather than absorbed sound, were considered adequate (they met federal regulations); and the price per foot was of prime concern to governments. Clearly there was little opportunity for a premium-priced product with features that were not perceived as benefits by the customer.

This example shows that market studies are not the sole domain of the large firm. The costs can be kept down, and one person can gather considerable and valuable information from customers or experts in a week or two of hard work.

Preliminary Technical Assessment

The *preliminary technical assessment,* a second facet of Stage 1, subjects the proposed product to the business's technical staff—R&D, engineering, and operations—for appraisal. The purpose is to establish preliminary rough technical and product performance objectives; undertake a very preliminary technical feasibility study; and pinpoint possible technical risks. Specific tasks might include discussions among in-house technical and operations people (occasionally outside experts will be used); a preliminary literature search (for example, a titles search); a preliminary patent search; and acquisition and review of competitive literature. The key questions concern the technical viability of the product:

- Approximately what will the product requirements or specs be? (Note that the product definition may still be fairly vague and fluid at this early stage.)
- How would these requirements be achieved technically? Is there a foreseeable technical solution? Is invention or new science required?
- What are the odds that the product is technically feasible? At what cost and time?
- Do you have the technological capability to develop it yourselves? Or do you need a partner or outside supplier for some development work?
- Can the product be manufactured or produced? How, with what equipment, and at what cost? Or should you consider outsourcing or a partner?
- What intellectual property and product regulatory issues are involved? Note that regulatory and patent issues are introduced and considered at this early stage.
- What are the key technical risks? And how might we handle each?

The potential for partnering merits special mention. Although working with a partner can bring the necessary and missing skills and resources to the project, there are also risks and costs. Our research into partnering reveals *no performance enhancement* in the case of partnering projects.[1] Don't expect partnering to be a panacea for new product success; leave the door open to other options. When partnering, be sure to spell out clearly how value gets shared and confirm that both parties agree on commitments.

Preliminary Business and Financial Assessment

Following preliminary technical and market assessments comes the preliminary business and financial assessment. The strategic and competitive rationale for the project are mapped out. Similarly, a core competencies assessment—do you have what it takes to win here—is undertaken, which may identify the need for a partnering or outsourcing relationship. And then comes a preliminary financial analysis.

At this early stage, estimates of expected sales, costs, and required investment are likely to be highly speculative and largely conjectural. Nonetheless, it makes sense to undertake a cursory financial analysis here, as a "sanity check"–to

Table 7.1: Summary of Stage 1 Actions – Scoping

Preliminary market assessment	Quick scoping of the market prospects for the product: potential, acceptance, requirements; not detailed market research; detective and desk research only, relying on readily available sources
Preliminary technical assessment	Conceptual assessment of technical feasibility, probable technical solution, technical risks, manufacturability (or source of supply), and intellectual property issues
Preliminary financial/ business assessment	A sanity check: an extremely rudimentary and quick check of the business rationale and financial prospects; the possible payback period (no spreadsheets here!)
Recommendation and Plans for Stage 2	A Go/Kill recommendation; and proposed Actions Plans for Stage 2 (timeline; resources, people and person-days; deliverables and date for next gate)

ensure that you're not spending $10 million on a $1-million opportunity. This financial analysis amounts to little more than a payback calculation based on ballpark estimates: What's the investment required in the venture; what's the probable annual income; and how many years before we see our money back?

Table 7.1 provides a summary of Stage 1. At the end of this Scoping Stage, a recommendation for the project is developed, along with proposed plans of action for Stage 2. The project now moves to Gate 2, where it is again subjected to scrutiny. But this time, the decision is to move to a much more extensive and expensive stage, namely, Building the Business Case.

On to Stage 2: Building the Business Case

Building the Business Case is the last of the up-front stages before serious product development work begins. It is perhaps the most difficult and certainly the most expensive of the predevelopment stages. Moreover, this is the *critical homework* stage—the one that makes or breaks the project. Coincidentally, it is also the stage that we found is so often weakly handled. Stage 2 actions are summarized in Table 7.2.

What is a business case? The *business case* is the *key deliverable to* Gate 3, the decision point that opens the door to a full-fledged development project. The business case has three main components:

✓ product and project definition,
✓ project justification, and
✓ project plan—the path forward.

Table 7.2: Summary of Stage 2 Actions: build the Business Case

User needs-and-wants study	Voice of customer research to determine product requirements; face-to-face interviews (or camping out) – in-depth market research. Determines what is "value" and what is a "customer benefit"; seeks to define a winning product concept from customer's perspective. Probes customer needs, wants and preferences, choice criteria, likes, dislikes and trade-offs regarding product requirements and design; also the customer's use system and product's value-in-use (economics); seeks insights into competitive product strengths and weaknesses
Competitive analysis	A detailed look at the competition – both direct and indirect. Determines who they are, product strengths and weaknesses, anticipated future products, pricing, competitors' other strengths and weaknesses, how they compete and their performance
Market analysis	Pulls together all market information from the two studies above plus secondary sources. Determines market size, trends, segmentation and size, buyer behavior and competitive situation. Also relies on similar sources as in Stage 1, only much more in-depth
Detailed technical assesment	Translates these market inputs into a technical feasible product design or concept (on paper). May involve some physical technical work (modeling, lab work) and also techniques such as Quality Function Deployment (QFD). Maps out the technical solution and technical route; highlights technical risks and solutions; reviews intellectual property issues and develops IP strategy; assesses possible technical partners and develops partnering strategy. Also looks in depth at manufacturability and source of supply: production route, costs and capital (equipment) requirements.
Concept testing	The final market test prior to full commitment to develop the product. Tests the proposed product concept with the customer (product concept, model, virtual prototype). Involves face-to-face interviews; gauges interest, liking, preference, purchase intent and price sensitivity.
Financial/business analysis	Looks at the business rationale for the project. Includes strategic assessment (fit and impact). Also a core competencies assessment and partnering (or out-sourcing) strategy is mapped out, along with the role of international units. Finally a detailed financial analysis is developed: NPV, IRR and sensitivity analysis
Plans of action	Develops recommendation for project (Go/Kill) and a detailed Action Plan for Stage 3 (Development Plan); also tentative plans for Stage 4, Testing, and Stage 5 (both preliminary Marketing and Operations Plans). A launch date is specified.

Consider each component of the business case:

1. *Definition.* This answers the "for whom" and "what" questions. That is, the all-party agreement spells out whom the product will be targeted at and exactly what the product will be—its benefits, features, and design requirements. Remember the importance of having sharp product definition before beginning the development work! This definition was discovered to be one of the key factors in success; it provides a target for development and forces discipline into Stage 2. Otherwise, the development team faces a vague product definition, one that is often a moving target.

   Inherent in the product definition is the need to put "meat" on the product idea—to move from the fairly preliminary and sketchy product definition (the one we had in Stage 1) to a *sharp, clear, and complete definition* by the end of Stage 2. Also implicit in this definition is the need to build in the ingredients of product superiority. This is the opportunity to shape the product's requirements, features, and specs into a set that delivers unique and real benefits to customers.

   The product and project definition includes the following:

   ✓ the project scope—the bounds of the development effort (is it a single new product or a family of products?)
   ✓ target market definition—precisely whom the product is aimed at
   ✓ the product concept—what the product will be and do (written in the language of the customer)
   ✓ the benefits to be delivered, including the *value proposition* for the customer
   ✓ the positioning strategy (including the price point)
   ✓ product features, attributes, performance requirements, and high-level specs

2. In the case of high-tech and IT industries, where markets change rapidly, it is important to pin down the product definition as clearly as possible before development begins. One should specify in advance which part of the product requirements and specs are fixed and which are fluid before development begins (one hopes that more than 50 percent is fixed, on entering development) and then build steps into the development process to gather data so that the fluid parts can be pinned down as development proceeds.

3. *Justification.* This second component of the business case answers the "why" question. That is, why should your company invest in this project? This question boils down to a review of business, financial, profitability,

and risk considerations. Because financial data are likely to be in error, this justification should include nonfinancial criteria and considerations as well: qualitative issues such as strategic rationale, competitive advantage, leverage, and market attractiveness. Solutions such as partnering and outsourcing are also part of the justification assessment.

4. *Project plan.* This final component of the business case answers the "how" and "by whom" questions. It lays out the plan of action from development to launch, usually in the form of a time line or a critical path plan. Required resources—money, people, and equipment—are spelled out, and a launch date is specified. Also included are plans for the preliminary marketing launch and for operations, manufacturing, or source of supply. Given the uncertainties of future events, however, most often these plans are very tentative. The recommendation is that the plan for the next stage (Stage 3, Development)—including activities, events, milestones, time line, and required resources—be defined in some detail and that plans for subsequent stages be sketches or "throw-away" plans.

What makes up this pivotal Stage 2? Figure 7.2 maps out the key actions. Building the business case involves, first of all, thorough market studies: a user needs-and-wants study, using voice-of-the-customer research, to define what must be built into the product; a competitive analysis; and a concept test of the product to gauge market acceptance. Technical work, largely conceptual, translates the market "wish list" into a technically feasible concept. A business case is developed for the project; the product definition is agreed to, and a thorough project justification and detailed project plan are developed.

Let's look at each of these Stage 2 actions in more detail.

Voice-of-the-Customer Research: A User Needs-and-Wants Study

A user needs-and-wants study is the voice-of-the-customer market research that is so often omitted, with disastrous consequences. Its purpose is to probe the customer in order to put meat on the idea—to take a rather skimpy idea and develop a complete description of the product, including its benefits, value proposition, features, performance characteristics, and design requirements. The problem is that most of us already have a fixed idea of what the customer is looking for, so we conveniently skip over this critical market study. We usually get it wrong, because we have not listened to the customer!

A superior product—one that delivers *unique benefits to customers*—is the number one success factor. Never forget this fact! But how do you define this unique and superior product? The user needs-and-wants study provides the big opportunity; it enables you to fashion your sketchy product idea into a concrete and winning new product concept. The goal of this study is to identify customer needs, wants, and preferences, what they're looking for in a "winning" product, and what will absolutely delight them!

FIGURE 7.2   The Key Blocks in Stage 2: Building the Business Case

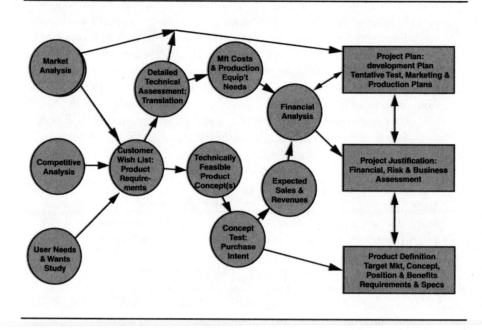

The ultimate objective is to deliver a product with real value—a solid value proposition—to the customer (Figure 7.3). Product value is in turn derived from the benefits built into and surrounding the product. And these in turn come from the product's design: its features, attributes, and performance characteristics and even its positioning.

It is crucial to understand the means-ends chain connecting value, benefits, and product features and performance (shown in Figure 7.3). One must listen to the customer in order to get the product design right! That's why this user needs-and-wants study is so critical.

Specific research questions to address in this study include the following:

- What is value to the customer? What does he or she really value and how much?
- What is a benefit? That is, what specific product deliverables would the customer see as being of benefit—enough to pay more for?
- What features, attributes, and performance characteristics translate into benefits and value for the customer?

Only by understanding the interrelationships between physical characteristics (that is, product features) and customer perceptions (that is, a customer-perceived benefit) are you in a position to sit down and design the winning new product.

FIGURE 7.3   The Means-End Link That Determines Product Value

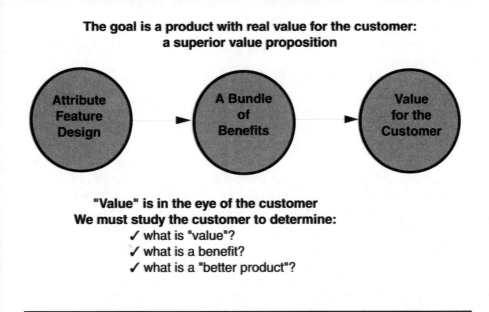

The user needs-and-wants study identifies these relationships and answers the key research questions above about value and benefits. You can start with qualitative research—for example, focus groups of customers—to gain some insights into product value and desired benefits. But a focus group is only a start and certainly not a substitute for a broader-based study. Face-to-face, in-depth, and on-site interviews are usually required in order to gain the depth of understanding needed to proceed with product design.

The specific information objectives of this user needs-and-wants study often include the following:

✓ to identify customer problems that require a new solution or a new product
✓ to determine unmet or unarticulated customer needs
✓ to identify customer wants and preferences in a new product
✓ to identify the order-winning criteria and their relative importance
✓ to pinpoint areas of likes and satisfaction with current (competitive) products and areas of dislikes and dissatisfaction with these products
✓ to study how the customer uses the products and what problems he or she faces in its use
✓ to understand the customer's economics of use and the total cycle costs to the customer

Here are ten specific questions that frequently are addressed in customer interviews as part of a user needs-and-wants study:

1. How is the potential customer now solving his or her problem? What is the current solution? For example, what particular product is he or she using, and why?
2. What unsolved problems is the customer or user experiencing with the current solution? Are there opportunities here for a new solution or new way of doing things?
3. If the customer had a choice, which product or brand would he or she buy now? Why? Which one or ones would he or she not buy? Why not?

These types of questions are important in that they are methods of inferring what the customer is looking for and what he or she wishes to avoid. Here we're trying to uncover what the customers' unmet and unarticulated needs are and what they see as having value, what a new solution might look like, and what their "hot buttons" are!

4. What are the customer's choice criteria—the criteria that the customer uses to make a purchase decision? What is the relative importance or weight of each criterion in the decision?
5. How do current (competitive) products rate on each of the choice criteria? Which competitor scores highest on each criterion? Who's the lowest? What is it about these products that causes the customer to rate them so high or low on each criterion?

These fairly traditional questions on choice criteria and competitive ratings are important for several reasons. First, an understanding of how the customer makes his or her purchase choice and what criteria are used is a critical input into product design; at a minimum, your new product must address and score high on the important criteria. Second, understanding how competitors' products score identifies areas of potential opportunity—for example, a competitive product weakness—that can be exploited with an improved design. A knowledge of the reasons that underlie these competitive ratings also provides valuable insights to the product designer regarding what to build into your new product and what to avoid. Finally, different patterns of responses among customers may suggest the existence of two or more market segments. There may be a market niche that has been missed by competitors—one that can be successfully targeted by you.

6. What does the customer specifically like about competitive products or current solutions? What does he or she dislike? What problems does the customer have when using competitive products?

Often competitive products do have many positive design aspects, which can be borrowed and built into your new product. There's nothing wrong with copying the good facets of a competitor's product, providing one goes well beyond a mere copy. For example, in developing its successful luxury automobile, the Lexus, Toyota took a hard look at luxury cars around the world, particularly European ones. Toyota borrowed the best ideas from these; many of the design concepts in the Lexus are simply copied from other luxury cars. A knowledge of the positive facets of competitive products is obviously a valuable input to the designer. Similarly, identification of customer dislikes and problems in competitive products opens up opportunities for significant design improvement. Remember: The objective is to design a superior product; that means it must be superior to the leading competitive products. An understanding of where the competitor fails—its Achilles heel—is half the battle!

7. What specific features, attributes, and performance is the customer looking for in a new product? Which of these are "must haves" and which are only "desirable but not essential"?
8. What trade-offs is the customer prepared to make (for example, among various possible performance deliverables, or product features, or features versus price)?

An understanding of the customer's stated requirements—both musts and shoulds—is obviously a critical design input. But note that this customer-stated wish list is usually fairly sterile, and it is not specific enough to build a winning new product design. A knowledge of customer trade-offs reveals the relative preferences among various product features and attributes and indicates relative value or importance of different design features to the customer.

9. How does the customer use (and abuse) the product? What is the customer's "use system" in which the product must operate? And how does it fit into (or interact with) other components of the system?
10. What are the customer's economics? How does your potential product affect his or her economics in use?

These last two questions are both critical and difficult. The first looks beyond the product itself; it probes the role the product plays in the total system. And it applies to all kinds of products, from prepared food entrées (where the kitchen and household are the system) to telecommunications components and software. The economics or "value in use" is fundamental to understanding how you can deliver a product that yields better economic value—for example, by saving the customer money over the total life of the product or in some other facet of his system.

A positioning study can also be an integral part of this user needs-and-wants investigation. In a positioning study, one determines the key dimensions by which customers perceive and differentiate among competitive products or brands. For example, in pharmaceutical products, often these key dimensions are "side effects" and "efficacy." Positioning studies also attempt to identify the positions of the competitors' products in the buyer's mind—how he or she views various offerings in terms of the key dimensions. Finally, positioning studies try to pinpoint possible new and desirable positions—niches or holes in the marketplace that are not occupied by a competitive product.

Using Voice-Of-Customer Research to Define Your New Product

Fine in theory, you say. But how do I put this into practice? There is no standard formula for listening to the voice of the customer in order to uncover unmet needs and translate these into potential winning solutions. But there are some patterns. In the Chapter 5, I gave you the example of the Fluke Documenting Process Calibrator; recall how on-site visits, or "fly-on-the-wall" research, with potential users revealed the problem that led to the new product. Here's another example, but from a different industry.

> Transitions Optical, a joint venture between PPG Industries of Pittsburgh, and Essilor International, Paris, has a stunning success in the eyeglasses market with its *Transitions III* plastic lenses that adjust to sunlight for prescription eyewear. Extensive market research revealed that consumers were unhappy with the traditional product—*Photo Gray Extra* from Corning. This twenty-year-old technology was perceived as heavy, for older people, and "worn by farmers." The concept of variable-tint eyewear—whose tinting changes to accommodate bright sunlight or darker rooms—was appealing to consumers.
>
> Market research was undertaken in numerous countries to *identify customers' needs* in this lucrative market. The research showed that consumers were looking for light-weight, modern, variable-tint eyewear, whose tinting changed quickly; at the same time, the lens had to be really clear when worn indoors. PPG, a world leader in the production of glass and coatings, was capable of developing the photochromic technology, and Essilor possessed the distribution network.
>
> But would the proposed product be a winner? To find out, numerous *concept tests* were undertaken with the proposed product—shopping mall interviews and focus groups of consumers—to confirm customer liking and purchase intent not only in the United States but in France, Germany, and the United Kingdom. When *Transitions III* was launched in the mid-1990s, it proved to be perfect for the market and very quickly achieved the leading market share.

In designing this critical user needs-and-wants market study, here are some tips and hints:

1. Think carefully about your *information objectives*. Remember that information has value only to the extent it improves a decision. Outline the key design decisions you must make, and then identify the information that you need to make these design decisions. Put these information objectives in writing. Only then are you ready to begin crafting the questions you wish to address to customers.

2. Use a *structured questionnaire* for interviews. You may think that you're good at interviewing—at directing the conversation and remembering answers. But if you plan on interviewing more than one or two customers, you'd better develop a questionnaire. Why?

   ✓ *completeness*: to ensure that you cover all the questions you want answers to
   ✓ *consistency*: to ensure that each respondent is questioned in the same way, with the same wording
   ✓ *recording*: to provide a consistent method of recording responses

3. Are you seeking the *right information*? Do a "preposterior" analysis; that is, before charging out to do interviews, imagine that the study is done, that you have the answers to the questions. Given these answers, can you make the design decisions? If there are any doubts, now is the time to rethink and revise your questionnaire—not after the interviews are finished!

4. Make sure the interviewees are *representative*, not just a handful of people or customers selected strictly for convenience. Get a list of prospective users in your target market, and select randomly from the list (or partition the list into subgroups or strata—for example, small, medium, and large users—and randomly select from each subgroup).

   In the case of *industrial clients*, never rely on one or two interviews per client firm. Remember: One person does not speak for his or her company! There are many influencers in the purchasing company, and focusing on one or two people in the mistaken belief that they represent the company can lead to very erroneous information.

5. Get your *technical people involved* in the interviews, too. Market information is too important to be left solely to the marketer. This is especially true for technology-based products, and where customers are technically sophisticated. The marketer may be best for setting up the interviews, designing the questionnaire, and handling the general questions, but the technical person has much more depth of knowledge about what is technically possible and what is not, and can engage the customer in a much more probing and profound conversation, which

can lead to identification of desired product features and performance that the marketer would have missed.

6. Study the *customer's system or use environment*. Don't just stop at asking questions about what product features or performance he or she wants. Investigate the use system and how the product fits into the whole system. And try to gain an understanding of how the system works, so that you can better appreciate the needs for and demands placed on your product.

When Xerox introduced its color copier, it made the mistake of doing market research on only the product. A fine job was done on determining what product attributes and levels of performance were desired in the ideal product. What Xerox missed entirely was the nature of the office system into which this color copier had to fit. What they failed to detect was that the office system was a black-and-white one—not color; there were few color originals to copy. This was discovered after launch, at which time Xerox found itself facing the difficult task of changing the office system; it had to encourage the use of color originals, for example, through color kits.

☞ **Suggestion:** Does your company do a solid job in terms of a user needs-and-wants study? Do you go to your customers, and through face-to-face meetings, try to understand their problems, needs, wants, likes, dislikes, and preferences before development begins—in short, everything you'll need to know to sit down and design a truly superior product? Or are you like most firms: You arrive at a concept or solution internally; you then use market research strictly to test the product concept, but you don't really listen to the voice of the customer to help you develop and refine the concept.

In your next significant new product project, why not build in a user needs-and-wants study before development begins? Let the results of this study help shape your product design, translating an otherwise mundane idea into a real winner!

Competitive Analysis

A second key to building a superior new product is competitive analysis. There are several purposes to such an analysis. The first is to understand the competitor's product and its strengths and weaknesses. If your objective is to deliver product superiority, then the benchmark for comparison—the competitor's product—must be totally understood. Second, a knowledge of how the competitor plays the game—how they compete and where and how they are getting customers—can provide valuable insights into the keys to success in this business. Finally, the competitor's strategy and how the competitor's product fits into its portfolio may provide clues about the expected competitive response to your product launch: For example, will it invoke a strong defense?

Here are some of the key questions to address in a competitive analysis:

1. Who are the key players—the direct or indirect competitors—whose product yours will replace (or take business away from)?
2. What are their products' features, attributes, and performance characteristics? What are their products' strong points and deficiencies?
3. What is their product offering likely to be by the time you get to market (anticipate their new products, features, and performance)?

It's important to understand just who the "enemy" is and the exact nature of the product that yours must overtake. Its strong points are clues as to what to build into your product; its weaknesses reveal areas to exploit in a superior design.

4. What other strengths and weaknesses does each competitor have—for example, sales force, customer service, technical support, advertising, and promotion? For what is each competitor held in high regard? What are its weak points?

You must compete not only on the basis of product but also on non-product elements. Although product advantage is clearly desirable, sometimes the main points of competitive advantage will be found in other elements of the marketing mix.

5. How does each competitor play the game? For example, on what types of customers (or segments) does each competitor focus? And what is the basis for competition? That is, how does each competitor get business—by low pricing? through product advantage? by having a larger or highly skilled sales force? or through heavy promotional effort?
6. How well are the competitors doing? What are their market shares, and what has been the trend for each of their shares? Why is each doing so well (or poorly)—what's the secret to its success (or demise)?

Here the focus is on what it takes to win. Take a close look at the different strategies and approaches of the players and observe their results. From this come valuable lessons about what succeeds and what fails in this marketplace.

7. What are the competitors' cost pictures? Their production volumes and capacities? Their profitability—both contribution and net? How important is this product to their operations and to their total profitability?

These often-confidential data give insights into the strategic importance of the competitors' products to the industry, their ability to respond (for example, how far they could cut price), and the likelihood of the competitor mounting an aggressive defense against your new product.

There are no formal methods for competitive analysis; it's more like playing detective and tracking down a variety of leads. Here are some suggestions:

- Get your hands on all possible *competitive literature* and competitive *advertising*. This is in the public domain; your own sales force should be able to help with trade literature, and clipping (or securing) advertisements displayed in print (or electronically) is straightforward.
- Do an Internet search through various *trade publications*, looking for information on competitors: announcements, new product introductions, plant expansions, or financial results.
- Try to acquire your *competitors' products*. If they are for sale and not too expensive, this is not a problem. A friendly customer may also provide access to a competitive product. If the product is intangible—a new service product—utilize "mystery shopping" by posing as a customer and experiencing your competitor's service product firsthand.
- Construct your *competitor's product road map*—their recent product introductions and their timing, along with features and performance. Try to project this road map into the future.
- Visit *trade shows*. Where else can you find under one roof the best and the newest that your competitors have to offer? It's all there—open for public viewing.
- Talk to your own *sales and service people*. They spend much time in the field and have the opportunity to see competitive products, practices, and prices. They also attend conferences and trade shows and often have friends in other firms. In many cases, they are storehouses of valuable competitive information.
- While doing your *user needs-and-wants study*, be sure to build in questions that seek opinion from your target customers about competitors: ratings and insights on competitive products, their sales force, service, and pricing.
- Talk to *suppliers* about your competitors. From suppliers you might be able to learn about the installed competitor capacity (what equipment and capacity it has) and current production volume (based on materials purchased). Some indication of the competitor's production operation and operations costs might also be gleaned from listening to suppliers.
- Use *financial sources* to learn about your competitors. For example, obtain a copy of their annual report. Ask your stockbroker for his or her investment firm's written appraisal of the competitor. To be publicly traded, many stock exchanges require considerable information on the operations of a company (much of which would be considered confidential); ask your investment house to secure this information—for example, the 10K report—from the stock exchange. And undertake a key-word search through the many financial papers and magazines—

Fortune, Business Week, the *Wall Street Journal*—based on your competitors' names.
- Hire a *consulting firm* that specializes in competitive intelligence. Often such firms have detailed intelligence files as well as considerable experience in employing some of the methods listed above.

Market Analysis

The two market studies discussed above—the user needs-and-wants study and the competitive analysis—are crucial to designing a superior product. But more information about the market is required in Stage 2. The numerous secondary and other sources of market information highlighted in the Scoping Stage (Stage 1) can be re-accessed, but the search should be much more thorough for Stage 2. The goal here is to develop a detailed portrait of the marketplace—a market analysis—which includes the following:

- ✓ market size, growth, and trends
- ✓ market segments: their size, growth, and trends
- ✓ buyer behavior: the who, what, when, where, and how of the purchase situation
- ✓ the competitive situation

When you develop a detailed marketing plan, this market analysis becomes even more essential. We revisit market analysis in Chapter 10, where we take a closer look at developing the marketing plan.

Detailed Technical Investigation

The user needs-and-wants study coupled with the competitive analysis should yield a set of guidelines—a wish list of what should be built into your new product to truly delight the customer and to upstage the competitor. Properly designed and executed, your market research should reveal what the "winning product" is from the customer's perspective as well as the product requirements that will yield product superiority over the competition.

This customer wish list must now be translated into something that is technically and economically feasible. This is where market needs and wants and technical possibilities must be married in order to arrive at a proposed product design. In short, technical people must find a means of satisfying expressed customer needs and preferences. This is a creative process involving the entire project team, not just technical people. It may involve the following activities:

- ✓ creative problem solving
- ✓ brainstorming
- ✓ techniques such as Quality Function Deployment
- ✓ detailed literature search and a patent search

    ✓ seeking help from outside experts
    ✓ some physical technical work, including some definitive experiments, models, or crude mock-ups

To a large extent, this successful technical translation depends on the technological prowess and brain power of your technical people. A clear definition of what is required to meet customer needs and yield competitive advantage will certainly sharpen and focus this creative process.

The questions that are addressed in this detailed technical investigation include the following:

1. What is the probable technical solution that will yield a product to meet marketplace requirements?
2. What is involved in arriving at this technical solution? Is invention required or is this simply a matter of applying fairly well-known technology?
3. What are the technical risks and potential roadblocks? How might these be dealt with? Can alternate technical solutions be pursued in parallel?
4. If you are partnering in development, what is the technological competence of your partner? What role will the partner play in tasks, deliverables, and commitments?
5. What are the key steps involved in arriving at a prototype product? How long will each step take and how much will each cost? What are the personnel requirements?
6. What legal, patent, regulatory, and safety issues might arise and how would you deal with each? Do you have a patent or intellectual property strategy in place?
7. Will the product be manufactured or produced (source of supply) in your plant or operations facilities? Would new facilities, equipment, and production personnel be required? What would the production volume be and at what capital cost? Do you need a partner or outsourcing for successful production?
8. What is the cost per unit of producing the product?

The end result is a solid idea of what the product will be from a technical standpoint, what the probable technical solution and technical route are, and a reasonably high confidence that this solution and route are technically feasible. Although some technical work—for example, lab work, experimental work, or modeling—may occur here, technical work should be limited in Stage 2. Be careful that work that is more appropriate to Stage 3 doesn't move forward into this business case stage. The depth of technical work here in Stage 2 was nicely expressed by Rohm and Haas's Biocides business unit in their new product process:

If lab work is conducted in Stage 2, the purpose is not to produce a prototype or final product; rather the spirit is to spend a limited amount of time to see if one can arrive at something remotely close to the desired product, enough to provide confidence that with more effort, it could be done.

My usual rule of thumb is to spend no more than 10 percent of the Stage 3 development costs in Stage 2; that is, spend 10 percent to gain the knowledge and confidence to justify spending the remaining 90 percent. But don't spend the 90 percent here!

Quality Function Deployment

Quality function deployment (QFD) is one technique adopted by a number of firms that helps to *translate customer needs and wants into a technique, concept, or design.*[2] Thus, QFD has particular applicability to Stage 2. It was developed in 1972 in Japan and brought to the United States by Ford and Xerox in the late 1980s.[3] The claim is that in some applications, QFD has reduced design time by 40 percent and design costs by 60 percent while maintaining and enhancing design quality.[4] Others claim that QFD's greatest success occurs when the model is used *conceptually*, rather than in its detailed form as it is usually described.

The First House: House of Quality.   QFD uses the model of four "houses" to integrate the informational needs of market, engineering, R&D, and management. The House of Quality (HOQ) is the first house, shown in Figure 7.4. This represents the translation between the marketing input (customer needs, wants, and perceptions) and R&D factors (design attributes and specs) through a relationship matrix. Griffin and Hauser stress that "the HOQ (as well as QFD) is an integrative process in which marketing and R&D participate as equal partners in all aspects of the communications process. . . . Much of the benefit of the HOQ comes from the mutual understanding of the problem and of one another that comes as marketing and R&D work together for a joint solution."[5] In developing this first house, the HOQ, we must listen to *both* voices—the customer's and the engineer's.

The Voice of the Customer
The results of the user needs-and-wants study provide critical inputs to QFD and the first house:

- *Identifying customer needs.* Customer needs are first identified. A customer need is a description of a benefit the customer may want fulfilled by the product. The user needs-and-wants study outlined above provides this needs-and-wants list.
- *Structuring the needs.* To make the lengthy list of needs manageable (often there are 100–400 items), they are structured into a hierarchy of primary, secondary, and tertiary needs. The primary needs are strategic ones—the top five to ten needs that set the strategic direction for the

FIGURE 7.4   The House of Quality in Quality Function Development

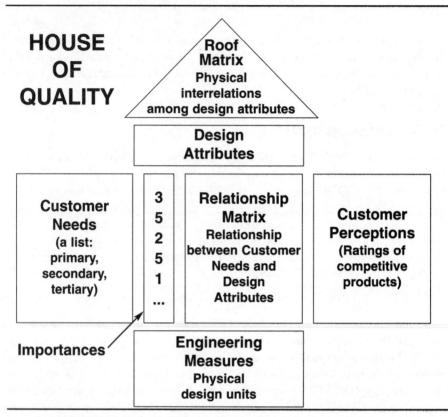

SOURCE: Adapted from A. Griffin, "Evaluating QFD's use in firms as a process for developing products," *Journal of Product Innovation Management* 9, 3 (1992): 17–28.

new product. The secondary needs are tactical—essentially elaborations of the primary needs; there may be twenty to thirty of these. Tertiary needs simply provide the details.

- *Importances of the needs.* These are indicated on the HOQ diagram (Figure 7.4) and come from the user needs-and-wants study.
- *Customer perceptions.* These describe how the customer rates competitive products in terms of their abilities to meet customer needs. Again these come from the user needs-and-wants study (for example, see questions 5 and 6 in that section).

The Voice of the Engineer
Specific input from R&D includes the following:

- *Design attributes.* Customer needs are translated into measurable design requirements. These are measured in physical units that become targets for R&D work, but they are not solutions. These are listed at the top of Figure 7.4.

- *Engineering measures.* The engineering measures (bottom of Figure 7.4) gauge competitive products on the same physical units specified by the design attributes.

- *Relationship matrix.* The project team then judges which design attributes in Figure 7.4 influence which customer needs. These influences or impacts are shown in each cell or element in the relationship matrix (center of Figure 7.4).

- *Roof matrix.* The roof matrix shows the interrelationships among the design attributes. For example, adding more of one attribute may take away from another.

Once the HOQ is complete, the project team can use the relationships to establish design targets, that is, specific performance values of the design attributes that the product will deliver. "To make these decisions, the team considers the cost and difficulty of achieving these targets, the influence of these targets on other design attributes, the influence of these targets on fulfilling customer needs (relative to competition), and any other relevant input of which the team is aware."[6]

Other Houses. The first house of QFD links customer needs to design attributes, and thus arrives at a technically feasible design concept or product definition. There are three other houses (not illustrated). The *second house of QFD* links the design attributes from the first house to solutions. Design attributes are placed on the left side of the house, and solutions are placed at the top of the house. When this second house is linked to the HOQ, these solutions are based on customer needs. This second house is thus a useful tool either at Stage 2 or even at Stage 3, Development, in the new product process.

The *third house* links design solutions from the second house to process operations (marketing, R&D, manufacturing, and delivery are coordinated). This time, design solutions are placed on the left, and process operations are located at the top of the house. The *fourth house* links process operations to production requirements to complete the cycle.

QFD has gained many proponents: "QFD works because it provides procedures and processes to enhance communication between, and structure decision making across, marketing and R&D and because it provides a translation mechanism from the language of the customer to the language of the engineer. It overcomes many of the barriers to communication. . . . The enhanced communication leads to reduced cycle time."[7] However, others see it as too complex and cumbersome and therefore use it more as a conceptual tool.

Testing the Concept with the Customer

Will the new product be a winner? Before pushing ahead into Stage 3 with product development, you must be certain that the product will meet customer needs and wants better than competitive products and will achieve your sales targets. Remember that your product is the new entry into the market, and it has to give the customer a reason to switch.

A problem faced by many firms is one of interpretation and translation. A thorough market study is undertaken that identifies customer needs and wants. The project team then translates these into a tentative product design—a set of product specs, perhaps using QFD. But something goes wrong in the translation. The final product isn't quite what the customer wants, or it lacks that special something that differentiates it from what the customer is already buying. It just doesn't quite delight the customer or push the customer's "hot button."

For the needs-identification-and-translation process to work well, two assumptions must be true:

1. The customer understands his or her needs and is able to verbalize these to you during the user needs-and-wants study.
2. You interpret these needs correctly and do a good job in translating these needs into the final product specs.

Both assumptions are rather doubtful. Even the most knowledgeable customer may not totally understand or be able to articulate his or her needs, and these may not be accurately conveyed during the face-to-face discussions. Even if needs are understood, there may be errors in translation; the needs and wants may be misinterpreted by you, resulting in the wrong set of product specs. The concept test is the final test prior to the development stage that validates that the product concept (and hence, the proposed product) is indeed a winner; it checks that customer needs were correctly understood, interpreted, and translated, and makes final course adjustments in the product design before it is too late.

There is another good reason to introduce a concept test here. There's one school of thought in market research that argues, "Customers don't know what they're looking for until they see it." The customer says, "Show me the product, and I will tell you whether it's right or not." Thus, although all the user needs-and-wants studies may yield valuable insights into customer needs, they may still miss the mark. Get something in front of the customer and gauge feedback before your charge into development. That's the role of the concept test.

Prospecting Versus Testing.   It makes sense to build in a concept test as part of Stage 2 and before proceeding to product development (see Figure 7.1). There is a fundamental difference between this concept test market study and the user needs-and-wants study outlined above. The user needs-and-wants study is a *prospecting* one: No product or product concept was available to show the customer, but hints, clues, and insights were obtained from the customer about what should be built into a winning product design.

Once the technical investigation has yielded a technically feasible concept, then a full proposition concept can be shown to the customer—a model, a set of drawings, a storyboard, a spec sheet, a dummy brochure, or a virtual proto-type—and his or her response can be gauged: "Given what you've told us, this is what we've come up with in terms of a proposed product. What do you think of it? Would you buy it?"

The concept test is not a prospecting study but rather a *test or validation* that the proposed product concept is indeed a winner; intent to purchase is estab-lished. Note that at this early stage you still don't have a developed product. The purpose of this concept test is to see if you're heading in the right direction. By this time you should have, at minimum, a written description of the product and its benefits, features, performance characteristics, and likely price. In addition, you may have something concrete to show the customer—line drawings, artists renderings, a model, a PowerPoint slide show, a crude working model, or even a virtual prototype of the product on your laptop.

Designing the Concept Test. The design of a concept test is similar to that of the user needs-and-wants study. At a minimum, you might use several focus groups of customers to gauge reactions to the proposed product. Although such focus groups give useful feedback on the product, remember that the limited sample size, the fact that group members are often not representative of the entire market (for example, a self-selected group), and the nature of the group dynamics (for example, one powerful person can sway the group) mean that the group's vote on the product may not be a true reflection of your target market. A broader and more representative sample of customers should be contacted through a survey: mail, telephone, e-mail, personal interview, or some combi-nation of these.

Concept tests differ from user needs-and-wants studies in two major ways: First, in a concept test you have something to show the customer to solicit feed-back; second, you are seeking very different types of information than in a user needs-and-wants study.

Presenting the New Product Proposition. For the most reliable results, try a *full proposition concept test.* That is, go beyond a simple written description—the traditional one-hundred-word paragraph portraying the product concept. In order to respond intelligently, the customer must fully understand the product as it will be. The better you are able to convey what the final product will be and do, the more accurate gauge of purchase intent you will get. Get as close to the "final product" as you can in your concept presentation:

- Use written descriptions in conjunction with visuals: artists' renderings of the product, line drawings, dummy spec sheets, dummy brochures, or perhaps even a PowerPoint slide show showing the product in simu-lated use.
- For consumer goods, pictures or drawings showing the product and its packaging can be displayed. Better yet, use a storyboard slide show pres-entation with a sound track.

- Use models (for example, crude working models) or rapid prototypes to show to the customer. Often a crude prototype or sample can be put together quickly and inexpensively as part of the detailed technical investigation in Stage 2. Pillsbury calls these "protocepts."
- Get creative and use the capability of your laptop and available software. Create a virtual prototype on your laptop; use CAD to draw the product and have it rotate in space before the customer's eyes. Or show the product operating. For software concepts, developing a few screens helps to anchor the product in the user's mind and enables the customer to experience it.
- If your project risk and amounts at stake are great enough, try a full proposition presentation using a video show or an interactive presentation on your laptop.

For example, GM used an interactive, computer-based presentation on its electric car project to bring the customer into the future through a simulated shopping trip. The customer was actually able to test-drive the car (using a simulator not unlike software flight simulators). The cost of the interactive presentation was significant; but it was still much less than the cost of developing a prototype automobile!

What Information to Seek. A concept test seeks customer reaction to the product in an attempt to assess market acceptance and expected sales revenues. Information objectives typically include the following:

1. a measure of the customer's interest in the proposed product and a determination of why interest level is high or low
2. a measure of the customer's liking for the product concept, and what facets he or she likes most, and what he or she likes least
3. a comparative measure of the customer's preference for the concept relative to competitive brands or products the customer now uses, and the reasons for these preferences
4. an indication of what the customer might expect to pay for the product
5. an indication of the customer's purchase intent at a specified price
6. information useful in finalizing the positioning strategy.

Figure 7.5 shows a typical questionnaire format. Note that there is a combination of closed-ended questions (to which the customer selects an answer, for example on a 1–5 or 0–10 scale) and open-ended questions (which result in a verbal answer or discussion). The closed-ended questions provide concrete, numeric data that can be aggregated and analyzed across many customers. But numbers alone tend to be sterile; hence open-ended responses are also sought to lend richness and greater understanding.

FIGURE 7.5   The Typical Concept Test Questionnaire

Face to face interview:
the user.customer is asked to review the product concept - make sure they understand the concept!

1a. first, are you interested in the proposed product? You can answer on this five-point scale (show them the scale):
☐ not interested at all   ☐ not too interested   ☐ somewhat
☐ quite interested   ☐ very interested

1b. Why so interested (or not interested)? _____

2a. To what extent do you like the product?
☐ not interested at all   ☐ not too interested   ☐ somewhat
☐ quite interested   ☐ very interested

2b. Identify the things you like the most about it: _____

2c. What things do you like least about it? _____

3a. You are already pruchasing (or familiar with) Brand X. How would you compare the new product with Brand X?
☐ not interested at all   ☐ not too interested   ☐ somewhat
☐ quite interested   ☐ very interested

3b. Why did you like it more (or less than Brand X? _____

4. Assume this new product was already available. How much would you expect to pay for it (you can ask this price question relative to a product they are familiar with or now buy)?_____

5a. Let's assume the new product is on the market at a price of $Y. What is the likelihood that you would buy it?
☐ not interested at all   ☐ not too interested   ☐ somewhat
☐ quite interested   ☐ very interested

5b. Why. . .what made you answer the way yo did (in 5a)? _____

5c. (If negative): What would yo like to see changed in the product? Any suggestions?_____

Be sure to use a structured questionnaire to ensure that all relevant questions and issues are covered and that answers are recorded in a consistent way. Even when conducting personal interviews, it is good practice to follow a standardized questionnaire or interview guide, perhaps even showing the customer the written questions on your laptop computer. Seek quantitative answers where possible; let the customer indicate his or her response on the various scaled measures, using a pointer and a scale, for example, to express his or her opinion.

It is also good practice to design a standard format for a concept test and to use that format consistently from product to product. In this way you will develop a history of data and establish benchmarks for comparison. For example, what does it mean when 30 percent of those surveyed check the "definitely would buy" box? Is this a good result or poor one, and what market share might this score translate into?

> Hewlett-Packard investigated the development of a new computer pointing device to replace the mouse, namely, fixed mounted cylinders that are twirled with the operator's thumb. The product had not yet been developed, but customer reaction was sought through a full-proposition concept test. Customers were shown a video, which demonstrated a mock-up and simulation of the product, and a simulation on a computer screen was used to vividly portray how the new device would work. Note that although H-P did not actually have a prototype or product to test with the customer, this concept test came very close to it—well before development had begun!

Using the Results of a Concept Test. Use the results of a concept test with caution. They merely provide an indication of likely product acceptance. There are no guarantees, and the results should not be used blindly. For most new products, particularly concepts in categories familiar to the customer, concept tests are likely to *overstate the market acceptance.* For example, a result of "30 percent of respondents definitely would buy" is not likely to translate into a market share of 30 percent for several reasons. First, respondents tend to have a positive response bias. There are many reasons for this: the so-called Hawthorn effect, whereby people under observation tend to respond more positively or enthusiastically than those not being studied; the desire to give socially acceptable or pleasing answers to the interviewer; and the fact that it's easy to say yes when there's no money or commitment involved. Second, although a respondent might say that he'll buy your product, in the case of a frequently repurchased product, he may continue to buy the competitor's as well, that is, split his purchases. If he buys both products equally, the original result of "30 percent definitely would buy" actually translates into a 15 percent market share. Third, not all potential buyers in the defined target market will be exposed or exposed sufficiently to the new product. Advertising, promotion, and sales force may reach less than half of the total target market. The "intent to purchase" figure must be cut down by a factor that reflects market exposure (or audience reach) on launch.

There are other problems as well that render the concept test results suspect. A common problem is obtaining feedback from the wrong respondents. This is particularly troublesome in industrial buying settings, where the one person interviewed may not speak for the entire company. Another problem is over-selling the product concept—either promising things that the final product won't or cannot deliver, or using too much hype in the presentation of the concept (this is a test, not a sales pitch!).

For more innovative products, however, that represent new or unfamiliar product categories to the customer, the concept test results may actually *understate the product's acceptance.* Unfamiliar concepts tend to elicit a negative response initially, and it may be only after the customer has had a chance to use the product for a while (or see others using it) that he or she begins to appreciate the product's benefits. In short, there is a learning process here that occurs over time—one that cannot be measured in the short time frame of a snapshot concept test. For example, the initial consumer reaction to the introduction of automatic teller machines by banks was very negative—it was an alien, somewhat scary concept. It was only after we used these machines for several years that we saw their advantages, and our comfort level increased. A purchase-intent concept test today would yield very different results to one done in the early 1970s (which would have predicted a very low market acceptance).

Here are some tips and hints in undertaking a concept test to gauge expected market acceptance:

1. *Be realistic* in preparing the concept presentation. The concept presentation should reflect the real-world environment that will exist when you launch your product. Control your zeal, highlighting benefits and performance characteristics that will be realistically included in the final product, which you will be able to communicate to the customer at launch.

   The importance of being realistic is obvious. But countless examples exist where lack of realism was the culprit. A well-known firm in the female personal products business investigated the viability of a new woman's body lotion. A concept test was undertaken, where the concept description showed a unique product with a number of benefits. Based on the high-scoring concept test, the company moved the product into development and finally test market. The commercials for the test market were skillfully prepared, but in a 30-second time slot, only one of the key benefits could be stressed. The test market was a failure.

   The company assumed there was something wrong with the advertising or marketing support, so it took a second shot. The elements of the marketing mix were revised and the advertising stressed a different benefit.

   Again the product failed. The reason was clear; there was no way to convey all the features and benefits that had been displayed in the concept test in a live launch situation—a 30-second commercial, with lower viewer attention levels and less time to tell the story, made the task impossible.

The key lesson to be learned here is this: Don't develop or test a concept presentation that can't be replicated in the real world!

2. *Don't oversell.* Remember that this is a test to gauge customer reaction to the product concept; it is not a test of your selling ability, nor is it a preselling exercise. Overselling what the product can do and the use of a too powerful presentation can lead to inflated and misleading results.

> A telephone company had developed the concept for a new office data retrieval system, using a telephone with a built-in LCD display. A concept test on target users was undertaken. A slick and professional video presentation was developed, showing a simulation of the product in action in an office—complete with a powerful sound track and a dramatization showing happy, satisfied users. Potential customers were brought into a small theater, shown the half-hour video, and then asked to respond to typical concept test questions.
>
> The results were extremely positive, and the company proceeded into development and launch of the INET 2000 product. But market launch results were very disappointing. The lesson learned here is that customers were responding not so much to the concept but to a very powerful and persuasive selling presentation. The concept was actually a poor one, but the video was superb!

In a similar vein, the use of emotionally loaded words in the concept presentation may actually backfire; it may act as a lightning rod, eliciting negative reaction and biasing the results downward:

- ✓ A new financial service may not be "sophisticated" and "elegant." The language is too powerful or simply inappropriate, causing customers to focus on this issue and fail to perceive other benefits.
- ✓ A supermarket ice cream brand could be "luscious," "rich," and "thick," but "gourmet" in a supermarket line may simply not be believable.

3. *Be clear.* Customers must fully understand the concept for their responses and feedback to be meaningful. Too often a product description is given that is vague, confusing, or superficial, and then the customer is queried about whether he or she would buy the product. The results are pure guesses on the part of the customer.

A food manufacturer undertook a concept test with a frozen yogurt bar, whose major benefits were its delicious taste and the fact that it contained no artificial preservatives. Unfortunately the body copy talked about a "nutritious quintessential frozen confection on a stick." What exactly is a "frozen confection"? Is it like an ice cream? Or is it better than or different from ice cream? And what does "quintessential" mean? I had to look the word up in the dictionary.

Keep it simple, clear, and understandable, and use whatever communication tools—including visuals and models—that might help explain the concept most clearly to the prospective customer.

4. *Contact the right potential customers or users.* Make sure that the customers you involve in the concept test are indeed representative of your target market. If your target user is upscale, up-market, higher-income professionals, there is no sense in sampling average consumers. Similarly, in an industrial setting, if your target market is an entire industry, then undertaking a concept test solely on leading-edge or innovative users is foolish; they're likely to give a much more positive response than the typical customer. Further, make sure that you seek opinion and feedback from a variety of people within the buying firm; there are often many purchase influencers in the decision to buy a new product.

With all its weaknesses, the concept test is still the best way of gauging likely product acceptance before you have actually developed a product. For familiar products in familiar categories (which are the bulk of product development efforts), it has proven quite predictive. The top box score (the percentage of people who replied "definitely would buy") is your best early indicator of how your product will fare, short of a test market or full launch.

Unfortunately, there are no simple formulas for translating this top box score into a predicted market share. Some market research firms have developed elaborate models for estimating initial trial rates for certain types of consumer goods; this initial trial rate combined with repurchase intent yields expected market share. But such formulas and norms tend to be very specific to certain industries and even product categories within industries.

For frequently repurchased consumer goods, for example, a top box score of 40 percent or higher is considered a strong score. In hundreds of studies comparing concept test results with test market results, such "strong" concepts result in an initial trial rate in excess of 30 percent, and there is a high likelihood of positive test market results. By contrast, "average" concepts—those receiving a top box score of 30 to 39 percent—achieve an initial trial rate of somewhat less than 30 percent and result in positive test market results about one-third of the time. Any consumer brand scoring less than 30 percent "definitely would pur-

FIGURE 7.6   Concept Test Relationships: Test Market Results Versus Purchase Intent

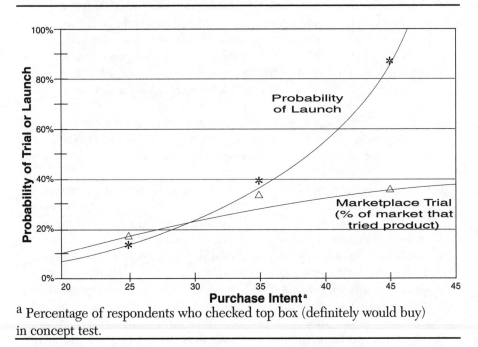

^a Percentage of respondents who checked top box (definitely would buy) in concept test.

chase" on the concept test gets a poor initial trial rate of well less than 20 percent and about one chance in ten that test market results will be positive. Figure 7.6 shows some of these relationships for frequently repurchased consumer goods.

Perhaps as important is the information obtained from the open-ended questions in a concept test, questions such as, "What did you like most about the product?" and "Why did you rate brand X as better?" If the concept is failing the test, then answers to these questions provide critical insights into what needs to be done to improve the product. Even for a successful test, these answers provide clues about how to fine-tune the product design to make it even more attractive to the customer. Finally, the comments that potential customers make in response to the product provide hints into how the product might be positioned and communicated to users—what customer "hot buttons" have been hit.

☞ **Suggestion:** Are you using concept tests effectively in your new product process? Do you take the time to verify that the proposed new product really is the right one before you charge off into development? Or do you assume that you have it right and that you'll take your chances?

Build a concept test into your next important new product development *before development begins.* You don't need a prototype or sample product—just a firm idea of what the product will be. Present the product proposition as clearly as possible to selected customers, and remember: Be realistic; don't oversell; be clear; and make sure you're speaking to the right people. Measure the customer's interest, liking, preference, and purchase intent; use scaled questions, and get quantitative answers (even in office interviews). You'll be surprised at the insights you'll gain about your proposed product's commercial prospects. But exercise care in the use of these concept test results; intent-to-purchase figures don't translate directly into market share!

Business and Financial Analysis

The various market studies—user needs-and-wants, the competitive analysis, the market analysis, and the concept test—help to map out the product definition. The target market is now sharply defined; the product concept and positioning strategy are confirmed; the benefits to be delivered and the value proposition are defined and validated, as are the physical attributes of the product—features, specs, and performance requirements. What remains is a business and financial justification of the project before one moves fully into the development stage.

The strategic rationale and competitive reasons for undertaking the project have been laid out in detail, as well as the core competencies assessment. If additional resources and capabilities are needed, plans have been established for partnering or outsourcing. (If outsourcing or partnering are required, a review of their capabilities and roles has been undertaken, and a letter of intent has been written by the end of Stage 2.) In addition, the role of international units in making the product a success is included here.

The financial analysis is obviously crucial as you move into Gate 3. Reasonable estimates can now be made for many of the inputs for a financial analysis. Market size and share estimates, together with pricing analysis, should yield expected revenues. The product's design characteristics are now known, so that the detailed technical assessment should yield cost estimates and reasonable projections of profit margins. The technical and operations assessment should also provide rough estimates of capital or equipment needs. Marketing requirements and the expected launch costs have been investigated, and additional project costs in Stages 3 and 4 have been forecast. These estimates are the inputs to a financial analysis.

Two types of financial analysis have merit as we move into Gate 3: the payback period and a discounted cash flow analysis (NPV and IRR), which can be used in conjunction with sensitivity analysis. I describe these financial techniques in the next chapter, where we explore project evaluation methods.

Plans of Action

The final component of the business case is the action plan. The rule is that a detailed plan of action is created for the next stage and tentative plans are developed for all subsequent stages. Following this rule, the business case plans consist of the following:

- ✓ a recommendation on the future of the project: go versus kill, or alternatively, hold
- ✓ the detailed development plan (described in Chapter 9)
- ✓ tentative plans for Stage 4, Testing and Validation (described in Chapter 9)
- ✓ a tentative manufacturing, operations, or supply plan
- ✓ a tentative marketing plan (outlined in Chapter 10)

On to Development

The market has been researched. The product has been defined. The technical route has been mapped out. The financial and business justification has been prepared. And the action plan or path forward for the next stage (and subsequent stages) has been developed. The business case is now ready. These are the deliverables to the pivotal Gate 3, or Go-to-Development decisions. This critical gate opens the door to a significant commitment of resources and to a full-fledged development program. Because the homework has been proficiently undertaken in Stages 1 and 2, development should proceed more smoothly. You now have clear and defined targets to speed toward.

Picking the Winners: Effective Gates and Portfolio Management

8

If a man look sharply and attentively, he shall see Fortune; for though she is blind, she is not invisible.
—Francis Bacon, *Of Fortune,* 1623

The Right Projects Right

There are two ways to win at new products. One is by doing projects right . . . putting together a solid cross-functional team, doing the up-front homework, building in the voice of the customer, getting sharp, early product definition, and so on. That's what the last chapter was about: *doing projects right.* The second way to win is to do *the right projects.* Even a blind man can get rich in a gold mine by swinging a pick-axe; it's not so much how you mine, it's the ability to pick the right gold mine.

This chapter is about the second way—about doing the right projects, or picking the right gold mines! This chapter takes a hard look at best practices for making go/kill decisions—making the gates effective—and portfolio management, or making sure that you have the right balance and number of projects.[1]

Focusing Resources on the Right Projects

New product resources are too valuable and scarce to waste on the wrong projects, but most new product projects are losers. Either they fail commercially in the marketplace, or they are canceled prior to product launch. Project selection—the ability to pick the right projects for investment—therefore becomes a critically important task for management.[2]

There are two major challenges here. First, if your business is typical, many of the projects in your portfolio are, at best, marginal ones and, at worst, unfit for commercialization. Although some duds are the result of poor project management, others are simply bad projects to begin with; they should have been killed much earlier. The ability to spot these losers early in the process (before too many resources have been spent on them) is one key to improved new product profitability.

Second, there are far more new product opportunities than resources to commercialize them. Tough choices must be made! One trap that many businesses fall prey to is trying to do too many projects and not having enough resources to do them well. *Pipeline gridlock* is the result: Projects take too long; too many projects wait in a queue; and too many projects are underresourced.

The gates must work! As go the gates, so goes the process. Gates are the quality-control checkpoints in the process, where poor quality or bad projects are halted. Gates are where resources are allocated to projects—where the pivotal go/kill and prioritization decisions are made. And gates focus resources on the right projects. Therefore, if the gates don't work, your new product process will fall into a state of disrepair very quickly.

Pipeline gridlock and the inability to make tough choices plague even the best product developers:

One of the first tasks of a newly appointed business unit manager at DuPont was to assess his portfolio of new product projects. He asked each senior scientist to submit a list of the new product projects he or she was working on, indicating how much time was allocated to each project and how long each project had been on the books.

To his chagrin, not one person submitted a list shorter than two pages long. The typical reply: "I'm working on twelve projects; they're all critical; I spend a few days per quarter on each; and they've been on the books for four years!"

Undaunted, the business unit manager went to round two: "Please submit a list of the *three* projects that you're working on." The request had barely been circulated when he began to receive angry phone calls and visits from the scientists: "How dare you cut me down to three projects! All twelve of my projects are of critical importance to the company!"

What the business unit manager discovered the hard way was that people could not, would not, and did not know how to make tough choices. They lacked the will; they lacked the criteria; and they lacked the methods. Priorities had never been set, and no focus was ever achieved in the business unit.

A Weak Area

Our benchmarking studies reveal that project prioritization is among the weakest areas of all the ones studied; it had a proficiency score of only 49 points out of 100. In too many businesses, project evaluations are weak, deficient, or even nonexistent. The research reveals that there are no serious gates or go/kill points and no consistently applied criteria for making decisions, and there is a strong reluctance to stop substandard projects; projects get a life of their own. The result is tunnels, not funnels; available resources are thinly spread, while the good projects are starved for resources.[3] In our NewProd projects studies, idea screening was identified as one of the most poorly handled activities of the entire new product process; idea screening was rated as "adequate" in only 12 percent of the cases![4] Furthermore, 37 percent of projects do not undergo a business or financial analysis prior to the development phase, and 65 percent of projects do not include a prelaunch business analysis.

Even when undertaken, project evaluation is not as easy as it seems. Many businesses have a mediocre track record in picking winners. For example, for every four projects selected for development, only one becomes a commercial success.[5] Management appears to be in error about 75 percent of the time. You'd be better off tossing a coin!

This failure at the gates—the inability on the part of many leadership teams to make tough choices and focus resources on the right projects—is the root cause for a host of new product problems:

- ✓ It means longer times to market, as too many projects wait in queues.
- ✓ It results in poor quality of execution; there just isn't the time or people to do a quality job.
- ✓ The up-front homework doesn't get done.
- ✓ The right kind of market input and voice of the customer is missing.
- ✓ Product definitions are unstable and often fuzzy.
- ✓ Launches are mediocre, as launch resources are spread too thinly.

These problems lead to higher failure rates, longer cycle times, and lower profits.

Tough Choices

Project selection is about tough choices. Its purpose is to concentrate scarce resources on the truly deserving projects. The result is better focus, improved prioritization of projects, and ultimately faster development for the chosen projects.

In an ideal new product process, management would be able to identify the probable winners early in the game and focus resources on those projects.

RECENT RESEARCH ON PROJECT SELECTION METHODS

Our study into project selection and portfolio management investigated the methods that companies employ, their strengths and weaknesses, and the performance results they achieve. That is, the portfolio methods used have been linked to performance results. Some of the discussion on project selection methods in practice in this chapter is taken from this research. The study was undertaken cooperatively with the Industrial Research Institute in Washington, D.C. (see Note 10).

Failure rates would be kept low, misallocated resources kept to a minimum, and the return maximized.

Three Approaches to Project Selection: A Quick Look

The three main approaches to project evaluation and selection at the gates include the following:

1. benefit measurement techniques,
2. economic models, and
3. portfolio selection and management methods.[6]

1. Benefit Measurement Techniques

Benefit measurement techniques require a well-informed management group to assess the project on a variety of characteristics.[7] Such methods typically avoid conventional economic data, such as projected sales, profit margins, and costs, but rely more on *subjective assessments of strategic variables,* such as fit with corporate objectives, competitive advantage, and market attractiveness. Included in this category are *checklists* and their extension, *scoring models.* I take a much closer look at these useful methods later in the chapter.

Benefit measurement techniques recognize the lack of concrete financial data at earlier stages of the project and the fact that financial analysis is likely to yield unreliable results. They rely on subjective inputs of characteristics that are likely to be known. As such, these techniques are most useful at the earlier gates, for example, the Idea Screen and even the Go-to-Development decision point. However, benefit measurement methods are limited by the fact that they treat each project in isolation and do not take into consideration the impact of the project on the overall resource allocation question.

2. Financial or Economic Models

Economic models treat project evaluation much like a conventional investment decision. Computation approaches, such as payback period, break-even analysis, return on investment, and discounted cash flow (DCF), including net present value (NPV) and internal rate of return (IRR), methods are used. To accommodate the uncertainty of data, probability-based techniques, such as decision tree analysis and Monte Carlo simulation, are proposed.

Although I recommend the use of certain of these financial methods—namely payback period, DCF, decision trees, and sensitivity analysis at some gates—recognize their weaknesses, too! Their main deficiency is simply *the lack of solid, reliable financial data*. Another weakness is that, like benefit measurement models, economic models treat each project in isolation; for example, a return or payback is calculated for a specific project, which is then compared to some magical hurdle rate. The approach does not deal with the overall resource allocation problem.

3. Portfolio Methods

Portfolio methods consider the entire set of projects, rather than each one in isolation. The original portfolio selection models were highly mathematical and employed techniques such as linear, dynamic, and integer programming. The objective is to develop a portfolio of new and existing projects to maximize some objective function (for example, the expected profits), subject to a set of resource constraints. Anyone familiar with these programming techniques will immediately recognize the intellectual challenge that the mathematician and management scientist would have solving this portfolio problem. However, in spite of the plethora of articles written, such techniques have not met with success; they simply require far too much data, including financial data on all projects (both potential projects as well as those in the pipeline), timing information, resource needs and availabilities, and probabilities of success.[8]

The portfolio issue remains an important one, however. It has led one popular book to predict that "R&D portfolio analysis and planning will grow in the 1990s to become the powerful tool that business portfolio planning became in the 1970s and 1980s."[9] The past few years have witnessed simplifications and improvements in the portfolio approaches described above that have made them more understandable and useful. These include methods to assess the total value of the portfolio (such as the Expected Commercial Value method); methods to yield the right balance of projects (such as portfolio maps and bubble diagrams); and methods designed to yield a strategically aligned portfolio (such as the Strategic Buckets method). Note that portfolio methods are not project evaluation tools per se (that is, they are not go/kill decision models). Rather, they are prioritization and resource allocation methods and hence can be used *in conjunction* with some of the other methods above, such as benefit measurement or economic models.

Popularity, Strengths, and Weaknesses of Project Selection Methods

Which methods are most popular as new product project selection tools? Our recent study into project selection, prioritization, and portfolio methods reveals decided preferences for certain approaches, although popularity does not necessary correlate with delivering superior results.[10]

- *Financial or economic methods.* These methods are extremely popular project selection approaches. But don't be fooled: The businesses with the *poorest performing portfolios* rely almost exclusively on financial selection approaches, according to our research. A total of 77 percent of businesses surveyed use such an approach in project selection, with 40 percent of businesses citing this as their dominant project selection and portfolio management method.
- *Business strategy.* In this case, the business's strategy is used as the basis for allocating money across different types of projects. Based on the strategy's priorities, money is allocated across different types of projects and into different envelopes or buckets. Projects are then ranked or rated within buckets. A total of 65 percent of businesses use this approach, but it is the dominant method for only 27 percent of businesses.
- *Bubble diagrams or portfolio maps.* Here, projects are plotted on an X-Y plot, much like bubbles or balloons. Projects are categorized according to the zone or quadrant they are in (for example, pearls, oysters, white elephants, and bread-and-butter projects; see Figure 8.1 for an example). A total of 41 percent of businesses use portfolio maps; hardly any use these as their dominant project selection method.
- *Scoring models.* Projects are rated or scored on a number of criteria (for example, low-medium-high; or 1–5 or 0–10 scales). The ratings on each scale are then added to yield a project score, which becomes the criterion used to make project selection and/or ranking decisions. A total of 38 percent of businesses use scoring models; in 18 percent, this is the dominant decision method.
- *Checklists.* Projects are evaluated on a set of Yes/No questions. Each project must achieve either all Yes answers or a certain number of Yes answers to proceed. The number of Yes's is used to make go/kill and prioritization decisions. Only 18 percent of businesses use checklists, almost none as the dominant tool.

FIGURE 8.1   Risk-Reward Bubble Diagram for Chemical Company

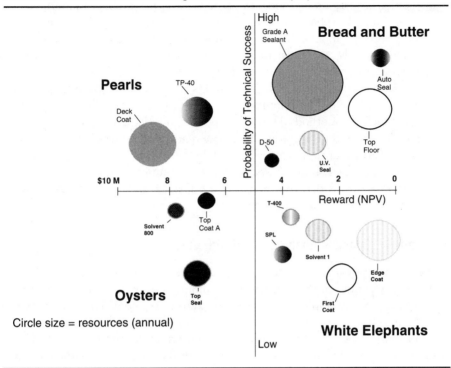

Traditional Portfolio Models: Great in Theory, But . . .

Although conceptually appealing, and perhaps the most rigorous, mathematically based portfolio models are more visible in textbooks and journal articles than in corporate offices. Studies done in North America and Europe show that managers have a great aversion to these mathematical techniques, and for good reason.[11] The major obstacle is the amount of data required on the financial results, resource needs timing, and probabilities of completion and success for all projects. Mathematical portfolio approaches also provide an inadequate treatment of risk and uncertainty; they are unable to handle multiple and inter-related criteria; and they fail to recognize interrelationships with respect to pay-offs of combined utilization of resources. Finally, managers perceive such techniques to be too difficult to understand and use.

Bubble Diagrams as Project Selection and Portfolio Models

The appeal of a portfolio approach lingers on, however, in the form of simplified versions that have been more recently packaged and promoted to industry.

Certain variants of the technique still suffer from many of the same problems that traditional portfolio methods do, namely, the considerable requirements of both financial and probability data. However, the simplified portfolio methods are much easier to understand and use; they don't require computer-based programming methods, and most important, they present results in the form of visually appealing portfolio maps (see Figure 8.1).

Our research reveals that bubble diagrams or portfolio maps, although recommended extensively by pundits and in the literature, see little use as the dominant decision method. They have both strengths and weaknesses, with strategic alignment and decision effectiveness at the top of the list of strengths (based on performance results achieved by businesses using this method). Weaknesses include a failure to deal with project numbers versus resources and spending breakdowns that reflect strategic priorities. Bubble diagrams are also more laborious to use than other models.

Economic or Financial Analysis—Use with Care

Economic models are the most popular project selection tools. They are familiar to managers, and they are accepted for other types of investment analysis in the business—for example, for capital expenditure decisions. However, they do have limitations. The toughest project selection decisions lie in the first few gates of the process when relatively little is known about the project. And it is here that traditional economic approaches suffer the most, because they require considerable financial data that must be quite accurate. Someone must make estimates of expected sales in year 1, year 2, and so on, and estimates are required for selling prices, production costs, marketing expenses, and investment outlays. Often these variables are difficult to estimate, especially in the early stages of a project. And even when estimates are made, they tend to be inaccurate. Various studies on firms' abilities to estimate expected new product sales and profits confirm that estimates were in error not by 10 percent or 20 percent, but by orders of magnitude![12] Therefore, economic models are usually considered most relevant for "known" projects (such as line extensions or product modifications—projects that are close to home and for which relatively good financial data are available) or at later stages of the new product process (for example for Gate 3 and later).

Our project selection research shows that financial methods have little to commend them. They suffer a multitude of weaknesses, yet ironically are the most popular of all methods, both overall and as the most dominant method. In particular, financial methods are ineffective decision tools, according to performance results achieved (that is, they yield the *wrong* decisions); they are not fully understood by management; and they fail to deal with important portfolio issues such as portfolio balance, gridlock and timeliness, and having the right number of projects for the available resources.[13]

There are more problems: Applying a financial screen to a high-risk or step-out project—perhaps your next major breakthrough product—will tend to kill it. The problem is not the project, which may well be a viable one; the problem is the application of the wrong evaluation technique. Here's why:

1. A financial analysis that is done prematurely on a project will reject all but the sure bets. On higher-risk projects, a probability-adjusted financial analysis in effect multiplies a string of probabilities together. Not surprisingly, the resulting financial reward is quite small. Alternately, worst-case financial scenarios for higher-risk projects tend to come out very negative. For example:

Procter & Gamble's two-in-one conditioner and shampoo technology platform is a technological breakthrough. It has spawned winning products such as Pert and Pantene. According to senior management, this program would not have passed the tough financial criteria applied to today's projects, simply because it was such an uncertain and high-risk project.

2. Traditional discounted cash flow (DCF) methods are *theoretically unsound* for determining the financial value of new product projects.[14] The argument is that they tend to substantially understate the value of higher-risk projects because they *fail to recognize the options nature of the investment decision*. Later in the chapter, I'll introduce more appropriate methods to deal with this criticism.

Financial analysis involving economic models is a powerful and useful tool in project evaluation, provided it is used at the right time and for the appropriate project type. However, if it is used too soon, or used for the wrong projects, it can do much damage. Qualitative and nonfinancial considerations must also enter the decision to move ahead.

The Benefits of Benefit Measurement

Benefit measurement methods are generally recommended for many of the gates in the new product process. At the earliest gates, benefit methods are the most logical evaluation tool because only a tentative commitment is required (early stages are relatively inexpensive ones) and because available information tends to be limited. At Gate 1, the idea screen, some companies use a sorting technique, such as Q-sort (below) to make gross distinctions between yea and nay project ideas. Checklists are also are a popular go/kill decision aid early in the process. And even at later gates—for example, Gate 3—benefit measurement methods, namely, scoring models coupled with checklists, have much to offer.

Our research into project selection methods reveals that of all methods, scoring models have much to commend them, and they fare remarkably well, in spite of their relative lack of popularity.[15] They yield a strategically aligned portfolio and one that reflects the business's spending priorities; they produce effective and efficient decisions; and they result in a portfolio of high-value projects.

A Closer Look at Benefit Measurement Approaches

Benefit measurement methods are popular and are recommended by a number of experts as a way to improve decision making at go/kill gates. Let's take a closer look at various types of approaches useful in screening new product projects. Benefit measurement methods are designed to *integrate subjective inputs of management* and include comparative approaches, simple checklists, and scoring models.

Comparative Approaches: Q-Sort and Analytic Hierarchy Approaches

Comparative approaches include such methods as Q-sort, project ranking, and paired comparisons. Each method requires the gatekeepers to compare one proposal to another proposal or to some set of alternative proposals. The decision maker must specify which of the proposed new product projects is preferred and, in some methods, the strength of preferences. In certain of these methods, a set of project benefit measurements is then computed by performing mathematical operations on the stated preferences.

The Q-sort method is one of the simplest and most effective methods for rank-ordering a set of new product proposals, especially at the idea screening gate.[16] Each member of the gatekeeping group is given a deck of cards, with each card bearing the name or description of one of the projects. Following a discussion on all the projects, each member then sorts and re-sorts the deck into five categories, from a "high" group to a "low" group (or into simple Yes or No categories), evaluating each project according to a prespecified criterion. (The criterion could be, for example, expected profitability, or simply go/kill.) The gatekeepers' results are anonymously tallied on a chart and displayed to the entire group. The group is then given a period of time to debate the results informally. The procedure is repeated, again on an anonymous and individual basis, followed by another discussion period. By the third round, the gatekeeper group usually moves to consensus on the ranking of the projects in each criterion. The method is simple, easy to understand, and straightforward to implement; it provides for group discussion and debate; and it moves the group toward agreement in a structured way.

Comparative methods such as Q-sort do have their limitations. Perhaps their weakest aspect is that gatekeepers must give an overall or global opinion on a project. Individual facets of each project—for example, size of market, fit with distribution channels, likelihood of technical success—are never directly compared and measured across projects. It is left to each decision maker to consider these individual elements consciously or unconsciously and to arrive somehow at a global assessment. This may be asking too much of some evaluators. Moreover, the group discussion may focus on a few facets of the project and overlook other key elements. A second problem is that no cut-off criterion is provided; projects are merely rank-ordered. It is conceivable that even those projects ranked highest will be mediocre choices in a field of poor ideas. Finally, a complaint voiced at some companies is that the decision process is not very transparent to those people outside the gatekeeping group; the entire process reeks of a political one, without the use of any criteria.

Analytic hierarchy approaches overcome some of the objections to Q-sort, for example, the lack of decision criteria. They are decision tools based on paired comparisons of both projects and criteria. Software such as *Aliah Strategic Thinking Process*[17] and *Expert Choice* enable a team of managers to arrive at the preferred set of projects in a portfolio.[18] Voting software and hardware (for example, hand-held wireless voting machines linked to software and a video projector) permit the management team to input their choices quickly and visually.

Benefit Contribution Models: Checklist Methods

One of the simplest approaches to evaluating new product proposals is the checklist method. This approach can be likened to questionnaires that follow a magazine article on some new dreaded disease. At the end of the article is a list of twenty questions. If you answer more than twelve Yes's out of twenty, then you should see your doctor—there's a good chance you have the disease. These types of diagnostic checklist questionnaires are found in fields from medicine to psychology to personal planning. They are the *original expert systems* and have proven to be remarkably accurate in terms of predicting or diagnosing some ailment or condition.

How are checklists developed? A group of experts constructs a list of questions that they believe are useful discriminators in predicting or diagnosing a situation. The system is validated using past cases: Does the list of twenty questions really discriminate between the yea and the nay cases? A cut-off score is established: How many Yes or No answers does it take to indicate the existence of a problem?

Checklists work well in new product evaluation, particularly at the early gates. Many companies use nothing more than a checklist of ten or fewer questions as the idea screen at Gate 1 (for example, recall Exxon Chemical's checklist of Start Gate questions—strategic fit, market attractiveness, technical feasibility, and no killer variables—in Chapter 5).

First, the project is presented to a group of gatekeepers. Following the project briefing, the evaluators answer the set of questions on the checklist, providing Yes/No or favorable/unfavorable answers. The answers are tallied, and a profile or score for the project is determined. A suitable pattern of responses (for example, a prespecified number of Yes replies) signals a go decision.

Checklist methods offer an attractive approach to new product evaluation. Implementation is straightforward; a number of criteria are considered, not just a single one; the list ensures that vital considerations are not overlooked; the evaluation is a consistent one, as all projects are subjected to the same set of criteria; and finally, the method does not require detailed financial inputs nor does it rely on a single financial criterion.

There are problems with checklists, however. The choice of questions for the list is arbitrary: They represent the compiler's best guess as to what factors are important to consider in evaluating a project. Some elements are likely to be more important than others (for example, having a sustainable competitive advantage versus having a fit with the business's manufacturing facilities), and the checklist does not build in a weighting scheme. The issue of what constitutes "an acceptable pattern of responses" remains a difficult one. Finally, the inputs or answers to the questions are subjective, may be largely conjecture and opinion, and may not even reflect careful thought.

Scoring Models

An extension of the checklist is the scoring model. Here projects are rated on a number of criteria, but this time on rating scales (for example, 0–10 or 1–5 scales). These ratings are then added together in a weighted fashion to yield an overall project score. The scoring model thus overcomes many of the criticisms of the checklist. Specifically:

- ✓ The scoring model allows for degrees in each characteristic; it is not just a Yes or No.
- ✓ It recognizes that some questions are more important than others and incorporates a weighting scheme.
- ✓ It provides a combining formula that yields a single project score, so that projects can be rank-ordered against each other or compared against some cut-off or minimum acceptable score.

In using a scoring model, the project is often first subjected to a set of must-meet criteria using the checklist approach above. These are the mandatory questions—a single No spells a kill. These questions are relatively easy to answer, and they weed out obviously unsuitable projects. Those projects that pass these must-meet questions are then subjected to a set of should-meet criteria using a scoring model. Independently of one another, the gatekeepers rate the project on each of a number of characteristics using numeric scales. The scores are tallied across gatekeepers, and an average score for each question is computed. The average score for each question is then multiplied by the weighting factor for that question and summed across questions to yield an overall score for the project, namely, the Project Attractiveness Score. This final score is used for two purposes:

1. *Go/kill decisions at gates.* The project attractiveness score is one input into the go/kill decision at each gate; for example, a score of 60 percent of maximum might be the cut-off or hurdle. Note that the decision is not quite as mechanical as a Yes/No based on this score; there is usually much animated discussion on each project.
2. *Prioritization.* Immediately following the go/kill decision, prioritization is decided. Here, the project attractiveness score for the new project (versus scores for already resourced projects) is a major input into how the new project is prioritized in the total list and whether it receives resources or is placed on hold.

Scoring models have been improved and refined. They are more user-friendly and more predictive, and they generate more useful output in the form of diagnostics. For example, NewProd™ is a computer-based scoring model that serves as both a diagnostic tool and a predictive model (see Appendix B).[19]

☞ **Suggestion:** If you are seeking to improve project selection and want to move beyond reliance on just financial tools, consider one of the benefit measurement tools outlined above. Perhaps the best combination is a set of must-meet questions, in the form of a checklist, followed by a scoring model to gauge the relative attractiveness of the project. And consider using the NewProd model as a predictive and diagnostic tool for the project team (Appendix B).

A Closer Look at Economic Models

The two most popular financial methods for new products are *payback period* and *discounted cash flow* (DCF), which includes net present value (NPV) and internal rate of return (IRR). Both payback and DCF are cash flow techniques as opposed to traditional accounting accrual methods; hence, they avoid disputes such as what can be capitalized and written off as opposed to expensed in year 1, or what depreciation rate to use. Moreover, DCF methods result in the "correct return" or yield from the project.

Payback and Break-even Times

Decision makers should consider three different measures of time, all of which are relevant to making go/kill decisions:

- *cycle time:* the time from project initiation to market launch. This metric answers the question, "How long is it to get to market and begin obtaining revenue?"

- *payback period:* the time from launch date to the full recovery of initial expenditures in R&D, capital equipment, and launch. It answers the question, "How long after launch is it to recover all your money?"
- *break-even time* (BET): the time from project initiation to when all expenditures are recovered. It answers the question, "From the time you first started spending money, how long is it to recover your money?"

Using payback and BET metrics as financial tools has four main advantages:

✓ The methods are simple and easily understood.
✓ They capture the notion of both *risk* and *return;* a faster payback or BET means both a higher return on investment and a lower risk (less need to count on distant, future, and highly uncertain revenues).
✓ They use a cash flow approach and, hence, avoid accounting method disputes.
✓ They project only as far into the future as the point of cash recovery; there is no need for five-to-ten-year projections as in DCF and NPV methods.

Discounted Cash Flow (DCF, or NPV and IRR)

A rigorous method of financial analysis for new products is *net present value or DCF methods.*[20] DCF analysis requires a year-by-year cash flow projection, but here the net cash flows for each year are discounted to the present using a discount rate (usually the minimal acceptable return or hurdle rate for the company). This stream of future cash earnings, appropriately discounted to the present, is then added, and initial outlays are subtracted to yield the net present value (NPV). If the NPV is positive, the project has cleared the hurdle or discount rate. Most computer spreadsheet programs come with a DCF capability, which also permits the calculation of the internal rate of return (IRR)[21]—the true yield on the project (as a percentage).

DCF analysis has certain advantages:

✓ It recognizes that time is money—that money has a time value—and it tends to penalize those projects with more distant launch dates and revenue streams.
✓ It is a cash flow method and avoids the usual problems of accounting and accrual techniques.
✓ It yields the "true" return as a percentage.
✓ It tends to place much less emphasis on cash flow projections that are many years into the future; that is, the result is not particularly sensitive to revenue and cost estimates made for many years out, particularly if the discount rate or IRR is high.

FIGURE 8.2   Determining the Expected Commercial Value (ECV)

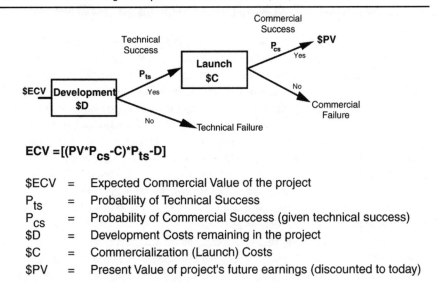

$$ECV = [(PV^*P_{cs}-C)^*P_{ts}-D]$$

$ECV	=	Expected Commercial Value of the project
P_{ts}	=	Probability of Technical Success
P_{cs}	=	Probability of Commercial Success (given technical success)
$D	=	Development Costs remaining in the project
$C	=	Commercialization (Launch) Costs
$PV	=	Present Value of project's future earnings (discounted to today)

SOURCE: Adapted from R. G. Cooper, S. J. Edgett, and E. J. Kleinschmidt, *Portfolio Management for New Products* (Reading, Mass.: Perseus Books, 1998).

To help identify project risks, *sensitivity analysis* is recommended. Sensitivity analysis is quite easy to do, especially if the project data are already in a spreadsheet format. In sensitivity analysis, key assumptions are tested. For example, what if the revenue drops to only 75 percent of projected? What if the manufacturing cost is 25 percent higher than expected? What if the launch date is a year later than projected? Spreadsheet values are changed, one at a time, and the financial calculations are repeated. Some managements require best-case and worst-case calculations, also done through sensitivity analysis.

If the returns are still positive under these different "what if" scenarios, the conclusion is that the project justification is not sensitive to the assumptions made. However, if certain "what if" scenarios yield negative returns, then these assumptions become critical: Key project risks have been identified.

In order to accommodate risk and uncertainty, DCF methods have been augmented to include Monte Carlo simulation, where numerous financial scenarios for the project are generated in order to better understand the financial risks, and the use of variable discount rates in the case of higher-risk projects. Commercially available Monte Carlo models include *At Risk* and *Crystal Ball*.

Options Pricing Theory: Expected Commercial Value

DCF or NPV methods have been recently criticized as being inappropriate for new product decisions. They assume an all-or-nothing decision situation and,

---

THE ACHILLES' HEEL OF NPV: OPTIONS PRICING THEORY VERSUS NPV

In recent years, some financial experts have recognized that the assumptions underlying traditional discounted cash flow (DCF) analysis (including NPV and IRR) are invalid in the case of new product investments. The net result is that NPV analysis *unfairly penalizes* certain types of projects, and by a considerable amount. Here's why.

In DCF analysis, the assumption is that the project is an all-or-nothing investment—a single and irreversible investment expenditure decision. In reality, however, investments in new product projects are made in increments; that is, management has a series of go/kill options along the way. As new information becomes available, the decision is made to invest more or to halt the project. These go/kill options, of course, reduce the risk of the project (versus an all-or-nothing approach). When DCF is used, this lost option value is an opportunity cost that should be incorporated when the investment is analyzed. But traditional spreadsheets used to generate NPVs do not!

By contrast, options pricing theory recognizes that management can kill the projects after each incremental investment is made—that management has options along the way. OPT is thus claimed to be the correct evaluation method, and a number of pundits have argued that NPV or DCF is "misused." Senior managers at Eastman Kodak go further and state that "the use of options pricing theory (OPT concepts) brings valuable insights into the R&D valuation process" and that "an options approach often yields a substantially higher valuation than a DCF approach." I have done a number of financial simulations, and I conclude that the Kodak view is correct: When the project is high risk one—that is, when the probability of technical or commercial success is low and the costs to undertake the project are high—then DCF and NPV *considerably understate the true value* of the project. This means that you will tend to kill otherwise valuable projects if you use the traditional NPV!

---

hence, are appropriate for capital expenditure decisions, but new product projects are purchased one piece at a time—in increments (see "The Achilles' Heel of NPV"). At each gate, management is in effect *buying options on the project;* these options cost far less than the full cost of the project and are therefore an effective way to reduce risk. The argument is that options pricing theory (OPT) rather than NPV is the appropriate way to evaluate the worth of a new product project at each gate.

One way to approximate an incremental or OPT approach is to structure the decision problem using a decision tree, according to Kodak.[22] This Expected Commercial Value method (ECV) seeks to determine the value or commercial worth of projects (see Figure 8.2) and is one of the more well-thought-out financial models. It features several twists that make it particularly appropriate to evaluating new product projects; unlike traditional NPV or DCF, this method recognizes that new product projects are *investments made in increments.*

In practice, the ECV decision tree considers the future stream of earnings from the project, the probabilities of both commercial success and technical

FIGURE 8.3   Illustration Using NPV and ECV Methods

The Situation:

Income stream, PV (present valued)	$40 million
Commercializaton costs (launch & capital)	$5 M
Development costs	$5 M
Probability of commercial success	50 %
Here the overall probability of success is	25 %

Traditional NPV, no probabilities:

The NPV is simply 40 - 5 - 5 =	$30 M

NPV with probabilities:
probability of success x payoff, minus probability
of failure x costs of failure which is: (.25 x 30) - (.75 x 10)   zero

The right way - the ECV or OPT way:
according to the formula and chart in Figure 8.2
{[(40 x .5) - 5] x .5} - 5 $2.5 M

Conclusions:
• The NPV method, without considering probabilities, grossly overestimates the value of the project
• With probabilities, the NPV method understates its value - project should be killed according to NPV
• But not so, according to the ECV (OPT - options pricing theory) method - the project really is worth $2.5 million!

SOURCE: Adapted from R. G. Cooper, S. J. Edgett, and E. J. Kleinschmidt, *Portfolio Management for New Products* (Reading, Mass.: Perseus Books, 1998).

success, along with both commercialization costs and development costs. The example shown in Figure 8.2 breaks the project into a two-stage model: Development and Commercialization (you can use three or four stages).

A sample calculation is given in Figure 8.3. Note *how different the ECV is from the NPV.* For example, the project's present-valued income stream is $40 million; after subtracting development and commercialization costs, its NPV becomes $30 million. Thus, at first glance, one might be tempted to place a commercial worth of $30 million on the project. When probabilities of success are introduced, the probability-adjusted NPV drops to zero—kill the project! But according to the ECV method, the *real value* of the project is $2.5 million—a major difference from either the $30 million or the zero figure!

☞**Suggestion:** Use payback period or BET in your first pass financial analysis (for example, in Stage 1). Your detailed financial analysis in Stage 2 should utilize a DCF method (NPV and IRR) along with sensitivity analysis. Better yet, move to options pricing theory, which recognizes the incremental nature of decisions and treats high-risk projects more fairly. But most important, recognize the inherent weakness of all of these financial approaches; the data inputs are typically very much in error, especially in the early stages of a project when the key decisions are made. And that's why exclusive use of these financial tools as the dominant project selection tool yields the worst performing portfolios!

Designing the Go/Kill Decision Points

Now it's time to start thinking about how to use the various evaluation methods outlined above—benefit measurement, economic and portfolio models—in a decision process for your business. In short, how does one integrate these models and tools into your *Stage-Gate*™ process to yield effective gates and gate decisions? In this section, we first look at some prerequisites—at the purpose of gates and requirements for a good gating system—and then move to the design of gates—structure and criteria.

Purpose of a Gate

Gates provide an assessment of the quality of the project, ensuring that your business does the right projects . . . and does them right! Gates deal with three *quality* issues: quality of execution; business rationale; and the quality of the action plan:

Quality of execution: Have the steps in the previous stage been executed in a quality fashion? Have the project leader and team done their jobs well?

Business rationale: Does the project (continue to) look like an attractive one from an economic and business standpoint?

Action plan: Are the proposed action plan and the resources requested reasonable and sound?

Note that these questions are separate issues and should be debated separately. For example, often a project team does a superb job but has their project put on hold simply because there are better projects to do. Unless the debate on quality of execution is separated from business rationale, the team may have the impression that they are being chastised by senior management for the job they have done.

Requirements of Effective Gate Methods

Many approaches to project evaluation and idea selection have been developed, as you have seen earlier in this chapter. When designing an approach to project evaluation and selection, and when electing the method that best suits your business, be sure to consider the following points.

Each decision point is only a tentative commitment in a sequential and conditional process. Each go/kill decision is only one in a sequence of such decisions.[23] A go decision is not an irreversible one, nor is it a decision to commit all the resources for the entire project. Rather gate decisions can be viewed as a series of *options decisions,* beginning with a flickering green light at the idea screen, with progressively stronger commitments made to the project at each successive decision point. In effect, you buy discrete pieces of the project at each gate; the entire new product project is incrementalized in order to reduce risk.

The gating procedure must maintain a reasonable balance between the errors of acceptance and errors of rejection. An evaluation procedure that is too weak fails to weed out the obvious losers and misfits, which results in misallocation of scarce resources and the start of a creeping commitment to the wrong projects. On the other hand, an evaluation procedure that is too rigid results in many worthwhile projects—perhaps your next breakthrough product—being stopped or rejected. This is especially true at the very early gates, where the project is little more than an idea; here it is extremely fragile and vulnerable and often too easy to kill.

Project evaluation is characterized by uncertainty of information and the absence of solid financial data. The initial decisions to move ahead with a project amount to decisions to invest that must be made in the absence of reliable financial data.[24] The most accurate data in the project are not available until the end of the development stage or even after testing and validation as the product nears commercialization—information on manufacturing costs, capital requirements, and expected revenue.[25] But at the early gates, data on projected sales, costs, and capital requirements are little more than educated guesses (if they exist at all). This lack of reliable financial data throughout much of the new product process emphasizes the need for methods of new product screening and predevelopment gate evaluation that are substantially different from those required for conventional commercial investment decisions.[26]

Project evaluation involves multiple objectives and therefore multiple decision criteria. The criteria used in project go/kill decisions should reflect the business's overall objectives and, in particular, its goals for its new product efforts. An obvious new product objective is to contribute to business profitability and growth. But there could be other specific ones, including the opening up of new windows of opportunity, operating within acceptable risk boundaries, focusing on certain arenas of strategic thrust, or simply complementing existing products. Moreover, as was seen in Chapters 3 and 4, many qualitative characteristics of a new product project—such as product advantage, market attractiveness, and leverage—are correlated with success and financial performance, and hence should be built in as goals or "desired characteristics" as part of the evaluation criteria.

The evaluation method must be realistic and easy to use. Project evaluation tools must be user-friendly. In short, they must be sufficiently simple and time efficient that they can be used by a group of managers in a meeting setting. Data requirements, operational and computational procedures, and interpretation of results must all be straightforward.

At the same time, the evaluation method must be realistic; for example, it cannot entail so many simplifying assumptions that the result is no longer valid.

Many operations research evaluation tools fail on this point, largely because their simplifying assumptions render the method unrealistic.

The Structure of a Gate

A little structure at gate meetings goes a long way to improving the effectiveness and efficiency of your business's decision making. Well-designed gates and gate meetings have a common format with three main components:

1. *Deliverables.* Project leaders often do not understand the expectations of senior management; hence, they arrive at gate meetings lacking much of the information that senior management needs in order to make a timely go/kill decision. To avoid this situation, *deliverables must be defined in advance* for each gate. These are what the project leader and team must deliver to the next gate; they are the results of actions in the preceding stage. The list of deliverables for a gate becomes the set of objectives for the project leader and team. A *standard menu of deliverables* is specified for each gate. In addition, at the preceding gate, both the path forward and the deliverables for the next gate are decided. A fairly typical menu of deliverables for the vital "money gate," Gate 3, is shown in Table 8.1.

   At Exxon Chemical, although each gate has a menu of standard required deliverables, the gatekeepers devote considerable attention toward the end of each gate meeting reaching consensus with the project team regarding just what will be delivered to the next gate. In this way, the expectations are made very clear for the project team.

2. *Criteria.* In order to make good decisions, gatekeepers need decision criteria—criteria that are operational (that is, are really used at gate meetings), visible, and clearly understood by all. These criteria are what the project is judged against in order to make the go/kill and prioritization decisions. These criteria are usually organized into a standard list for each gate, but they change somewhat from gate to gate. The list includes both financial and qualitative criteria, and it is broken down into required (must-meet) characteristics and desired (should-meet) characteristics.

3. *Outputs.* Too often, project review meetings end with a rather vague decision. Ask any three people who attended the meeting about what decisions were made, and you're likely to hear three different answers. Thus, gates must have clearly articulated outputs. Outputs are the results of the gate meeting and include a decision (go/kill/hold/recycle) and a path forward (an approved project plan, and a date and the list of

TABLE 8.1   Typical Deliverable for Gate 3 (The Go-to-Development Decision Point)

- Results of detailed market analysis
- User needs, wants, benefits desired & defined
  (based on customer interviews)
- Concept test results & purchase intent data
- Competitive analysis (who, shares, pricing)
- Preliminary marketing plan (one page)
- Results of technical analysis (technical feasibility demonstrated)
- Probably technical route; risks identified
- Product definition: target market, positioning, price point,
  product requirements
- Estimates of likely R&D costs, timing, resources
- Probable manufacturing route
- Estimates of manufacturing costs, equipment & capital requirements
- Legal, regulatory, environmental assessments
- Financial analysis (IRR, NPVC, sensitivity analysis)
- Plan of action for next state (in detail)

---

required deliverables for the next gate). There are only four possible decisions from a gate meeting;[27] the decision cannot be to "defer the decision":

- *Go* means just that; the project is approved, and the resources, both people and money, are committed by the gatekeepers.
- *Kill* means "terminate the project"; stop all work on it, and spend no more time or money here. And don't resurrect the project under a new name in a few months!
- *Hold* means that the project passes the gate criteria—it's a good project—but that better projects are available and resources are not available for the current project. A hold decision is a prioritization issue.
- *Recycle* is analogous to "rework" on a production line: Go back and do the stage over again, but this time do it right. Recycle signals that the project team has not delivered what was required of them.

Types of Gate Criteria

Each gate has it own list of criteria for use by the gatekeepers. These criteria are what the gate decision is based on and include go/kill and/or project prioritization criteria. Gate criteria are of two types:

- *Must-meet:* These are Yes/No questions; a single No can signal a kill decision. Checklists are the usual format for must-meet items.
- *Should-meet:* These are highly desirable project characteristics, but a No on one question won't kill the project; rather these questions are scored and a point count or project score is determined. Scoring models handle the should-meet questions well.

Note that criteria can be *quantitative* (for example, IRR > 22%) as well as *qualitative,* capturing issues such as the strategic alignment of the project.

In the design of a gating scheme, the must-meet criteria, or *checklist questions,* typically capture strategic issues, feasibility questions, and resource availabilities. Examples include the following:

- Does the new product project fit the strategic direction of the business?
- Is its development technically feasible?
- Do you have the resources required to undertake the venture?

A No to these questions—for example, a lack of strategic fit—is enough to kill the project.

By contrast, the should-meet criteria, or *scoring model questions,* describe the relative attractiveness of the project. Examples include the following:

- Is the market attractive—a large and growing one? How attractive?
- Is this familiar technology to us? Do we have some of the technical skills in-house?
- Can the product utilize existing plant and production equipment/technology? How easily?
- Will the product have sustainable competitive advantage? How much?

A No or negative answer to any one of these should-meet questions certainly won't kill the project. But enough low scores may indicate that the project is simply not attractive enough to pursue.

Gate criteria are designed to be used by the gatekeepers at the gate meeting. After the project is presented and debated, the criteria should be discussed one by one and scored, and then a decision is reached based on the criteria scores. Progressive companies use scorecards or computer-assisted scoring at gate meetings, so that scores can be displayed and differences debated.

☞ **Suggestion:** Most firms do not have a visible list of go/kill and prioritization criteria for selecting projects (other than financial criteria, which are probably not the best ones to use, especially at early gates). If you lack a visible list of criteria, develop one. Consider using a set of must-meet questions in a checklist format as culling questions, followed by a list of should-meet questions in a scoring model format to help determine relative project attractiveness. Be sure to use these criteria at your gate meeting, discussing each question, and reaching

TABLE 8.2   Sample Gate 1, 2, 3 Must-Meet Criteria

- Strategic alignment (fits the business strategy)
- Existence of market need (minimum size)
- Reasonable likelihood of technical feasibility
- Product advantage (unique customer benefits, good value for moeny for the customer)
- Meets environmental health & safety policies
- Positive return versus risk
- No show stopper (killer variables)

---

closure on it. If you do this, chances are your gatekeeping group will make more objective and better reasoned decisions.

Culling Questions: Must-Meet Criteria

As you think about the gating process, remember that project selection is a culling process. The approach is to subject projects initially to simple, easy-to-ask questions; in this way, the list of projects is pared down to a more manageable subset, which are then subjected to more thorough evaluation.

The first part of each gate—the initial culling questions—is a simple *quality check* that the deliverables are in place and that the activities underlying these deliverables have been executed in a quality fashion: the "deliverables check." Next, a set of must-meet questions determine whether the project meets minimum standards in terms of strategic alignment, magnitude of the opportunity, technical feasibility, and so on. These questions are designed more to weed out obvious loser and misfit projects than to give a strong green light. Table 8.2 shows my recommended set of must-meet criteria for Gates 1, 2 and 3; this is a composite list based on the experiences and gate designs at a number of leading companies. These gate criteria are applied in a relatively gentle fashion at Gate 1, but with increasing rigor at successive gates.

Attractiveness or Prioritization Questions: Should-Meet Criteria

The next set of questions asks whether the project is a good business proposition; they confirm that the project yields positive value for the company. No project scores top marks on every business criterion, so here is where the should-meet or scored criteria apply . . . a point count system based on a scoring model. In your scoring model, you should try to capture criteria that you believe are characteristics of a "good" or "high-priority" project. Strategic fit and strategic importance, along with financial attractiveness, are obvious criteria. But you might also want to include some of the factors that drive performance (from Chapters 3 and 4), for example, product and competitive advantage, ability to leverage core competencies, and market attractiveness. The list shown in Table 8.3 is a well-crafted list of Gate 3 criteria, based on criteria used at leading companies and also on my critical success factors. You can abbreviate the list for earlier gates.

The Gatekeepers

Who are the people that tend these critical gates—the gatekeepers who make the go/kill and resource allocation decisions and who are essential to making the new product process work? Obviously the choice of the gatekeepers is specific to each business and its organizational structure. But here are some rules of thumb:

- The first rule is simple: The gatekeepers at any gate must have the *authority to approve the resources* required for the next stage. That is, they are the owners of the resources.
- To the extent that resources will be required from different functions, the gatekeepers must *represent different functional areas*—R&D, marketing, engineering, operations, and perhaps sales, purchasing, and quality assurance. There's not much sense having a gatekeeper group from just one functional area, such as marketing or R&D!
- The gatekeepers usually *change somewhat from gate to gate*. Typically Gate 1, the idea screen, is staffed by a small group, perhaps three or four people who need not be the most senior in the organization. Here, the spending level is quite low. By Gate 3, however, where financial and resource commitments are substantial, the gatekeepers typically include more senior managers, such as the leadership team of the business.
- There should also be some *continuity of gatekeepers* from gate to gate. In short, the composition of the evaluation group should not change totally, requiring a total start-from-the-beginning justification of the project at each gate. For example, some members of the leadership team—perhaps the heads of the marketing and R&D departments— might be at Gate 2, with the full leadership team at Gate 3.

Projects of differing magnitudes require differing levels of gatekeeper groups. For example, one major financial institution has two levels of gatekeepers from Gate 3 on:

- a senior Gate 3–5 gatekeeping group for larger, high-risk projects (total cost greater than $500,000)
- a middle-level gatekeeping group for lower-risk and/or smaller projects (this is also the Gate 2 gatekeeping group for both project types).

TABLE 8.3   Gate 3 Should-Meet Prioritization Criteria

1. Strategic:
- degree to which project aligns with the business's strategy
- strategic importance of project to the business

2. Product Advantage:
extent to which the new product. . .
- offers unique benefits to users/customers (not available on competitive products)
- meets customer needs better than competitive products
- provides excellent value for money to the customer

3. Market Attractiveness:
- market size
- market growth rate
- competitive situation (tough, intense, price-based competition is a low score

4. Synergies (Leverages Core Competencies):
- leverages our business's marketing, distribution, and selling strengths/resources
- leverages our technological know-how, expertise, and experience
- leverages our manufacturing/operations capabilities, expertise, and facilities

5. Technical Feasibility:
- size of the technical gap (small gap is a high score)
- complexity of the project, technically (less complex is a high score)
- technical uncertainty of outcome (high certainty is a high score)

6. Risk versus Return:
- expected profitability (magnitued: NPV in $)
- percent return (IRR% or ROI%)
- payback period (or BET) how fast you recover your initial expenditure/investment (years)
- certainty of return/profit/sales estimates (from "pure guess" to "highly predictable")
- degree to which project is low cost and fast to do

A final issue is the need for the same gatekeeping groups across all projects. Two companies I have worked with implemented their *Stage-Gate*™ processes with different gatekeeping groups for different projects. At Kodak, each project had its own gatekeeping team, but no one gatekeeper group had an overview picture of all the projects; the result was that resource allocation across projects became impossible. At Telenor, the Norwegian telephone system, the situation was similar, with each project having its own gatekeeper group; in this case, the evaluation teams quickly turned into steering committees and "cheerleaders" so that no projects were ever killed! Both companies have revised their gatekeeping methods and have moved toward "standing gatekeeper groups" that review all Gate 3, 4, and 5 projects.

But It's More Than Just Project Selection

Picking the right projects is more than simply individual project selection; rather, it's about the *entire mix* of projects and new product or technology investments that your business makes—in short, portfolio management.[28]

- Project selection deals with the fingers: go/kill decisions on individual projects.
- Portfolio management deals with the fist: looking at the entire set of project investments together.

Much like a stock market portfolio manager, those senior managers who succeed at optimizing their new product investments—select the winning new product projects, achieve the ideal balance of projects, and build a portfolio that supports the business's strategy—will win in the long run.

What Is Portfolio Management?

A vital question in the new product battleground is, How should the business most effectively invest its R&D and new product resources? That's what *portfolio management* is about—resource allocation to achieve your business's new product objectives. That is, which new product (or other) projects should the business fund from the many opportunities it faces? And which ones should receive top priority and be accelerated to market? It is also about business strategy, for today's new product projects decide tomorrow's product and the market profile of the business. Finally, it is about balance, specifically, the optimal investment mix between risk and return, maintenance and growth, and short-term and long-term new product projects.

Portfolio management is defined as follows:

Portfolio management is a dynamic decision process, whereby a business's list of active new product (and development) projects is constantly updated and revised. In this process, new projects are evaluated, selected, and prioritized;

existing projects may be accelerated, killed, or de-prioritized; and resources are allocated and reallocated to active projects. The portfolio decision process is characterized by uncertain and changing information, dynamic opportunities, multiple goals and strategic considerations, interdependence among projects, and multiple decision-makers and locations. The portfolio decision process encompasses or overlaps a number of decision-making processes within the business, including periodic reviews of the total portfolio of all projects (looking at all projects holistically, and against each other), making Go/Kill decisions on individual projects on an ongoing basis, and developing a new product strategy for the business, complete with strategic resource allocation decisions.[29]

Integrating Portfolio Management into Your New Product Process

By putting a *Stage-Gate*™ process in place, you are taking the first step toward effective portfolio management. First, quality of information should improve, enabling fact-based go/kill decisions. This is especially true if you really adhere to the principles of *Stage-Gate*, namely, doing the up-front homework, building in voice of the customer, and so on. Second, the gates should at minimum kill poor projects—gates provide the needed rigor and scrutiny—thereby improving the overall quality of your portfolio. Finally, a gating process engages senior management in the right way. Where *Stage-Gate* processes fall short, however, is in project prioritization and resource balancing. That's the role of portfolio management methods.

Our research reveals that a number of companies are experimenting with different approaches to portfolio management. These attempts are quite new, and thus the approaches are tentative.[30] Virtually all the firms finding success here had already implemented a systematic new product process and had designated one gate as the point where portfolio management kicks in. Typically, this is Gate 2 (which precedes Stage 2, Building the Business Case) or Gate 3 (Go to Development).

From this point on, however, there is a divergence of opinion, with many different portfolio tools and techniques employed. Two broad portfolio approaches were observed in practice, and each has its own merits.[31]

In the next section, I summarize the various portfolio tools used. I then outline the two fundamental approaches to portfolio management. Note that although the two approaches share some of the same tools, and on the surface look similar, they are fundamentally different in terms of how they are put into practice.

Different Goals, Different Portfolio Tools

A variety of portfolio tools, charts and techniques are employed to assist in the review of all projects. Our research uncovered three goals of portfolio management, and different tools appear best suited to each of the goals. The three goals are value maximization, balance, and strategic alignment.

FIGURE 8.4   Prioritized Scored List of Projects: A Rank-Ordered List

Project	Leader	Strat Fit	Prod Advtg	Market Attract	Core Comp	Tech Feasib	Re- ward	Project Attract	People FTE	Cum FTE	Status
Episilon	Peters	9	9	10	10	9	9	93.3	20	20	Go #1
Gamma	Cooper	10	10	7	7	7	7	80.0	20	40	Go #2
Alpha	Smith	8	7	7	8	8	9	75.0	15	55	Go #3
Delta	Scott	7	7	9	9	8	5	74.0	12	67	Go #4
Beta	Jones	7	7	6	6	8	6	66.7	20	87	HOLD
Omicron	Baily	8	6	6	8	7	5	66.7	20	107	HOLD

(resource limit: 70 FTE)

1. **Set up a spreadsheet - list your active, "on hold" & proposed projects**
2. **Rank these projects according to some criterion (e.g., Project Attractiveness Score or ECV)**
   - √ **in this example, 6 screening criteria are used**
   - √ **the Project Attractiveness Score - the average of these out of 100 - is used as the ranking criterion**
   - √ **all 6 are good projects with scores over 65 points out of 100**
3. **Include projects until you are out of resources (here measured by FTEs - full time equivalent people).**
   - √ **here the first 4 projects are Go (note the resource limit of 70 FTEs); and the last 2 are put on hold**

SOURCE: Adapted from R. G. Cooper, S. J. Edgett, and E. J. Kleinschmidt, *Portfolio Management for New Products* (Reading, Mass.: Perseus Books, 1998).

Goal 1: *Value Maximization*—To allocate resources so as to maximize the value of the portfolio in terms of some business objective, such as profitability. Tools used to assess "project value" include familiar ones seen earlier in this chapter:

- *NPV:* The project's net present value (or some other financial metric) is determined and must exceed some minimum acceptable value. Projects are also ranked by NPVs.
- *ECV:* Expected Commercial Value is a variant of NPV and introduces probabilities of technical and commercial success along with an incremental decision process (options pricing theory).
- *Scoring model:* Decision makers rate the project on a number of questions that distinguish superior projects to yield a quantified Project Attractiveness Score. This score is a proxy for the "value of the project to the company," but it incorporates strategic, leverage, and other considerations beyond just the financial measures.

The way prioritization works is this: The values of all projects to the business are computed according to one of the three methods above. Projects are ranked according to this "value" or metric, for example, NPV, ECV, or Project

FIGURE 8.5   Procter & Gamble's 3-Dimensional Risk-Reward Bubble Diagram

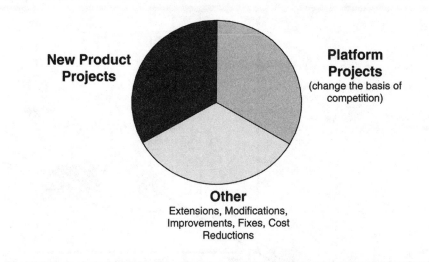

New Product Projects

Platform Projects
(change the basis of competition)

Other
Extensions, Modifications, Improvements, Fixes, Cost Reductions

The business's strategy dictates the split of resources into buckets; projects are rank ordered within buckets, but using different criteria in each bucket (method used by AlliedSignal-Honeywell)

SOURCE: Adapted from R. G. Cooper, S. J. Edgett, and E. J. Kleinschmidt, *Portfolio Management for New Products* (Reading, Mass.: Perseus Books, 1998).

Attractiveness Score, until there are no more resources (see Figure 8.4). Any project above the "out-of-resources" line is a go; any projects below the line are on hold or killed. It's tough but effective!

Goal 2: *Balance*—To achieve a desired balance of projects in terms of a number of parameters: long-term projects versus short-term ones; high-risk projects versus sure bets; and across various markets, technologies, and project types.

Visual charts display balance in new product project portfolios. These visual representations include portfolio maps or bubble diagrams, such as the risk-reward bubble diagram used at Procter & Gamble, plotting NPV, probability of success, and time to market (see Figure 8.5), or the traditional bubble diagram seen earlier in the chapter (Figure 8.1). Other visuals include pie charts that show the breakdown in numbers of projects or spending by project types, product lines, or markets.[32]

Goal 3: *Strategic Alignment*—To ensure that the final portfolio of projects reflects the business's strategy, that the breakdown of spending across projects, areas, and markets mirrors the business's strategy, and that all projects are "on strategy."

The Strategic Buckets approach is used by some leading firms to ensure that portfolio spending mirrors their strategic priorities. Here, management pre-

FIGURE 8.6   Strategic Buckets Method of Portfolio Management

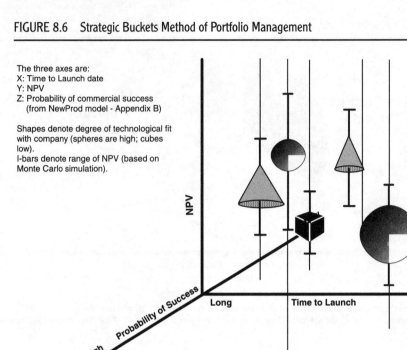

The three axes are:
X: Time to Launch date
Y: NPV
Z: Probability of commercial success
  (from NewProd model - Appendix B)

Shapes denote degree of technological fit with company (spheres are high; cubes low).
I-bars denote range of NPV (based on Monte Carlo simulation).

allocates funds to various "buckets": project types, markets, technologies, or product lines. These splits are based on strategic considerations. For example, GE-Honeywell splits development resources into three buckets: platform projects, new products, and minor projects (see Figure 8.6). Projects are categorized by bucket and then rank-ordered within a bucket. Thus, multiple lists or portfolios of projects are created, with each portfolio managed separately.

But We Have Constrained Resources!

Superimposed across all three goals, of course, is the factor of resource constraints. That is, management must try to achieve these three goals, but must always be wary of the fact that if too many projects are approved for the limited resources, then gridlock is the result—and we have surely lost.

The problem of too many projects and too few resources can be partly resolved by undertaking a *resource capacity analysis,* as outlined in Chapter 4, critical success factor #13. Recall that this analysis attempts to quantify your projects' demand for resources (usually people, expressed as person-days of work) in relation to the availability of these resources:[33]

1. *Do you have enough of the right resources to handle projects currently in your pipeline?* Begin with your current list of active projects. Determine the person-days each month required to complete them

according to their time lines. Then look at the availability of resources. You usually find major gaps and hence potential bottlenecks.

2. *Do you have enough resources to achieve your new product goals?* Begin with your new product goals. What percentage of your business's sales will come from new products? Now determine the person-days required to achieve this goal. Again, you will likely find a major gap between demand based on your goals and capacity available. It's time to make some tough choices about the reality of your goals or whether more resources are required.

This capacity analysis usually highlights key problems:

- ✓ It detects far too many projects in the pipeline, which leads to an immediate prioritization and pruning effort.
- ✓ It causes senior management to rethink its fairly arbitrary new product revenue and profit goals for the business.
- ✓ It identifies areas that are major bottlenecks in the innovation process, leading to decisions to increase or shift personnel.

Putting the Portfolio Tools to Work

How are these various portfolio tools used in conjunction with a gating process? There are two fundamentally different approaches.

Approach 1: The Gates Dominate

Here, the philosophy is that if your gating or *Stage-Gate*™ process is working well, the portfolio will take care of itself. Therefore, make good decisions at the gates! The emphasis of this approach is on *sharpening gate decision making* on individual projects.

In Approach 1, senior management or gatekeepers make go/kill decisions at gates on individual projects. Also at gates, the project is prioritized and resources are allocated. Gates thus provide an in-depth review of projects, one project at a time, and project teams leave the gate meeting with committed resources—with a check in hand! This is a *real-time decision process*, with gates activated many times throughout the year. By contrast, the periodic Portfolio Review, held perhaps once or twice a year, serves largely as a check to ensure that real-time gate decisions are good ones.

This "gates dominate" approach is often used by companies that already have a *Stage-Gate* process in place that is working well. They then add portfolio management to their gating process, almost as a complementary decision process. Our research found this approach used most often in larger companies, in sci-

FIGURE 8.7 The Two-Part Decision Process at Gates

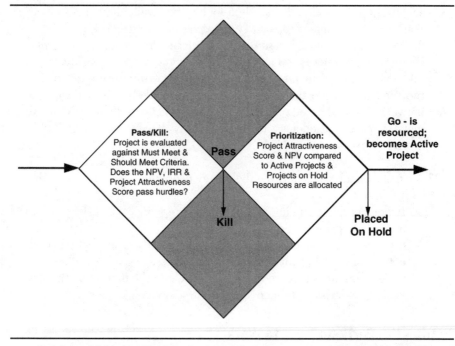

SOURCE: R. G. Cooper, S. J. Edgett, and E. J. Kleinschmidt, "New problems, new solutions: Making portfolio management more effective," *Research-Technology Management* 43, 2 (2000): 18–33.

ence-based industries, and where projects are lengthy (such as the chemical process industry).

Here's how it works: Projects proceed through the *Stage-Gate* process as portrayed in Figure 5.4. Projects are rated and scored at gates, usually by senior management, especially at more critical gates (Gate 3 and beyond).

To introduce portfolio management, gates become two-part decisions (see Figure 8.7). The first part or half of the gate is a *pass-versus-kill decision*, where individual projects are evaluated using the financial, checklist, and scoring model valuation tools described above. The second half of the gate meeting involves *prioritization* of the project under discussion in relation to all other projects (Figure 8.7). In practice, this means making a go-versus-hold decision; if a go decision is made, then resources are allocated to the project. A rank-ordered list of projects is created to compare the relative attractiveness of the project under discussion to the active projects and those on hold (see Figure 8.4). Here, projects can be ranked on a financial criterion (for example, NPV or, better yet, the ECV) or on the Project Attractiveness Score derived from the scoring model.

Additionally, the impact of the proposed project on the total portfolio of projects is assessed. The questions are: Does the new project under discussion improve the balance of projects (or detract from balance)? Does the project improve the portfolio's strategic alignment? Bubble diagrams and pie charts are the tools used for visualizing balance and alignment, as outlined above.

Note how the gates dominate the decision process in this approach; go/kill decisions, prioritization decisions, and resource allocation decisions are made in real time, right at the gate meeting. But other projects are *not* discussed and reprioritized at the gate; only the project in question is given a priority level relative to the rest.

Portfolio Reviews in Approach 1

What about looking at all projects together? That's the role of Portfolio Reviews. In this approach, the Portfolio Reviews serve largely as *a check that the gates are working well.* Senior management meets perhaps once or twice a year to review the portfolio of all projects using the various pie charts, bubble diagrams, and lists described above:

✓ Is there the right balance of projects?
✓ Is there the right mix?
✓ Are all projects strategically aligned (do they fit the business's strategy)?
✓ Are there the right priorities among projects?

If the gates are working, not too many decisions or major corrective actions should be required at the Portfolio Review. In our research, some companies indicated that they don't even look at individual projects at the Portfolio Review but consider only projects in aggregate!

Recap: Approach 1

To recap, the gates are where the day-to-day go/kill decisions are made on projects in Approach 1. Gates focus on individual projects—one at a time—and are in-depth reviews. At gates, each project is evaluated and scored before moving on to the next stage—a real-time decision process. At gates, poor projects are spotted and weeded out, and good ones are identified and prioritized accordingly. Note that resource decisions—committing people and money to specific projects—are made right at these gate meetings. Thus, the gates become a two-part decision process, with projects evaluated on absolute criteria in the first part (pass/kill decisions), followed by a comparison with other active and on-hold projects in the second part (go-versus-hold decisions).

Portfolio Reviews, by contrast, are periodic meetings held perhaps twice per year. They serve as a check on the portfolio and oversee the gate decisions being made. If the gates are working well, the Portfolio Reviews are largely a rubber stamp.

Note that the portfolio reviewers and the senior gatekeepers are most often the same people within the business. The result of the gating process working in tandem with the Portfolio Reviews is an effective, harmonized portfolio management process (see Figure 8.8).

Approach 2: Portfolio Review Dominates

The philosophy of the second approach is that every project must compete against all the others. A single decision on all projects replaces one of the gates in the gating process.

Here, senior management makes go/kill and prioritization decisions at the Portfolio Reviews, where *all projects are up for auction* and are considered on the table together. This Portfolio Review occurs two to four times a year. The gates in the *Stage-Gate* process serve merely as checks on projects—ensuring that projects remain financially sound and are proceeding on schedule.

The result of this approach, where the Portfolio Review dominates, is a more dynamic, constantly changing portfolio of projects. The method may suit faster-paced companies, such as software, IT, and electronics firms, but it requires a much stronger commitment by senior management to the decision process, spending the time to look at all projects together and in depth several times a year.

Approach 2 uses many of the same portfolio tools and models described above, but in a different way. The result is a more dynamic portfolio of projects. In this approach, the project enters the portfolio process typically after the first stage (at Gate 2), when data are available.

The main difference from Approach 1 is that early in the life of projects, a combined Gate 2 and portfolio decision meeting takes place. All new Gate 2 projects, together with all projects past Gate 2, are reviewed and prioritized in relation to one another. Every project at Gate 2 and beyond is thus in the auction, and all these projects are ranked against each other. Active projects, well along in their development, can be killed or reprioritized here, and resources are allocated here rather than at the gates.

The role of gates in Approach 2 is very different from Approach 1. Successive gates (after Gate 2) are merely checkpoints or review points.

✓ Gates check that the project is on time, on course, and on budget.
✓ Gates check quality of work done—the quality of deliverables.
✓ Gates check that the business case and project are still in good shape.

If a project is weak on any of these points, it could be killed at the gate, recycled to the previous stage, or flagged for the next Portfolio Review/Gate 2 meeting.

FIGURE 8.8   Method 1—An Integrated Portfolio Management Process

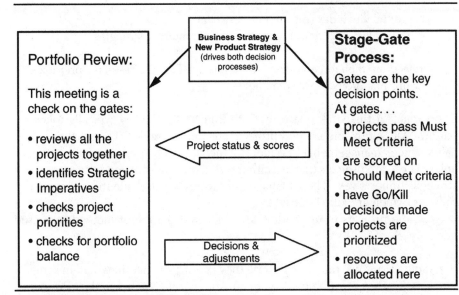

SOURCE: R. G. Cooper, S. J. Edgett, and E. J. Kleinschmidt, "New problems, new solutions: Making portfolio management more effective," *Research-Technology Management* 43, 2 (2000): 18–33.

An "All Projects" Gate 2 Meeting

The major decisions, however, occur at the combined Gate 2/Portfolio Review, which is a more extended, proactive meeting than Portfolio Reviews in Approach 1. And although this is a periodic process, it is almost real time because this meeting is usually held every three months.

EXFO Engineering, a mid-sized entrepreneurial and very successful instrument manufacturer, has implemented both a *Stage-Gate* process and portfolio management Approach 2. Four times a year, the leadership team of this business, chaired by the CEO, evaluates the complete slate of new product projects during their Portfolio Review meetings. Any project at or beyond Gate 2 is included in this prioritization exercise. Projects are rated according to the following criteria:

✓ confidence in the project team and in their proposed costs, revenues, and schedules
✓ revenues (times a commercial risk factor) versus expenses (development and commercialization costs, including a technical risk factor), over a two-year period

✓ match to the strategic plan (specific growth directions, with a weighting factor on each)
✓ profitability index (return on investment)
✓ availability of technical resources and commercial strengths

Projects are then force-ranked against one another. The result is a prioritized list, with some projects placed on hold.

The format of this vital, quarterly Gate 2/Portfolio Review typically follows a pattern. All Gate 2 and beyond projects are "on the table." The portfolio managers (senior management) first identify the "must-do" projects—the untouchables. These are projects that are either well along and still good projects, or are strategic imperatives. Then management votes on and identifies "won't-do" projects, which are killed outright.

Next, the projects in the middle are evaluated. Different methods are used here:

- Some firms use the same criteria they use at gate meetings, and in some cases, the most recent gate 0–10 scores; that is, the Project Attractiveness Score from each project's most recent gate meeting is used to rank-order the projects.
- Other managements rescore the projects right at the Portfolio Review/Gate 2 meeting (using a shorter list of criteria than the list found in the typical scoring model).
- Forced ranking on criteria is also used. Here management ranks the projects *against one another*—1 to N—on each criterion. Again, a handful of major criteria are used, such as those used by Kodak at its Portfolio Review:[34]

    ✓ strategic fit
    ✓ product leadership (product advantage)
    ✓ probability of technical success
    ✓ market attractiveness (growth, margins)
    ✓ value to the company (profitability based on NPV)

My colleagues and I recommend the forced-ranking method because it yields better discrimination than a traditional scoring model, forcing some projects to the top of the list and others to the bottom. One of the weaknesses of a scoring model is that projects tend to score in the middle; every project scores 60 out of 100. But any of these three methods yields a list of projects, rank-ordered according to objective scores. Projects are ranked until one runs out of resources. This ranked list is the first cut or *tentative portfolio*.

Following this, it is necessary to check for portfolio balance and strategic alignment. The proposed portfolio is displayed using some of the bubble dia-

FIGURE 8.9   The Portfolio Display After Completing the Ranking

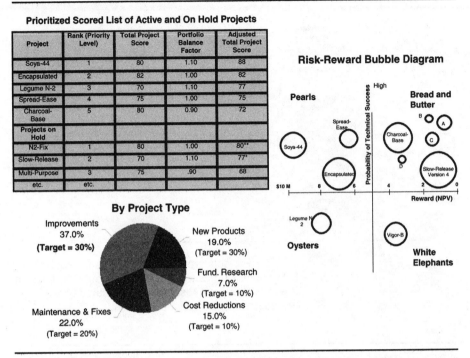

Prioritized Scored List of Active and On Hold Projects

Project	Rank (Priority Level)	Total Project Score	Portfolio Balance Factor	Adjusted Total Project Score
Soya-44	1	80	1.10	88
Encapsulated	2	82	1.00	82
Legume N-2	3	70	1.10	77
Spread-Ease	4	75	1.00	75
Charcoal-Base	5	80	0.90	72
Projects on Hold				
N2-Fix	1	80	1.00	80**
Slow-Release	2	70	1.10	77*
Multi-Purpose	3	75	.90	68
etc.	etc.			

Risk-Reward Bubble Diagram

By Project Type

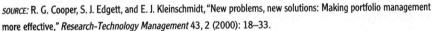

Improvements
37.0%
(Target = 30%)

New Products
19.0%
(Target = 30%)

Fund. Research
7.0%
(Target = 10%)

Cost Reductions
15.0%
(Target = 10%)

Maintenance & Fixes
22.0%
(Target = 20%)

SOURCE: R. G. Cooper, S. J. Edgett, and E. J. Kleinschmidt, "New problems, new solutions: Making portfolio management more effective," *Research-Technology Management* 43, 2 (2000): 18–33.

grams and pie charts described above (summarized in Figure 8.9). The purpose here is to visualize the balance of the proposed portfolio and also to check for strategic alignment. If the tentative portfolio is poorly balanced or not strategically aligned, projects are removed from the list and other projects are bumped up. The process is repeated until balance and alignment are achieved.

Recap: Approach 2

To recap, the Portfolio Review/Gate 2 meeting is where the key decisions are made in Approach 2. It's held two to four times a year. It is here that the key go/kill decisions are made, and consequently, it is a senior management meeting. With all projects at or beyond Gate 2 on the table, the meeting:

✓ spots must-do and won't-do projects;
✓ scores (force-ranks) the ones in the middle;
✓ checks for balance and strategic alignment (using various portfolio charts and bubble diagrams);

FIGURE 8.10   Method 2—Portfolio Management Intersecting with the New Product Process

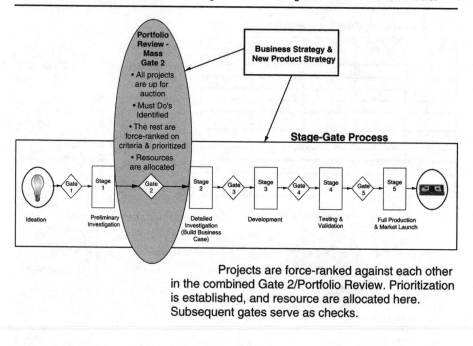

Projects are force-ranked against each other in the combined Gate 2/Portfolio Review. Prioritization is established, and resource are allocated here. Subsequent gates serve as checks.

SOURCE: R. G. Cooper, S. J. Edgett, and E. J. Kleinschmidt, "New problems, new solutions: Making portfolio management more effective," *Research-Technology Management* 43, 2 (2000): 18–33.

✓ decides the portfolio: which projects, what priorities, how much resources.

The gates serve mainly as a check. Projects are checked as they progress from stage to stage to ensure that they are on time, on budget, and remain good projects. Go/kill decisions are still made at gates to weed out poor projects. Gates rely on criteria, and the scores at these gates are often used as inputs to the Portfolio Review meeting.

Approach 2 thus lashes together the two decision processes: the gating process and the Portfolio Review. Gate 2 is really the integrative decision point in the scheme, the point where the two decision processes intersect (see Figure 8.10).

Pros and Cons: Approach 2 Versus Approach 1

Approach 2 has some advantages over Approach 1. Management indicates that it is easier to prioritize projects when looking at all projects on the table together (rather than one at a time at real-time gates). Additionally, some people have difficulty with the two-part gate approach in Approach 1 (Figure 8.7). For example, how does one find resources for a good project when that is the only project being considered at the meeting? Finally, some managers like the notion that prioritization of all projects is redone regularly. No project is sacred!

There are also disadvantages to Approach 2 and areas in which Approach 1 is superior. Many managements believe that if projects are to be killed, then the project team should be there to defend the project (or at least to provide updated information), such as happens at an in-depth gate meeting. Another criticism is that Approach 2 requires a major time commitment from senior management; for example, senior management in the mid-sized firm in the instrument business cited above takes three days every quarter to conduct its Portfolio Review/Gate 2 meeting! A final advantage of Approach 1 is that gate reviews provide a much more in-depth assessment than is possible when all the projects are considered at a single meeting.

Just Do It!

New product portfolio management has become a vital concern, particularly among leading firms. For example, senior executives in top-performing businesses consider new product portfolio management to be "of critical importance."[35] Although a number of tools have been described that help to select projects and visualize a portfolio, the choice of tool may not be that critical; indeed, the best performers use an average of 2.4 tools each. No one tool can do it all!

Two different approaches to portfolio management—one where the gates dominate and one where the Portfolio Review dominates—have also been outlined. Both have their merits, and both are recommended. Regardless of which portfolio management method or which specific tools you favor, do move ahead: Choose a method and implement it! Our research shows clearly that those businesses that feature a systematic portfolio management process—regardless of the specific approach—outperform the rest.

Development, Testing, and Validation

Everything that can be invented has been invented.
—Charles H. Duell, Commissioner of the U.S. Patent Office (urging President McKinley to abolish the Patent Office)

The whole history of invention has been a struggle against time.
—Charles Babbage, grandfather of the computer (1791–1871)

On to Stage 3: Development

The project is Go to Development. The up-front homework has been done, and the product has been clearly defined: target market, product concept and positioning, benefits, and product requirements.

Stage 3, Development, begins. Here the business case plans are translated into concrete deliverables. Remember: The deliverable at the end of Stage 3 is a prototype product that has been at least partially validated with customers and through extensive in-house, alpha, or lab tests. As experienced project managers will attest, however, even in the most astutely defined project, much can go wrong from this point on. Two major problems often beset projects during the Development Stage.

1. *The product definition isn't quite right.* Problem number one is that the final product may not receive the same enthusiastic reception from potential customers that the product concept did in tests undertaken in Stage 2. This apparent inconsistency may be because the project team incorrectly translated the concept into a product—for example, ignored or downplayed certain customer requests. Alternately, technical problems may have been encountered during development that forced a

relaxing of certain performance requirements or an omission of features desired by customers. Worse, in the concept test, the customer may have been responding to an upbeat, perhaps even unrealistic, concept presentation, but the final product or prototype fell far short of the promised product as portrayed in the concept test.

2. *Things change.* The second problem occurs because the world does not stand still. Note that the entire project has been defined and justified on the basis of how things were (or were anticipated) just prior to the Development Stage. But development takes months, in some industries years, and much that is unexpected can occur during this time frame. The market may change partway through development, making the original estimates of market size and product acceptance invalid. Customer requirements may shift, rendering the original set of product specs obsolete. Competitors may introduce similar products in the meantime, creating a less receptive market environment. These and other external changes mean that the original product definition and justification are no longer valid.

These two pervasive problems present major challenges to the project manager going into the Development Stage. Challenge number one is to ensure that the product prototype or final design does indeed meet customer requirements. This requires *seeking customer input and feedback throughout the entire Development Stage.* One cannot be sure about the success of a new product until it reaches the marketplace. Thus, it becomes imperative to build into the game plan a number of checks and tests to ensure that the project is still on target as it moves through Development and toward Launch. This is one of the key messages of this chapter: Build in checks and evaluations during and following product development. The name of this game is "no surprises."

Challenge number two is to move through Development and into Launch as quickly as possible. Rapid development is essential in order to gain competitive advantage and to enjoy the product's revenues as soon as possible. Most importantly, *rapid development minimizes the impact of a changing environment;* if the product's development time can be reduced from eighteen months to nine, the odds of things changing are similarly greatly reduced. For example, one of the problems with General Motors in the 1980s was the six-year cycle time from concept to launch; by the time the car was ready for market, consumers' tastes had changed, as had the competitive situation—so GM cars always looked a step or two behind the times. That's a second important message of this chapter: Reduce cycle time during the Development Stage.

Seek Customer Input Throughout the Development Stage

Seeking customer input and feedback is a vital and ongoing activity throughout Development, both to *ensure that the product is right and also to speed devel-*

opment toward a correctly defined target. Don't be afraid to reach out to large numbers of customers to answer key design questions that arise during the Development Stage. The original voice-of-customer research that was done prior to product development may not be enough to resolve all your design dilemmas. Technical problems may arise during the Development Stage that necessitate a significant product design change. Note that with better up-front homework, many of these technical roadblocks would have already been anticipated, and appropriate measures would have been built into the development plan to deal with them, hence minimizing the number of "on the fly" and unexpected changes needed during the Development Stage. Nonetheless, unforeseen technical glitches invariably occur.

Avoiding the Edsel

If the impact of the product design change is likely to be visible to the customer, then check it out—don't assume! If market conditions are changing as a result of shifts in customers' tastes and preferences or because a new competitive product hits the market, don't be an ostrich. There's no disgrace in admitting that the up-front market investigations didn't answer every possible question. It's a fact of life that markets change and unforeseen technical problems occur. Fluid markets—changing needs, new competitive launches—present a particular challenge in software, high-tech and IT industries. That's why I recommended in Chapters 4 and 7 that for such fluid markets, one should pin down as much of the product definition as possible based on solid up-front homework; but there will be a variable part of the product definition as well, even as the project enters the Development Stage. Activities that help to define the variable part of the product specs—for example, rapid prototypes and tests with customers—must be built into Stage 3, Development, to ensure that the product is right for the customer.

The Edsel is the classic new product failure. In its day, the Edsel was one of the most carefully market-researched automobiles ever. Unfortunately, in the years between initial design work and product launch, customers' tastes changed, and so did the economy. Moreover, key design decisions were rarely checked out with customers—the styling of the car (which many people found repulsive), the electric push-button transmission located in the steering wheel hub, even the name of the car. What would have been the outcome if Ford had reached out to its customers at every step of the design and development process? The answer is obvious, as we witness the stunning success of the Mustang in the 1960s and the Sable and Taurus in the 1980s—superb product development efforts, where the customer was an integral part of the development process, every step of the way!

Astute product developers also recognize that additional market surveys may be required, even during the Development Stage. For example, in the development of a novel milk-packaging system using polyethylene plastic bags, DuPont of Canada's project team ran into a technical snag. The original concept was for milk to be packaged in one-quart plastic bags, and these bags would have a tear-off tab for easy opening and resealing. The predevelopment market research tested and confirmed this product concept.

During development, however, technical difficulties arose that made the tear-off tab almost impossible. Rather than merely assuming that a change in product design would be acceptable to the consumer, the project team undertook a market survey of users to determine the importance of the tear-off tab. A hastily commissioned market survey revealed that the tear-off tab was desirable but not essential and that product acceptance by the consumer would not be significantly affected by its absence. The tab was removed from the design, and the product went on to be a great commercial success in Canada.

Designing Customer Tests

An often forgotten facet of customer testing is the *seeking of continual customer feedback during development*—that is, constant and iterative tests of the product as it takes shape during the lengthy Development Stage. Recall from Chapter 7 the argument that that "customers don't know what they're looking for until they see it." Thus, the message is simple: Get *something* in front of the customer as early as possible in Stage 3, Development, even if it's not the finished product. Only then will the customer have something that he or she can react to and start providing valuable feedback on. So test, test, test with the customer throughout the Development Stage—and start early.

In-house product testing (or lab or alpha tests) is normally an integral facet of product development. But an in-house test only confirms that the product works properly under controlled or laboratory conditions. It says little about whether the product works under actual use conditions or whether the customer finds the product acceptable. Customers seem to have an innate ability to find product weaknesses, things the engineering-testing group could never have imagined. The "acid test" of the product design is with the customer.

There are many relatively simple customer tests that can be built into the game plan during Stage 3. Let's imagine that you are partway through the development of a fairly complex product—for example, a new lawn-and-garden tractor aimed at homeowners. Key components—the new automatic transmission and dashboard instrument panel—have already been designed, developed, and tested in house. Both of these components are highly visible in the final product; they determine how the transmission shifts and how the dash looks and functions. Here's what you can do to assess the degree of customer acceptance:

1. Bring potential users (and your dealers) to the development site (or to a convenient location, such as a suburban hotel) to view and try out key components. You might mount the transmission on an existing tractor

and display a mock-up of the dashboard. Let the customer look, touch, and try. Record their reactions and comments. Obtain basic background information (demographics and other segmentation data), and then measure interest, liking, preference, and purchase intent much like in a concept test (using the question format shown in Chapter 7 in Figure 7.5). Include probing questions, noting areas of particular likes and dislikes. If the customer has problems or voices complaints when he or she sees or tries the product or component, note these as well.

2. The same procedure can be used with focus groups of customers. Start with an introductory group session. Then move to the display area so customers can touch and try. Finally, reconvene the group for a discussion of the merits and shortcomings of the tested components. The group session is more efficient than individual interviews (more inputs in a shorter period of time) and often leads to a more interesting and insightful discussion (the group members stimulate one another). But be careful of group dynamics: A single powerful member can sway the entire group to a positive or negative reaction to the prototype.

3. When the number of customers is small, try setting up a "user's panel"—an ongoing group of potential customers that acts as a sounding board or team of advisors during the development process. Whenever designs, design decisions, or components need to be checked, convene the customer panel to get its reaction.

4. Customer partnerships are perhaps the most certain way of seeking continual and honest customer input during the development phase. Customer partnerships work particularly well when both the customer and the developer have something to gain from a cooperative development effort. Seeking customer input in such an arrangement is quite straightforward; the customer becomes an integral part of your design team.

As you become more comfortable involving the customer in your Stage 3, Development, you can begin to accelerate the process. For example, in the case of computer software development, you might develop a small facet of the product in a few days—rapid prototypes of several screen displays. But don't treat these as a secret; show them to the customer, and seek immediate feedback as you proceed to the next step in development. The *ideal action is fast, highly iterative, and parallel;* a rapid or partial prototype is quickly fashioned, followed by immediate customer feedback, followed by development of another part of the product or a more complete prototype, and so on—a back-and-forth pattern, as illustrated in Figure 9.1.

The example above was for software; it is easy to visualize how one might bring facets of an incomplete software product to customers for reaction in a series of rapid prototypes and tests. But this same procedure works for most industries. Don't wait until the very end of development to begin to expose your

FIGURE 9.1   The Iterative Nature of the Rapid-Prototype-and-Test Pattern

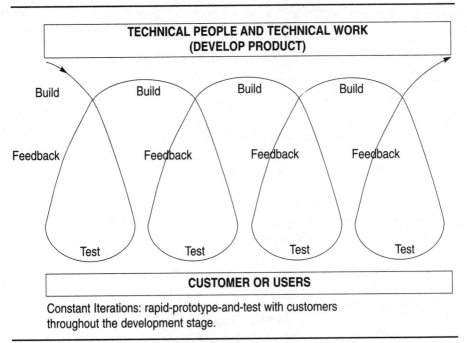

Constant Iterations: rapid-prototype-and-test with customers
throughout the development stage.

product to the customer. Get something in front of the customer early: a rapid
prototype, a lab sample, or a rough working model.

One concern often voiced is this: "What about creating unrealistic customer
expectations?" This is a valid question. When undertaking these early prototype-
and-test iterations, it must be made very clear to the customer exactly what
stage of the development program you are in, that this is an early prototype test
and not a field trial or offer to sell. That's why I encourage several members of
the project team to make the presentation to the customer and not to leave this
test to the sales force! Another tip: Show your customer an outline of your new
product process; many companies have developed glossy brochures of their
Stage-Gate™ processes precisely for this reason. Indicate to your customer
exactly where the project is—in Stage 3, not Stage 5. Chances are your customer
uses a similar new product process and will understand immediately.

☞ **Suggestion:** Although this rapid, iterative prototype-and-test process is
practiced by a minority of industries, such as software producers, the methodology has applicability to a much broader range of industries and settings. The
point is: Break the development of the product into pieces or parts; rapidly
develop partial prototypes, working models, lab samples, or parts of the product; then test these quickly with the customer. This iterative series of rapid-prototype-and-test steps will quickly move you down the field in Stage 3 to your
goal of the right product, and in a much shorter time frame.

Shortening Development Times

The second challenge introduced at the beginning of this chapter is to shorten development times so as to minimize the chances that the development target has changed. Thus, a sense of urgency is essential throughout Stage 3. This is one of the longest and potentially most troublesome phases of the project, but with the homework done up-front and with a solid product and project definition in place, many of the pitfalls and time wasters typical of the development phase have been eliminated.

"Speed is everything! But not at the expense of quality of execution."

We saw in Chapter 4 five sensible ways to reduce cycle time. Build these into your new product process. This is the first way to reduce cycle time:

1. *Do it right the first time:* Build quality of execution into every task and step of the project. The best way to save time is by avoiding having to go back and do it a second time.
2. *Homework and definition:* Doing the up-front homework and getting clear project definition saves time downstream; it means clear product design targets and less recycling.
3. *Organize around a multifunctional team with empowerment:* The cross-functional team is essential for timely development; it cuts down on "siloing" up and down the vertical organization and promotes parallel processing (rather than sequential problem solving).
4. *Parallel processing:* The relay race, sequential, or series approach to product development is dead; a more appropriate scheme is a rugby game or parallel processing. More gets done in an elapsed period of time, and the process becomes multifunctional.
5. *Prioritize and focus:* The best way to slow projects down is to dissipate your limited resources and people across too many projects. By concentrating resources on the truly deserving projects, not only will the work be done better, but it will be done faster.

In addition to these, here are some "nuts-and-bolts" ways to reduce cycle time. Consider making them part of your process.

- *Use flow-charting:* Map out each and every activity in a project. Then challenge the project team to figure out how every activity can be reduced in time—try to cut the time of each in half. Remove the time wasters! Any project or process can be accelerated by shortening each stage.[1] Shortcuts, or omitting the unnecessary, are obvious time savers.
- *Use planning tools:* Utilize critical path-planning and project management time-line software. Look for opportunities for undertaking tasks concurrently or for beginning one task before another ends.

- *Add flexibility:* To ensure greater speed, overlap stages; bring activities forward into an earlier stage, especially those with a long lead time; have multiple gate approvals—for example, a combined Gate 2 and 3 meeting—at one time; and use intelligent corner cutting. It's okay to relax the rules of a well-defined process and move to the third-generation scheme, once you have your *Stage-Gate* process up and running.
- *Deadlines must be regarded as sacred:* Time-based innovation is impossible without a disciplined adherence to deadlines.[2] Unfortunately, most companies only pay lip service to this principle. By sacred deadlines, I mean that a predetermined date is adhered to as a guideline for planning, with no excuses. The plan is developed, complete with the tasks to be done and their deadline dates. Delays are dealt with through extra input of effort and resources, not postponement.
- *Make funding flexible:* Set aside envelopes of money (or resources) so that one does not have to wait for a new budget year for money to start a promising project.
- *Move ahead anyway:* If gatekeepers cannot make timely decisions (for example, cannot arrange a time for a meeting, or don't show up to the meeting), the decision is an automatic go. Make this a company rule.
- *Keep it simple:* Find opportunities for unbundling products and projects. For example, instead of a project that requires three inventions, break it into three separate new product projects: introduce three successively better generations of products. The rule here is: Project complexity doubles and triples the cycle time, so work to reduce the complexity of projects!

☞ **Suggestion:** When implementing your new product process, *make every effort to reduce cycle times* of projects. The mere fact that you're now using a *Stage-Gate* process that builds in quality of execution, up-front homework, early definition, multifunctional teams, parallel processing, and focus means automatic cycle-time reduction. But do more than this. Use the approaches outlined above during your implementation: flow-charting, planning tools, process flexibility, sacred deadlines, flexible funding, fast gate decisions, and complexity reduction. But be sensible, too. Often the "quick fix" methods designed to speed things up—for example, cutting corners or omitting steps—yield precisely the opposite effect and, in many cases, are very costly. Note that there is also a dark side to accelerated product development (see sidebar).[3]

Worship the Time Line

In spite of these measures to reduce cycle time, there still is the commonly voiced complaint that the development phase takes far longer than expected; R&D or the design group is invariably accused of lacking a sense of time urgency. I often hear this criticism leveled at R&D or other technical groups

---

THE DARK SIDE OF ACCELERATED PRODUCT DEVELOPMENT

Some words of warning are in order concerning placing too much emphasis on accelerated product development and speed to market. According to new product guru Merle Crawford, the quest for cycle-time reduction leads companies to focus on the mundane—to develop trivial products and line extensions rather than genuine breakthrough products. It also results in short-cutting certain key activities—product testing, careful product definition, market studies—at the expense of quality of execution and with negative consequences, such as higher failure rates. And it is disruptive to the team concept; undue time pressure and adherence to unrealistic timelines create great anxiety in project teams, with team members often blaming each other for missed milestones. This results in greater people costs and chewed up resources.

---

by marketing and management people. Part of the problem may be indeed that technical people have a longer-term orientation and don't exhibit quite the same degree of "hustle" and responsiveness that marketers and business people do. But the problem may also be a management and planning one as well, for at the heart of every good development project is a *sound development plan*.

The physical development of the product must be driven by a well-crafted development plan. This is the project plan approved at Gate 3, which includes the following:

✓ a chronological listing of activities, actions, and tasks, including their time line. (Gantt charts, which provide a time line and show activities along this line as bars, defining a start time and an end time, are appropriate for relatively simple projects, whereas critical-path plans are needed for more complex projects).

✓ resources required for each action or task, notably personnel, person-days, and dollars

✓ milestones to be achieved throughout the development phase (and built into the time line). These milestones are measurable and definable points in the project where a review of the project is conducted to determine if it is on track, on schedule, and on budget.

The time line or time schedule is a critical element in the plan. It must be aggressive, causing team members to stretch a bit. But it must also be realistic. Too often a very compressed R&D plan is put together in response to management's demands. Unrealistic completion times are assigned to tasks. But within months or weeks of implementation, the truth is known; the plan of action is pure fiction, and its entire credibility is lost. So be aggressive, but be realistic, too, in designing the time line.

Another problem is the great difficulty in estimating how long it will take to complete certain tasks and how many person-days will be required. For example, some technical tasks may have an uncertain time frame—how long and how much work will it take to arrive at a technical solution? There are no easy answers to providing reliable time estimates here, other than three solid rules of thumb:

- The entire project team should develop the time line as a team—working together (instead of the project leader developing the schedule on her own). This is one of the first agenda items of the newly formed project team: developing the time line.
- The time estimates must be realistic and objective; try to remove emotion and undue pressure by others from this estimation exercise.
- Apply a "fudge factor." Invariably, activities take longer or involve more work (person-days) than originally estimated. For some activities, there is a consistent pattern of underestimation of times. Smart companies keep a record of "estimated time" versus "actual time to accomplish the task." These records provide historical data useful for future estimates and for deciding how large a "fudge factor" to use. (This data is collected at the Post-Launch Review.)

Milestones: Critical Checkpoints

Milestones are important metrics in the time line. Milestones are those checkpoints along the way where you check to make sure that you're on schedule and on budget. One rule of thumb that some firms employ is that if several milestones in a row are missed, the project is flagged. The project is clearly in some sort of trouble, and the project leader must call for a full review of the project (in my model, the project cycles back Gate 3, so that gatekeepers can reconsider the wisdom of continuing with this project, now in trouble). In this way, milestones can be used to blow the whistle on projects that are heading off course, before the problem becomes too serious.

To be effective, a milestone must be measurable and have a time frame attached. For example, in the development of a new software product, the proposal "to have most of the code written and partially debugged" is a very poor milestone. Words such as "most of" and "partially" are not measurable, and further, there is no time frame. Rather, the milestone should be quantifiable; "to have 30,000 lines of code written and fully debugged by day 95 of the project" is more appropriate.

Milestones are not to be confused with the periodic review meetings that technical managers often hold. These review meetings typically are scheduled on a calendar basis rather than in "real time" and after certain tasks have been completed. Typical is the "quarterly review of all projects." These meetings are more for information purposes rather than for control, but they do serve a useful role. Senior technical people are able to review progress to date during the Development Stage and to provide insights, advice, and mentoring to the technical players on the team.

Practice Discipline

Project plans—time lines and milestones—are meant to be followed. When a project falls way behind schedule, too often it is because the project team just went through the motions of developing a plan of action complete with a time schedule simply to meet management's requirements that such a plan be prepared. Then it is business as usual, and the plan and time line are conveniently forgotten. Wrong! There must be constant self-discipline and accountability for these time schedules. Time lines are there for a purpose. One of the common traits I've observed among successful project leaders is a dedication to the plan and to the schedule. Some examples:

A textbook case of a successful new product undertaken in DuPont's automotive paint refinish business was driven by a (then) relatively inexperienced project leader. One of her keys to success, she told me, was her dedication to her schedule throughout the development phase of the project. She and her team used project management software to lay out the plan for the two-year development phase. Every Monday morning at 7:30 A.M., the entire team would meet to review progress: What did we accomplish last week; where are we on the time line; and what needs to be achieved by this time next week? Each Monday the critical path plan was updated, and a new time schedule was generated. "It was this discipline—this religious adherence to the time line—that drove the project so quickly and successfully," she exclaimed. The project was one of the most successful and time efficient that the division had ever experienced.

The R&D manager at Adhesives Systems (formerly a small, high-tech subsidiary of B.F. Goodrich) is in effect the technical leader on each project. The division has an enviable record of fast-paced, successful developments. His secret to success: good planning and tight control of projects. Every project must have a detailed plan of action before it begins. Once a project is underway, he has a weekly meeting with the technical players on the project, and every two weeks there is a full team meeting—marketing, R&D, and manufacturing players. But the weekly follow-ups are critical, he claims: "When the project is falling short, I know about it, and they (the players) know that I know about it! We have a (time) plan and I push hard to stick to it."

Many project teams and leaders have resorted to user-friendly software to help map out their projects, such as MS-Project. Besides being excellent tools to help structure and plan the project, these software packages also have the advantage of permitting weekly updates to the project's schedule and plan.

Parallel Actions During Stage 3

Remember that while the physical development and testing of the product proceeds in Stage 3, many other activities are concurrently being undertaken by other members of the project team. And there's a lot of work and many tasks here! Some of these are invariably overlooked until too late—hence the need for having a clearly defined game plan for Stage 3. Here are some typical activities that you should also build into your Stage 3. Not all of these will apply to you; it depends on the nature of your projects and your industry.[4]

Market Development

In Stage 3, continue to monitor and research the market and the competitive situation to confirm product acceptance and a positive market situation. Early prototypes or lab samples are taken to a handful of trusted customers for initial reaction and feedback.

Also in Stage 3, the detailed market launch plan comes together. This is a first cut at the full market launch plan, including pricing, distribution, promotion, sales force, and so on. (Note that I recommend a tentative or "throw-away" market launch plan as a deliverable at the end of Stage 2, even before the Development Stage begins!). Obtain any legal approvals needed for your marketing and sales literature; for technical products, develop plans for technical service and support to meet customer expectations. You should also be working with foreign affiliates on the above items to develop market launch plans for these countries, securing volume and pricing commitments. Also, if you have a commercial partner, design the launch plan elements with that partner—who does what, and commitments on both sides. Finally, Stage 3 is the time to begin to identify appropriate test site customers for product testing in Stage 4 (including foreign sites).

Intellectual Property and Product Regulatory Issues

This is the stage to finalize the details of the technology protection strategy (intellectual property) and its implementation. Here you begin to undertake full implementation of your technology protection strategy. And also, finalize and implement the plan for product regulatory issues (including securing necessary approvals and resolution of regulatory issues, including foreign regulatory issues).

Production/Operations Process (or Supply Route)

In Stage 3, the production or supply process is defined and designed in detail (the process should be designed on paper, with process economics studied).

Production costs and capital expenditures are spelled out much more accurately than in Stage 2. Contact vendors to determine costs and lead times on equipment items. If you are in a process industry, develop the process in the lab in Stage 3, using bench-scale pilots.

Stage 3 is the stage to define and resolve plant environmental, health, and safety (EH&S) issues. If needed, develop and implement a plan to obtain plant regulatory approvals.

Finally, Stage 3 sees the development of a detailed operations and supply plan, along with quality assurance requirements and a quality assurance plan. The facilities for plant or pilot trials in Stage 4 are designed. And consider ordering some long lead-time equipment items for plant, pilot, or operations trials required in the next stage. It is important to note that the project could be canceled at Gates 4 or 5, so the risk of ordering some equipment items early must be weighed against the cost of lost lead time and a postponed launch.

Update Your Detailed Business and Financial Analysis

With better data now available (based on a developed product and a defined production or supply process), you should redo your Stage 2 financial and business analysis:

- ✓ Determine the payback period (years to recoup your investment).
- ✓ Undertake a discounted cash flow analysis (spreadsheet), including determination of NPV and IRR percent (identify your key financial assumptions).
- ✓ Perform a sensitivity analysis on key financial assumptions (for example, price, volume, and costs).
- ✓ Assess the impact of the product and project on other products and businesses in your company (for example, does it cannibalize or support the sales of other products?).
- ✓ Identify your pivotal business and financial risks.
- ✓ Prepare your capital appropriation request (or CAPEX) for equipment required in Stage 4 (earlier if the equipment requires a long lead time).

Develop Action Plans

Developing action plans is a key part of Stage 3. Map out your plan for Stage 4, Testing and Validation (actions, resources, people, timing, schedule, and milestones). Many firms also develop a discontinue plan. This is an exit plan that deals with customers and their expectations, production equipment purchased, and product inventory in house or in the field in the event that the project is canceled in Stages 4 or 5.

Other plans developed here (and sometimes even earlier) are the postlaunch plan and the life cycle plan:

✓ The postlaunch plan deals with issues that occur immediately after launch—what will be done, what needs to be measured, and what fixes or corrections are anticipated.
✓ The life cycle plan moves well beyond the immediate launch phase and paints a picture sometimes through to product exit: new product releases, continuous improvements, and next generation products.

On to Stage 4: Testing and Validation

A prototype or sample product has been developed. Thanks to the ongoing lab and customer testing that took place throughout Stage 3, the product has at least been partially proven even before it enters the Testing and Validation Stage. The purpose of Stage 4 is to provide final and total validation of the entire project: the commercial product, its production, and its marketing. Typical activities in this stage include extended in-house product tests, customer field trials or usage tests, test markets, and trial or pilot production.

Testing with Customers

Not only must the product work right in the lab or development department, but it must also work right when the customer uses and abuses it. The product must also be acceptable to the customer (simply "working right" doesn't guarantee customer acceptance). Finally, the product must excite and, indeed, delight the customer; he or she must find it not only acceptable but actually *like it better* than what he or she is buying now. In short, customer reaction must be sufficiently positive so as to establish purchase intent.

For some products, the first time the customer can see and try the product is after the prototype or sample is completed. But this is risky! Don't wait until the product is fully developed before showing it to the customer. This grand unveiling could lead to some very unpleasant surprises rather late in the game. Nonetheless, there are some situations where customers cannot be a part of the development phase, and hence, Stage 4 is the first chance you have to seek customer reaction. This might be true in the case of highly confidential developments or perhaps some consumer goods (where the final sample or prototype is required before customer reactions are meaningful). It may also be true for more complex products, where the product is such that individual components (or working models) cannot be tested with customers. An example of the latter is an office telecommunications/information system, for which separate components including software, desktop hardware, large switching devices, and communications networks mean very little to an office customer until they are working together as a system.

Remember: By delaying customer tests until the end of Development—until Stage 4—the risks increase. Try building in customer tests during Development. For example, customer testing of this office telecommunications system during Stage 3, Development, might allow customers to try a working model of the desktop unit complete with simulated screens on your laptop, and a mock-up of the output, and so on.

One of the pitfalls here is the reluctance of the project team to unveil their "baby" too soon to customers, just in case the reaction is negative:

> A well-known firm was developing a new camera-microscope system for use in a lab. In the homework phase, team members had interviewed lab users to solicit their inputs and brought in expert microscopists to seek performance requirements. So far so good. But no concept test presenting specs and performance characteristics of the proposed product was ever done. Here the team leader argued that the customer would actually have to "experience the product" in order to respond intelligently.
>
> Thus, he sought to develop a "working model"—this was supposed to be a very crude but working version of the product—so that the customer could have hands-on experience. The problem was that the so-called working model ended up being almost the final prototype, and by this point the project was into the millions of dollars. The project leader's reluctance to show early versions of the product or even product concepts to customers is understandable, but his arguments were faulty. Admittedly, a working model will yield better feedback, but concept tests and bringing customers in to see bits and pieces of the product, as it takes shape, also yield useful insights and solid feedback regarding product design. Further, by deferring customer feedback and reaction to so late a point in the process, he placed the project and company in a needlessly high-risk situation.

Preference Tests

A preference test—in which customers, either individually or as a group, are exposed to the finished product and their interest, liking, preference, and purchase intent measured—does several things. First, it provides a more accurate reading of likely market acceptance than the predevelopment concept test or any of the customer tests done during development. You now have the "commercial" or finished product to show the user. By contrast, in the concept test, the customers saw only a description or a model of the proposed product—something fairly intangible. And even during the Development Stage, you only had pieces of the product, or a working model, but not the final product. During the Stage 4 preference tests, however, customers are exposed to the real product—one they can touch, taste, or try. Much more information is presented to them, and because they are better informed, their answers and reactions are likely to be better predictors of eventual market acceptance.

A preference test also provides clues to minor design improvements that can make the product even better. If the suggested design improvements turn out to be major, it's back to the drawing board for a total redesign and more customer tests, or perhaps a decision to move ahead on the development of release #2.

The final purpose of preference tests is to determine how and why the customer responds to the product. For this purpose, tape recordings of customer responses are invaluable. The words and phrases the customers use in their comments provide valuable hints about how the product should be communicated to the customer. The attributes or features that first strike the customer can be used in designing ads, brochures, or sales presentations.

Once the preference testing is complete, what does one do with the data? Can market acceptance or market share be estimated from the data? Many of the same guidelines outlined in conducting a concept test also apply to the preference test in order to maximize the value of preference testing.

- *Be careful not to "oversell" the product to the customer.* If you make too forceful or biased a presentation, what you're probably measuring is how good a salesperson you are, not whether the customer really likes the product.

  In the case of a new telecommunications product, for example, the project manager (who also was the product champion) conducted user tests and follow-up interviews himself. He was delighted with the consistently positive customer reaction. A second wave of tests and interviews, done by a third party, revealed much more negative results. It was found that the enthusiastic product champion had so oversold his product's benefits that he virtually coerced the respondents into positive responses.

- *Be sure that the customer is sufficiently well informed* about the product to be able to judge it. This is a particular problem with innovative products. If the potential customer doesn't understand the product, its use, or its benefits, his or her responses won't mean very much. An "information session" held prior to the product test should give the customer relevant facts concerning the characteristics, use, and purpose of the product if these are not immediately apparent.

- *Be cautious in measuring price sensitivity* in customer preference tests. A common ploy is to ask an "intent to purchase question" about a product priced at say, 99 cents. Then the question is repeated, and a price 5 cents higher is named. Not surprisingly, the proportion of "definitely would buy" responses goes down as the price goes up. This type of questioning is invalid, however. By quoting the first price as 99 cents, the interviewer has established a *reference price* in the buyer's mind that is likely to bias all subsequent price questions. Had half the respondents been presented one price, and the other half the higher price, the positive responses would have been much closer. The same problem arises when a list of possible prices is presented and the respondent is asked, "What's the most you'd pay for the product?" The reference range of prices influences the answer.

If price sensitivity is an issue—that is, if you want to measure intent to purchase as a function of price—one price should be presented to one group of respondents, a second price to another group, and so on. Even with these controls, however, measuring price sensitivity is tenuous at best.

- *Don't take "preference" and "intent-to-purchase" data literally.* A 52 percent preference level does not translate into 52 percent of market share. The concerns relating to concept test results also apply here (these were outlined in Chapter 7). The results usually must be discounted to adjust for "yea saying," the lack of dollar commitment on the part of the buyer, and split purchases.

  Some firms use the following rule of thumb: A minimum of 50 percent of the target market must prefer the product, either "somewhat" or "very much," over the brand or make they currently buy or use. If the figure is below 50 percent, the new product is in trouble. History is perhaps the best guide for translating preference and intent data into market-share estimates. This points to the need to conduct user tests for every new product and to build up a history of data.

- *Interpret results of preference tests of difficult-to-distinguish products carefully.* For example, one cigarette manufacturer consistently obtained preference results on new products in the 45 to 55 percent range—a respectable result, so management thought. Eventual market shares were disappointing, however. An investigation of the testing procedure was undertaken. It was found that when a preference test was conducted on cigarette A versus cigarette B, 40 percent of the people preferred A, 40 percent preferred B, and 20 percent liked both equally. The catch was that A and B actually were the same cigarette! The point is that people will often indicate a preference, where no difference exists, particularly in product categories that offer few product cues to help users distinguish between products. Thus, the preference results of 45 percent obtained in the cigarette example aren't very meaningful: 40 percent was by chance, and only 5 percent was true preference. In product categories where cues do exist, however, preference results are more meaningful.

Extended Trials, Field Trials, or Beta Tests

Extended user trials (or beta tests or field trials) enable the customer to use a product over a longer time period, usually at his or her own premises. The customer's reactions and intents are thus likely to be based on better information. Extended tests are particularly appropriate for complex products, for products that require a learning period, and when it takes time for the customer to discover the product's strengths and weaknesses. An extended trial may also uncover product deficiencies not apparent in a short customer test or a lab test.

To undertake an extended trial, a sample of potential customers is identified and qualified (that is, they agree to participate). The product is then given or loaned to the customer. He or she proceeds to use it at home, in the office, or in the factory. A debriefing session is held with the user (either in a personal interview or by phone). The usual questions—interest, liking, preference, and intent—are posed. Probing questions can be asked about the product's strengths and weaknesses, its ease of use, its frequency of use, and suggestions for improvement.

Skipping the extended field trials is tempting, but the results can be disastrous:

One major marine coating manufacturer was anxious to get his new product to market before competition *at all costs!* The entire industry had been alerted to the fact that traditional ship-bottom coatings would no longer be accepted; they were toxic to plant life. Somehow manufacturers had to figure out how to keep plant life from growing on ship bottoms without using toxic materials.

The answer: very slippery paint. The company focused on a new generation of ship-bottom coatings based on silicone technology. In a rush, they moved to accelerated field trials, testing the new coating on various steel plates that were dipped into seawater. No ship tests were untaken, however. The product was launched, and one of Europe's largest shipowners was the first major customer.

All went well for the first year, until the developer began to get some complaints from the major user. "That slippery paint you sold us—guess what? It's slippery on both sides!" After one year of ocean duty, the paint was peeling of the ships. And that meant dry-docking the vessel, stripping off the paint, and repainting the ship. The costs were enormous, and the claims by customers began to mount.

The coating company survived . . . barely. But the damage to both its bottom line and reputation was substantial. It is another example of moving a bit too quickly—in this case, through the field trials in haste—and getting caught later.

Another example:

A manufacturer of heavy equipment developed a prototype tree-harvesting machine. The unit was designed to fell trees with a knifelike action, strip the branches, cut the tree into sections, and load the sections onto a carrying device. The unit was thoroughly tested by company engineers in nearby forests and pronounced satisfactory. The unit was then loaned for customer tests to a forest products firm. All went well at the first site. When the unit was operating at a second site during rainy weather, serious product deficiencies became apparent. The combination of a certain soft soil (common in many forests) and wet weather caused the unit to become hopelessly mired in the mud. The test revealed that major changes were required in the traction design of the product—expensive changes, perhaps, but far less costly than the prospect of having dozens of the units stuck in the mud of forests around the world.

When undertaking field trials or extended trials in the case of complex, technical, or industrial products, a little care taken at the beginning in the design of these trials can make the results so much more valid. Here are some tips:

1. *Pick the test sites carefully.* Certainly, convenience is a factor, but strive for representativeness too. If you pick only "friendly customers," then you're likely to get positively biased responses and may be in for a shock after market launch.
2. *Get a written agreement with the customer in advance.* This agreement should specify, first of all, that this is a product test (many new products are placed with potential customers by aggressive salespeople, but the customer is not fully apprised that this is only a test!). Next it should indicate something about the timing, test duration, test conditions, what will be measured, by whom and how. How many times have we witnessed disputes over test results because a different testing procedure or metric was used? It could have been avoided if these had been spelled out in advance.
3. *Be there!* Even if the tests are being done at two in the morning, be on site. Strange and unforeseen events have a habit of befalling otherwise straightforward product tests when the project leader isn't there to check up on things. Get your presence written into the agreement beforehand (item 2 above).
4. *Get the customer to sign off on the test results,* and most important, on the interpretation of these results—for example, that the test was a success or a failure. Two people can witness the same event and draw quite different conclusions from it. Get agreement, and get it in writing!
5. *Specify in advance what happens in the event of a successful test.* For example, if the beta tests are successful, is the customer expected to sign a purchase order and keep the new hardware or software? Or if the field trials are positive, does this automatically lead to commercial production runs by the customer?

Customer Tests: Not the Place to Cut Corners

User tests and contacts, both during development and after the prototype or sample is ready, often prove critical to the success of the product, so don't cut corners here! Studies show that this customer test phase—whether it's done and how well it's executed—is significantly correlated with new product success. Moreover, analyses of new product failures reveal that *in half the failures, the customer test was poorly undertaken or skipped altogether.*[5] The objectives of these customer tests usually include some or all of the following:

✓ to determine whether the product works well in actual use conditions (if not, what improvements are required?)

✓ to gauge whether the product is acceptable to the customer (and why, or why not?)

✓ to measure the customer's level of interest, liking, preference, and intent to purchase (and the reasons for these)

✓ to gauge price sensitivity—how preference and intent are affected by price

✓ to determine those benefits, attributes, and features of the product to which the customer responds most strongly (information useful in the design of the communications strategy for the product)

☞ **Suggestion:** The customer test phase is not a difficult step, nor is it unduly expensive. Given its pivotal role in identifying product deficiencies while there is still time to correct them, and in assessing likely market acceptance, I recommend that customer tests be built into your game plan, at a minimum, following the Development Stage, and if possible, during and throughout the development process. Remember: Check with the customer, and check again—no surprises!

The Final Trials

By now, the product has been tested with the customer and has been pronounced satisfactory. Minor design improvements have been incorporated. At the same time, the marketing plan for the product is coming together. (Chapter 10 is devoted to the development of a marketing plan; note that this marketing planning exercise gets underway in parallel with product development.)

Finally, the time is ripe to test the product, its production, and the launch plan under commercial conditions. For the first time you pull together all the elements of the marketing mix—product, price, advertising, promotion, sales force—and test their combined effect. At the same time, you produce a limited quantity of the product in a trial or pilot production run. The aim, of course, is to determine whether the strategy and programs as envisaged will generate the sales and profits you expect. If the answer is no, then you can choose between modifying the strategy and killing the project. It's still not too late to turn back.

There are two possible ways to test the launch strategy. Both are essentially experimental. Both cost less and are less risky than a full-blown launch. Both serve to provide a fairly valid test of the launch strategy, while leaving time for course corrections to be made before the launch. And both are reasonably good predictors of eventual sales or market share.

The first method is a *pre-test market* or *simulated test market*—a simulated shopping experiment that has gained popularity among consumer-goods producers. The second is a test market or *trial sell*, which although more expensive has wider applicability for different types of products. Let's look at each in more detail.

The Pre-Test Market

A pre-test market (or simulated test market) is a relatively inexpensive yet surprisingly useful method for predicting market share and sales from a *new consumer product*. There are a number of commercial versions of pre-test market studies offered by various consulting or market research firms. Examples include BASES, ASSESSOR, and TEMP.

Potential customers in a pre-test market study are brought to a testing facility, where they are exposed to advertising for the new product or to a concept statement. In some approaches, the advertising is built right into a television show, and consumers think they are there to view a pilot. Following the exposure, consumers are given the opportunity to go on a simulated shopping trip through a dummy store. They are given coupons or credits and asked to select some merchandise. Of course, the new brand is displayed in the store, along with a variety of other typical store products. If a consumer chooses the brand under test, he or she is interviewed a few weeks later, after using the product.

A pre-test market study yields important information. First, the simulated shopping trip provides a measure of the effectiveness of the advertising and the package in generating sales. Second, information on product use, liking, and repurchase intent is obtained. The initial trial rate combined with the repurchase intent permits estimates of sales or market share. Finally, these techniques produce valuable segmentation data. Demographics and other pertinent information about study participants are obtained, and a more exact definition of the target market is developed. Each of the commercially available pre-test market techniques varies somewhat in terms of method, computation, and purpose. BASES is used primarily to predict Year 1 and ongoing volume, whereas ASSESSOR and TEMP predict ongoing market share.

Why have such techniques become so popular, particularly among consumer-goods producers? Cost is the big factor. A pre-test market costs about $100,000 or so; a test market can cost ten times that amount. Moreover, pre-test markets are surprisingly predictive. Although the experiment is somewhat artificial—a simulated shopping trip, phony money, a dummy store, and so on—experience has shown that the results are very close to the market share finally achieved after launch. One major consumer goods firm estimates that pre-test markets demonstrate an "accuracy rate" of plus or minus 2 percentage points. That is, if the predicted share was 10 percent, the actual share will be between 8 percent and 12 percent.

Other reasons for using a pre-test market include speed (it doesn't take as long to set up and conduct as a test market); the depth of data provided (segmentation data on triers and repurchasers); exposure (in a pre-test market, there is far less chance that the competition will learn about your new brand, and even less likelihood that competitors will get their hands on a sample); and control. The last point merits mention. In a full-fledged test market, there are many variables beyond the control of those conducting the test. One of these is competitive activity. Stories are told of deliberate competitor interference: Competitors cut their prices, increase promotional activity, and even sabotage the test displays, all in an effort to thwart the test market or invalidate its results. A pre-test market, in contrast, is much more controlled; the store, the competitive brands on the shelf, and the displays are all within the control of the company conducting the test.

The one serious problem with a pre-test market is its limited applicability. Pre-tests are typically limited to relatively inexpensive consumer goods—the kinds of products found on supermarket shelves. The dummy store, the simulated shopping trip, and the fake money are clearly inappropriate techniques to use with big-ticket consumer items or industrial products. For those products, a trial sell, or test market, is the best means of testing the proposed launch plan and product.

Test Markets

Test markets (or trial sells) are the ultimate form of testing a new product and its marketing plan prior to committing to the full launch. Of the testing techniques, a test market comes closest to testing the full launch strategy before it actually takes place.

A test market is essentially an experiment. As in any experiment, there are subjects, treatments, and a control group. A small representative sample of customers is chosen. They are the *subjects*. They are exposed to your new product and to the complete launch plan, which includes all the elements of the marketing mix. This is the *treatment*. (Several different treatments can be used on different groups to see which works best.) The *control group* is all people not exposed to the test market.

There are usually two reasons for conducting a test-market study. The most common objective is to determine (or verify) the expected sales of the new product. A reliable forecast of future sales is critical to the final go/kill decision at Gate 5. If the test market shows poor sales performance, the project can be killed or perhaps recycled to an earlier stage for necessary revision of the product or its launch plan.

A second objective is to evaluate two (or more) alternative launch plans by testing two different treatments to see which gives better results. This type of test marketing is less common. For one thing, it's clearly more expensive. Besides, the hope is that by the time you're ready to test market, strategy questions will have been resolved. Nonetheless, in some cases the test market is used to decide which market strategy works best. The choice of an appropriate positioning strategy is one of those cases.

Some years ago, a food company planned to introduce a new instant breakfast drink. The product had some taste advantages over competitors; it also was more convenient to prepare and store in the home. One possible strategy was to position the product as a "great-tasting breakfast drink"; the other was to position it as "a convenient, easy-to-prepare breakfast drink." Four test market cities were chosen. Two were subjected to the "great taste" positioning strategy; the other two featured the "convenience" strategy, and the test market results contributed to the decision to use the "great taste" strategy for the national launch.

Test markets can also be used for industrial products, in which case they're usually referred to as trial sells. A trial sell goes hand in hand with a pilot production run of the product. If a limited quantity of the product can be produced, samples can be made available to a handful of company salespeople in one or two sales territories for trial sell. The elements of the trial sell are as close to those of the actual launch as possible: the price, the advertising literature, the direct mail, and sales presentation are identical. The only difference is that national advertising and promotion cannot be used for a single sales territory. As with a consumer test market, negative sales performance in a trial sell will signal either a kill decision or significant changes in the launch plan before the product is sold nationally.

Designing a Test Market

When the decision is go for a test market, a number of decisions will have to be made to ensure accuracy and reliability of results.

Locations. The test-market locations must be chosen. In the case of consumer goods, cities usually are selected; for industrial products, sales territories can be used. Locations should be chosen to be representative of the entire market. For consumer goods, this means representative in terms of demographics and other segmentation variables. Cities must be selected with the availability of appropriate local media in mind. For industrial goods, a "representative" sales territory means representative in terms of industry breakdown, size of buying firms, and so forth.

Two or more sites usually are selected for the test. If two alternative strategies are being tested, if the risks are high in the project, if uncontrollable variables are likely to be a factor, or if representativeness is a problem, then more than two sites probably will be required.

Execution. The test market itself amounts to an execution of the marketing plan, but only for the selected locations—a "mini-launch" or soft launch. All of the elements of the marketing mix should be as close to those of the final launch as possible, including pricing, advertising, channels, and sales presentations. The duration of the test market must be established; tests can range from several months to several years, although shorter tests usually are preferred. Products with longer repurchase cycles necessarily mean a longer test market period.

Measuring Results

Decisions must also be made on what data to gather. For consumer goods, warehouse shipments are a rough indicator of performance, but that figure also includes product already in the distribution pipeline. Sales to end users—retail sales measured through store audits—are the preferred measure. With industrial goods, sales to end users can be more directly measured, since the distribution channels tend to be shorter.

Some firms include end-user surveys in their test markets. Now that the product is actually in the hands of a customer, the time is ripe to obtain critical information. The task is to conduct follow-up interviews with users to find answers to some or all of the following questions:

- Who bought the product (demographics and other segmentation data)? Such information helps to confirm or refute the original definition of the target market.
- Why did he or she buy it? A knowledge of the "why's" leads to insights into the effectiveness of the communications and positioning strategies and into buyer motivations and preferences.
- Did the customer like the product after he or she tried it? Why or why not? Such information is critical to a confirmation of the soundness of the product's design, features, attributes, and benefits.
- Would the customer repurchase the product? Answers to this question enable a determination of the long-run market share to be made.

Incorporating an end-user survey into a test market provides far more information than the test market alone, which only measures sales results. The results of a survey can prove invaluable if the market launch strategy needs modification or adjustment.

Identifying the User

Identification of the end users can be a problem for manufacturers of some types of goods. If follow-up interviews are to be conducted, provision must be made in the design of the test market to determine who should be interviewed. For industrial goods, the "who" information can be recorded as part of the sale, either through your own sales force or with the help of distributors. (The "who" information might include not just the purchasing agent but also the individual or departmental user.) For big-ticket consumer goods, a mail-back in the guise of a warranty card provides this data. For smaller items, in-store intercepts can be used, or some form of redeemable mail-back can be included in the package.

E-Commerce Test Markets

Many opportunities exist to test and validate in e-commerce developments. For example, custom-tailored prototypes can be developed for select beta-test customers and delivered over the Internet. And results of the test—usage rates, patterns of usage, functions and features used most often, and so on—can be monitored electronically.

In the same vein, a semicommercial prototype product can be developed and offered for sale to a limited clientele—a test market over the Internet. Customer purchase rates, along with segmentation information—who bought the product and why—can be easily measured. A customer satisfaction questionnaire can be built right into the product, so that instant feedback on customer liking and future purchase intent is obtained.

To Test or Not to Test?

Having examined the elements of a successful test market, we now move to the most important decision: whether to undertake a test market at all. One common school of thought argues that test markets aren't worth the time, trouble, and cost. Test markets are expensive, particularly in terms of competitive lead time. Moreover, a test market exposes your product to competitors, thus giving them time to respond. If speed and the competitive situation are crucial factors, then consider omitting the test market; this may prove to be "intelligent corner cutting." For example, for the typical e-commerce product, a test market may simply be a time waster. The product is ready, so why not launch right away? The risks of proceeding may be quite low. But be aware of the risks, and try to *build other steps into your game plan* that address the customer acceptance issue much earlier in the process—for example, better up-front market research, constant customer feedback during development, and well-executed beta or field trials.

Financial costs are another big factor. In the case of tangible products, test markets cost hundreds of thousands, and sometimes even millions, of dollars.

The value of the information generated by a test market must be weighed against the cost of conducting the test market. E-commerce products are much easier and cheaper to test-market, and hence the decision may not be as difficult.

Another argument against test markets is that they exemplify the "horse and the barn door" situation. By the time the test market results are in, the door is being locked just after the horse has fled. Basically, the development budget has been spent, the product is fully developed, the creative work has been done, the packaging costs incurred, and the plant tooled up, at least for limited production. What's left? It's almost too late in the game to make changes now. The time to have killed or modified the project was much earlier in the process. This argument is persuasive in cases when expenditures up to the point of commercialization (for example, development) are particularly high in relation to launch costs.

A final argument against undertaking a test market is the questionable validity of results. As noted above, much can go wrong with a test market. Many variables in the experiment are beyond the control of those conducting the test. Often those variables cannot be known until the test market is well under way, and by that time it's too late to do anything.

Test markets or trial sells are not necessarily needless or wasteful. Give serious thought, however, to the pros and cons of undertaking such a test. Test markets should not be an automatic or routine part of every new product's game plan.

A test market is useful when the uncertainties and the amounts at stake are high. A test market is warranted in the following types of circumstance:

1. *When there is still a high degree of uncertainty* about the eventual sales of the new product as the launch phase approaches. When you've conducted all the appropriate tests but are still unsure about the product's market acceptance, a test market may be called for. On the other hand, if you built market studies into earlier stages of your game plan—a concept test in Stage 2, rapid prototype and tests during Development, and user and preference tests during Stage 4 (and these have been well executed)—then you should be fairly sure about market acceptance and hence may not need a test market.

2. *When the horse is still not completely out of the barn*—when there are many expenses yet to be incurred in the project before and during the full launch. If many expenditures remain to be committed in the project—for example, if a plant needs to be built or a production line retooled or set up; if an expensive national advertising campaign needs to be mounted; if a sales force needs to be hired and trained—then a test market can be used to provide valuable inputs to these final go decisions. On the other hand, if the production facilities are in place, and the if launch is relatively inexpensive (that is, if future expenditures are low), the cost and time involved in a test market may not be justifiable.

Certain technical considerations must be borne in mind when deciding to go with a test market. Limited or trial production may not be practical for some products. As one manufacturer of telecommunications equipment put it: "For telephone handsets, there's no problem doing a test market. We can run a couple of thousand of these units down a quickly set-up production line quite easily. For major capital equipment, however, such as a new digital switch, the day we make our first production unit, that's the day we're in full-scale production. There's no halfway."

Limited marketing in one or two cities, regions, or sales territories must also be possible. For goods that rely on electronic media, local print media, direct mail, local distribution channels, and personal selling, the marketing effort can be made to focus on one region. If national advertising and promotion vehicles are key to the product's launch, then a test market may be ruled out.

Suggestion: If the risk remains high as the project approaches the Launch Stage, consider building into your game plan a final trial: a pre-test market or a test market, accompanied by pilot or limited production. A pre-test market is recommended for consumer goods as a cost-effective predictor of market acceptance. For other types of goods, however, a full test market or trial sell is really the only method of accurately predicting the final sales results.

Go to Launch

The final evaluation decision gate—Go to Launch—is largely a financial one. Armed with the results of preference or end-user tests, test markets or trial sells, and pilot production runs, you can now make estimates of production and marketing costs, sales volumes, final prices, and profit margins with a high degree of confidence. Before the product moves to full-scale commercialization, a thorough financial analysis is essential.

By now, the market and production tests have yielded positive results. Armed with these results, the final NPV, IRR, and sensitivity analyses are carried out. The expected return clearly exceeds the minimum acceptable level, even with pessimistic estimates of key variables, so the decision is go for commercialization. It's time for the final play of the game—into the market!

The Final Play—
Into the Market

Plans are nothing. Planning is everything.
—Dwight D. Eisenhower

The Marketing Plan

The marketplace is the battleground on which the new product's fortunes will be decided. Thus, the plan that guides the product's entry to the market is a pivotal facet of the new product strategy. In this chapter, we'll look at the factors involved in developing a marketing plan for your new product.

First, what is a marketing plan? It's simply a plan of action for new product introduction or launch. It specifies three things:

- ✓ the marketing objectives
- ✓ the marketing strategies
- ✓ the marketing programs

The marketing plan itself is a document that outlines or summarizes your objectives, strategies, and programs. The marketing-planning process is a series of activities undertaken to arrive at the marketing plan. Much of this chapter will deal with the process of developing a marketing plan—setting objectives, developing marketing strategies, and formulating marketing programs.

Timing Is Everything

When does the marketing-planning activity begin? This chapter occurs rather late in the book because the market launch is one of the final stages in the new product game plan. However, this is not to imply that marketing planning should be the final step prior to launch. If you leave it to the bitter end, you're likely to find you've done too little, too late.

> During one of my investigations into how companies develop new products, I made an appointment to interview a senior executive in charge of new products. The company was a large manufacturer of heavy equipment. I arrived at headquarters for the interview and was quickly directed to the engineering building several blocks away. "Mr. X, who's in charge of new products, is located in our Engineering Department," I was told. That should have been my first clue. During the interview, Mr. X spent several hours reviewing the development process. He focused almost entirely on the engineering, prototype-development, and product-testing phases. Finally I asked, "When do the other departments—manufacturing and marketing—get involved?" He replied, "Manufacturing? They enter the scene after the product is tested and we've developed a set of manufacturing drawings. And marketing? Those sales folks get involved as the product's getting ready for production—almost as the first unit comes down the production line." In subsequent conversations, it came as no surprise to learn that the firm's new product performance was indeed dismal and that many problems could be traced to a lack of an effective and carefully conceived launch plan.

Start Early

Marketing planning is an ongoing activity that occurs formally and informally throughout much of the new product process. Informally, it begins during the first few stages of the game plan, right after the idea or Discovery Stage. By the time the project enters Stage 2, formal marketing planning is already underway as part of Building the Business Case. The development of a full marketing plan occurs simultaneously with product development to emphasize that a formal marketing plan should be in place long before the product is ready for market introduction or even for a trial sell.

☞ **Suggestion:** Where in the new product process does marketing planning occur in your business? Does it begin, as it does in many firms, at the very end of the new product process? Or do you start marketing planning in parallel with the development of the product? If it's a matter of "too little, too late," why not incorporate the marketing-planning activities alongside the development activities of your new product process?

An Iterative Process

The marketing-planning process for a new product is an iterative one. The plan is not carved in marble at the early stages of the new product process. Even the formal marketing plan that should be in place prior to product test and trials is likely to be tentative. The first version of the plan probably will see many changes before it is finally implemented in the Launch Stage. In short, there will be many times when you will rethink and recast your marketing objectives, strategies, and programs before implementation.

Setting Marketing Objectives

The marketing objectives that you specify for a new product must mean something. Why bother going through the aggravation of setting objectives at all? Objectives are part of a marketing plan for good reason.

The Role of Objectives

First, an *objective is a decision criterion*. When a manager is faced with two alternative courses of action, he or she weighs the consequences of each action against his or her objectives. The manager then picks the alternative that comes closest to meeting those objectives. Thus, marketing objectives help managers make decisions about specific marketing actions.

Second, a common and well-understood set of objectives for a new product *creates a sense of purpose*—a goal for the team players to strive toward. The written objectives communicate this goal. This common understanding is critical, particularly if the new product team is a large and diverse one. In too many new product projects, the players are on quite different wavelengths simply because the product's marketing objectives are not clearly specified, not written down, and not communicated. You've probably heard the saying, "Having lost sight of our objectives, we redoubled our efforts." This remark applies in many new product situations.

Finally, marketing objectives become *a standard for measurement*. Milestones or benchmarks are critical during the Launch Stage, when course corrections may be necessary. How will you know if you're on course if you haven't specified where you should be at any given time?

Good Objectives

What makes a "good objective"? Marketing objectives must

    ✓ set criteria for making decisions,
    ✓ be quantifiable and measurable, and
    ✓ specify a time frame.

A typical objective might be expressed as: "To gain a leadership position in the market." This sounds laudable, but it's a poor objective. First, it is not useful as a decision criterion. Second, it isn't quantified. What does "leadership" mean?

Does it mean "50 percent market share or better," or does it mean "the highest market share among competitors"? And what does "market" mean? The whole market? Or a specific and narrow segment of the market? Third, because the objective isn't quantified, it can't be measured. For example, one year from now, after the product is on the market, how will the product manager know if the product is meeting its objective? Finally, no time limit has been specified. Is the objective to be reached in Year 1 or in Year 10?

There is a much better way to express the same marketing objective: "To obtain a 20 percent unit market share in the owner-operator segment of the class 8 diesel truck market by the end of Year 2 in the market." Phrased in this way, the objective is a guide to action. Alternative plans can be assessed on their likelihood of achieving a 20 percent share; the objective is quantified and measurable; a time limit is specified; and market share can be measured during Year 2 to determine whether the product is on course.

Typical marketing objectives for a new product should include some or all of the following:

✓ unit or dollar sales of the product by year after launch
✓ share by year (be sure to specify the whole market or a segment, and whether the share is measured in terms of units or dollars)
✓ product profitability—percentage margins, annual profits by year (dollars or percentage), and payback period

☞ **Suggestion:** Review several of your firm's past marketing plans for new product launches. Take a hard look at the "marketing objectives" section of the plan. Did the stated objectives establish good criteria for making decisions? Were they quantifiable and measurable? Did they specify a time frame? If not, strive for sharper objectives in future marketing plans using the list of typical objectives above as a guide.

Refining the Objectives

The process of setting objectives will involve iteration, or recycling. The setting of objectives is shown as the first step in the marketing-planning process in Figure 10.1. In practice, however, you must revisit this objective-setting stage a number of times as you move toward your final marketing plan.

At the early stages of the project, some rough numbers may be available that permit ballpark estimates of objectives. These early estimates may be little more than educated guesses, but at least you will have made your first attempt at setting some objectives for the product. As more and better information about the market, the product's expected advantages, and projected costs becomes available, the objectives will become better defined and more valid. Market studies, financial analyses, cost analyses, and other activities that are part of the new product process are inputs to the constant refinement of marketing objectives. By the time the product is ready for launch, the marketing objectives will have undergone extensive changes from the first rough estimates made at the beginning of the project.

Realistically, marketing objectives for a new product represent a *merging of what is desired and ideal* and *what is possible.* In the final marketing plan, the objectives for the product—sales, market share, margins—and the forecasts for the product become one and the same.

The Situation Size-Up

The situation size-up is a key facet of the marketing-planning process. Typically, it is shown as the step that precedes the development of strategies. In practice, however, size-ups are done often and at virtually every phase of marketing planning. A size-up is a situation analysis; it pulls together the relevant information and asks, "So what? What does all this information mean to the development of my plan of action? What are the action implications?" Many situation size-ups are long, boring, and overly descriptive and fail to answer the question, "So what?" They begin with the heading "Background," then move to "Description of the Market," and so on. They're full of information and long on description, but short on action implications. Make sure that your situation size-up includes the pertinent information but always tell the reader, "Here's what this means in terms of an action plan for our new product." The major areas—both internal and external—that should be covered in a situation size-up in a new product marketing plan are shown in Figure 10.1.

The Market Analysis

The market analysis lowers the microscope on the market for the new product. A good market analysis addresses the following questions and issues.

- *Market overview.* How large is the market? How fast is it growing? What are the key market trends, both quantitative and qualitative? And what are the market drivers?
- *Market segments.* What market segments exist in this new product's marketplace? How is each segment unique? How fast is each growing, and what are their drivers? What other segment trends are evident?
- *Buyer behavior.* The who, what, when, where, why, and how of the purchase process within each segment are set out. Who buys? Who are the purchase influencers? What do the buyers buy, and when, and where? Why do they buy what they buy? What are their choice criteria (the order-winning criteria), and what are their preferences, wants, and needs?

FIGURE 10.1   Developing the Marketing Plan

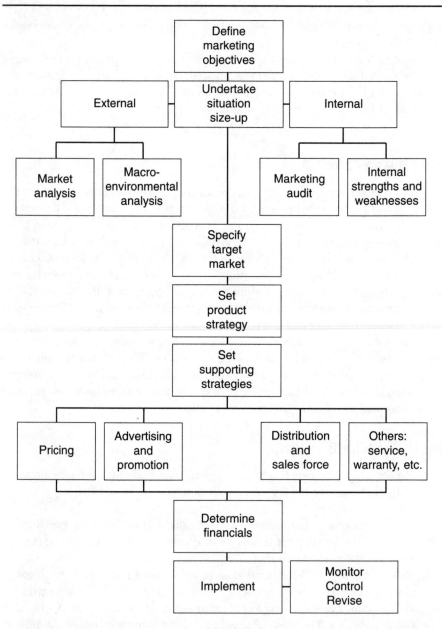

- *Competition.* Who are the competitors in each segment? What are their strengths and weaknesses? How good are their products? How does the customer rate their products? What are the competitors' strategies in pricing, advertising, and distribution? How well are they doing in terms of market share and profitability? Why?

There are two points to remember: First, much of this market information will not be readily known at the outset of the new product project. By the time the project is ready to enter the Development Stage, however, market studies should have been undertaken in Stage 2, and a thorough market analysis, with action implications, should have been completed.

The second point is that *a good market analysis goes a long way toward charting a winning market strategy.* If the market analysis lacks insight and information, the marketing plan probably will be vague and not very hard-hitting.

A sound market analysis is the foundation upon which a winning launch plan is built. Don't skimp at this step.

Macroenvironmental Analysis

A macroenvironmental analysis looks beyond the immediate marketplace or the new product. Trends and factors outside the firm and the product's market that may have an impact on the market and product are analyzed. These include the following:

✓ the economic situation,
✓ the political, legislative, and legal situation,
✓ demographic trends,
✓ social trends, and
✓ technological developments.

For example, when assessing the economic situation in the case of a new home gardening product—say, a rototiller—one would look at, among other things,

✓ the gross national product (as an overall indicator of wealth) and the disposable income (current and projected) of targeted families,
✓ costs and prices of garden produce and inflation rates, and
✓ fuel-cost projections.

Under the "demographics" heading, one would look at the age breakdown of the population, population locations, and so on.

Several general questions should be asked for each trend category in the macroenvironmental analysis:

✓ What is the situation or trend?
✓ What is the timing of the situation or trend, and how certain is it to occur? Is it here now or is it a "maybe" and far in the future?
✓ What are the implications of the situation or trend? Is it a threat or an opportunity? For example, what impact does the aging of the population have on the purchase of labor-saving home gardening products? For the design, positioning, and pricing of such products?
✓ What action is called for in light of the situation or trend?

The macroenvironmental analysis tends to be less concrete and less focused than the market analysis, and some of the conclusions or action implications will be fuzzy and contradictory. Nonetheless, the analysis is a useful one to build into your marketing planning. It doesn't take much time or effort, and on occasion some critical factors with a major bearing on the project are identified.

Internal Assessment

An internal assessment focuses on the company's internal strengths and weaknesses, particularly as they pertain to the project in question. A marketing audit typically is part of this assessment; it pinpoints your marketing "assets" and "liabilities."

- Can your relationships with your customers be used to advantage with the new product? Or your image and brand name?
- Look at your sales force. Is it good, bad, or indifferent? What are its strengths and weaknesses? Will it be able to do a good job with the new product? If not, what should be done?
- What shape is your customer service in? Are significant changes and improvements required to support the new product?
- Assess the status of your distribution or channel system, pricing policies, advertising approaches, and so on. What needs to be done to bring them up to speed for the new product project?

The idea behind the marketing audit is to identify marketing strengths and resources that you can build on and use to advantage in the new product. Remember: The shrewd strategist always *attacks from a position of strength*. An essential step in the strategy-development process, therefore, is to understand what your strengths really are and to identify and correct any weaknesses in your business's marketing resources that could have a negative impact on the new product launch.

Another facet of the marketing audit is to look at your marketing performance over time—at current products and, perhaps, at other recent launches. Consider market shares, margins, and marketing costs against the strategies employed. The point here is to learn from your history and to build these insights into a winning marketing strategy for your new product.

The internal assessment must also consider other facets of the company that will have a bearing on the launch plan for the new product. For example, you should be aware of the strengths and weaknesses of the manufacturing or operations department—supply capacity and reliability of supply, quality-assurance problems, availability of raw materials, people shortages, and so on. Similarly, the strengths and weaknesses of other groups in the company, such as engineering, R&D, and finance, are equally critical. The object is to avoid being handicapped in your market launch by problems in other company departments.

☞ **Suggestion:** Using past new product marketing plans in your company as test cases, assess the "goodness" of the situation size-ups that were undertaken. Was the market analysis a good one? Did it touch on the points outlined above? Was the environment reviewed and assessed? Was a "strengths-and-weaknesses" audit undertaken? Most important, did the situation size-up point to action implications? If your situation size-ups have typically been weak, why not begin with an outline or map of what you want to see in such an analysis? Remember that a solid situation size-up makes the job of strategy formulation much easier.

Defining the Target Market

The importance of target-market definition is a key element of the product definition, a vital deliverable to Gate 3 (see Chapters 4 and 7). Clearly, one must have a precise definition of the target market before designing the product and before developing the launch plan. *From market segmentation, all else flows;* segmentation is fundamental to effective marketing planning. Yet many people get it wrong! Before embarking on a plan of action, it is essential that you know "the object of your affection."

How is a target market selected or defined? The first step is *segmenting the market,* that is, identifying the segments. The second step is *selecting the appropriate segment* to become the target market.

Segmenting the Market

Market segmentation is a popular topic among marketing strategists and too complex to be fully discussed in this short chapter. Let's look at the highlights.

In the old days, economists spoke about markets as though they were relatively monolithic and homogeneous: "The market for X will behave this way or that way." Markets aren't homogeneous entities, however. They are people or groups of people buying things. No two people or groups of people are exactly alike, especially when it comes to their purchasing patterns. As consumers, we're all individuals; we have unique motivations, tastes, preferences, and desires. To treat all these different people or buying units as though they were painted with the same brush is naive. Moreover, to try to appeal to those different customers with the same strategy—one product, one price, one communications approach—is counterproductive.

Market segmentation is the delineation of groups or clusters of people within a market such that there is relative homogeneity within each group and heterogeneity between groups. That is, the people within one cluster or segment exhibit more or less the same buying characteristics but are quite different from the people in other clusters or segments. The company that develops a strategy tai-

FIGURE 10.2   Different Ways of Viewing a Market

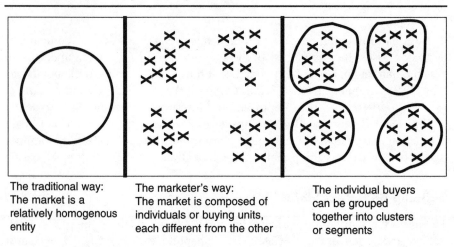

The traditional way:
The market is a
relatively homogenous
entity

The marketer's way:
The market is composed of
individuals or buying units,
each different from the other

The individual buyers
can be grouped
together into clusters
or segments

lored to a specific buyer or type of buyer is likely to be more successful than the firm that has only a single strategy in the marketplace. Henry Ford's remark, "You can have any color as long as it's black," may have worked for the Model T and the early days of the automobile industry, but it fell flat once General Motors implemented a strategy of market segmentation in the 1920s: "A car for every purse and person." The idea behind segmentation is shown pictorially in Figure 10.2.

This quick look at segmentation theory reveals that segmenting a market is a lot more difficult than picking a few convenient variables—age, sex, income (or, for industrial products, company size or Standard Industrial Classification [SIC] code)—and splitting the market into groups or categories. That is one method of segmentation, but the results usually aren't very helpful.

Bases for Segmenting Markets

Four broad categories of variables are useful in segmenting a market.

1. State of Being.   Included in this category are familiar sociological variables such as age, sex, income, occupation, education level, and the stage of the family cycle. The analogous variables for industrial goods are company size, industry classification (SIC code), and type of buying unit. Geography is another convenient variable: urban, suburban, exurban, and rural; regions of the country; and even regions of the world.

These "state of being" variables are the easiest to use; they're familiar and easily measurable, and published statistics relating to the variables are usually available. Frequently, however, they don't yield useful segments. The statement,

"We're introducing a new brand of after-dinner liqueur aimed at women," is nonsense. The target market "women" assumes that all women's tastes are the same when it comes to after-dinner liqueurs, and that's simply not true. Remember, seek clusters of people that are relatively homogeneous. When it comes to buying your type of product, the buyers within a segment should behave much like one another.

2. State of Mind. The variables in this category describe potential customers' attitudes, values, and lifestyles. This type of segmentation is called "psychographics." Consider the over-the-counter drug market. Psychographically, some people are hypochondriacs, some are skeptics, some are authority seekers. Each type is a different segment, to which a different product or different marketing strategy can be targeted.

A popular consumer segmentation scheme is the VAL 2 psychographic inventory, developed by the Stanford Research Institute.[1] Eight types of consumers are identified, based on their self-identify and their resources:

1. Actualizers: high resources with a focus on principle and action; active, take-charge expression of taste, independence, and character; college educated
2. Fulfilleds: high resources with a focus on principle; mature, satisfied, well-informed people for whom image has little importance; married, older, and college educated
3. Believers: low resources with a focus on principle; traditional, moralistic with a predictable lifestyle tied to family and church; non-innovative; older and high school educated
4. Achievers: high resources with a focus on status; successful, career-oriented; low risk-takers; respect authority and status quo; highly image-conscious; college educated
5. Strivers: low resources with a focus on status; impulsive and trend-conscious; seek social approval; money defines success; younger
6. Experiencers: high resources with a focus on action; young, enthusiastic, risk-takers; single and impulsive purchasers
7. Makers: low resources with a focus on practical action; conservative, practical, family-oriented; work with their hands, high school educated
8. Strugglers: poor, little education, few resources; focus on living for the moment; cautious; older.

3. Product Usage. Product usage segmentation looks at how the product is bought or used. The three major bases for usage segmentation are as follows:

- *Volume segmentation.* The popular 80:20 rule applies for many markets—20 percent of the customers buy 80 percent of the product. Buyers can be divided into categories of heavy user, light user, and non-user.

- *Loyalty.* Some customers are loyal to your firm, some are loyal to a competitor, and some move back and forth. The three different segments may deserve three different strategies.
- *Market factor.* Different people respond to different elements of the marketing mix. In many markets, there are price-sensitive buyers, quality-conscious buyers, convenience buyers, service-seeking buyers, and so on. These types of buyers are different segments and should be treated accordingly.

4. Benefit Segmentation.   Perhaps the most useful method of segmentation for use with a new product is benefit segmentation. Benefit segmentation recognizes that *people have different reasons and motivations for buying* a product, and therefore they seek different packages of benefits. When purchasing a new automobile, some people are looking for basic transportation—a reliable, practical, low-cost, safe car. Others seek a prestigious high-performance car loaded with creature comforts.

Benefit segmentation is particularly useful for new product strategy. Using this approach, the target market defines the benefits that must be built into the new product. Usually, these benefits can be translated into specific product features, which aids the product design process. The positioning and communications strategies also are largely defined by the benefit segment selected. Consider, for example, two target market definitions for a new alcoholic beverage:

- Target market A: "The product will be aimed at middle-income, American women in the 20 to 30 age group."
- Target market B: "The product will be aimed at women seeking a mild, nonfattening, sweet-tasting, smooth beverage to be used in a relatively upscale social setting."

The definition of target market A is an example of demographic segmentation. The definition is too vague to be useful in designing the product or creating an ad campaign. The definition of target market B is an example of benefit segmentation. The product can almost be designed and advertised simply by reading the statement. Benefit segmentation has its drawbacks, however. It invariably requires extensive market research. That research is difficult—many intangible variables must be measured. It's much easier to measure people's ages or occupations than it is to measure the benefits they seek.

☞ **Suggestion:** No doubt there is a great deal of discussion in your firm about market segmentation and about selecting the right target market when developing a marketing plan for a new product. But have you ever tried to segment the market based on the different packages of benefits customers want from a given product? Try benefit segmentation. You'll find its a very powerful tool in designing a new product strategy. Some market research will be required to determine what benefits are sought and which people seek what benefits. Or for consumer goods, consider psychographic segmentation, such as the VALS 2 scheme; it has some creative and insightful approaches to target and market your product.

Selecting the Right Target Market

A segmentation analysis should yield a number of potential market segments. At the same time, different versions of the product may be conceived to suit two or more segments. As Figure 10.1 illustrates, when one thinks of market segments one also thinks immediately of how to target the segments—for example, what product benefits and features can be built into the product to suit it to a particular segment or segments. The next task is to select the appropriate target market from among these options.

> Fibernyle, a division of Lawson Mardon Packaging, a major international packaging division, developed a packaging breakthrough—a plastic aerosol container designed to replace metal aerosol cans. The new product offered numerous benefits: better aesthetics, non-rusting, better feel, and internal cleanliness. Many possible market segments (and positioning strategies) were identified for the aerosol cans, from large-volume, low-price commodity segments such as toiletries (for example, shaving cream and hair spray) to specialty, low-volume (but potentially high-value-added) niche segments such as medical products (for example, contact lens sprays).
>
> The choice of segment (and positioning of the product) proved crucial to the entire project. Segment choice determines the nature of product specs that must be met and the product testing required, the benefits that will be emphasized, the pricing strategy, and even production equipment acquisition (high-volume versus low-volume).

Criteria for Market Selection

What are the criteria for selecting the target market (and product concept) from among a list of options? What criteria should Fibernyle management use for their plastic aerosol? Several straightforward criteria apply:

- *Segment attractiveness:* Which segment is the most attractive in terms of its market size, growth, and future potential?
- *Competitive situation:* In which segment is the competition the least, the weakest, or the most vulnerable?
- *Fit:* Where is the best fit between the needs, wants, and preferences of each segment and the benefits, features, and technological possibilities of your product?

- *Ease of access:* Which of the segments is the easiest for your company to reach in its selling effort, distribution channels, and so forth?
- *Relative advantage:* In which segment do you have the greatest advantage over competitors in terms of product features and benefits, as well as other facets of your entry strategy? Note that "fit" and "ease of access" are not enough; they suggest mere adequacy. You must also look for areas in which you have a strong likelihood of outdoing your competitors.
- *Profitability:* It all boils down to profits! In which segment are you most likely to meet your sales and profits objectives?

Product Strategy

The definition of the product strategy—exactly what the product will be—goes hand in hand with the selection of the target market. Remember our discussion of the product definition: The product definition defines the target market and the product strategy. Target market definition and product strategy, together, are the leading edge of strategy development and are front and center in the development of the marketing plan (see Figure 10.1).

What is meant by "product strategy"? For a new product there can be three or four components to the term.

The Product's Positioning

Product positioning is a combination of market segmentation and product differentiation. "Positioning" in the marketplace means "how the product will be perceived by potential customers versus competitive products." It's the continuation of the sentence, "Our product is the one that . . . ." The position is usually defined in terms of key underlying dimensions by which customers perceive and differentiate among competitive makes. For example, traditionally a Volvo is an automobile that is . . . what? It's safe, reliable, and lasts a long time (and is perhaps somewhat boxy and boring). By contrast, a BMW 500 series is . . . ? It certainly isn't boxy and boring. No, it's been carefully positioned by BMW as the ultimate driving machine. The two cars have very different positioning, yet technically the they are fairly similar. Note how in recent years Volvo is striving to change its traditional positioning by combining the "safe and reliable" strategy with a "fun to drive and sporty" positioning.

Step 1 in defining the product strategy is the specification of the product's positioning—usually a sentence or two defining how the product will be positioned in the market and in customers' minds, relative to competitive products and in terms of benefits offered. If you can't write down a clear, concise, and meaningful positioning statement, chances are you're headed for trouble. A fuzzy positioning statement is usually an indication of fuzzy thinking—no product strategy or, at best, only a vague notion of strategy.

Product Benefits and Value Proposition

The benefits that the product will deliver to the customer should be delineated. Remember: A benefit is not a feature, although the two can be closely connected. A feature is part of the product's design—a physical thing. A benefit is in the eye of the beholder—some characteristic that is of value to the customer. The acid test of a benefit is this: "If the customer won't pay more for it, chances are it's not a benefit!" For example, in the design of a new garden tractor, a benefit might be ease of use by elderly people. Corresponding features that translate into this benefit might be a clutchless transmission, a hydraulic lift mechanism for the mower deck, and power-assisted steering.

Hand in hand with product benefits is the value proposition: What is the product's value to the customer? This value proposition is usually a single and simple sentence that explains why the customer would buy this product over another—what's the inducement?

Features and Attributes

Step 3 is to translate the desired benefits and the value proposition into features, attributes, and product requirements. This step is likely to result in a much longer list of items, one that gets very close to defining the product specifications. Here is where QFD may help (see Chapter 7). For example, in the case of a highway truck, if one benefit of the proposed vehicle is that it is "quick and easy to repair and maintain," then the corresponding list of features or product requirements might include the following:

- ✓ a quick-disconnect radiator: 2–4 butterfly bolts, several hose connections, and the rad is out
- ✓ facility to drop the engine between the frame rails—the engine is out in half an hour
- ✓ color-coded hoses and wiring with quick connecters—snap in, snap out for easy replacement
- ✓ modularized electrics in the dashboard so that faulty modules can be pulled and replaced in minutes
- ✓ 90 degree tilt engine bonnet for easy engine access

This three-step procedure—defining the position, outlining the benefits and value proposition, and itemizing the product features, attributes, and requirements—is a logical lead-in to the development of product specifications. This fourth and final facet of the product strategy is an exact definition of what the product will be, and something tangible the development group can work toward. In some projects, detailed product specs may not be possible at this point, and creative solutions by the development team may be required.

The Internet and Product Strategy

Products can be custom designed for customers, almost instantaneously, using Internet-based direct selling or marketing. Witness the example of Dell Computers. Through the Internet, the consumer can custom tailor his new computer—specifying what memory, speed, modem, hard drive, and other features he wants. This is a far cry from the "take what we offer" based on a handful of standard models available in most computer retail outlets.

The implication is this: Suppliers can now offer a much wider range of product or service packages—an infinite array of product variants and bundles of features. Let the customer design their own product, much like Dell does. This gives you enormous competitive advantage over the "fixed package" approach of your competitors.

> Recently I went to the private banking service of a major North American bank to inquire about their high-end service offerings. They offered me a service package option—for which I had to pay extra—that covered the waterfront. The salesperson stressed that I could get guaranteed personal loans up to a large dollar maximum. I explained that I had paid off all my loans and that I typically don't borrow money—I am a partner in a consulting business with a positive cash flow. He went on to explain that this private banking service package offered *preferred interest rates* on any loans I could want. I told him again I didn't want to borrow money. I asked about investment counseling and investment services, especially in international markets. He said the package did not cover that. I left.

The point is that this bank had designed a "fixed" service offering, likely based on extensive market research. The trouble is, they came up with a product aimed at the "average person" in this target market. But *no one is average*, including you and me, and so often the product does not quite fit us perfectly. Now imagine that you are a banker and that you can offer your small business clients an infinite array of product features—put "product design in your customer's hands"—so that they can pick and choose (and only pay for) the features and options they really need. What a deal for the customer! And what an advantage for you.

Now one can launch products and modify them on the fly . . . literally designing the product in real time. For example, the approach is to launch Version 1 of the new service, and then let the customer make choices on options or features they want through the Internet. Some of the product options offered on your web page may not even be available yet, but by recording the number of "customer votes" for certain features or options, the fast-paced developer can design and release Version 2 to suit these customer requests. This real time product development offers significant advantages in terms of responding to market needs in record time.

The Supporting Elements of the Market Launch Plan

By now the leading edge of the marketing plan has been developed—the target market and product strategy. The top of the pyramid in Figure 10.1 is in place. Now come the supporting strategies, the remaining blocks in the structure. These are the elements of the marketing mix that will support the product launch. Let's have a quick look at the more critical ones.

Channels and E-Channels

You know that e-commerce has really arrived when icons of the old economy make enthusiastic pronouncements like Jack Welch, CEO of General Electric: "You have to be in e-commerce in every element of your business, in all of your supply chain, in all of your information flow, in all of your communications, in all of your customer interactions. This is not some activity outside the business—this *is* the business. It's like breathing when you come to work!"[2]

The advent of e-commerce and the Internet has introduced many new possibilities in product development.[3] It has also presented some major challenges! The obvious opportunities are in the *launch phase or roll-out* of the new product: the use of an e-commerce channel to direct-sell your new product and the implications of using that channel. Just in case you become too focused on the Internet as a direct-marketing channel, note that there are other less obvious but potentially higher-impact marketing and design implications, as in the banking example above, and some are very provocative to the product developer.[4] But here are some that impact directly on channels:

1. The supplier can now sell directly to the end user or ultimate customer. The traditional intermediary or middleman can be cut out or "dis-intermediated." An estimated 22 percent of automobiles in the United States are sold through the Internet. What does this mean to General Motors, whose traditional strength has been its dealership on every corner? Dell Computers and Gateway are posing major threats to other PC makers who use traditional channels (Hewlett-Packard and Compaq). IBM has switched its distribution of laptops from traditional retail outlets to the Internet. Schwab launched its on-line stock purchase service, and now over half of its business is conducted through this channel. The Thomson Corporation announced that it has sold its chain of sixty newspapers, while it is developing e-information and e-commerce products as quickly as it can. Morgan Stanley Dean Witter predicts that at some point within the next three to five years, the Internet will account *for all GDP growth!*

The bottom line is this: Your market launch, channel, and marketing options are suddenly much different than they were a few years ago. If your new products have the potential to be sold through the Internet—and most do—then chances are your competition is already working on development of an e-channel! Products that are being sold over the Internet include myriad products and services: plastics and paper, banking services, commodity chemicals, investment brokerage, cattle, insurance, computers, books, toys, mobile and other telephone services, bandwidth, small package delivery, travel and tourism, and even steel.

At a minimum, you *must include e-commerce* and the Internet in your new product development. The good news is that this opens up all kinds of new product/new channel possibilities for you, potentially leading to competitive advantages and increased sales and profits. The bad news: Your traditional channel strategies may have become obsolete for your next product launch!

Here is what e-commerce means to your new product launch plans: You must rethink your distribution channel emphasis. At a minimum, use the Internet to provide product information through an on-line catalogue or sales brochure. But look hard at the option of using the Internet as a selling channel where prices can be set, deals made, and sales closed.

Companies in the service sector must pay special attention to Internet sales. Because service products are intangible, they are *particularly well suited for sale over the Internet*. When you buy a tangible product—a new dress, a new suit, or even a new car—chances are you want to experience it first—try it on or take it for a test drive. But with services, there is no test drive or try on. Customers have become accustomed to buying new service products for years without trying them first; hence, services are particularly amenable to Internet sales.

For companies in business-to-business industries, where you are dealing with large customers, you can be sure that Internet-based supply chains must be part of your market launch plan. Some major purchasers have set up web-marketplaces: Think of an electronic bazaar or auction—a place where buyers and sellers exchange information, bid on goods, seal deals, and arrange delivery.[5] For example, Auto Exchange has been established by General Motors, Ford, and DaimlerChrysler as a procurement hub. There are other B2B web-marketplaces, too: GEPolymerland (by GE Plastics); Petrocosm (an oil and gas marketplace owned by Texaco and Chevron); and Rooster.com (a Cargill and DuPont web site where farmers can buy equipment and supplies). Whether the web-marketplaces are owned by you, the supplier (as in GEPolymerland); by several suppliers (as in Rooster.com), by a consortium of purchasers (as in Auto Exchange), or by an independently operated procurement or selling hub (such as PlasticsNet), the implications are clear. For many of you, a mandatory element to be built into your launch plan is an e-channel.

2. There are no geographic monopolies anymore. Even if you're the only bank or travel agent in town, or the major brokerage company in a metropolitan area, it no longer guarantees you customer loyalty or a guaranteed market. Through e-commerce, service providers in other parts of the country, and from even other countries, can invade your private domain. Likewise, you can access their local markets, too, opening up all kinds of new market opportunities for the innovator.

ING, a Dutch bank, has mounted a major marketing initiative on the Internet to attract customers in Canada. Through television advertising and a web-page address, the bank has picked up thousands of retail clients who normally banked at domestic Canadian banks.

The removal of geographic boundaries means a much higher potential for profit for the successful innovator. Traditionally, businesses were restricted to the areas that their sales offices, distributors, or outlets covered . . . but no longer. This geographic freedom *multiplies the potential market size* for your new product by orders of magnitude. It also means that you may have to innovate more often and more quickly, because now your competition can come from anywhere; it's no longer just the organization down the street or even across the country.

Pricing Strategy

How does one go about pricing a new product? It is difficult to generalize, but there are some basic guidelines.

1. What is the product's target market and positioning strategy? Before you reach your pricing decision, both the target market and the product's positioning strategy must be specified. For example, if the product is aimed at a "niche" market, one with specialized needs, and if the positioning is a highly differentiated one, in essence you have a mini-monopoly situation; For that target market, yours is the one and only product. A premium price strategy is likely the route to follow. Conversely, if the product is not well differentiated from competitive products, and if the target market is served by others, a competitive pricing policy is appropriate.

Just in case you're tempted to enter the market on a "low-ball" price basis (that is, using a low price as a means of gaining market share), remember that price is the easiest strategy for a competitor to counter, whereas a product advantage may take years to match. Similarly, an advantage gained through a clever promotional program, a unique channel, e-marketing or superior distribution effort, or a massive selling campaign may force the competitor to play catch-up ball for months or even years. In contrast, a price advantage is usually temporary; it can be countered tomorrow morning with a simple e-mail to all salespeople, dealers, and distributors announcing a similar price cut.

Our NewProd studies confirm the fact that a low price entry strategy for a new product doesn't work all that well. For example, low price was not found to have any impact on new product success. Similarly, our NewProd study of the chemical industry found that of all the elements of product advantage found in new chemical products, low price was one of the few that was not correlated with success.[6] The message here is not that price is unimportant. Of course it is! Offering good value for money and being price-competitive are essential to success. But *low price as the leading edge of strategy for new products may not be a winning strategy.* There is a big difference between being price-competitive (offering good value for money) and electing a low price strategy!

It does make sense, however, to use price as a leading weapon when you have a sustainable and real cost advantage: when your costs are truly lower than competitors' by virtue of product design, low-cost access to raw material, cheaper labor, or higher production volumes. Unfortunately, most firms are not in the position of being *best cost producers,* especially in the case of a product new to the company. A low price decision means sacrificing immediate profits in order to "buy" market share for the future, or to open a window for future new products. (These topics are discussed in more detail below.)

2. *What are the other strategic issues?* There are a number of strategic issues that may affect your pricing decisions.

Skimming versus penetration

One school of thought argues that a pricing policy that yields low selling prices, high volumes, and low production costs is desirable. The profit per unit is low, but bigger profits come from volume. Usually, a larger investment in production facilities is required. The idea is to dominate the market through penetration pricing and to reap the long-term rewards of a leading market share. An assessment of your own strengths and weaknesses, your financial capacity and risk averseness, the slope of the learning or experience curve (costs versus cumulative production volume), the price sensitivity of the marketplace, and possible competitive reactions will dictate whether such a policy is a viable option.

The high-volume, low-price policy has many adherents. The PIMS studies (Profit Impact of Market Strategy) point to market dominance and high market shares as the key to profitability.[7] Similarly, the BCG model (the Boston Consulting Group's approach to strategic planning) relies heavily on experience curves and on gaining market share as the keys to having a portfolio of "star products."[8]

The alternative to high volumes and low prices is a skimming policy. The new product is aimed at the market segment for which the product has the most value, and which will pay a premium for it. Profit per unit is high, but volumes are lower. Investment in production facilities is also lower, so the risk is often lower. Although the product may never dominate the entire market, it may dominate the one segment and prove very profitable.

A combination of the two strategies is also possible. A skimming strategy is implemented to start with, attacking the high-value market segments. The initial risk is low. If the product gains acceptance, and when the investment is partly paid back, then a penetration policy is adopted: increase production, drop prices, and go for dominance across the entire market. Timing is critical. The shift must take place before competitors invest in the development and production of similar products.

Overall business strategy

The new product's pricing must be established in the light of your business's overall strategy. The new product is not a "stand-alone" item; it is part of a grander plan. For example, senior management may have decided that a specific market or product category is top priority and will commit significant resources, at a loss if necessary, to gain a foothold in the market. The new product may be the advance landing party that will sustain heavy losses while paving the way for more profitable future entries. Normal pricing practices may give way to larger issues.

3. *What is the product's value?*   All new product pricing boils down to an assessment of the product's value or worth to the customer. Value, like beauty, is in the eye of the beholder—the customer, in this case. Value is subjective; perceptions vary with the buyer. The price is objective, set by the seller. Ideally, the price accurately reflects the product's value.

Because two people can look at the same product, however, and judge it to have a different value, the first question to ask is, Who values the product? If you've done an effective job in defining the target market, that question will have been answered. The next question is, What is the product's value or worth? In assessing value to the customer, one usually looks at what the customer's options are. If similar products are available to the customer, then your product's value is simply the price of the alternative to the customer, plus or minus a bit, depending on the advantages of your product, service delivery, reputation, and so on, relative to the competitor's product. In pricing in highly competitive markets characterized by relatively homogeneous products, start with competitive prices and work upward or downward from there.

If your product is significantly different from what is now on the market, it is often possible to impute a value by comparing the product's worth relative to the product the customer is now using to solve his or her problem.

> For example, some years ago, a firm introduced a new building material aimed at builders of prefab homes. The product was a 4 by 8 foot panel of very thin bricks attached to a backer sheet and was designed to replace conventional brickwork on the exterior of a prefab home. The product's main advantage was that it could be factory-installed, thus eliminating on-site labor. The product was an innovation, so there were no directly competitive products upon which to base a pricing policy. The customer's alternative was conventional bricklaying at the job site; the value of the new product to the customer was calculated based on those material and labor costs.

When the new product has economic benefits to the customer—for example, measurable cost savings, as in the brick panel example above—a value-in-use can be calculated and used as a standard for the product's value to the customer. The product's value sets the upper limit on price.

4. If in doubt, research the customer.   Often, the only way to assess accurately the product's value to the customer is through market research. This research can be combined with the concept test or the product tests. There are several ways to gauge product worth and price sensitivity:

- Ask the potential buyer, "What is the maximum price at which you would buy this product?" Naturally, you'll get different answers from different people, but plotting "percentage of respondents (cumulative)" versus "maximum price" gives an indication of price sensitivity (or price elasticity).
- In measuring the intent to purchase, expose different groups of people to different prices. For example, divide your research sample into three groups. Present the product concept to group A at price 1, to group B at price 2, and to group C at price 3. Measure the intent to purchase, and plot "the percentage who said definitely yes" versus "price level." Again, this curve gives an indication of price sensitivity.
- Use trade-off analysis in your concept tests. Different versions of the same product are presented to the respondent. The product can be varied along a number of possible dimensions, of which price is one. Sophisticated data analysis is used to determine the utility (or worth) of different features or attributes to the user.
- A test market or trial sell (perhaps as part of your field trials or beta tests) also can be used as an experiment to test different price strategies.

5. What is the contribution profit?   The place to start a pricing analysis is at the top line, not the bottom line, of a profit analysis. The first question to ask is, At what price might the product sell? Based on the assessment of the product's value to the customer, there will probably be a range of possible prices—several possible prices to consider.

Next, consider the contribution profit per unit. Contribution profit is the selling price less variable costs per unit (direct labor, materials, sales commissions, and so on). This contribution profit at each proposed selling price is crucial. It tells us the relative volumes we must sell at each price in order to make the same annual profit. The contribution profit analysis thus gives significant clues as to the direction in which our pricing policy should move.

Now it's time to start thinking about possible sales volumes at the different prices. Often the sales volumes need only be educated guesses. The total contribution profit is found by multiplying relative volumes at the different prices by the contribution per unit. This figure signals the best price (or at least the price that yields the maximum expected contribution profit).

Usually, estimates of expected volumes at different prices are highly uncertain, even after conducting extensive market research, so use sensitivity analysis. That is, chose pessimistic, likely, and optimistic estimates of volumes at each price, and produce three sets of contribution profit calculations. Chances are that you'll see that the "best price" doesn't change all that much as you move from pessimistic to optimistic scenarios.

6. Consider promotional pricing. There can be a big difference between the ongoing or "normal" price and the introductory price of a new product. The pricing calculations, market research, and positioning strategy may all point to a premium price. But management may lose heart and feel that the price is too high to induce initial sales. A lower, less than optimal, price may be chosen. If obtaining initial trials is a major problem, don't sacrifice a well-conceived pricing strategy to do so. An introductory "promotional" price can be used to induce those first sales.

Promotional pricing can take many forms. For consumer goods, it can be coupons, a cents-off deal, or a company rebate. For industrial goods, a simple explanation that an introductory price is being offered to the first customers to buy the product or to beta-test customers will suffice.

7. E-commerce affects pricing strategies. Since the Internet has, for some product categories, become a real-time auction, your pricing strategies may have to change. One might plan a product launch where pricing is fluid—where customer demand (or its lack) creates real-time pricing adjustments during the launch phase. Pricing is infinitely fluid! To accomplish this, you might have to build a real-time, on-line pricing learning model into your launch.

Another option is to become part of a web-based auction, which is like a traditional auction—set up to help the seller get the best price (such as eMerge's cattle auctions). Or you might consider becoming part of an on-line exchange, which offers constant price adjustments as supply and demand ebb and flow (such as Altra Energy Technologies or Rooster.com).

☞ **Suggestion:** Although pricing is one of the most critical decisions of the new product's marketing strategy, all too often the pricing decision is handled in a sloppy fashion. Moreover, too often managers get locked into a "cost plus" mentality; prices are based on costs rather than on what the product is worth to the customer. In this section, seven key points to remember have been highlighted. Use this list the next time you face a new product pricing decision. The result will be a much more thoughtful approach to pricing and usually a better decision.

Advertising and Marketing Communications: Getting the Message Across

A company can have the best product in the world and sell it at a fair price. If no one knows about it, however, the battle is lost. The product's virtues must be communicated to its target market. Advertising is an effective communication tool.

E-Communications

Your marketing communications and advertising strategy must change as you shift to new economy marketing techniques. Yesterday, you controlled the advertising or marketing communications through traditional electronic or print mass media and through direct mail, but the Internet has changed all that. No longer do you control what information the customer sees—rather, he or she does! With the click of a mouse, the customer can turn off your message and switch to a competitor's web page. Even more unsettling is that people and businesses are turning to the web for product information like never before, which means that traditional media are increasingly taking a backseat. Procter & Gamble, one of the world's largest advertisers, spent about 2–3 percent on Internet advertising in 2000, but that figure is expected to rise to 20–30 percent of its total advertising dollars in the near future.

Steps in Developing Your Communications Plan for Launch

Normally, the marketing communications plan is developed by an advertising agency or an in-house advertising or graphics department. The new product project leader is often tempted to wash his or her hands of the advertising function—to subcontract this facet of the marketing plan and assume that "those advertising folks will handle it."

This attitude is wrong. An effective advertising campaign begins with the project leader. Although the details of the media plan and development of the "creative" (the artwork and copy) may be the task of others, the communications strategy itself is the project leader's responsibility. Here are some simple "before" and "after" steps that can be taken to ensure a more effective advertising effort for the new product.

Before meeting with the advertising agency (the term "agency" is used to denote either an outside or in-house group), here's what to do:

1. Specify the communications objectives. Advertising can do many things. It creates awareness, knowledge, and understanding. It can shape attitudes and create a desire or a preference for a product. In the case of direct marketing, it can even create a sale. Advertising can do all these wonderful things—for a cost! Before talking to the agency, pin down *what you want your marketing communications to do for you and your new product.* The product's advertising objectives should be specific and quantifiable. Some examples include the following:

- ✓ to create an awareness, within three months of launch, among 50 percent of the defined target market, that Product X is now available
- ✓ in six months, to have 30 percent of municipal water engineers, buyers, and consultants aware that a new water pipe is corrosion resistant and has doubled the life of a traditional ductile iron pipe

The role of advertising in the total selling effort must be decided before specifying detailed advertising objectives: How much of the communications job will advertising do, and how much will be done by the sales force or other mechanisms? For example, do you want your web page to help create awareness and provide a minimal amount of product knowledge? Or will awareness be created through another medium and your web-page will provide detailed product information? (Some pharmaceutical companies use television or magazine ads to create awareness and refer the target user to their web page for much more in-depth product information.) Or will your web page take the customer from awareness right through to purchase—a direct selling tool?

2. *Specify the target market and positioning strategy.* Good advertising people will insist on knowing these in detail. Without a clear definition of the target market, how can they design a media plan? And without a positioning strategy, how will they know what the message is to be?

3. *Describe the target market.* The project leader must provide as much detail as possible on the target market and how it behaves: demographics, locations, occupations, and so on. Other types of segmentation may have been used, such as benefit or volume segmentation. That's fine for most of the elements of the marketing strategy, such as product design, pricing, and so on. But remember, the advertising industry, and certainly the media plan facet, still relies heavily on traditional segmentation variables in the choice of appropriate media. For consumer products, readership and viewership are still reported in terms of age, sex, and income and for industrial goods by industry and by the audience's occupation or position.

4. *Communicate the product to the agency.* The agency should study the product thoroughly before embarking on campaign development. You can help by providing as much detail as possible on how the product works, how it is used, and what its benefits, features, and attributes are.

With these four key steps in place, it's time to turn the advertising development over to the agency. The agency will devise a media plan—which media will be used, the frequency and timing of appearance, and the budget allocation—and the advertisement itself. When the agency presents the results of its efforts, the project leader must once again become a key player in development of the advertising plan.

5. *Review the plan and approve.* The review and approval of the proposed advertising and communications plan is next. The steps are as follows:

Review the media plan.

The essential question is whether the proposed media plan will reach the target audience with the desired frequency. The plan should specify the *expected reach* and *frequency* of the campaign: how many potential customers the campaign will reach, who these people are, and how often they will receive a message.

First, look at each medium recommended by the agency and, in particular, at the readership or viewership of that medium. Then compare that with the defined target audience and the advertising objectives. Second, determine how often the target customer will be hit with a message. The choice of frequency is largely based on experience. A good rule of thumb is that it takes at least three impressions for a person to get a message. A mere awareness of your product is likely to require a minimum frequency of three; more ambitious objectives— knowledge of product benefits or features, liking, or preference—will require a higher frequency.

Review the creative.
Does the message back the product's position? Does it get across the product's benefits to the reader or viewer? An ad may be extremely creative and artistic and may even win awards. However, the real purpose of an ad is effective communication of the product. Don't feel shy about asking probing questions and critiquing the ad's potential effectiveness as a communication piece.

Run tests on the creative.
If the advertising budget for the product is large enough, you may want to test the ad. For example, the pre-test market procedure described in Chapter 9 can be used to perform a test of an ad's effectiveness. Another method is to measure customers' preferences for products on a list before and after viewing the ad. The advertising agency will be able to design appropriate testing procedures.

For low-budget campaigns, the testing should be done on a smaller scale and at a lower cost. There's no sense spending $50,000 to test the effectiveness of a $200,000 ad budget! Advertising for industrial products, for example, is often a low-budget element and may take the form of a brochure, a direct mailing, a web page, or trade journal advertising. You should still test, however. Obtain feedback on your proposed ad by exposing it to a handful of customers, either individually or as part of a focus group, to measure its suitability and effectiveness. When designing a web page, be sure to test it on a few potential users first. Most web pages are anything but user friendly, and many communicate very poorly.

Assess the worth of the objectives.
Now comes the tough question. The proposed plan from the agency will include a budget. Review the advertising budget with the original objectives in mind. You can then decide whether to accept the costs as reasonable in light of the objectives or to back off on some of the objectives—perhaps they were too ambitious to start with.

6. *Build in measurement.*   The only way to know whether the advertising plan is achieving its objectives is to build in some techniques of measurement.

Decide, with the agency, how advertising effectiveness will be measured. This will usually involve a market research study. For example, if one of the advertising objectives was that "in six months, 30 percent of municipal engineers will know that our pipe has double the life of the competitor," then plan to take a representative sample of municipal engineers in six months. Ask them what they know about the new kind of pipe. If significantly less than 30 percent of the sample don't know that is has double the life of the competitor, then the ad didn't achieve its objective. Commercial services are an alternative to market research. Such services regularly measure viewership or readership of ads in various media.

☞ **Suggestion:** You've probably heard someone remark that 50 percent of advertising dollars are wasted. The problem is that no one knows which 50 percent! It's true that advertising is very much an art. Well-informed advertising decisions can be made, however. Use the "before" and "after" steps and rules outlined in this section; be tough on the advertising people, and see if you can't improve this important element of the launch effort.

Sales Force Decisions

For the majority of new products, sales force decisions will be straightforward: The product will be sold by the company's existing sales force and/or through its existing distribution system. In the gating or project selection process, several important questions will have been asked. Will the product be sold to a market we now serve? Will the product be sold to our existing customers? Will the product be sold by our sales force and/or through our present distribution system?

If the answers to these questions are "yes"—and they are for most new product projects that pass the early gates—then the sales force plan boils down to tactical issues:

- ✓ training the sales force in the selling of the new product,
- ✓ providing the sales force with the appropriate selling aids,
- ✓ devoting effort to the new product (for example, developing a call plan with the sales force to introduce the product), and
- ✓ motivating and incentivizing the sales force (doing "internal marketing" to ensure that the sales force enthusiastically supports the new product).

Don't underestimate this last item. In some companies, this internal marketing effort—getting the sales force on your side—is as critical (and almost as time-consuming) as the external marketing program!

For some new products, however, the use of the existing company sales force and/or distribution system may be inappropriate. If changes or additions to your sales force are to be made, two important questions must be answered:

- What is the nature of the selling job for the new product?
- Is the nature of the selling job compatible with the talents, training, and the way the current sales force (or distributor) operates?

An example:

A manufacturer of scientific lasers and instruments marketed a product line of nitrogen lasers and other light sources in a low price range, typically $1,000 to $5,000 per unit. Its "sales force" consisted of a network of manufacturers' reps throughout North America, Europe, and Japan who called on scientific accounts. As scientific products went, the sale was a relatively simple one. The product was easily understood by buyers; it was easy to explain and demonstrate on site by salespeople; it was a low-risk purchase item; and the client's purchase decision was typically quick and uncomplicated.

A new product introduced by the firm represented a significant departure. Unlike the simple lasers, this new optical instrument was a system—a sophisticated unit, priced at about $200,000. It could not be demonstrated on site; many people were involved in a lengthy purchasing process; considerable explanation of the system's features was required; and it was a high-risk purchase decision for the customer. Naively, the company moved the new product through its usual sales force system. The product manager was available to the reps for backup. Not surprisingly, the reps failed to perform. The selling task was so different from that for the usual products the reps handled that they were simply unable to cope with the new product.

In making sales force decisions for your new product—whether to use your existing sales force, hire a new sales force, work with a partner, or use a third party (a middleman)—the decision rests on a few critical factors:

- ✓ the fit between the nature of the selling job for the new product and the talents, training, and operating methods of the sales force—how they sell now,
- ✓ the degree of control over the selling effort that you need to exercise, and
- ✓ the relative costs of each option, and whether those costs are fixed or variable.

Other Supporting Strategies

The main elements of the launch are now in place: the product and target market definition, the pricing strategy, the marketing communications program, and the sales force effort. The remaining elements, not discussed in detail here, are physical distribution, promotion, customer service, and warranties. Each of these remaining elements is critical to the success of the new product, of course, and each must be built into the launch plan. Fortunately, most of the remaining elements are in place as ongoing programs in your company, and it's simply a matter of making use of what's already there for your new product.

Marketing Planning and the *Stage-Gate*™ New Product Process

You will have noticed that the marketing-planning process, outlined in Figure 10.1, closely parallels the *Stage-Gate* new product process. Indeed, if Figure 10.1 is superimposed on the new product process shown in Figure 10.3, key marketing-planning steps correspond to the various stages of the new product process. For example, the first few steps of developing the marketing plan—setting objectives and undertaking a situation size-up—correspond to the two up-front stages of *Stage-Gate*. Target market definition and defining product strategy are critical facets of Stage 2, Building the Business Case—the key stage just preceding product development. Thus, the marketing-planning process gets underway much earlier in the game than many people might imagine.

The Final Step: The "Financials"

The financial statements are an integral part of any launch plan. They cover two topics:

- ✓ what the plan will cost to implement (the budget), and
- ✓ what the plan will achieve (sales and profits projections).

The "financials" are detailed pro-forma profit-and-loss statements for the new product for Year 1, Year 2, Year 3, and so forth—in essence, a financial plan for the project.

Most new product project leaders and teams are somewhat suspicious of financial people. They tend to view them as too narrow (strictly financially driven), too short-term, and too prone to kill a project prematurely, and so the project team tries to avoid financial people, financial scrutiny, and financial analysis. Although the new products game is very much future-oriented, and as noted in Chapter 8, financial analysis must be used with caution, this is one time when a solid financial analysis and a financial plan are essential.

The financial plan is important for several reasons. First, it serves as a budget for the new product—an itemized accounting of how much will be spent, and where. Second, the financial plan is the critical input for the final go/kill decisions as the project moves closer and closer to full launch and commercial production. The expected return from the product can be computed from the financial plan. Finally, the financial plan provides benchmarks. These benchmarks are critical to the control phase of the launch plan—making sure that the

FIGURE 10.3   How the Development of a Launch Plan Overlaps the *Stage-Gate* Process

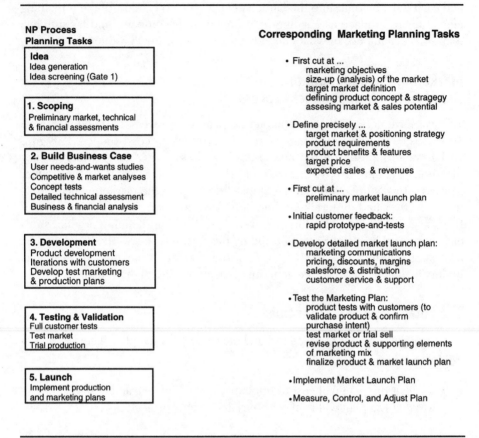

NP Process Planning Tasks

Idea
Idea generation
Idea screening (Gate 1)

1. Scoping
Preliminary market, technical & financial assessments

2. Build Business Case
User needs-and-wants studies
Competitive & market analyses
Concept tests
Detailed technical assessment
Business & financial analysis

3. Development
Product development
Iterations with customers
Develop test marketing & production plans

4. Testing & Validation
Full customer tests
Test market
Trial production

5. Launch
Implement production and marketing plans

Corresponding Marketing Planning Tasks

• First cut at ...
    marketing objectives
    size-up (analysis) of the market
    target market definition
    defining product concept & stragegy
    assesing market & sales potential

• Define precisely ...
    target market & positioning strategy
    product requirements
    product benefits & features
    target price
    expected sales & revenues

• First cut at ...
    preliminary market launch plan

• Initial customer feedback:
    rapid prototype-and-tests

• Develop detailed market launch plan:
    marketing communications
    pricing, discounts, margins
    salesforce & distribution
    customer service & support

• Test the Marketing Plan:
    product tests with customers (to
    validate product & confirm
    purchase intent)
    test market or trial sell
    revise product & supporting elements
    of marketing mix
    finalize product & market launch plan

• Implement Market Launch Plan

• Measure, Control, and Adjust Plan

new product is on course. A launch plan should also include contingency plans for actions to be taken if the results deviate from the expected course.

In developing a launch plan, and particularly for the first attempt or first iteration for a specific new product, the financial plan is often the acid test. Any major discrepancies in strategic thinking are discovered and dealt with at this point; for example, there may be major differences between the objectives and the financials. The original sales and profit objectives set out at the beginning of the planning exercise may be miles apart from the sales and profits spelled out in the financial projections. Or there may be inconsistencies between costs of achievement and expected results. The financials often reveal that the costs of implementing the plan are simply not warranted by the results the plan will achieve.

The existence of such discrepancies is no surprise. The marketing-planning exercise is very much an iterative one. This was the first attempt—a roughed-out, tentative plan. Now go back to the beginning of the planning exercise, and start again—the refining process. Rethink the objectives; redo the size-up; reformulate the launch programs; recalculate the financials. These iterations take time and effort, so it's important that you begin this marketing-planning exercise early in the new product process—ideally before Gate 3.

As the product moves closer and closer to the launch, and with each successive iteration and refinement to the plan, the launch plan starts to crystallize. And if the homework, tests, and trials have been properly executed, it should be a matter of clear sailing into a successful launch . . . with another winner on your hands!

Implementing the *Stage-Gate*™ New Product Process in Your Company

There is nothing more difficult to carry out, nor more doubtful of success, nor more dangerous to handle than to initiate a new order of things. For the reformer has enemies from all those who profit by the old order, and only lukewarm defenders in all those who would profit by the new order, this lukewarmness arising partly from their fear of their adversaries, who have the laws in their favor, and partly from the incredulity of mankind, who do not truly believe in anything new until they have had actual experience of it.
—Machiavelli, *The Prince,* 1532

Let's Implement *Stage-Gate*™

So when do we start? Let's do it!

You've just about finished reading this book; you've talked to a few of your colleagues; you've read a few of the articles referenced here, and a few more. Your company has re-engineered many of its processes and methods, and this *Stage-Gate*™ approach seems to tie in nicely. The prospect of adopting a formal new product process or *Stage-Gate* process in your company is increasingly appealing.

Next you contact a few acquaintances at other firms that have implemented such new product game plans—companies such as 3M, Kodak, Hewlett-Packard, Exxon Chemicals, Corning, Guinness, Lego, Black & Decker, Lucent,

Procter & Gamble, various divisions in DuPont, and others. You learn from these companies that *Stage-Gate* processes do indeed work; they reduce the errors and omissions, they reduce the rework and failure rates, and they even decrease the cycle time. But you also learn from these other companies that *it's not quite as easy and straightforward as it seems.*

For the first part of this chapter, let's consider the results of implementing a formal new product process. Later in the chapter, I'll lay out a step-by-step procedure for implementing *Stage-Gate* and also look at some of the key implementation issues.

Some Evidence: Research Results

Do formal new product processes really work? The PDMA best practices study strongly endorses the *Stage-Gate* approach. Recall from Chapter 3 some of Griffin's conclusions: Although new product development processes are a relatively recent phenomena, they are seen as being necessary for effective new product development (NPD). Her study finds that "the Best [companies] are more likely to use some type of formal NPD process than the Rest (68 percent versus 44 percent)." She notes, however, that "nearly 60 percent of the firms surveyed use some form of *Stage-Gate™* process for NPD. They are more likely to have moved from simpler *Stage-Gate* processes to more sophisticated facilitated or third-generation processes, and are more likely to have had processes in place for a longer period of time."[1] Griffin's major study's results are also supported by a number of other, somewhat smaller studies, also cited in Chapter 3.

The evidence is fairly compelling. The best firms all seem to have a *Stage-Gate* process, or one like it, in place. Indeed more than half the companies in Griffin's study had adopted a *Stage-Gate* process. But wait . . . our experience suggests that this figure is misleading. Sixty-eight percent of firms *say* they have a *Stage-Gate* process in place, but my best guess that only half of them have got it right; the rest are going through the motions. The difference is in the implementation, which is the topic of this chapter.

Are the Performance Results Positive?

The overwhelming evidence suggests the performance results are positive. *Stage-Gate* processes really work, according to the managers who took part in our in-depth study of their firms' new product processes.[2] However, this was a fairly biased sample; these were firms deliberately chosen because they had indeed implemented a *Stage-Gate* process, and they appeared to have done it well—in short they represent "best practice."[3]

Managers were first asked to assess the *overall contribution* of their formal new product process to their company's development program. A five-point scale ranging from 1 to 5 (from "highly negative impact" to "highly positive impact") was used. The results are clear: Managers wholeheartedly endorse the

FIGURE 11.1   Overall Contribution of Systematic New Product Process

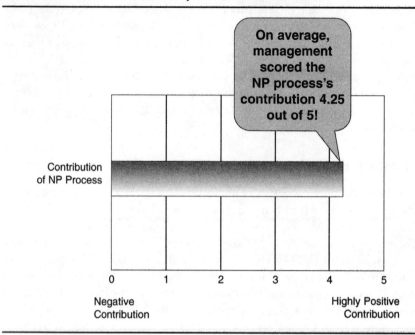

SOURCE: R. G. Cooper and E. J. Kleinschmidt, *Formal Processes for Managing New Products: The Industry Experience* (Hamilton, Ont., Canada: McMaster University, 1991).

new product process, the mean score being 4.25 out of 5 (see Figure 11.1). Comments were enthusiastic:

> "It's critical for success!"
> "It keeps us on track and streamlines the process [of product development]."
> "The process requires marketing people to do analysis up front—what the market needs is very clearly defined now."

No system designed to improve product innovation is without its weaknesses. And there were some cautious assessments, too:

> "A positive contribution . . . a little bureaucratic, but otherwise good."
> "It has created some time consuming steps, but the overall effect is good."

The *specific performance results* achieved by implementing *Stage-Gate* processes are also impressive. Managers were asked to describe the results of implementing a new product process in their own firm—an open-ended, "top-of-mind" discussion. The discussion comments were coded and categorized to identify and rank areas of major impact.

Improved product success rates, higher customer satisfaction, and meeting time, quality, and cost objectives are the most frequently cited areas of positive impact (see Figure 11.2). More than one-third of managers, without any prompting, indicated that the process's strongest impact was on the *success rate* of new products and on the *customer satisfaction* achieved. Managers revealed that a much stronger market orientation had been built into their new product game plan and that key activities such as market studies and concept tests were now an integral facet of their product development efforts. The results were positive:

"Product success is more likely now."
"We've managed to greatly improve customer satisfaction."
"Our products really meet market needs, and they succeed more often—fewer failures."

Being *on time and on budget*—that is, meeting project and product objectives—is seen as another payoff from formal processes, as cited by 34 percent of managers. New product processes brought discipline into product development, where previously there had been chaos, and more attention was focused on time schedules, deadlines, and project costs and objectives:

"The projects are on target [now]: on time, and on quality and cost targets."

Being *faster-to-market* and obtaining *better profit performance* from new products are other comments volunteered by the study's participants (see Figure 11.2). There were almost no negative comments in this open-ended discussion of the impact of the formal new product process.

These top-of-mind comments provide some assurance that *Stage-Gate* approaches do work. But there's more! The *degree of improvement* in six key areas was rated on five-point scales (1 = no improvement, 5 = great improvement) to provide quantitative measures of performance impact. The results, given in Figure 11.3, are provocative and provide strong support for implementing a *Stage-Gate* model. On all six dimensions of performance, there was significant improvement. Although answers varied, there were very few instances where "no improvement" was cited. The major benefits of implementing a new product process, in rank order, include the following:

1. *Improved teamwork*. Managers saw significant improvement in interfunctional teamwork. The fact that new product processes stress cross-functional activities and use multifunctional criteria and gatekeepers at each gate promotes and demands this teamwork:

"There is a much smoother transition from lab to manufacturing. Manufacturing is involved [in the project] almost from the beginning."

FIGURE 11.2   Positive Impact of Systematic New Product Process

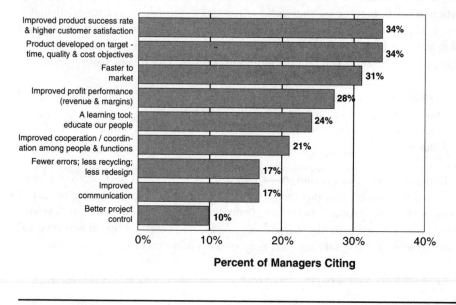

34% of managers intervvviews cited "improved success rates"; 34% also said "on time, cost & quality targets as the major impacts of a formal new product process

Improved product success rate & higher customer satisfaction — 34%
Product developed on target - time, quality & cost objectives — 34%
Faster to market — 31%
Improved profit performance (revenue & margins) — 28%
A learning tool: educate our people — 24%
Improved cooperation / coordination among people & functions — 21%
Fewer errors; less recycling; less redesign — 17%
Improved communication — 17%
Better project control — 10%

Percent of Managers Citing

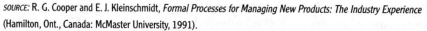

SOURCE: R. G. Cooper and E. J. Kleinschmidt, *Formal Processes for Managing New Products: The Industry Experience* (Hamilton, Ont., Canada: McMaster University, 1991).

"Common priorities are now supported by all functions."
"There are more multifunctional discussions and information exchange, and earlier commitment by marketing and manufacturing."

2. *Less recycling and rework.* The amount of recycle and rework—going back and doing it again—was greatly reduced. New product processes generally have a number of quality checks built into the process to ensure that critical activities are carried out, and in a quality fashion, thereby reducing the incidence of recycle:

"There are fewer design changes late in the project—we get the specs definition right."
"The number of engineering change notices after release to manufacturing has dropped. We keep a detailed record of these."

3. *Improved success rates.* Managers noted that the proportion of new products that succeeded was higher and that the profitability from new

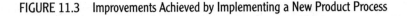

FIGURE 11.3   Improvements Achieved by Implementing a New Product Process

Management noted major improvements on many metrics when a systematic new product process was implemented

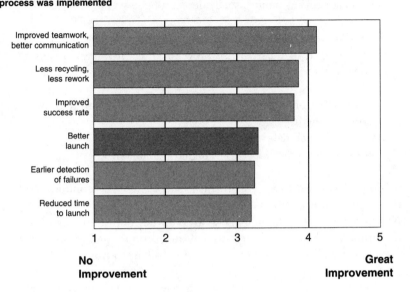

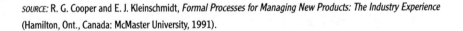

SOURCE: R. G. Cooper and E. J. Kleinschmidt, *Formal Processes for Managing New Products: The Industry Experience* (Hamilton, Ont., Canada: McMaster University, 1991).

products was also greater. The fact that *Stage-Gate* processes build in better project evaluations at the gates (hence, cull out potential failures earlier) and focus more attention on key success activities, such as market studies, sharper and earlier product definition, and customer tests, accounts for this improvement:

> "The number of projects that exceed [sales and profit] targets has risen considerably."
> "There are fewer customer complaints now. Our products are 'right' when production starts."
> "We measure our new product performance based on profit contribution . . . we know the success rate is up."

4. *Earlier detection of failures.* Potential failures were spotted earlier, and either they were killed outright or steps were taken to avert disaster. The use of gates with clear go/kill criteria, typical of most firms' processes, helped to sharpen the project evaluations:

"Checkpoints throughout the process are key to spotting failures."
"We actually kill projects now. In the past, we'd just let them continue."
"Our major review points usually detect weaknesses in projects."

5. *Better launch.* Marketing planning and other market-oriented activities are integral to most firmsß' new product processes, resulting in more involvement in the project by marketing and a better launch:

"There is better internal coordination between marketing and manufacturing."
"We meet launch dates now, and on budget."
"Customer acceptance levels are higher [at launch]."

6. *Shorter elapsed time.* This result is surprising. The common view is that a more thoroughly executed new product project takes more time. Not so, according to the managers interviewed. Better homework, more multifunctional inputs, better market and product definition, and less recycle work all serve to shorten the idea-to-launch time:

"Compared to similar projects prior to having our new process, our times to launch are down."
"The number of iterations in development has been reduced."
"We stay on schedule more often now."

This conclusion on cycle time reduction, although somewhat surprising, has been backed up by another study—this one an extensive internal study within one firm.[4] Here, the time to market for a large number of new product projects was considered, both before and after the implementation of a formal new product process. Cycle times, of course, depend on project complexity, and so a measure of complexity was developed, and cycle times are plotted against this measure (see Figure 11.4). Two plots are shown—"before" and "after" the introduction of a systematic stage-and-gate new product process. The results include the following:

- The stage-and-gate process reduced the cycle time. It reduced the slope of the relationship between time and complexity by about one-third; and it reduced the intercept by one-third (see Figure 11.4). The end result is that the introduction of a formal *Stage-Gate* process cuts cycle time by about one-third for simple projects and by *considerably more than one-third for more complex ones!*
- The formal new product process also made the complexity-time relationship much more predictable. The lower of the two lines in Figure

FIGURE 11.4   Cycle-Time Reduction Using a *Stage-Gate* New Product Process

The use of a Stage-Gate process reduces time to market by about 35%.
It also reduces the "scatter of points" on the chart - predictability of cycle time is much better!

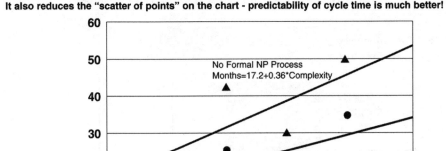

Complexity (% change from previous product)

SOURCE: A. Griffin, "Metrics for measuring product development cycle time," *Journal of Product Innovation Management* 10, 2 (March 1993): 112–125.

11.4—the results seen *after* a new product process was introduced—provides a much better fit for all the data points than the upper "before" line. The unexplained variance, "noise," or unpredictability, in time to market was reduced from 65 percent to 35 percent.

These time-to-market metrics in Figure 11.4 admittedly are limited to the experiences of a single company. But such measures are hard to come by. This metric study, together with our study's more qualitative assessments across a number of firms and business units, provides concrete evidence that *Stage-Gate* processes really do work and also lead to time compression!

The Nature and Use of the New Product Process

The performance results of implementing a new product process are impressive. But what are the characteristics of the process used? Chapter 5 portrayed the typical *Stage-Gate* process, but this was a generic process. Clearly, each company modifies and adapts the process to its own needs.

FIGURE 11.5   Formality and Rigidity of the New Product Process

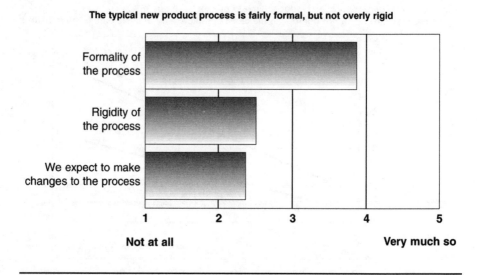

The typical new product process is fairly formal, but not overly rigid

SOURCE: R. G. Cooper and E. J. Kleinschmidt, *Formal Processes for Managing New Products: The Industry Experience* (Hamilton, Ont., Canada: McMaster University, 1991).

Formality

The formality and rigidity of processes varies from firm to firm. On average, managers thought that their process was quite formal, but not overly rigid (see Figure 11.5). In discussing formality, managers cited the following characteristics of their processes:

- ✓ The process includes formal gate meetings, complete with exit or go/kill criteria, with sign-offs required (52%).[5]
- ✓ The process provides detailed descriptions of the tasks and activities to be completed at each stage or phase (44%).
- ✓ The process requires documentation and reports, which are spelled out in the process (for example, through templates for deliverables) (14%).
- ✓ The process specifies a set of "deliverables" or inputs for each gate. These deliverables become the objectives of the project team (10%).

Many managers commented that although the process was formally laid out, paperwork was kept to a minimum.

Lack of flexibility in the process is not a major concern. Only a small minority of managers saw their processes as totally rigid; that is, all stages and all gates

FIGURE 11.6   Reasons Why Businesses Implemented a Systematic New Product Process

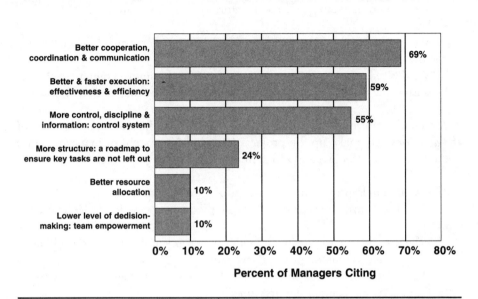

SOURCE: R. G. Cooper and E. J. Kleinschmidt, *Formal Processes for Managing New Products: The Industry Experience* (Hamilton, Ont., Canada: McMaster University, 1991).

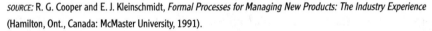

must be adhered to, regardless of the project and situation. Typical comments included the following:

> "Each project has its own requirements and, hence, differing degrees of adherence to the total system."
> "The decision to bypass certain activities or review points can be made with the approval of management."

Rationale for a New Product Process

What were the motivations that underlay the implementation of a *Stage-Gate* process? The majority of reasons lie within six main categories; three motivations dominate (see Figure 11.6).

The most often cited motivation is the desire for *better cooperation, communication, and coordination* among people directly and indirectly involved in a new product project. Most often, these people reported to different functional areas, and the need for teamwork was frequently mentioned:

"We needed a common understanding among the different departments involved in the project."

"We wanted marketing and manufacturing to be more involved and much earlier."

"We needed to 'blur the lines' between different departments so that we could work as a team."

"We desired a system to coordinate activities and improve communication, because many people are involved in a project and over a long period of time."

A second major motivation is the desire to improve the *quality and timing of the activities* that make up the project. A total of 59 percent of managers cited a need for more effective and efficient execution of project tasks:

"We wanted to improve our efficiency, product quality, and timing."

"[The need was] to accelerate the new product process for faster market entry."

"[The process would] provide for better homework at the front end, yielding sharper product definition prior to development."

"We had too much recycling . . . going back and doing it again. We wanted better quality of execution the first time."

The desire for more *control and information* is the third major reason for implementing a *Stage-Gate* process: a system that yields discipline, controls activities, and provides information for top management (cited by 55 percent of managers). Typical comments included the following:

"[The process] was needed to ensure that projects met company goals."

"We needed better checkpoints throughout the process."

"Top management wanted to be kept informed and involved in the development process."

"We desired a tracking of the status of all projects."

The need for structure—a road map to guide the project—was mentioned by a minority of respondents (24 percent). Here the major concern is that key activities or tasks were left until too late, or forgotten altogether. A new product project is complex, often entailing dozens of tasks at different stages. A standardized lists of tasks, broken down by stage, helps to ensure no critical errors of omission.

Other reasons cited for implementing a new product process include the desire to improve resource allocation or budgeting decisions (cited by 10 percent) and the need to *move decisions lower* in the organizational structure to the project team level (cited by 10 percent).

Implementation Problems

A vital question concerns how such *Stage-Gate* processes were implemented. For example, was it a management edict, or was there bottom-up development and support? The most common mechanism was a new products committee, which made the decision to implement and then designed a process (26 percent of firms). Other approaches included a top-down directive (15 percent) and a gradual development—the process simply appeared and grew over time (15 percent).

Initial response to the new system was by no means universally positive within firms. On a five-point scale, the initial response averaged a mid-range 4.5, where 1 meant "poorly received" and 5 meant "very well received." Comments broke down as follows:

✓ well or fairly well received (58%)
✓ perceived as bureaucratic by many people (14%)
✓ the process needed revision initially (10%)
✓ mixed reception: well received by some, poorly received by others (7%)
✓ poorly received (4%)

The range of responses suggests that even the best-designed new product process can be expected to meet with mixed reviews on introduction. The subsequent positive results achieved, however, changed the views of the skeptics.

The majority of firms did not provide formal training for their people when they first introduced their *Stage-Gate* process. The breakdown was as follows:

✓ learned the process on the job (55%)
✓ some formal training provided, but mostly learned on the job (24%)
✓ only meetings and discussions held when introduced (11%)
✓ formal training provided (10%)

This *lack of training and education explains some of the initial skepticism* and the lack of universal acceptance when the system was first introduced. Respondents also indicated that it was a mistake to have provided so little in the way of formal training.

Most managers (90 percent) indicated that there had been start-up problems when their new product process was first implemented. In 80 percent of these cases, the problems were not deemed to be serious. When queried further, the majority of managers (55 percent) indicated that the problems were applications problems rather than with the process itself. That is, they or their staff had difficulty undertaking some of the tasks that the new process plan required and that the process itself was not problematic. Again, this points to the lack of education, training, and facilitation as a possible cause. But 45 percent of managers saw the process itself, not its application, as the root of the problem.

A number of steps were undertaken to overcome these problems and weaknesses in initial implementation. Seventy-eight percent of firms worked on team building and teamwork solutions; 17 percent undertook organizational redesign; 17 percent obtained greater involvement of more senior managers; and 10 percent simplified the design of the process.

The goal of higher new product success rates, shorter development times, and more profitable new products will continue to be an elusive one. The design and implementation of *Stage-Gate* new product processes has produced enviable results for the few firms that we studied. The evidence is clear: stage-and-gate new product processes really do work. But implementation clearly remains a challenge!

Designing and Implementing a *Stage-Gate* Process

You've seen the positive results in other firms. Now it's time to charge ahead in your company.

- If your current product development process is more than two years old, or if it does not yield the results it should, or if it's missing some of the ingredients of a winning process described in the preceding chapters, then maybe it's time for a total process overhaul.
- If you don't have a new product process at all, then now is the time to consider installing one.

But recognize at the outset that the design and implementation of a world-class *Stage-Gate* new product process is certainly no easy task.

The development of new products is one of the most important endeavors of the modern corporation; it is also a most difficult task to do successfully! Similarly, designing and implementing a *Stage-Gate* or new product process is also the most difficult—conceptually and operationally—of any process redesign in your company. Don't assume that this is the typical "process re-engineering task"—it isn't! Here are some comments from experts in *Stage-Gate* around the world:

"Seventy-five percent of all companies, working on their own, have major errors and deficiencies in their [new product] system and the way they implemented it."
—Jens Arleth, Managing Director of U3-Innovation Management, Copenhagen

"Implementing a new product process is a challenging task. It requires strong commitment from the top, and a total willingness for change in the business.

FIGURE 11.7   A *Stage-Gate* Process for Designing and Implementing *Stage-Gate*

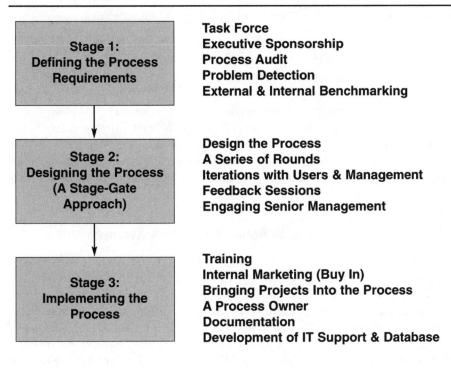

Stage 1:
Defining the Process
Requirements

Task Force
Executive Sponsorship
Process Audit
Problem Detection
External & Internal Benchmarking

Stage 2:
Designing the Process
(A Stage-Gate
Approach)

Design the Process
A Series of Rounds
Iterations with Users & Management
Feedback Sessions
Engaging Senior Management

Stage 3:
Implementing the
Process

Training
Internal Marketing (Buy In)
Bringing Projects Into the Process
A Process Owner
Documentation
Development of IT Support & Database

Integrating the different perspectives and aspirations of the relevant players and creating a shared understanding of *Stage-Gate* principles and merits are keys to success."
—Dr. Angelika Dreher, SIMMA & Partner Consulting, Austria

"For every dollar and every hour you spend designing your new product process, expect to spend ten times that amount on implementation. Get help!"
—Dr. Scott Edgett, researcher and principal consultant, Product Development Institute, Inc.

Think before you act. Don't underestimate the amount of work involved in the design and implementation of a *Stage-Gate* new product process. On the surface it looks easy, but, to use the metaphor of a gracefully swimming duck, underneath there's a lot of paddling going on!

To help companies over this hurdle, we have designed a *Stage-Gate process for designing and implementing a Stage-Gate process!* (Figure 11.7) After all, you're introducing a new concept into the company, so why not use a *Stage-Gate*

approach to do it! The design and implementation of a new product process—
let's abbreviate this to NPP—proceeds in three stages or phases:

Stage 1: The Foundation: Defining the Process Requirements
Stage 2: Designing the *Stage-Gate* New Product Process
Stage 3: Implementation of *Stage-Gate*

Note that I show these as three discrete stages in Figure 11.7. However, as in
any product development, the stages overlap. In fact, implementation has
already begun in Stage 1. The mere fact that a task force has been set up to look
into ways to improve product innovation in your company has created certain
expectations (and fears) among potential user groups. . . . The journey has
begun!

Stage 1: The Foundation: Defining the Process Requirements

Understanding the problem is the first step to a solution. Stage 1 is a first and
necessary step. Its purpose is to understand what needs fixing and to map out
the "specs" for the new process. This step is often skipped over by process
redesign task forces with disastrous results. The normal situation is that everyone on the task force thinks that they know what the problem is and what needs
fixing. Only later are they surprised to learn that they missed the mark—
that others in the company had quite different views. Here are the key tasks in
Stage 1:

1. Seek senior management commitment.

One key to the successful implementation of *Stage-Gate* is having senior management on board. If the executives of the business are not leading the charge
here, expect a very tough and frustrating battle trying to move *Stage-Gate* forward. Thus, the very first step is to get the executive or leadership team of the
business committed and to single out one or two very senior people as *executive
sponsors* of the effort.

2. Assemble a task force.

You cannot design and implement *Stage-Gate* on your own. It requires a critical
mass of people—the "do-ers"—in conjunction with senior management support. Your executive sponsors should agree to a task force and agree to release
time for people to serve on this work group.

Who should be on this task force? Clearly the task force must be carefully
selected to include knowledgeable, bright, thoughtful, experienced, and influ-
ential people from the different functions involved in product development

(and the different geographic areas, too). Additional members might include an executive sponsor (who represents senior management and lends credibility and authority to the task force) and an outside expert, consultant, or facilitator (someone who has been through the exercise before). The task force should be representative of the functions, the various businesses or product areas, and geographies. There should also be a respected, passionate, and strong task force leader.

How large should this task force be? This task force should not be a committee with a cast of thousands; rather, this is a lean, action-oriented task force. But there must be enough people to obtain diversity of opinion, function, and geography. The best task forces that I've seen operate with about five to ten people. Three or four is too few—there is not a broad enough perspective; more than ten is too many—the group becomes cumbersome, and it's almost impossible to schedule meetings.

> One of the best NPP task forces that I have served on was in the Biocides business unit at Rohm and Haas. Team members were carefully selected: the sales and marketing managers from Europe, the sales and marketing managers from North America, and two R&D managers. The executive sponsor was the director of R&D, and I was the outside facilitator. One weakness was that certain functions (notably manufacturing) and certain regions (specifically the Pacific and South/Central America) were not represented, but total representation would have required a task force twice the size. Special efforts were made to keep these other people involved in the task force's work.

What about time commitments by the task force members? Anticipate a fairly intense effort, especially at the beginning. Task force members' calendars need to be freed up for key dates well in advance. There's a lot of work to be done, perhaps more than you expect. At Glaxo-Wellcome in the United States, for example, the task force leader was assigned full time for one year to the effort, and her task force members had considerable time freed up over this period. Once you're into Stage 2—the actual design of the process—work becomes quite heavy, with the task force meeting off-site, typically in two-day sessions for a series of rounds. I'll have more on these rounds later.

4. Hold a "kick-off" seminar/workshop.

A kick-off seminar achieves a number of goals. It helps to generate organizational buy-in right at the start. It is an excellent way to sound a "wake-up call" to the organization, creating awareness of need for improvement. Finally, by building in a "problem-detection" session, the workshop starts to identify problems and key issues with current practice.

One serious trap that a well-intentioned NPP task force can become entangled in is the failure to keep the rest of the organization informed. In short, the task force becomes so focused on their objective that they fail to communicate with others outside the task force. And those in the company with a real interest in new products, but who aren't on the task force, quickly view the task force as a distant "ivory tower." As a result, six months later, when the new process is about to be launched, there already exists a significant constituency of naysayers.

The key rule here is this: Keep your internal clients informed and involved! Don't forget that the rest of the folks in the organization are your customers or clients—the people that will ultimately use this *Stage-Gate* process. Therefore, before the task force even starts out on its journey, hold an information session—a new products day or kick-off event that covers the following topics:

- ✓ your business's new product objectives versus your new product performance (this often identifies a gap)
- ✓ your current new product practices (perhaps based on some internal study or audit, as outlined below)
- ✓ the need for a new way of handling new products
- ✓ the concept of the *Stage-Gate* process and its positive impact at other firms (use the results presented earlier in this chapter)
- ✓ an introduction of the task force, its mandate and composition, and the role of other players present

One activity I've often successfully built into this kick-off event is the problem-detection session. Here, teams at the event break out, identify a list of key problems, and most important, recommend potential solutions. They then reconvene and present their results to the other teams. One result, invariably, is the recognition of the need for a new product process. Organizational buy-in has already begun!

4. Conduct an internal audit of current practices.

Start doing the up-front homework, laying the foundation for the task ahead. Undertake a study of current new product practices and deficiencies in the company. You have several options here:

- Consider conducting an audit or study within the business to determine the major problems, barriers, pitfalls, and deficiencies that plague the way you currently do new product projects. This list of problems provides an excellent incentive to get started on the design and implementation of a new product process; it also provides some guidelines and objectives for the task force.

- Use our *ProBE* methodology.[6] The Product Development Institute has developed *ProBE* in response to the repeated requests by businesses to undertake an internal audit of product development. *ProBE* is an inexpensive way to conduct a quick assessment and audit of new product practices and performance in your business (your performance and practices are compared to numerous other firms, using our database; see Appendix A)
- Dissect a handful of your past projects. That is, use our NewProd methodology outlined in Chapter 5, and do what Hewlett-Packard and others did. Hewlett-Packard undertook a retrospective analysis of past projects to determine success drivers and also things that were not working well. Select some projects that have been commercialized, and challenge the project team to undertake a retrospective flow-chart analysis—from idea to launch. Then the project team reviews each and every activity all the way through the project, posing questions such as, Did we do a good job here? How could we have done this better? This postmortem provides many valuable insights into what's going wrong and what works in your current innovation process.
- Utilize the kick-off seminar, described above, to advantage. Allow break-out teams to identify key problems in the problem-detection session. This is a quick way to air a lot of issues quickly and get consensus on the relative importance of issues to be resolved.

Some examples include the following:

Procter & Gamble's current new product process traces its roots to a major retrospective study of new product successes and failures. Sixty past new product projects were studied in depth (550 P&G people took part in the study) to find out what was going well and what was lacking in their current methods. This extensive study laid the foundation for the company's current new product process.

When Guinness decided to adopt and adapt a *Stage-Gate* process for their brewery businesses, they first held a kick-off seminar on product innovation. A problem-detection session was built in, which helped to flesh out some of the major issues that plagued product development in the business. Next, a multinational task force was assembled. A *ProBE* analysis was undertaken to assess current practices, while other members of the task force undertook retrospective analyses—"walk-throughs" of past projects—to identify good practices and areas of deficiency. Some benchmarking of other companies—for example of Pillsbury, a food company but also a member of the Guinness-Diageo group—was undertaken. These preliminaries identified a number of weaknesses in product development practices that the new process must rectify; it also pinpointed many good practices, which were subsequently built into Guinness's *NaviGate* process by design.

5. Benchmark other firms.

Some task forces spend some time benchmarking other companies. This I recommend, as it allows you to see *Stage-Gate* in action and to discuss with others some of the problems and pitfalls along the way. But a word of caution is necessary here: Benchmarking can take a lot of time. Furthermore, benchmarking is, in effect, "field research," and unless you are an experienced field researcher, you're likely to make a lot of mistakes and even reach erroneous conclusions.

Fortunately, there have been numerous benchmarking studies done by others. For example, our own research is published, and parts have been presented in earlier chapters. So has the PDMA's. Thus, although I suggest a few company visits for benchmarking, don't re-invent the wheel. Look to the literature (item 6 below) too!

6. Conduct a thorough literature review.

There have been countless studies over the past decades into new product practices and performance. A number have been cited in earlier chapters. Go back and look at some of the findings in Chapters 2–5 and review those cited earlier in this chapter. For example, start with Griffin's PDMA best practices study and some of the investigations she considered.[7] My colleagues and I have also written several other books. One on portfolio management and project selection provides insights into gate criteria and how to integrate portfolio methods into *Stage-Gate*.[8] Another book, *Product Leadership*, aimed at the leadership team of the business, provides guidance about the role of senior management as gatekeepers and strategists in the process.[9] A more recent book focuses on developing new service products.[10]

7. Map the next steps.

Following these preliminaries—getting top management buy-in, selecting the task force, undertaking a current practices audit, and the workshop kick-off—the task force is ready to move. But first they must develop a mandate and plan of action. The action plan deals with the next steps, namely, Stage 2 and the detailed design of the process (next section). Also, the task force should be clear on their mandate for the next stage and should seek concurrence from senior management. Here's the mandate or task force charter mapped out at Hallmark, the greeting card and gift company:

Hallmark New Products Task Force: Our Task Force's Charter

1. Develop a new product road map—a game plan to drive new product projects from idea to launch. This road map should outline:
   - the decision points, including gatekeepers, criteria and outputs; and
   - the stages or phases, including key activities, best practices, and deliverables.

2. Develop an implementation plan for the road map, including items such as:
   - getting buy-in at all levels,
   - communication and promotion to users,
   - documentation (for example, guide book, brochures),
   - training,
   - database,
   - and others.

8. Secure senior management sign-off.

Now it's time to go to a "gate" . . . to present the results and conclusions of Stage 1 in Figure 11.7 to the leadership team of your business and to your executive sponsors. These deliverables include an identification of the problems and what needs fixing; the specs and requirements for the new process—what the process must be and do; the forward plan or action plan for the next stage, including timing and resources required; and your mandate or charter. The "gate" sees sign-off by senior management . . . and its go to Stage 2. Note that getting sign-off at this point is absolutely critical; you're wasting your time without it. Also, this is the point where senior management must really decide how committed they are to moving forward with a *Stage-Gate* approach, because now they begin to see the true cost to the business and the level of commitment required from them.

Stage 2: Detailed Design of Your *Stage-Gate* Process

Now for the design of the process. This task sounds relatively straightforward; in fact, some people are even tempted to "lift" the model right out of this book and proclaim, "Voilà, we have our system!" But hold on. Unless you want to face disaster a few months down the road, there are quite a few other facets to this design phase.

The vital thing to remember is *ownership*. If people have not had a hand in crafting the process, there's not much likelihood that they'll willingly adopt it! Your task force's most important goal is implementation of a world-class new product process. But if your goal is merely to design the perfect innovation process, you'll probably succeed at that goal but fail overall. From the minute your task force meets to map out your new process, every effort must be made to ensure implementation. And that means you must involve and engage the user community—gatekeepers, team leaders, and project team members—in the design of the new process.

Obviously you cannot invite all of them to every task force meeting. But by proceeding in rounds, you can engage them in the process, seeking their input and feedback as the process takes shape.

Here's what Round 1 might look like—a two-day off-site, work meeting of your task force:

- ✓ The mandate agreed to by senior management is discussed and understood by all.
- ✓ A conceptual model of the new process is mapped out and agreed to—something similar to the flow diagram in Figure 5.4.
- ✓ The purpose, flavor, or spirit of each stage is agreed to.
- ✓ The essence of each gate and who the gatekeepers might be is agreed on.
- ✓ Time permitting, some of the key activities in each stage of the model are listed.
- ✓ Next steps are agreed to.

What you have accomplished is to map out the *conceptual design* or skeleton of the proposed NPP. Immediately after the meeting, a designated task force member writes up draft #1—a dozen pages and a flow diagram not unlike the diagram shown in Figure 5.4. The write-up identifies and names the stages and gates; provides the spirit or flavor (the purpose) of each stage and gate; and lists some activities in each stage. But details, such as in-depth descriptions of activities, deliverables, and gate criteria, as well as organization and procedures, are not yet spelled out.

The draft #1 write-up is quickly circulated to task force members; each provides quick comment and feedback, and corrections are immediately made. Draft #2 now goes out within days, and I recommend that it be accompanied by a PowerPoint presentation outlining the highlights of the new NPP.

At this point, each task force member begins to share the new process with their colleagues, subordinates, and bosses. That is, each task force member hosts "show and tell" sessions and seeks feedback from their constituencies (their "clients"). The feedback is circulated to the task force, and the agenda and objectives for the next two-day meeting are set.

End of Round 1.

A round typically takes about 2–3 weeks if you have discipline and adhere to a tight time line. One of the most demanding tasks is the quick write-up of material and getting it out to people in less than one week following the first meeting. Estimate about one round for the conceptual design and another three to five rounds for the detailed design. Implementation, or Stage 3 below, varies considerably by company.

The conceptual design or skeleton of the model has been accepted by the organization and by senior management by the end of Round 1. Now it's time to put some meat on this skeleton, so more rounds are scheduled. Here, the following questions are addressed as your detailed *Stage-Gate* model takes shape:

- *Stage descriptions.* Specifically, what actions or activities are required at each stage? Often an overview or brief description of each activity is developed to provide the project team with a flavor for what is expected and to incorporate current best practices.
- *Deliverables.* What deliverables are the result or endpoint of each stage, and what will be delivered to each gate? In what level of detail? Some task forces develop guides, templates, or even forms for many of the deliverables. (For example, if you decide to move immediately to a paperless process—a web-based process—you likely need to develop some forms with designated fields for the deliverables, simply so the project documentation can be conveniently and electronically prepared and stored).
- *Gate descriptions.* What are the gate criteria—the must-meet and should-meet items outlined in Chapter 8? How will projects be prioritized? Once a project is given a go decision at a gate, is this a firm and binding decision (or can the project be reprioritized in a month or two if a better project comes along)? And how do gates mesh with quarterly reviews of projects, project milestones, and annual budget setting? Finally, how do you begin to integrate portfolio management into your new NPP?
- *Gate procedures.* Who are the gatekeepers for each gate? How is the meeting run—for example, is there a chairperson, a referee, or a facilitator present? What method should gatekeepers use to score the project against the criteria? How are decisions made? Should the project team be present for the entire meeting? And so on.
- *Organization.* What should the composition of cross-functional teams be? Where in the process should the team be formed? Who does the work on the project prior to this point? Who should be the project team leaders? Is it the same leader from beginning to end of the project? How much empowerment should the team be given? How should team members be relieved of their normal duties? Who does the annual performance evaluation of each team member? And how are team members recognized and rewarded?
- *What's "in" the process?* Which projects does this new process handle? All projects or just some types? And what about process developments (where the project may result in an improved manufacturing or operation process)? How are platform projects and science or exploratory projects handled (see Chapters 5 and 6)? And what about small proj-

ects—extensions, fixes, and modifications? Do they go through the full process, or should there be a three-stage version of the process for low-risk projects? How much flexibility is there?

Remember: Throughout these rounds, as the process takes shape, there is *constant information flow between task force members and the various constituents in the organization*, including senior management, potential gatekeepers, team leaders, and team members. The goal here is to seek both feedback and buy-in. And it is particularly important to have someone on the task force interfacing with the executive sponsors and the senior management group—keeping them appraised of progress and how the process is coming together. I even try to engage the leadership team in specific tasks; for example, let them help you map out the Gate 3 go/kill criteria. Once again, if they're involved, there's a much higher chance that they'll take ownership.

After these series of design rounds, potential users of the process—both team members and senior management—should have seen the process several times and have provided feedback each time. My rule of thumb is three times; it takes three impressions for this new process to begin to sink in. As a result of this design procedure, your task force has a *Stage-Gate* process design that has been crafted with the benefit of many people's input and feedback, making it a much better and more robust process design. In addition, and most important, buy-in has already begun.

Documentation and presentation are important, and so one result of this design phase is normally the development of a fairly detailed "new product process document," from which you can develop a users' guide and manual in Stage 3. Toward the end of Stage 2, implementation issues begin to be aired, and an implementation plan is developed as the final task in Stage 2.

Speeding Up the Stage 2 Design Phase

The desire to move quickly has led some firms to novel approaches to getting *Stage-Gate* up and running more quickly. Thus, instead of spending three or more months on the design of the process, they merely purchase an off-the-shelf *Stage-Gate* model from another firm or outside vendor. For example, one major Japanese company purchased Dow Chemical's new product process (Dow has a world-class process, and the Japanese firm was already in joint ventures with Dow and knew of Dow's excellent process). Similarly, the Product Development Institute has various versions of stage-gate-in-a-box available for different industries. Invariably, the company must still modify and adjust the process to suit its own culture and organization, but the end result is usually a better process (if you start with a world-class process, you're likely to end up with one), and one that is in place much faster. The task force can then spend their energies where the real challenges are—implementing the process.

Stage 3: Implementation

Implementation is by far the longest, most difficult, and most expensive phase. It consists of a set of events and activities designed to inform people about the NPP and train them in its use; to seek buy-in and commitment from the organization; and to bring projects—both new and existing—into the new system. The implementation phase normally is initiated at some event or company conference whereby members of senior management indicate their commitment, and an overview of the process is presented. But each company's implementation plan must be designed to suit its own culture and needs. The mechanics—the design of a process—are relatively easy, but the behavioral side—getting commitment and change in behavior—isn't!

Bringing Projects into the NPP

Decisions must be made about how to bring current projects into the system. The use of piloting as one technique to gain organizational commitment is outlined below. This is a gradual approach to bringing projects on board, in which only a few test projects are initially introduced to the NPP. Some people find this approach takes too long. On the other hand, you can begin piloting projects as you are designing the process (in Stage 2, above), especially if the relevant project leaders are also on the task force.

Other companies simply announce a starting date, and all new projects are "in the system" after that date. Leaders of all existing projects must declare where they are in the process—what stage or gate—by that date. An additional requirement is that all existing projects must clear one gate within, say, six months of the starting date. This gate may be the next gate, or if the project is not far enough into the stage, then the preceding gate.

One of my favorite approaches is the use of "welcome gates." Project team members attend a two-day training session on the new process. At the end of the session, the concept of welcome gates is announced. Before they depart the training session, each project team must declare where their project is within the new process—in which stage and heading toward which gate. Next they must declare when they'll be through that gate (usually a time limit of "next three months" is defined). But here's the difference: The welcome gate is positioned as a nonthreatening gate, where projects are not required to have all the deliverables completed. That is, for this entry gate, the rules are relaxed a little. But once past this entry gate, the project must adhere to the principles of the new process.

Announcing a new way of doing things obviously creates anxiety among potential users. The first fear among project teams and leaders is that "my project might be canceled." Often the commitment is made that the welcome gate will be a very gentle one, with very few kills expected. In one Japanese company, we even had to remove the word "kill" as a decision option at gates *for the first year* of implementation. Instead we replaced "kill" with the phrase "the project receives no resources." Different cultures require different methods of implementation.

Getting Commitment and Buy-In

The entire organization must be committed: senior managers, coaches, and players. No new order of things will be successfully internalized in an organization unless there is commitment and buy-in from those at the top, from those at the middle level, and from those lower down who must use the new system.

If those at the top—senior management—don't commit to this new product process, then very quickly the word will spread through the organization that the system isn't for real—that the most senior people don't support it! Moreover, top management has the authority to commit the vital resources, without which the new process will barely limp along. My personal observation is that there has never been a successful implementation of a formal NPP (or *Stage-Gate* process) without the commitment and dedication of top management. As one champion of a *Stage-Gate* system confessed:

> The breakthrough came when senior management actually started to use the language of the process . . . when they started asking questions such as "Is the project in Stage 2 or 3?"; "When's the next gate?" and "Are the deliverables in place?" It was then that we all got the message that the senior people were serious about using our new process.

Top management commitment alone isn't enough, however. Sure, the CEO can place his or her blessing on the new system and say the right words at senior management meetings. He or she can even dictate the implementation of the new process and allocate people to do so. All these items are a step in the right direction. But alone they won't yield a successful new product process.

Managers at the next levels down in the organization must also be on board. These are the decision makers for the majority of new product projects—the business unit manager, the marketing and sales managers, the R&D or engineering manager, the manufacturing and QA managers, and so on. These are the people who tend most of the gates or key decision points in the process, not the CEO or executive vice presidents.

If these key middle-level people have not committed to the concept and procedures of the NPP, then all is lost. For if they run gate meetings badly—they are poorly prepared, fail to use the stated gate criteria, shoot from the hip, let half-baked projects slip through gates with half the deliverables missing (or worse yet, let projects simply slide around gates), ask inane questions, seek irrelevant information, or kill projects for the wrong reasons—then even the best designed NPP will quickly break down and fall into disuse. Unfortunately, I have seen all of these abuses within supposedly well-managed firms.

Fact: The greatest change in behavior is required not at the project leader and team level but at the decision-making level. Managers who tend the gates face the greatest learning challenge. Thus, the buy-in of these middle-level managers is critical to the success of the *Stage-Gate* implementation. As go the gates, so goes the process!

Management commitment alone is not enough. The senior executives can say all the right things and even commit people and money. But that is no guarantee of success. The middle-level managers—the people who tend the gates— can run sharp, disciplined gate meetings. But there's more to success than this. Never forget: Implementation really happens in the trenches. Implementation means ordinary team members and project leaders buying into the process: R&D people, engineers, marketing people, and manufacturing folks—the real "do-ers" in the organization—ultimately make it happen. If they are not committed to making this new product process work—if they see it as useless, bureaucratic, or another "flavor of the month" from management upstairs— then the process is doomed to failure. They'll simply pretend to be using the process; they'll go through the motions and say the right words, but in reality, it's business as usual.

Here are some of the ways firms get people onboard and committed to their new product process.

1. Position the NPP as one facet of your Quality Management, ISO-9000, or Six-Sigma program.   Quality Management, ISO-9000, and Six-Sigma programs are increasingly popular these days, especially among senior management. The insights that these quality programs bring include the following:

- ✓ a recognition that *all work is a process,* and that any process can be managed to be more effective and efficient
- ✓ the understanding that it takes a lot of time and work to successfully implement a new process—it's not a quick fix. But the *results are worth the effort.*

These "truths" that the quality management proponents have brought into organizations also apply to the NPP. In "selling" your new product process, position it as part of the firm's overall program on quality management. Argue that the NPP is simply the application of quality management approaches to new products. Indeed, some ISO experts argue that compliance with ISO standards demands the implementation of a stage-and-gate process!

Show that new product development is merely a process and that this process too can be managed more effectively. Talk about gates not as harsh hurdles but as quality-control checkpoints in the process—to ensure that the project is a quality one. And finally, make the point that, like Six Sigma methods, implementation of the NPP will be difficult and long and will require resources, but that the results are worth the effort.

2. Sell everyone on the need for more new products! Surprising as this seems, not everyone in the organization is as convinced as you are of the need for new products. The "champions of the process" by definition are the most supportive of a strong new product effort; the rest of the organization is often not quite as eager or convinced that new products are top priority. The implication here is that not only must you sell the concept of a *Stage-Gate* process, but you must also promote the notion that "new products are vital for the health, prosperity, and even survival of the organization." There is much evidence available to support this view. Use it.

☞ **Suggestion:** Use industry data to make your case for the need for new products, for example, how new products are having a major impact on company fortunes—on sales, profits and even share prices!

Look at your own track record. What percentage of sales come from new products? What is your objective? What has been your growth driver? Compare your performance—profits, growth, and so on—to competitors or other business units in your corporation. Once everyone is convinced that new products are essential, the next question is, How do we get more winners? And that's where the NPP is proposed as the solution.

3. Use facts to underpin the potential benefits of the NPP. There are many skeptics in any organization. As the quotation from *The Prince* that opens this chapter suggests, this skepticism arises from the "incredulity of mankind, who do not truly believe in anything new until they have had actual experience of it." If your colleagues don't have direct experience, then bring experiences in from other organizations where *Stage-Gate* processes have been used with success. That is, don't promise imaginary benefits based on speculation and hearsay; deal with facts and solid evidence.

To substantiate the need for formal new product processes, for example, take apart any unsuccessful project. At the root of its problems, you'll probably find serious process deficiencies: poor quality of execution; certain key activities not done at all or done too late; poor or nonexistent gates or decision points; and so on. If you can't provide the evidence from your own company, then at least rely on research studies done in others. Use our NewProd studies outlined in Chapter 3, where the overriding conclusion is that most firms' product development processes are in serious trouble and that success and failure depends to a large extent on process.

There is not much published evidence of the performance results of implementing new product processes, but those studies that have investigated the impact of *Stage-Gate* processes provide universally positive results. The data on how formal NPPs affect results (provided earlier in this chapter) give you the ammunition to prove your point. And the PDMA best practices study provides a ringing endorsement of *Stage-Gate* approaches.

4. Deal with the barriers and preconceptions. The initial reaction to an NPP by some in the organization may be less than positive, as the study earlier in the chapter showed. Common views are, first, that an NPP is unnecessarily bureaucratic, and second, that it will now take longer to develop and launch new products. Both preconceptions are wrong! Nonetheless, these are the nightmares of people charged with running NPPs in other firms. There is a real danger that the process will indeed become bureaucratic and that it will extend the time to market. Thus, *every effort must be taken to minimize bureaucracy and to speed products to market.* Recall the discussion on speed in Chapter 9 and make sure that you build in at least some of these speed enhancers into your process. Further, come armed with the evidence and make the point strongly that in well-run NPPs at other companies, the "system" has evolved to a slick, streamlined process that accelerates products to market.

5. Buy-in starts at the top. Encourage and train senior people to start "talking the talk and walking the walk" of the NPP. They must "model the way" and set the example for others. If they use the language of the NPP, ask the "process questions" (for example, ask about stages and gates), and refer to gate criteria (even in casual conversation or ordinary meetings), then the rest of the organization gets the message.

6. Get the commitment to the NPP written into the business's mission and strategic plan. This is not a major item, but several companies have found that it is an effective way of focusing the spotlight on the NPP.

7. Use pilots. Identify a handful of projects, and use these as test or demonstration cases of "how to do it." Make sure that these projects are really well run: Select good potential projects—ones destined for success; choose pilot projects with able leaders and proficient teams; provide good mentoring and facilitation; and commit the right resources. Throughout their development, hold these projects up as shining examples to the rest of the organization; they are illustrations of the use of the NPP, as well as proof that the new process works!

Getting organization buy-in and commitment is the first prerequisite for successful implementation of a new process. This involves changing attitudes, values, and actions. It relies on effective communications, presentations, and internal marketing. These requirements lead us into the next two critical items: communication and training.

Communicating your NP Process

Effective communication and presentation of the NPP are cornerstones of its success. I've witnessed several instances when initial attempts to implement a well-designed NPP were dealt fatal blows by poor communication vehicles. The written documentation (for the introduction of the system) was too lengthy; it was complex, hard to follow, and not user-friendly; and it simply turned the reader or audience off before he or she had completed page 1.

Remember: First impressions are lasting ones, and the initial documentation or presentation sets the stage for all that is to follow. Here are some actions items to ensure successful communication.

1. Design a promotional brochure.   Virtually every company with a successful new product process has embraced the "internal marketing" facet. They have designed simple, appealing introduction communication pieces for their NPPs. Most have been professionally designed and have an artistic quality equal to a company sales brochure. The argument here is that in any organization, internal marketing is every bit as important as external marketing, so do it professionally.

Remember: You're marketing a "new product" within your own company—in this case, a new way of doing things—so use marketing tools. A four-page color, glossy brochure helps. This brochure creates the first impression. It's how the task force first introduces the process at meetings and training sessions and to senior management. And the brochure also comes in handy with sales people, who must explain the new process to customer partners. Indeed, many sales people find their company's *Stage-Gate* brochure to be an effective selling tool.

- Guinness went to their ad agency to design the brochure for their new product process, originally called the RAPID process. A professional brochure was the result, which depicted the five-stage process in picture format. Everyone who sees the brochure agrees that it's a very effective and creative communication piece.
- Wavin, a Shell-Europe subsidiary in the PVC business, developed a novel booklet that features a cartoon character who leads you through their NPP. Although the version I saw was not written in English, the visuals were so clear that I was easily able to follow their seven-stage process. Wavin has also developed appealing posters that are displayed on company bulletin boards. The same cartoon character leads you through the process on these full-sized posters.
- Exxon Chemical developed a more conservative, but nonetheless effective, four-page glossy brochure that highlights the company's NPP and its rationale. Exxon uses this not only for internal marketing but also with customers (for example, in the event of a joint development project with a customer).

2. *Produce a user's quick guide.* A user's guide is also needed. This is not so much for promotional purposes, but more to lay out the highlights of the new process for users. For example, the guide outlines the stages, gates, stage activities, gate criteria, and gatekeepers. But keep this guide short. This is not the place to overwhelm the reader with thirty pages of deliverables templates and forms!

> Procter & Gamble's initial written presentation was a detailed user's manual in a thick loose-leaf binder. Although it was well written and an invaluable guide to the would-be product developer, it saw most of its service on office bookshelves rather than in project team meetings. It was politely ignored; most recipients, it was suspected, hadn't read past the table of contents.
>
> Internal marketing research was then conducted on managers to find out what was appealing—what they would read. Various concepts and mock-ups were presented to managers.
>
> The "rebirth" of Procter & Gamble's SIMPL process introduced a simple, easy-to-read guide that laid out the stages, gates, and expectations clearly and simply. It is a pleasure to read.

The quick guide is the introduction—the teaser. It is a simple road map, intended more to provide an overview of the process, and is not a substitute for the detailed and operational instruction manual.

3. *Design a user-friendly instructional manual (and move to an e-manual).* Do you remember, in the old days, when you acquired a new piece of software for your PC? It most likely came with a user's manual—a gray-brown three-ring loose-leaf binder measuring about six inches square (and about three inches thick!). Did you find this inviting . . . did you have trouble restraining yourself from reading it cover to cover?

The software people have smartened up a lot in the last decade; they've designed manuals that are easy to read, well illustrated, and actually useful! Maybe we can learn from their experience. In fact, some software programs have no manual at all—it's all on help screens.

The description of the NPP delivered by the typical task force at the end of Stage 2 (see Figure 11.7) tends to be simply that—a detailed description of the NPP. But it's usually not a very good user's manual—it never was intended to be one; rather, it is a working document.

Companies with successful *Stage-Gate* processes invariably put considerable thought and effort into appropriate documentation. Some examples include the following:

- Exxon Chemical has developed an NPP user's manual that is as slick as any professional software manual today. It is professionally typeset; there are illustrations, diagrams, boxed inserts, and other devices to make it appealing, easy to read, and understandable. The booklet is about fifty pages in length and inviting to read.

- Guinness developed an electronic user's manual with point-and-click capability. The entire manual is web-based on the company's Intranet system. It is also interactive, so that users can download templates and forms, complete them, and then send them to (or share them with) other people.

The point here is, don't assume the working document that your task force develops is the user's manual. It probably isn't! And if you try to make it the user's manual, experience suggests that you'll fail. Engage someone to translate your document into one that will serve users well. Take a look at software user's manuals, pick the ones you like, and use them as a model for your NPP documentation.

4. Develop a professional live presentation package. During the first year of implementation, you'll be presenting and "selling" your NPP, possibly to numerous audiences within the corporation. The problem is that most managers are not very good at making such formal, large-audience presentations. And why should they be? They're not professional actors and not seasoned performers. Get some professional help and develop tools—from a PowerPoint presentation to a video show—that will heighten the professionalism and effectiveness of your presentation.

> Recently, I observed three different NPP task forces making oral presentations to various groups in their companies. In two cases, the presentations did not go as well as was hoped. One was simply boring; the presenters didn't excite the audience. In the other, the task force leader "died on stage" in front of an audience of more than fifty people. He was simply poorly prepared. He had terrible, almost unreadable visuals; an unrehearsed talk; and serious content problems in the presentation (for example, the audience consisted of a number of senior salespeople, yet the NPP failed to include the sales department in product development!). By the end of the presentation, there was real hostility in the room!
>
> In contrast, the task force at Glaxo-Wellcome had developed a superb PowerPoint presentation to "pitch" the process to senior management and the executives of the company. This presentation was one of the most professional I've ever seen; it utilized very effective use of color and graphics, a professional script and story line, and excellent layout. Although the Glaxo new product process is an excellent one, no doubt this presentation had much to do with successfully selling it to the company.

Remember the purpose of these presentations. The official purpose is instructional and informational—to teach people about this new process. But let's not kid ourselves. The *real purpose is selling*—to get organizational buy-in!

If you don't secure buy-in, then the instructional facet of these presentations is wasted. Therefore, treat this effort very much as a sales pitch.

5. Come up with a good name for the process.   Would a rose by any other name still be a rose? Maybe and maybe not! Many of those involved in NPP implementations concur that even seemingly trivial issues—the name chosen for your process—are important. You're selling a "product" here, so worry about its brand name! Some names used by different companies include the following:

- SC Johnson's Wax: ATOM—accelerate to market
- Guinness: NaviGate
- Dofasco (a steel company in Canada): SWIFT—seeking winning innovations for tomorrow
- Exxon Chemical: PIP—product innovation process
- Peco Energy (Pennsylvania Energy Corporation): Gateways
- Bayer (U.S.): STARGate—strategic applications and research gate process
- Toray Chemical (Japan): PASS—project assist system for success
- Kennametal (a tool maker): ACE—achieve a cutting edge
- Royal Bank of Canada: RPR—right projects right
- Product Development Institute: RAPID—road map for accelerating products into development

Some companies have gone as far as researching different names internally. Even the names of some of the components of the system have come under scrutiny. For example, Corning found the term "gate" had a negative connotation and, hence, uses the term "diamond decision point"; both Skil Tools and Black & Decker use the term "tollgate" instead of gate. (B&D researched different words and found that potential users saw a tollgate as a positive thing: "Once you paid your money, you had a clear and open highway until the next tollgate.") The Thomson Corporation uses the term "decision point" instead of "gate," while Nortel Networks uses the term "business decision point."

Provide Training

The need for training and facilitation in the use of the NPP cannot be understated. Yet in our study, many companies confessed to weaknesses in their initial training attempts; they simply underestimated the training needs of users. The majority did not provide training as part of implementation, and this was cited as one of the reasons that their NPPs were not favorably received. Training is important for two reasons:

- *We dislike the unknown.* We tend to have a negative predisposition toward things we don't know or don't understand. If your audience— the intended users—doesn't understand the system (or worse yet, has incorrect views or misperceptions about it), then you're in for an uphill battle in implementation. Training, if nothing else, creates familiarity and a sense of comfort about new and foreign things.

- *People don't know how to use the process.* Your NPP requires many people—team leaders, team members, and gatekeepers—to do new and different things, or to do old things in a new way. Without instruction, guidance, and facilitation, there is a high likelihood that people will simply get it wrong; they'll do a poor job on these new tasks. Learning by doing is great in theory, but the problem is that you may not have this luxury. *The NPP must work reasonably well the first time.* If it doesn't, users will become frustrated, and the process will be blamed. Good luck trying to implement it then! Training provides people with the necessary skills and knowledge to carry out the new tasks that the NPP demands of them.

Everyone who has been through the implementation of an NPP agrees that training is important. But there is little unanimity on the nature and format of that training. What topics should be covered in the training program? Three general areas emerge:

- *Soft skills.* The NPP demands certain "people skills" or "soft skills" that may be new to some players. These are often part of project management skills training and include team leadership, interpersonal skills, time management, meeting management, and conflict resolution.
- *Hard skills.* The NPP requires certain people to undertake (or at least oversee) tasks they haven't done before (particularly in the case of technical people). Hard skills topics include financial and business analysis, market research and market information gathering, market segmentation and target market selection, competitive analysis, exploiting e-business opportunities, project management (including the use of software for project management), designing and conducting field tests, and designing a marketing plan.
- *The use of the NPP.* Users must be trained in the use of the new process. Specific topics here might include the structure of the process, expectations at each gate (deliverables), gate criteria, the details of each stage, how a gate meeting works, and so on. Here, users include both team members and gatekeepers.

There are mixed views on how much soft-skill and hard-skill training should be included during the implementation phases of the NPP. Some companies argue that these skills are acquired and available on a routine basis as part of their company's normal training programs. But there is unequivocal support for the notion of a training program in how to use the NPP system:

- Exxon Chemical has put together a two-day training program on the use of their NPP. Within three years, more than 1,000 people had been put through this program.
- Corning has charged its human resources department with the implementation of its NPP. Not only do they provide hands-on facilitation, but they also have designed and put in place a three-day training program on the NPP, with an almost-full-time instructor.
- When Reckitt & Colman (now Reckitt-Benckiser) rolled out their *Stage-Gate* new product process, a two-day professionally delivered seminar was designed. It was presented about twenty times in London for the European divisions, followed by sessions in New Jersey and Toronto; subsequently it was also presented in Johannesburg, São Paulo, Auckland, and Sydney.

A variety of different training methods and formats are recommended for the implementation of your NPP. Some firms use a program of formal seminars, which NPP users take in advance of their projects. This seminar format is relied on mostly for the initial introduction of the NPP (for example, the two-day Exxon NPP course and three-day Corning NPP course). These introductory seminars consist of a combination of lectures, discussions, company cases, team exercises, and role playing (for example, running a gate meeting). Additionally, some firms, such as Hewlett-Packard, offer a full complement of hard-skills courses (and some soft-skills seminars) appropriate for product development teams.

Other companies provide "just-in-time" (JIT) training to each project team at the time it is needed. This entails a combination of custom-tailored seminars together with standard training packages.

Some firms rely heavily on the use of facilitators to help the project teams and gatekeepers:

- Corning provides facilitators to work closely with the project team. The facilitator acts as a consultant, a mentor, and a trainer.
- Guinness has a process manager in every major business unit. One role of the process manager is to mentor and assist project teams and to help them when they are having difficulty. Another role is to conduct training when it is required.

Good materials and documentation can go a long way as a substitute for formal or JIT training. For example, Guinness's web-based documentation is almost a "self-help, do-it-yourself" training program for team members, and so is the *Accolade* software package. Other companies develop extensive illustration materials taken from real company cases, with examples of a business case, a project plan, competitive analysis, and so on. These models show clearly and visibly what is expected of teams, reflecting the adage, "don't tell me, show me an example!"

Develop IT Support for the Process

Information technology can provide support in a number of important ways, from information display to archiving project documentation to tracking projects. Try to build in the benefits of a comprehensive IT support system for product innovation as you design and implement your new product process. You have many options; here are some that I've seen in progressive companies.

An e-manual.   Develop an e-manual for your process on your Intranet, and get rid of that thick, loose-leaf binder (which nobody reads anyway!). Although the e-manual itself may be every bit as detailed as the hard-copy version, it does not appear so. Users see only what they need. It's a user-friendly solution to the need for a comprehensive manual that does not overwhelm the reader.

A paperless process.   Move to a paperless process, where all documentation developed by the project team is handled and stored through a web-based IT system. For example, the system has all the templates required for gate deliverables, and project team members simply work directly on the system templates, eliminating the need for hard copies. Completed documents are delivered to the process manager and to gatekeepers as needed . . . all electronically.

IT tracking.   Consider an IT system to track projects and provide information displays on projects. International Paper's web-based system allows users— team members or gatekeepers—to see any facet of any project in a moment.

Gate facilitation.   Gates can be facilitated by IT. For example, Rohm and Haas uses video conferencing for international gate meetings. International Paper is experimenting with web-based gates that enable gatekeepers to electronically prescore projects before the meeting even begins. And something as simple as an Excel spreadsheet along with a video projector can be used to display the scores of gatekeepers on the rating criteria right at the gate meeting—an excellent tool to facilitate discussion and reach an effective gate conclusion.

A project database.   If you plan to measure results (next section) and track projects, then a database on projects in your pipeline is essential. Here, vital statistics on projects, timing, resources allocated, progress achieved, and performance results are stored. The data are usually collected by the process manager (often right at gate meetings) and entered into the database.

Portfolio management.   Portfolio management is a key challenge, and it, too, relies on IT support. First, in order to develop some of the tables, charts, and diagrams useful for portfolio management (Chapter 8), data on projects is required—hence, the database above. And IT is used to provide some of these portfolio tools—to display bubble diagrams, rank-ordered lists, and pie charts of resource breakdowns—so useful at gate meetings and portfolio reviews. Consider acquiring NewPort Max, portfolio management software (www.prod-dev.com).

Toolbox. Finally, IT can provide a one-stop shopping toolbox for product development. These tools include project management or time-line software, the *NewProd™* diagnostic model (Appendix B), and standard financial models with probabilistic capabilities, among others.

What about the availability of off-the-shelf software packages that handle most or all of the IT support functions listed above? It's a question I am always asked. Remarkably, there has, until now, been a real shortage of comprehensive, all-inclusive software packages in support of a stage-and-gate process. A few tools have been available for some time, such as *MS-Project,* but these are limited to specific functions or tasks. Our institute has looked at a number of proposed software packages—software developers are always approaching us for our views and advice—and some have progressed to Beta tests as this book goes to press. But there's only one package that we have seen fit to endorse and recommend so far: *Accolade Gate-Based NPD System* by Sopheon-Teltech.[11]

Metrics—How Well Are You Doing?

Is it too early to start thinking about new product metrics? Certainly not! I strongly subscribe to the view that "you cannot manage what you cannot measure," and "what gets measured gets done." Some firms have made the mistake of not implementing measurement of their new product process until too late in the game.

At a *Stage-Gate™* benchmarking session in Atlanta attended by leading firms, metrics was a hot topic. Each company identified the metrics that it used to capture how well it was doing at new products. The conclusions:

First, there is no universal view on what should be measured. These different companies—all leaders—gauged a variety of different things. However, there were certain metrics that the majority of businesses used (shown in Tables 11.1 and 11.2).

Next, virtually every business began with a much longer list of metrics than it now uses. The message seems to be: Err on the side of too many metrics at the beginning, and over time, you'll decide which ones are the most useful to your management group.

TABLE 11.1   Post-process Metrics: How Well Are You Doing at New Products?

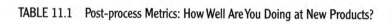

How Well Are You Doing at New Products?

Short Term (measured immediately):

1. Timeliness:
    * cycle time (months) — from Gate 3 to Launch (not too useful; must be a relative measure)
    * on-time launch (actual vs. scheduled launch date—the variance in months)
    * actual time relative to fastest possible cycle time for that project

2. Develop & Capital Costs:
    * staying within budget (variance)

Longer Term (measured much later; e.g., two years into launch, based on latest expected results):

1. Financial:
    * profitability (NPV, IRR, payback period, break-even time).
        - vs. projections made at Gates 3 and 5
        - vs. your hurdle rate
    * sales (units, dollars, market share)
    * manufacturing costs
        (both items vs. Gate 3 and Gate 5 projections)

2. Success Rates:
    * percent of products launched that became commercial successes
      (you must define "commercial success")
    * percent of Development projects that became commercial successes
    * attrition curves (numbers of projects vs. stage in the process: the "fall off" rate—see Figure 1.3)

3. Percentage of Your Sales Generated by New Products
    (you must define "new product")
    (also, you must define the time horizon: e.g., launched in the last 3 years)

4. Percent of Growth (or profits) Generated by New Products
    (similar to item 3 above)

TABLE 11.2   In-process Metrics: Is the Process Working?

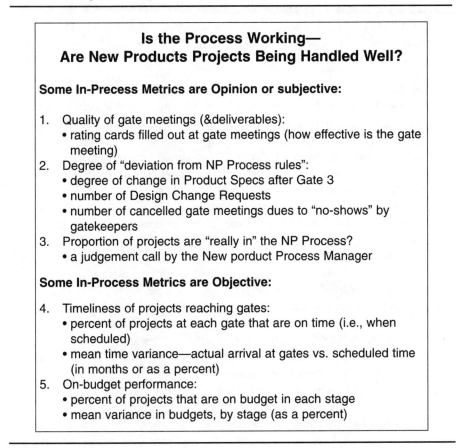

**Is the Process Working—
Are New Products Projects Being Handled Well?**

Some In-Precess Metrics are Opinion or subjective:

1. Quality of gate meetings (&deliverables):
    • rating cards filled out at gate meetings (how effective is the gate meeting)
2. Degree of "deviation from NP Process rules":
    • degree of change in Product Specs after Gate 3
    • number of Design Change Requests
    • number of cancelled gate meetings dues to "no-shows" by gatekeepers
3. Proportion of projects are "really in" the NP Process?
    • a judgement call by the New porduct Process Manager

Some In-Process Metrics are Objective:

4. Timeliness of projects reaching gates:
    • percent of projects at each gate that are on time (i.e., when scheduled)
    • mean time variance—actual arrival at gates vs. scheduled time (in months or as a percent)
5. On-budget performance:
    • percent of projects that are on budget in each stage
    • mean variance in budgets, by stage (as a percent)

Metrics used by various firms fall into two broad categories:

1. *Post-process metrics.* These answer the question, "How well are you doing at new product development?" They are "post-process" in the sense that they can be measured only after the product is launched. These include both short-term metrics (measurable immediately after launch; for example, "the proportion of products launched on time") as well as longer-term metrics (which might take several years after launch to determine; for example, "the proportion of launches that became commercial winners"). Table 11.1 provides some commonly used post-process metrics.

Data on these post-process metrics are gathered on individual projects but are most often reported in aggregate, for example, percentage of sales achieved by new products launched in the last three years, or the average variance in on-time performance. These post-process metrics are very important measures. The trouble is that if these are the only metrics you employ, you might be waiting three or four years to find out how well you are doing—and that's too long to wait in order to take corrective action. Therefore, most companies use *in-process* metrics, too.

2. *In-process metrics.* These answer the question, "Is our process working . . . really?" These in-process metrics can be measured almost immediately, and they capture how well new product projects are unfolding—for example, whether they are on time at gates, and whether deliverables to gates are in good shape. Obviously, achieving high scores on these metrics is not the ultimate goal, but they are immediately measurable (that is, you don't have to wait three years to find out the results). Think of these as *intermediate metrics* and early warning signals about ultimate results. Table 11.2 provides some good examples of in-process metrics.

> Dow Corning uses its "red-green" chart as a visual metric to spot projects in trouble, or gates and stages in trouble (Figure 11.8). Here, the various gates in their *Stage-Gate*™ process are shown across the top of the grid, while the projects are listed down the side. Inside each box is the expected date for the gate meeting—when the project should have reached that review point. The actual date—when it really arrived—is also shown. When a project is "on time," color the box green; when it is late, color the box red.

Reading across the rows, one can spot projects that are clearly in trouble—missing key gate review dates. Reading down the columns shows the gates that are missed, suggesting that the previous stage is very much in trouble. For example, in the grid in Figure 11.8, projects B and C are clearly off course; and Stage 2, feasibility, appears to be the most problematic stage in the process.

A Process Manager

No process, no matter how good and how logical, ever implemented itself. It needs someone to make it happen—that's the role of the process manager. I repeat what I said in Chapter 5: To my knowledge, *there has never been a successful installation of a Stage-Gate process without a process manager or facilitator in place!* And for larger companies, this is a full-time position.

Unfortunately, many companies miss this important point. They spend considerable time and money designing the process and then drop the ball when it comes to putting a process manager in place. In the case of some firms, the NPP had been designed and had been in the implementation phase for sev-

FIGURE 11.8 "Red-Green" Monitoring Chart

	Gate2	Gate 3	Gate 4	Gate 5	PLR
Project A	Aug 1/97 Septr 1/97	Dec 1/97 Feb 1/98	Sept 1/98 Sept 1/98	Dec 1/98	--
Project B	July 1/97 Sept 1/97	Aug 1/97 Nov 1/97	Dec 1/97 Feb 1/98	Mar 1/98 Jun 1/98	Jun 1/99
Project C	Feb 1/97 Apr 1/97	Jun 1/97 Aug 1/97	Dec 1/98 Feb 1/98	Jun 1/98 Jul 1/98	Jul 1/99
Project D	Jun 1/97 Jun 1/97	Jul 1/97 Nov 1/97	Feb 1/98 Mar 1/98	Jul 1/98 Aug 1/98	Aug 1/99 --
Project E	Sept 1/97 Sept 1/97	Nov 1/97 Dec 1/97	Aug 1/98 Sept 1/98	Dec 1/98	--
Project F	Nov 1/97 Dec 1/97	Mar 1/98 May 1/98	Dec 1/98	--	--

☐ denotes late to the gate by more than 1 month   ☐ denotes on time at gate

SOURCE: R. G. Cooper, *Product Leadership: Creating and Launching Superior New Products* (Reading, Mass.: Perseus Books, 1998).

eral years but was limping along and led by a committee (often the task force that had designed it). But it was only when a dedicated champion was appointed to devote his or her energies to the NPP that it really was implemented.

Here is a quick list of some of the responsibilities that this process manager or "keeper of the process" is charged with. The process manager is a busy person; she

✓ leads the implementation effort of the NP process throughout the business
✓ is responsible for the maintenance of the process upon implementation
✓ provides for, and participates in, required training
✓ trains new employees
✓ acts as a focal point for feedback on the process, making necessary improvements to the process (for example, feedback received at gates and at the post-launch review)
✓ develops and maintains the database and metrics

✓ uses portfolio analysis techniques to provide data for portfolio analysis and gate meetings

✓ tracks each new product project throughout the process and measures performance and ultimate success

✓ establishes practical and consistent guidelines for deliverables (for example, templates)

✓ facilitates and referees the gate meetings

✓ acts as a coach and resource to project teams

✓ serves as a resource to project teams to help remove roadblocks and blockers

✓ develops and maintains the documentation for the NP process (for example, manual, e-manual, guide, and brochures)

✓ oversees the IT support system for product development

✓ seeks out and disseminates new tools for product development and project management

✓ promotes the use of the NP process at every opportunity, seeking buy-in from key people

Give serious consideration to having a full-time manager of the NPP, certainly during its initial years. Committees and task forces tend to do a rotten job of implementation!

Ten Ways to Fail!

I wrap up this chapter with a tongue-in-cheek exposé of all the ways that people manage to ruin the implementation of a *Stage-Gate* process. Before you chuckle here, remember: These are all true—someone, somewhere, did each one and wished they had not!

1. Design the *Stage-Gate* process on your own, in your own office, and in a vacuum. You know best—task forces are a waste of time!
2. Don't do any homework or auditing. You already know what the problem is in your company, so jump immediately to a solution.
3. Don't bother looking at other companies' process designs—their stages and gates, criteria and deliverables, activities, team structures, and so on. Again, you have nothing to learn here.
4. If you do assemble a task force, meet over several months in private. Then present "your grand design" and assume everyone in the company will applaud—even though they have not been involved in the design.
5. Don't seek outside help; just read the book and design your process based on the generic one. Piece of cake! If you do seek help, hire a re-

engineering consultant who knows nothing about new product management.

6. Don't waste time testing and seeking feedback from others in the company as your task force designs the process. After all, you're the task force . . . what do these "outsiders" know? Your process design is likely to be near perfect!

7. When others do have questions or criticisms, treat these people as "cynics" and "negative thinkers." Refuse to deal with these objections, and never, never modify the process . . . it's yours, and cast in stone.

8. Don't provide training—most of this "*Stage-Gate* stuff" is obvious. Anyone ought to be able to do it just by reading the manual.

9. Speaking of manuals, make sure the new product process guide is thick and full of checklists and forms. If in doubt, overwhelm the reader and user.

10. Don't bother installing a process manager. The process is so good that it will automatically implement itself.

After you're well into implementation, revisit this list and see how many misdeeds you're guilty of!

A Final Thought on Implementation

Many investigations, including my own NewProd studies, have provided clues and insights into how to mount a successful product innovation effort. Now you move ahead and translate these and other insights and lessons into a carefully crafted new product process—a game plan that provides a road map and discipline, focuses on quality of execution, builds in the up-front homework, is strongly market-oriented, and is backed by appropriate resources.

The implementation of a *Stage-Gate™* process is far more complex than its mere design, however. Implementation means effecting organizational change, which is perhaps the most difficult of all challenges in today's corporation. Being a change agent requires much planning and work, as this chapter has made clear. If the experiences of other firms are any guide, however, the results of a successfully implemented new product process are well worth the effort. But don't underestimate the effort required!

A Product Innovation and Technology Strategy for Your Business

I find the great thing in this world is not so much where we stand, as in which direction we are moving: To reach the port of heaven, we must sail sometimes with the wind and sometimes against it but we must sail, and not drift, and not lie at anchor.
—Oliver Wendell Holmes, *The Autocrat of the Breakfast Table,* 1858

Win the Battle, Lose the War?

What if . . .

✓ What if your business had implemented a *Stage-Gate*™ new product process to guide projects to market?
✓ And what if all your business's new product projects followed the process and were executed well—good up-front homework, solid marketing input, tough go/kill gates, and so on?
✓ And what if your business committed the necessary resources to product development—both quality and quantity of resources?

Would the result be a high-performing business unit? Not necessarily. One of the three cornerstones of success in new product warfare is still missing, and that cornerstone makes the difference between winning individual battles and winning the entire new product war.

The missing cornerstone is the *business's product innovation and technology strategy*. And it's lacking in too many businesses I have studied. The product innovation strategy charts the strategy for the business's entire new product efforts. It is the master plan: It provides the direction for your enterprise's new product efforts, and it is the essential link between your product development effort and your total business strategy.[1]

This chapter begins with a look at the need for a product innovation strategy and the hard evidence in support of strategy—facts that make it imperative that you develop a product innovation and technology strategy for your business.[2] The components of an innovation strategy are then defined, followed by a glimpse into some of the broad strategic options or scenarios that your business might elect in product innovation. I then reveal the benchmarking evidence to see what types of product development strategies deliver the best results and to understand what strategic success factors the winners had in common. Next, approaches to developing a product innovation strategy are outlined— approaches where you define and elect arenas of strategic thrust for your new product efforts and possible attack plans.

So let's move forward, elevating ourselves above the battle—above the level of the individual new product project, tactics, and the *Stage-Gate*™ process— and play the role of the general, looking at strategy and direction for the business's entire new product effort. Let's go win the war!

The Importance of a Product Innovation Strategy for Your Business

Businesses that are most likely to succeed in the development and launch of new products are those that implement a company-specific approach, driven by business objectives and strategies, with a *well-defined new product strategy* at its core. This was one of the findings of an extensive study of new product practices by Booz-Allen and Hamilton; the new product strategy was viewed as instrumental to the effective identification of market and product opportunities.[3]

Our benchmarking studies also reveal that having an articulated new product strategy for the business is one of the three important drivers of new product performance. Recall the three cornerstones of performance from Figure 3.7 in Chapter 3. Businesses with a defined new product strategy—one that specifies goals and the role of new products, defines arenas of strategic thrust, and has a longer-term orientation—achieve better new product results. These businesses more often meet their new product sales and profit objectives; they boast new product efforts with a much greater positive impact on the business; and they achieve higher success rates at launch.

A number of companies do develop such innovation strategies. For example, *product innovation charters* were described by Crawford in his study of 125 firms.[4] He notes that managements are now beginning to pull all the multifunctional elements together in one document, which specifies the types of markets, products, technologies, and orientation the company will pursue with its new product strategy.

What Is a Product Innovation Strategy?

A product innovation strategy is a strategic master plan that guides your business's new product war efforts. But how does one define or describe a new product strategy? The term "strategy" is widely used in business circles today. The word is derived from the ancient Greek word meaning "the art of the general." Until comparatively recently, its use was confined to the military. In a business context, strategy has been defined as "the schemes whereby a firm's resources and advantages are managed (deployed) in order to surprise and surpass competitors or to exploit opportunities."[5] More specifically, strategic change is defined as "a realignment of a firm's product/market environment."[6] Strategy is closely tied to product and market specification; Corey argues that strategy is about choosing your *markets to target* and choosing the *products to target them with.*[7]

Business strategy here refers to the business unit's strategy, and the *product innovation and technology strategy* is a component of that business strategy.[8] By *business and new product strategy,* I do not mean a vaguely worded statement of intent, one that approaches a vision or mission statement. Rather, I mean operational, action-specific strategies. Recall from Chapter 8 that strategy is about where you spend money. Thus, a business's product innovation and technology strategy includes the following:

1. the goals for your business's total product development efforts
2. the role of product development: how new products tie into your business's overall goals
3. arenas of strategic focus: markets, technologies, product categories, including priorities
4. deployment: spending allocations (or splits) across these arenas (R&D funds or people, possibly marketing and capital resources for developments)
5. how to attack each arena in order to win

Let's elaborate on these five strategy elements.

1 and 2—Goals and role. The business's product innovation strategy specifies the goals of the new product effort, and it indicates the role that product innovation will play in helping the business achieve its business objectives. It answers the question, How do new products and product innovation fit into your business's overall plan? A statement such as "By the year 2007, 30 percent of our business's sales will come from new products" is a typical goal. Performance goals can also be stated, such as the desired number of new product introductions, expected success rates, and desired financial returns from new products.

3–Arenas and strategic thrust. The concept of strategic arenas is at the heart of a new product strategy. A business and new product strategy, at a minimum, specifies clearly defined strategic arenas for the business to focus on, including how it will focus its product development efforts. These are the battlefields where the attack is focused. That is, this strategy defines the types of markets, applications, technologies, and products on which the business will focus its new product efforts. The specification of these arenas—what's "inbounds" and what's "out-of-bounds"—is fundamental to spelling out the direction or *strategic thrust* of the business's product development effort and is the result of identifying and assessing product innovation opportunities at the strategic level.

These strategic arenas can be defined in terms of the following dimensions:

- ✓ markets or market segments
- ✓ product types, product lines, or product categories
- ✓ technologies and technology platforms

4–Spending priorities. Strategy definition goes further, however; it indicates the relative emphasis, or strategic priorities, accorded each arena of strategic focus. For example, if markets A, B, and C are identified as "strategic arenas," the relative priorities of these markets should be part of the strategy. This means that the strategy must be translated into *deployment decisions:* the relative spending priorities or splits (allocation of resources across arenas, for example, how much to spend in each of markets A, B, and C, or on technologies X, Y, and Z).

5–Plan of attack or entry strategy. The issue of how to attack each strategic arena should also be part of the business's product innovation strategy. For example, for one arena, the strategy may be to become the industry innovator—the first to the market with new products; and in another arena, the attack plan may be to be a "fast follower," rapidly copying and improving upon competitive entries. Other strategies might focus on being low cost or the differentiator or a niche player; others may emphasize certain strengths, core competencies, or product attributes or advantages.

The attack plan may map out a number of planned assaults in the form of *major new product initiatives* needed to succeed in a certain market or sector. These initiatives are often spelled out in the form of a product road map, specifying an entire series of new product releases and their timing. The attack plan may also logically lead to spending decisions regarding how much to spend on different types of projects (spending split by project types, such as platform developments versus new products versus maintenance and renewal projects). Additionally, entry strategies might be outlined and can include internal product development, licensing, joint venturing, and even acquisitions of other firms.

Why Have a Product Innovation Strategy at All?

Developing a product innovation strategy is hard work. It involves many people, especially top management. Why, then, go to all the effort? Most of us can probably name countless companies that do not appear to have a master plan for their new product efforts. How do they get by?

Doing Business Without a Strategy

Running an innovation program without a strategy is like running a war without a military strategy. There's no rudder, there's no direction, and the results are often highly unsatisfactory. You simply drift. On occasion, such unplanned efforts do succeed, largely owing to good luck or perhaps brilliant tactics.

Conducting a business's new product effort without a strategy will inevitably lead to a number of ad hoc decisions made independently of one another. New product and R&D projects are initiated solely on their own merits, with little regard to their fit into the grander scheme (portfolio management is all but impossible, for example). The result is that the business finds itself in unrelated or unwanted markets, products, and technologies. There is no focus.

Goals and Role: The Necessary Link to Business Strategy

What types of direction does a new product strategy give a business's new product efforts? First, the goals of your new product strategy tie your product development effort tightly to the overall business strategy. New product development, so often viewed in a "hands-off" fashion by senior management, becomes a central part of the business strategy, a key plank in the business's overall strategic platform.

The question of spending commitments on new products is dealt with by defining the role and goals of the new product effort. Often the R&D or new product budget is easy prey in hard economic times. Development and new product marketing spending tend to be viewed as discretionary expenditures— something that can be slashed if need be. However, if product innovation is established as a central facet of your business's overall strategy, and the role and goals of product innovation are firmly defined, then cutting this R&D budget becomes much less arbitrary. There is a continuity of resource commitment to new products.

The Strategic Arenas: Guiding the War Effort

The second facet of the new product strategy, the definition of arenas, is critical to guiding and focusing new product efforts. The first stage in the Stage-Gate™ new product process is the Discovery Stage or idea generation. But where does one search for new product ideas? Unless the arenas are defined, the idea search is undirected, unfocused, and ineffective.

Your business's new product strategy is also fundamental to project selection and portfolio management. That's why I show strategy as the top box in the portfolio management process of Figure 8.8 in Chapter 8. Strategy overarches the entire decision and selection process. For example, the first gate in the new product process is idea screening. The key criterion for this early go/kill decision is whether the proposed project has strategic alignment. This usually translates into, "Is this the kind of market, product, and technology that we as a business have decided is fair game for us?" Without a definition of your playing fields—arenas of strategic thrust—effective screening decisions will be difficult to achieve. The strategic alignment question remains a vital criterion for project selection at almost every gate throughout the *Stage-Gate* process. It dictates spending splits and the desired balance of the portfolio of projects, and hence is critical to portfolio management.

The definition of arenas also guides long-term resource and personnel planning. If certain markets are designated top priority arenas, then the business can acquire resources, people, skills, and knowledge to enable it to attack those markets. Similarly, if certain technologies are singled out as arenas, the business can hire and acquire resources and technologies to bolster its abilities in those fields. Resource building doesn't happen overnight. One can't buy a sales force on a moment's notice, and one can't acquire a critical mass of key researchers or engineers in a certain technology at the local supermarket. Putting the right people, resources, and skills in place takes both lead time and direction.

The Evidence in Support of Strategy

The argument in favor of a deliberate assessment of opportunities and the development of a new product strategy, although logical, may be somewhat theoretical. One can't help but think of all those companies that have made it without a grand strategy. Further, the notion of deciding what's inbounds versus out-of-bounds is foreign to many businesses. After completing his large sample study on innovation charters, Crawford noted that "the idea of putting definitive restrictions on new product activity is not novel, but the use of it, especially sophisticated use, is still not widespread."[9] Quinn's work on how managers *really* develop corporate strategy concludes that "the approaches they [managers] use frequently bear little resemblance to the rational-analytical systems so often described in the planning literature."[10] He goes on: "Overall corporate strategy tended to evolve as internal decisions and external events flowed together to create a new consensus for action." He argues that strategies evolve and crystallize over time, often in a piecemeal fashion and based on interim decisions. His argument is not that businesses have no strategies but that the way the strategy is developed often does not hinge on formal planning methods.

Regardless of how strategy is developed, the question remains, Does a new product strategy really matter? Perhaps current practice observed by Quinn is not ideal, and senior people *ought to* approach strategy development a little more formally! So where's the evidence in support of having a new product strategy? The studies that have looked at businesses' new product strategies have a clear and consistent message: New product strategies at the business-unit or company level are critical to success, and some strategies clearly work better than others. Consider these facts:

- Booz-Allen & Hamilton's study of new product practices found that "successful companies are more committed to growth through new products developed internally" and that "they are more likely to have a strategic plan that includes a certain portion of growth from new products."[11] The authors of this study go on to explain why having a new product strategy is tied to success:

  A new product strategy links the new product process to company objectives, and provides focus for idea/concept generation and for establishing appropriate screening criteria. The outcome of this strategy analysis is a set of strategic roles used not to generate specific new product ideas but to help identify markets for which new products will be developed. These market opportunities provide the set of product and market requirements from which new product ideas are generated. In addition, strategic roles provide guidelines for new product performance measurement criteria. Performance thresholds tied to strategic roles provide a more precise means of screening new product ideas.

- How various new product strategies are tied to performance was studied by Nystrom and Edvardsson in a number of industrial product firms.[12] Strategies emphasizing the synergistic use of technology, a responsive R&D organization, and an externally oriented R&D effort are generally more successful. Although the study was limited to a handful of strategy dimensions, the message is clear that strategy and performance are closely linked.

- The performance impact of product innovation strategies in 120 businesses was investigated in one of my own studies.[13] This study is one of the first investigations undertaken on a large number of businesses that considers many strategy dimensions and how the strategy of the business's entire new product effort is tied to performance results. The overriding conclusion is that product innovation strategy and performance are strongly linked. The types of markets, products, and technologies that firms elect and the orientation and direction of their product innovation efforts have a pronounced impact on success and profitability. Strategy really does count.

- Ten best practices were identified by management in a study of 79 leading R&D organizations[14.] Near the top of the list is "use a formal development process," an endorsement of the use of stage-and-gate processes. Even higher on the list is "coordinate long-range business planning and R&D plans"—a call for a new product or R&D plan for the business that meshes with the business plan. Although adoption of these best practices varies widely by company, the study revealed that high performers tend to embrace these best practices more than do low performers.

The #2 Cornerstone of Performance: A Clear and Well-Communicated New Product Strategy for the Business

Do you have a clearly articulated product innovation strategy for your business? If so, you're in the minority.[15] But businesses that boast such a strategy do better, according to our major benchmarking study.[16] Recall from Chapter 3 that having a new product strategy—a clear and visible one—is the #2 driver of businesses' new product performance. Businesses that have articulated new product strategies fare much better than those found lacking here: They have 32 percent higher new product success rates, meet sales objectives 42 percent more often, and meet profit objectives 39 percent better. The ingredients of a solid new product strategy are also correlated with both the impact and profitability of the business's total new product efforts (see Figure 12.1).

The benchmarking study found that there are *four main ingredients of a positive new product strategy.*

1. There are goals or objectives for the business's total new product efforts.

This ingredient of strategy—having clear goals—would seem to be fairly basic, but most businesses are found lacking here. Firms scored a mediocre proficiency rating here: only 58.8 points out of 100 (see Figure 12.1). Leading firms, such as 3M, make new product goals, for example, "30 percent of our division's sales will come from new products introduced over the next three years," an explicit part of their business goals. What's more, 3M ties the achievement of these goals to senior management's compensation, which may partially explain 3M's stunning track record in product innovation!

Ironically, having new product goals drives the *impact* of the business's new product effort more than its *profitability*. This is perhaps a reflection of the fact that these goals are most often stated as a percentage of the business's sales to be generated by new products; hence, the result is felt more in terms of sales impact than in profit. One might argue that goals expressed in terms of profit and return on R&D spending might also be appropriate here.

2. The role of new products in achieving the business's goals is clearly communicated to all.

FIGURE 12.1   Ratings of Strategy Ingredients and Effect on Performance

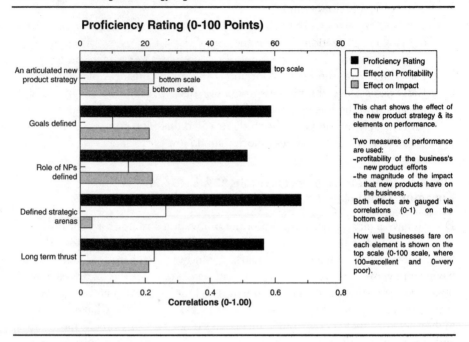

SOURCE: See endnote 21 in chapter 1

The whole point of having goals is so that everyone involved in the activity—in this case, new products—has a common purpose. But as our benchmarking studies revealed, project team members are often not aware of their business's new product objectives or the role that new products play in the overall business objectives. This is the *weakest ingredient* of new product strategy; businesses score a very poor 51.5 points out of 100 here (see Figure 12.1).

3. *There are clearly defined arenas—specified areas of strategic focus or strategic thrust, such as specific products, markets, or technologies—to give direction to the business's total new product effort.*

The new product strategy specifies where you'll attack and, most important, where you won't attack. Without defined arenas, the search for specific new product ideas or opportunities is unfocused. Over time, the portfolio of new product projects is likely to contain a lot of unrelated projects, in many different markets, technologies, or product types—a shotgun effort. And the results are predictable: a not-so-profitable new product effort.

One division of DuPont, a polymers firm, faced exactly this problem; much money was spent on R&D, but there was no focus because there were no defined arenas. Management soon recognized the deficiency. They then identified a number of possible arenas (product/market/technology areas to consider), assessed each in terms of their market attractiveness and the opportunity for leveraging the division's core competencies, selected several arenas, and then began to focus their new product initiatives within these chosen arenas.

Although this is an important strategy ingredient, businesses fare only moderately well here: a score of only 68.0 points out of 100.

4. *The new product effort has a long-term thrust and focus.*

This is a fairly weak ingredient of the four strategy ingredients, with a rating of only 56.5 out of 100 across all businesses (see Figure 12.1). Most firms have far too many short-term (and often low-value) projects in their portfolios. This is *the most important* of the four strategy ingredients. It is significantly linked to four important performance metrics: meeting sales and profit objectives, and the impact of the program on both company sales and profits, as well as to the two performance dimensions, new product profitability and impact.

☞ **Suggestion:** Doing business without a strategy is like a guiding a ship without a rudder. Our benchmarking study's results support this conclusion, and so do other studies. Simply stated, businesses that have goals for their total new product effort, that have clearly defined arenas of strategic thrust, that have a longer-term orientation, and that communicate this strategy to all, outperform the rest.

Do what 3M does. *Set goals* for your business's new product effort (for example, percentage of sales, profit, or growth that new products will contribute over the next X years). Make these goals clear to everyone involved. And consider tying them to senior management's compensation!

Emulate the DuPont example, and *specify strategic arenas*—areas of strategic focus, defined in terms of markets, technologies, and product types or categories. Base these choices on a strategic exercise. And consider going one step further: Move toward portfolio management, and decide priorities and *target expenditure splits* across these arenas.

Strategy Types: Prospectors, Analyzers, Defenders, Reactors

One way of looking at strategy is through a typology based upon the speed that an organization responds to changing market and external conditions by altering its products and markets. There are four strategy types, according to Miles and Snow,[17] and you may wish to elect one as the scenario or model for your own business. Which one are you? And which one should you be?[18]

Prospectors: These businesses are the industry innovators. They value being "first in" with new products and are first to adopt new technologies, even though there are risks and not all such efforts are profitable. Prospectors respond rapidly to early signals that point to emerging or new opportunities. In the automobile business, Honda and DaimlerChrysler-U.S. are considered to be prospectors.

Analyzers: These businesses are fast followers. By carefully monitoring the actions of major competitors, and by moving quickly, they often are able to bring a superior product to market—one that is more cost-efficient or that has better features and benefits—than the prospector's product. But analyzers are rarely first to market. Toyota and Ford are analyzer companies.

Defenders: Defenders attempt to locate and maintain a secure position or niche in a relatively stable product or market area. They protect their domain by offering higher quality, superior service, or lower prices. These businesses ignore industry changes that have no direct influence on their current operations. General Motors, Nissan, and Mazda are defenders.

Reactors: These firms are not as aggressive in maintaining established products and markets as competitors. They respond only when forced to by strong external or market pressures. Subaru was considered a reactor (although its strategy has changed to one of focusing on a niche area, namely, four-wheel drive).

These four types of businesses are useful descriptors when senior management is trying to envision which type of product developer your business aspires to be. Additionally, the way resources are split across project types varies by business, with prospectors undertaking proportionately more new-to-the-world projects as a percentage of their total portfolio. Average breakdowns by project type are shown in Table 12.1 for each of the four strategies. This may provide a useful guide or point of comparison for your business.[19]

☞ **Suggestion:** Having a clearly defined product innovation strategy pays off. If your organization does not have an explicit, written product innovation and technology strategy, complete with measurable goals and specification of arenas as a guide to your business's new product efforts, now is the time to begin developing one.

What strategy type is your business—prospector, analyzer, defender, or reactor? And which type should you be? Or is your strategic approach to new products a hit-and-miss affair—no strategy at all? Read on to see what strategic types, thrusts, and arenas appear to yield superlative results.

Winning Product Innovation Strategies and Their Performance Impacts

What are the secrets of a successful new product strategy? To answer this question, I investigated the product innovation strategies of 120 business units and assessed them on 66 strategy variables.[20] These strategy variables describe the types of markets, products, and technologies that the businesses elected for

TABLE 12.1   Project Types Undertaken by Each Business Strategy Type

Project Type	Prospector	Analyzer	Defender	Reactor
New-to-the-world	30%[a]	6%	7%	0%
New-to-the-firm	15%	15%	16%	8%
Additions to existing product line	22%	40%	38%	52%
Improvements to existing products	11%	15%	10%	14%
Repositionings	8%	8%	9%	12%
Cost reductions	15%	16%	20%	13%
Number of firms	30	22	22	4

[a]: Reads: 30% of the products that Prospectors develop are classed as "new-to-the-world". adds to 100% down a column. Source: Griffin and Page [i].

SOURCE: A. Griffin and A. L. Page, "PDMA success measurement project: Recommended measures for product development success and failure," *Journal of Product Innovation Management* 13, 6 (November 1996): 478–495.

their new product efforts and the businesses' direction, orientation, and commitment to these initiatives. The performance of the businesses' new product efforts was measured on ten different performance metrics. The conclusions, set out below, are based on concrete data and the results of a scientific investigation, not on wishful thinking, conjecture, or speculation. They should be useful to you in the formulation of your new product strategy.

Conclusion 1. There is a strong connection between the new product strategy a business elects and the performance results it achieves.

New product strategy and performance are closely connected. Four strategic thrusts and five different strategy types or scenarios were uncovered (described below), and each is strongly tied to performance. One strategy—Type A, the differentiated strategy—achieves remarkable results and serves as a model to other businesses.

The implications of this strategy-performance link are critical to the management of a business's new product efforts. The existence of this link points to the need to define clearly your business's new product strategy as a central and integral part of your overall business plan. The development of a new product strategy becomes a pivotal task for the leadership team of your business.

Conclusion 2. There are four strategic thrusts or orientations that impact performance, and these should be considered as you develop your business's new product strategy.

- *Technologically sophisticated strategies* do better. Businesses that are strong on this dimension employ sophisticated development technologies and develop high-technology, technically complex new products. These businesses are strongly R&D-oriented, proactive in acquiring new development technologies, and proactive in generating new product ideas. They develop innovative, higher-risk, venturesome products that offer unique features and benefits to customers. They employ state-of-the-art development and production technologies, and the business's product innovation effort is viewed by management as offensive (as opposed to defensive) and as a leading edge of the business's total strategy.
- *Market-oriented and marketing-driven strategies* do better. Businesses that are strong on this marketing dimension feature a new product process that is strongly market-oriented and one dominated by marketing people. These enterprises are proactive in market-need identification, and new product ideas are primarily market-derived. This orientation is characterized by businesses whose new product efforts are highly responsive and sensitive to market needs and wants; products are developed that are closely in tune with market wants.
- A *focused new product effort* is more successful. Strongly focused businesses develop new products that are closely related to each other—the opposite of a highly diverse approach. The products that these businesses develop employ related development technologies and related production methods. They are aimed at closely related markets, and the new products themselves are closely tied to each other.
- An *offensive orientation* outperforms a defensive stance. Businesses with an offensive orientation view their new product initiatives as aggressive ones—aimed at growth and gaining market share (rather than merely protecting a position). Their new product efforts feature an active search effort for new product ideas, and they are proactive in terms of market-need identification.

Conclusion 3. There are five separate strategy types or scenarios that businesses elect for their new product strategies.

The strategy types, in order of performance, include the following:

Type A: the differentiated strategy (15.6 percent of businesses studied). These businesses boast a technologically sophisticated and aggressive effort, a high degree of product fit and focus, and a strong market orientation (three of the four thrusts above). They target attractive high-growth, high-potential markets where competition is weaker. Resulting new products are premium-priced and feature strong differentiation and competitive advantage; they include high-quality products that meet customer needs better than competitors' and products with a strong customer impact that offer unique features and benefits to the customer.

Not surprisingly, this strategy leads to the best results: the highest percentage of sales by new products (47 percent versus 35 percent for the other businesses); the highest success rates at launch; a higher profitability level; and greater new product impact on the business's sales and profits.

Type B: the low-budget conservative strategy (23.8 percent of businesses). These organizations feature low R&D spending and develop copycat, undifferentiated new products. Their new product efforts are focused and highly synergistic with the base business, tending toward a "stay-close-to-home" approach. New products match the business's production and technological skills and resources; fit into the business's existing product lines; and are aimed at familiar and existing markets.

In spite of their lack of spending, organizations adopting this strategy achieve moderately positive results: a high proportion of successes, and low failure and kill rates. The new product effort is profitable, but it yields a low proportion of sales by new products and has a low impact on the business's sales and profits. This conservative strategy results in an efficient, safe, and profitable new product effort, but one lacking a dramatic impact on the business.

Type C: the technology push strategy. This is the most popular strategy, elected by 26.2 percent of the businesses studied. Businesses here feature a technologically driven approach to product innovation and are technologically sophisticated, technology oriented, and innovative. But their new product effort lacks a strong market orientation, and there is little fit, synergy, or focus in the types of products and markets exploited. Moreover, the markets targeted tend to be unattractive ones.

The technology push strategy generally leads to mediocre performance results: It fails to meet the business's new product objectives; it yields a high proportion of project cancellations and product failures; and it is less profitable than Type A or B above. This strategy results in a major new product impact on the business's sales, however. In sum, the technology push strategy produces a technologically aggressive, moderately high-impact effort, but it is costly, inefficient, and plagued by failures because of a lack of focus and a lack of marketing orientation and input.

Type D: the not-in-the-game strategy (15.6 percent of businesses). Businesses that adopt this strategy simply lack technological sophistication; they develop new products that are low-technology, copycat, and low-risk, and they rely on simple, mature technologies. These developments prove to be a poor fit with the existing technology and production base of the business. These enterprises lack an offensive stance, and they attempt to serve market needs that they haven't served before.

Predictably, Type D results are dismal. New products represent a low proportion of their annual sales, and a high proportion of their new products fail commercially. Finally, their new product efforts are rated the lowest in terms of meeting the business's objectives and in their impact on the organization's sales and profits.

Type E: The high-budget diverse strategy (18.9 percent of businesses). This is the "bull-in-a-china-shop" strategy. It features heavy spending on R&D, but in an unfocused fashion; there is no direction, no synergy, no fit. These businesses attack new markets and new technologies and use unfamiliar production technologies. These businesses are tied with Type D as the worst performers.

Conclusion 4. One strategy—Type A, the differentiated strategy— yields exceptional performance results.

The strategy that outperforms the others calls for a balance between *technological sophistication* and aggressiveness and a *strong market orientation*. The performance results of the businesses that elect this balanced strategy are dramatically better than the other four strategy groups in terms of the following:

- ✓ new product success as compared to competitors' efforts
- ✓ generating business unit sales (47 percent of sales from new products versus 35 percent for all other businesses)
- ✓ meeting the business's new product objectives and impact on the business's sales and profit
- ✓ the overall success of the effort

Several characteristics distinguish these Type A high performers from the rest. First, they develop new products that have competitive advantage or differentiation in two ways: high-quality, superior products (superior to competing products in meeting customer needs), and products that offer unique features and benefits with a high customer impact. Their products also tend to be premium priced. New products fit into the businesses' current product lines and are closely related to each other. To achieve this level of differentiation, these businesses feature a strongly market-oriented and marketing-dominated new product effort; they are technologically sophisticated, oriented, and aggressive; and they are highly focused. Finally, they select familiar markets with needs that the organization has served before; their targeted markets are high-potential and high-growth ones, but are not intensely competitive.

The orientation of these businesses' strategies serves as a guide to others. Differentiated-strategy businesses are the only ones to achieve a combination of a *strong market orientation* and a high level of *technological sophistication and aggressiveness.* These businesses possess technological prowess comparable to that of many other enterprises, yet they base their new product efforts on the needs and wants of the marketplace. Their new product ideas are derived from the marketplace; a proactive search effort is made for market need identification; a dominant marketing group is involved in the new product process; and the entire process has a strong market orientation.

Finally, the differentiated strategy yields positive results regardless of the characteristics of the business's industry or the business itself. Industry growth rate, technology level, and technological maturity of the industry all affect performance, but the most important factor is the choice of the right strategy. Moreover, this differentiated strategy gives consistently positive results regardless of enterprise type or industry. This winning strategy is also a universally applicable strategy.

Conclusion 5. Adopting some, but not all, of the elements of the winning strategy is not sufficient.

Certain elements of the Type A balanced strategy can be found in other strategy types. However, none of those types perform nearly as well as Type A. For example:

- Strategy Type B, the *low-budget conservative* approach, shares certain elements with Type A, namely, a good product fit and focus. Type B businesses also possess a high degree of technological and marketing synergy between their new product projects and the business's resource base. The result is second best, but far short of the winning strategy. In particular, although the success, failure, and kill rates of new products are positive, the low-budget, technologically unaggressive strategy simply lacks the R&D commitment and technological prowess of Strategy Type A. The result is a low-impact new product initiative—a case of winning the battle, but losing the war.
- Strategy Type C, *technology push*, businesses adopt a technologically aggressive stance, like the winning Type A businesses. But they lack a market orientation, develop products that are a poor fit with their marketing resources, and tend to target low-growth, low-need markets. The result is a moderately high-impact new product effort, but one with poor success, failure, and kill rates.

The conclusion is that a technologically driven and dominated strategy, on its own, is ineffective. Equally ineffective for many organizations is a conservative, stay-close-to-home approach to new products. The most successful strategy is one that marries technological prowess, a strong market orientation, and a high degree of fit and focus: Type A, the differentiated strategy.

Conclusion 6. The low-budget conservative strategy yields fairly positive results, especially for some types of businesses and industries.

Strategy B—the low-budget conservative approach—is one of the most popular strategies. It works well only for some types of businesses, however. Organizations adopting this conservative strategy . . .

- ✓ leverage their competencies in terms of development technology and production expertise
- ✓ have very focused development efforts (focused on few markets, product types, or technologies)
- ✓ develop products that fit into the existing product line (a stay-close-to-home approach)
- ✓ tend to target markets where the business can leverage its marketing strengths

But these businesses . . .

- ✓ have a low level of R&D spending
- ✓ are relatively unsophisticated technologically and lack a strong technological orientation
- ✓ develop products with the fewest advantages and the least differentiation: copycat products in their customer impact and features, and parity (undifferentiated) products in terms of quality and meeting customer needs
- ✓ compete on price (new products are priced lower than competitors')
- ✓ target highly competitive markets

On average, businesses adopting this low-budget conservative strategy achieve positive results in profitability (returns versus expenditures on new products) and new product success rates. The end result is a low-impact new product effort, however, with a lower-than-average percentage of sales from new products (31 percent versus 38 percent for all the other businesses). For certain types of enterprises, the low-budget conservative strategy works particularly well. Businesses with strengths in marketing (strong sales force, channel system, advertising, and market research skills) and businesses in technologically mature, slower-growth industries perform extremely well by adopting this strategy. Sound performance is restricted to their profitability and success rates, however; the total new product effort is still low impact.

One conclusion is that organizations that possess certain distinctive or core competencies—marketing prowess, for example—might rely on those strengths as the key to moving relatively ho-hum new products to the market. But the results for these Type B businesses are still inferior to the differentiated strategy enterprises that face similar markets and have similar strengths. Moreover,

for businesses lacking key strengths or facing developing, higher-growth industries, the low-budget conservative strategy typically yields results far inferior to
the differentiated strategy. Further, although a conservative strategy may work
well for some businesses and over the medium term, if markets or technologies
change dramatically, these businesses are caught in a vulnerable position—vic-
tims of the product life cycle trap.[21]

Conclusion 7. Certain types of arenas yield better performance.

Certain arenas or battlefields, when attacked or targeted, tend to result in victory. The characteristics of these "winning battlefields" or arenas—the kinds of
markets, technologies, and products that successful businesses focus their innovation efforts on—provide a list of vital criteria that are useful in the evaluation
and selection of arenas. There are two broad factors or main themes that distinguish high-performance arenas, according to the study:

1. the magnitude of opportunities in the arena—for example, whether
   markets in the arena are growing, and the existence of major market and
   technological opportunities in the arena, and
2. the strength or ability of the business to exploit the arena—for example,
   whether the business brings the right resources and skills to the table.

I use these two dimensions as broad criteria later in the chapter to help assess
strategic arenas as part of the strategy development process.

☞ **Suggestion:** Four major strategic thrusts are the common denominators in
businesses that are successful at new products:

1. technological sophistication,
2. a strong market orientation and a market-driven process,
3. focus, and
4. an offensive (versus a defensive) stance.

Have you built these orientations or thrusts into your new product strategy?

Now, take a step back for a moment, and consider your business's new product
efforts and strategy. Which of the five strategy scenarios—Type A through Type
E—comes closest to describing your business's approach? How do your performance results compare?

Next, compare your business's explicit or implicit new product strategy to Type
A, the differentiated strategy. Do you share the same orientations? Do you
select the same types of markets? Do you develop similar types of products? Go
through the list of distinguishing characteristics of these Type A businesses, and

see how you rate on each item. This exercise should shed light on your strategic strengths and weaknesses.

Is your business a Type B, facing mature markets, but with key marketing strengths? Have you elected the low-budget conservative approach to new products? If so, and if you're typical, the results of your new product efforts are probably adequate. But they could be even better if you adopt the differentiated strategy approach. And watch out for the long run, that you aren't blind-sided by changing markets and technologies.

Developing a Product Innovation Strategy for Your Business: Setting Goals

A few years ago, I boarded an early morning flight on a major airline. The captain began his announcement: "Welcome aboard flight 123 en route to . . . ah . . . ah . . . ." There was a long pause. The pause was punctuated by laughter and wisecracks from the passengers; the captain didn't know where the flight was going! Fortunately, within 30 seconds, he remembered our destination. If he hadn't, the plane probably would have emptied. Who would stay on a plane where the captain didn't know his destination? Many of us, however, seem content to stay onboard new product efforts that have no destination.

Defining goals for your product development strategy is essential. Most of us accept that premise. My strategy study and our benchmarking investigations both reveal that many organizations lack written and measurable goals for their innovation effort.

What types of goals should be included in an innovation strategy? First, the goals should be measurable so that they can be used as benchmarks against which to measure performance. For example, Booz-Allen & Hamilton note that firms are now measuring the results of their innovation efforts.[22] Second, the goals should tie the business's new product initiatives tightly to its business strategy. Finally, they must give both senior management as well as project teams a sense of direction and purpose and establish criteria for gate decision making.

Goals That Describe the Role of New Products

One type of new product goal focuses on the role that the new product effort will play in achieving the business goals. Some examples:

1. The percentage of your business's sales in Year 5 that will be derived from new products introduced in that five-year period. (Five years is a historically accepted time span in which to define a product as "new," although given today's pace, two or three years is more appropriate for most businesses). Alternatively, one can speak of absolute sales—dollars in Year 3 from new products—rather than relative sales or percentages.

2. The percentage of your business's profits in Year 2 or 3 that will be derived from new products introduced in that time span. Again, absolute dollars can be used instead of relative profits.
3. Sales and profits objectives expressed as a percentage of business growth. For example: 70 percent of growth in your business's sales over the next three years will come from new products introduced in this period.
4. The strategic role, such as defending market share, exploiting a new technology, establishing a foothold in a new market, opening up a new technological or market window of opportunity, capitalizing on a strength or resource, or diversifying into higher-growth areas.[23]
5. The number of new products to be introduced. (There are problems with this type of objective, however; products could be large-volume or small-volume ones, and the number of products does not directly translate into sales and profits).

By far the most popular is goal type #1 above—percentage of your business's sales in Year 2 or 3 to be derived from new products. It's the metric that 3M popularized. Goal type #2 is related to profit and thus seems even more appropriate, but it may be harder to measure—different accounting practices can change the measure of profits dramatically. Goal type #3 is closely linked to #1 and #2. And don't forget to consider goal type #4—it's more qualitative, but it merits some thought.

The specification of these goals gives a strong indication of just how important new products are to the total business strategy. The question of resource allocation and spending on new product efforts can then be more objectively decided.

Performance Goals

A second type of goal deals with the expected performance of the new product effort. Such goals are useful guides to managers within the new products group. Examples include

- success, failure, and kill rates of new products developed,
- number of new product ideas to be considered annually,
- number of projects entering development (or in development) annually, and
- minimum acceptable financial returns for new product projects.

Many of these performance goals flow logically from the role goals. For example, if the business wants 70 percent of sales growth to come from new products, how does that figure translate into number of successful products, number of development projects, success, failure, and kill rates, and number of ideas to be considered annually?

How to Set the Goals

Setting these goals is no easy task. The first time through, the exercise is often a frustrating experience. Yet these goals are fundamental to developing an innovation strategy, not to mention a logically determined R&D budget figure. New product goal setting usually begins with a strategic planning exercise for the entire business. The business's growth and profit goals are decided, along with areas of strategic thrust. These business goals and thrusts then are translated into new product goals, often using *gap analysis*.

> Senior management at Guinness (Ireland) developed an overall strategic plan for their brewing business. Ambitious growth and profit goals were decided. A review of current products and markets worldwide revealed that gaps would exist between projected sales and the goals. That is, current products and markets were projected into the future, and expected revenues and profits were compared to the desired level of sales and profits (the business goals). The gaps needed to be filled by new markets, new products, or new businesses. From this, a set of new product goals were determined.

Here are the types of metrics most often used by various types of businesses for their new product efforts; these may prove useful in setting your own new product goals.[24]

Prospector businesses—the innovators—most often use

- ✓ percentage of profits from new products
- ✓ percentage of sales from new products
- ✓ ability to open up new windows of opportunity

Analyzer enterprises—the fast followers with competitive advantage—look to

- ✓ ROI from development efforts
- ✓ whether the innovation effort fits or supports the business's overall strategy
- ✓ percentage of profits from new products
- ✓ success/failure rates

Defender organizations measure

- ✓ ROI from development efforts
- ✓ fit with or support of the business's strategy

Reactor businesses rely on

- ✓ ROI from development efforts

✓ success/failure rates
✓ fit with or support of the business's strategy

Additionally, Table 12.1, showing the breakdown of projects by type, is a useful guide to your discussion on goals. What types of new products—from new-to-the-world products to cost reductions—do you want for your business?

Defining Target Arenas for Your Business

The specification of strategic arenas or battlefields provides an important guide to your product innovation efforts. As Day notes, "what is needed is a strategy statement that specifies those areas where development is to proceed and identifies (perhaps by exclusion) those areas that are off limits."[25] The arenas guide the search for new product ideas; they help in project selection (for example, as noted in Chapter 8, a typical and important must-meet criterion in project selection is, Does the project fit within our business's strategy? The strategy is defined in part by the arenas). Finally, delineation of where the business wishes to focus its new product efforts is critical to long-term planning, particularly for resource and skills acquisition.

Defining the target arenas answers the question, On what business, product, market, or technology areas should the business focus its new product efforts? Conceptually, the task is one of *opportunity identification* followed by *opportunity assessment*.

Two issues immediately arise. First, one may question the need for focus at all. Note, however, that new product focus has been found to be an important ingredient of successful innovation strategies.[26] Focus provides direction for idea generation, criteria for project selection, and targets for resource acquisition.[27] A second criticism is that focus inhibits creativity: Some of the best ideas may lie outside the target arenas and will be rejected. The counterargument is that focus improves creativity by targeting energies on those areas where the payoff is likely to be the greatest.[28] Further, significant new product breakthroughs outside the bounds of the new-product strategy statement can usually be readily accommodated in an ongoing project screening process, or through free-time or scouting projects. Finally, inevitably there are products that "got away" in any new product effort, but there will continue to exist ample opportunities within the defined arenas for the business to exploit, provided management has done a credible job at arena definition.

There are three steps to defining the target arenas. The first is analysis—assessing your marketplace, as well as your own company. The second is developing a comprehensive list of possible arenas: opportunity identification. The third is paring down the list—assessing the opportunities to yield a choice of the target arenas.

Strategic Analysis

Strategic analysis is a well-known topic, so I won't dwell too long on it here. Strategic analysis entails the familiar SWOT analysis—strengths, weaknesses, opportunities, and threats. The purpose is to identify possible hot or interesting arenas—markets, technologies, or product areas—that might become your strategic arenas.

Analysis begins with an assessment of your marketplace and your customer's industry. Recall that Chapter 6, which focused on the Discovery Stage, outlined much of this external analysis. Indeed, there is a blurring between developing a product innovation strategy and Discovery, the first stage in *Stage-Gate* (see "Look for Disruptions in Your Customer's Industry" in Chapter 6):

- ✓ map your value chain
- ✓ identify industry drivers and shifts in these
- ✓ undertake market and industry trend analysis
- ✓ use Porter's five forces model
- ✓ develop profit pool maps and market maps—who makes the money in the industry or market (Figures 6.1 and 6.2)?
- ✓ identify opportunities and threats

Not only should this assessment identify possible new opportunities—arenas that are emerging—but it should also provide quality data for evaluating and selecting the right arenas.

The second component of this strategic analysis is an internal assessment, namely, looking at your own firm. The old adage "attack from a position of strength" rings true in product development. As so many of the studies cited here have concluded, leveraging your strengths and competencies increases success rates and new product profitability. So take a hard look at your business, and undertake a core competencies analysis. This means looking at strengths and weaknesses in all facets of your business:

- Marketing and Sales:

  - ✓ loyalty of key customer groups and customer relationships
  - ✓ brand name or franchise in the marketplace
  - ✓ product—quality, reliability, value reputations
  - ✓ distribution and channels (for example, access to key customer groups)
  - ✓ sales force (for example, coverage, skills, reputation)
  - ✓ advertising, communications, and public relations
  - ✓ service, support, and technical service
  - ✓ market shares, presence in certain markets or segments, reputation overall

- Product Technology:

  ✓ areas of product leadership, technologically (for example, features, functionality, product performance)
  ✓ technological capabilities
  ✓ access to new technologies
  ✓ unique technologies or technological skills
  ✓ intellectual property and proprietary positions
  ✓ in-house technological skill base

- Operations or Production Capabilities and Technology:

  ✓ production or operations resources, facilities, and capacities
  ✓ unique skills or abilities
  ✓ technological capabilities in production or operations
  ✓ unique production technologies, intellectual property, and protection
  ✓ raw materials access
  ✓ workforce—skills, knowledge, availability

Assess yourself on each facet, especially relative to your direct and indirect competitors. Then identify areas where you are better than the rest—core or distinctive competencies. These are your strengths. Then look for arenas where you can leverage these strengths to advantage.

Defining the Arenas . . . But What Is a New Product Arena?

How does one define a new product opportunity or arena? Corey proposes that we build two-dimensional matrices, with the dimensions labeled "products" and "markets" in order to identify new business arenas.[29] He notes that markets, together with the products that can be developed in response to needs in these markets, define the opportunities for exploitation: the arenas.

Telenor, the Norwegian telephone system, uses a product/market matrix to help visualize strategic choices and to define arenas on which to focus its new product efforts. One dimension of the matrix is *market segments:* home office; small business; residential; and so on (see Figure 12.2). The other dimension is the *product offering* or product categories: voice, data, Internet, wireless, and so on. The roughly 10 by 10 matrix identifies 100 cells or possible arenas; some are ruled out immediately as infeasible. The remaining set are evaluated, and priorities are established. The top-priority or "star" arenas are singled out for more intensive product development efforts.

In *Defining the Business,* Abell takes this matrix approach one step further by proposing that a business be defined in terms of *three* dimensions:[30]

FIGURE 12.2   Product/Market Matrix

Products

	Voice	Data	Internet	Wireless	Long Distance
SoHo			☆	☆	☆
Medium Business		☆		☆	
Large Business		☆		☆	
Multinationals		☆		☆	☆
Residential	☆			☆	

Markets

The axes of the diagram are "Products" and "Markets". Each cell represents a potential strategic arena.

Arenas are assessed for their potential and the company's business position. Stars designate top priority arenas - where new product efforts will be focused.

1. *Customer groups served.* For a computer manufacturer, customer groups might include banks, manufacturers, universities, hospitals, retailers, and so on.
2. *Customer functions served.* These might include applications support, services, software, central processing, core memory storage, and disk storage.
3. *Technologies utilized.* For core memory storage, several existing and new technologies might have application.

The result is a three-dimensional diagram, with new product arenas defined in this three-dimensional space.

Finally, Crawford's study of firms' innovation charters points to several ways in which managers define new product arenas in practice.[31] Arenas are specified by the following:

✓ product type (for example, liquid pumps),
✓ by end-user activity (process industries),
✓ by type of technology employed (rotary hydraulics), or
✓ by end-user group (oil refineries).

FIGURE 12.3   Defining New Product Arenas: The Three Dimensions

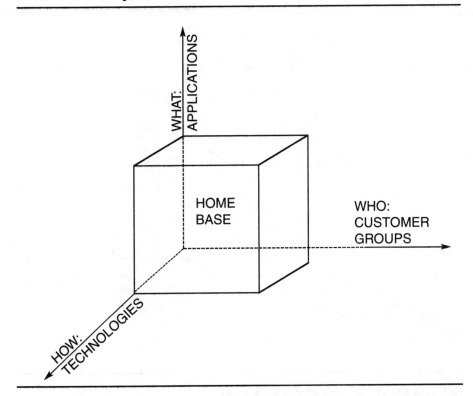

On its own, each of these arena definition schemes has its problems. For example, a product-type definition is limiting: Product classes or types die. Similarly, an end-user group definition could lead the business into a number of unrelated technologies, products, and production systems.

A review of these and other schemes for defining a business arena reveals that a single-dimension approach is likely too narrow. A two- or three-dimensional approach, variants of Corey's or Abell's, probably will suit most business contexts.[32] For example, a new product arena can be defined in terms of the following:

1. *Who:* the customer group to be served (markets or market segments)
2. *What:* the application (or customer need to be satisfied)
3. *How:* the technology required to design, develop, and produce products for the arena

These three dimensions—who, what, and how—provide a useful starting point to describe new product arenas. Sometimes, the last two dimensions—what and how—can be simply combined into a single dimension, product line, or product type.

FIGURE 12.4   The Arena Dimensions for Chempro

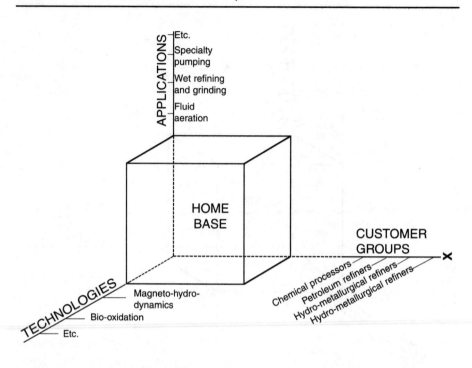

Defining Arenas: A Step-by-Step Illustration

Let's look more closely at some of the details of this process of searching for and prioritizing arenas. A two- or three-dimensional diagram can be used for this search and evaluation (see Figure 12.3). You might also use the product/market matrix of Figure 12.2, or any other convenient dimensions that define arenas for your business. Here I use the three dimensions of customer groups, applications, and technologies, which are shown as the X, Y, and Z axes of the diagram in Figure 12.3. Home base is located, and then other opportunities are identified by moving away from home base in terms of other (but related) customer groups, applications, and technologies. Chempro serves as our example.

Chempro is a medium-sized manufacturer of blending and agitation process equipment for the pulp and paper industry. The company's major strength is its ability to design and manufacture rotary hydraulic equipment. The market served is the pulp and paper industry. The application is agitation and blending of liquids and slurries. The company's current or home base is shown as the cube in Figure 12.4.

What new product arenas exist for the company? Clearly, the home base is one of these, and indeed the firm is active in seeking new product ideas for agi-

FIGURE 12.5   Arena Map: Identification of Possible Strategic Arenas for Chempro

	Current Customer Group	New Customer Groups		
	Pulp & paper industry	Chemical process industry	Petroleum refining companies	Metallurgical industry (ore refining)
Current Application **Agitation & blending of liquids**	Agitators & blenders for pulp & paper industry	Chemical mixers	Blenders for petroleum storage tanks	Hydro-metallurgical agitators
New Applications **Aeration of liquids**	Surface aerators, P&P waste treatment	Aerators for chemical wastes	Aerators for petroleum waste treatment	Aerators for flotation cells (hdyro-metallurgical)
Wet refining & grinding	Pulpers, repulpers & refiners			
Specialty pumping	High density paper stock pumps	Specialty chemical pumps	Specialty petroleum pumps	Slurry pumps

SOURCE: R. G. Cooper, "Strategic planning for successful technological innovation," *Business Quarterly* 43 (Spring 1978): 46–54.

tation equipment in the pulp and paper field. Most of these opportunities, however, are limited to modifications and improvements.

One direction that senior management can take is to develop new products aimed at alternative customer groups. These customer groups include the chemical, food-processing, petroleum-refining, and hydro-metallurgical fields. The options are shown on the X or horizontal axis of Figure 12.4.

Similarly, new products in related applications can be sought. These related applications include the pumping of fluids, fluid aeration, and refining and grinding, as shown on the vertical or Y axis of the arena matrix.

Considering these two dimensions—different applications and different customer groups—management now proceeds to define a number of new arenas. Working with a two-dimensional grid (Figure 12.5), management recognizes that besides the home-base arena, there are twelve other arenas that the company can consider for its new product focus. For example, Chempro can develop blending and agitation equipment (same application) aimed at the chemical or petroleum industries (new customer groups). Alternatively, the business can target aeration devices (new application) at its current customers, namely, pulp

TABLE 12.2   Characteristics of High-Performance New Product Arenas

I. Arena Opportunity (North-south or Vertical Axis):

1. Market attractiveness:
   - Size of the markets in the arena (dollar volume) — 5
   - Number of potential customers for the product in the arena — 9
   - Long-term potential of markets in the arena — 11
   - Growth rates of markets in the arena — 17

   Sub-total: Market attractiveness — 42

2. Technological opportunities:
   - Technology level of products sold in this arena (high tech = good) — 12
   - Nature of technologies in this arena (leading and state-of-the-art technologies=good) — 19
   - Technological elasticity (opportunity for developing new products in this arena: e.g., will a dollar spent yield high returns in terms of new products sales & profits?) — 27

   Sub-total: technological opportunities — 58

Total for Arena Opportunity — 100

II Business Strength (East-West or Horizontal Axis):

1. Ability to leverage your technological competencies, strengths & experience:
   - Degree of fit between production processes used in this arena & the production processes & skills of your business — 11
   - Degree of fit between R&D skills/resources required in this arena & the technical skills/resources of your business — 14
   - Degree of fit between engineering/design skills/resources required & your engineering/technical skills/resources — 4

   Subtotal: Technological leverage — 29

2. Ability to leverage marketing competencies, strengths & experience:
   - Degree of fit between the sales force and/or distribution channel system required for this arena & those of your business — 8
   - Degree of fit between the advertising & promotion approaches and skills required in this arena fit & those of your business — 14

   Subtotal: Marketing leverage

(continues)

3. Strategie leverage—potential for gaining for product
advantage or differentiation:
Envision the new products that you would/could develop
in this arena...

• Potential for impact—the magnitude of product impact on customers (e.g., on their operations, costs, workflow, etc.)	18
• Potential for differentiation—will new products here be unique (differentiated from) competitive products?	20
• Potential to meet customer needs better than competitive products	11
Subtotal: Potential for leverage via product advantage	49
Total for Business Strength	100

and paper companies. Each of these possibilities represents a new arena for Chempro.

Chempro might also be able to change its third dimension by moving from its home base of rotary hydraulic technology to other technologies. If the alternatives are superimposed along the third dimension atop the matrix, the result is a much larger number of possible arenas. (This third dimension expansion is not shown in Figure 12.5, as it's a little hard on the eyes!) Possible alternative arenas along the "new technologies" axis include magneto-hydrodynamic pumps and agitators for a variety of end-user groups and bio-oxidation reactors for the food industry, among others.

Selecting the Right Arenas

The task now is to narrow down the many possible arenas to a target set that will become the focus of the business's innovation strategy. To a certain extent, a pre-screening of these arenas has already occurred: The arenas have been identified as being related to the base business on at least one of the three dimensions.

The choice of the right arenas is based on a single must-meet criterion and two should-meet criteria. The must-meet criterion is an obvious one: Does the arena fit within the business's mission, vision, and overall strategy? The other two criteria were identified in my studies of successful new product strategies. These criteria are *arena opportunity* and *business strength* (see Table 12.2).

Arena opportunity is a strategic dimension that captures how attractive the external opportunity is for that arena. In Table 12.2, arena opportunity consists of the following:

✓ *market attractiveness:* the size, growth, and potential of market opportunities within the arena, and

✓ *technological opportunities:* the degree to which technological and
new product opportunities exist within the arena.

In practice, arena opportunity is a composite index constructed from the
answers to a number of individual questions. Table 12.2 shows a sample list of
questions found in my study of product innovation strategies (this list may not
be an exhaustive one). Typically, an arena is assessed against each question and
is given a rating; these ratings are then multiplied by the question weight shown
in the table and added to yield an *index of arena opportunity.* Arenas that feature large, growing, and high-potential markets, that are characterized by technological elasticity (bang for R&D buck spent[33]), and that feature high-tech
products based on leading-edge technologies score high on the arena opportunity dimension.

Business strength is the other strategic dimension. Business strength focuses
on the business's ability to successfully exploit the arena. The ability to leverage
the organization's resources and skills to advantage in the new arena is a key concept here. Business strength is again a composite dimension, consisting of three
factors (again from my study of innovation strategies):

✓ ability to leverage the business's technological competencies
✓ ability to leverage its marketing competencies, and
✓ strategic leverage—the potential to gain product advantage and differentiation.

Arenas that build on the business's core and distinctive competencies, that fit
well the business's marketing and technological strengths and resources, and
that offer the business a solid opportunity to gain product advantage or achieve
product differentiation are the ones that score high on the business strength
dimension.

Mapping the Strategic Arenas

How the various arenas score on the two criteria can be shown pictorially in the
arena assessment map of Figure 12.6. Arena opportunity is shown as the vertical or north-south dimension, and business strength as the horizontal or east-
west axis. The result is a four-sector diagram, not unlike traditional portfolio
models, but with different dimensions and different components to each
dimension.

Each sector represents a different type of opportunity:

• The arenas shown in the northwest sector (the upper-left), which feature high arena opportunity and business strength, are clearly the most
desirable. These are called the "good bets."

FIGURE 12.6   Arena Assessment for Chempro

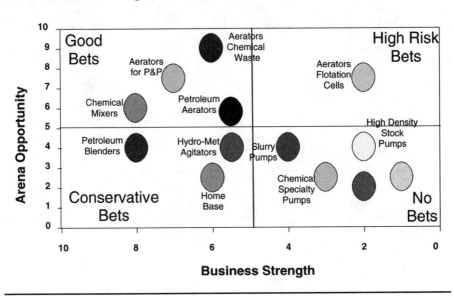

Chempro management elected three arenas in the "Good Bets" quadrant and one "Conservative Bet" to target with ne   products

- Diagonally opposite, in the southeast (lower-right) sector, are the "low-low" arenas—those arenas that neither build on the organization's strengths nor offer attractive external opportunities. These are the "no bets."
- The "high-risk bets" are in the northeast (upper-right) sector. They represent high-opportunity arenas where the business has no exploitable strengths.
- Finally, the soutwest (lower-left) sector houses the "conservative bets"— arenas where the business can utilize its strengths to advantage, but where the external opportunity is not so attractive. These are opportunities to be pursued at little risk, but which offer limited returns.

Using such a map, management can eliminate certain arenas outright (those in the "no bet" sector) and select a reasonable balance of arenas from the other three sectors. The "good bets," in the northwest sector, are usually the top-priority ones.

Assessing the Arenas at Chempro

At Chempro, strategic arena assessment is simplified by recognizing the company's technological and financial resource limitations. Chempro's main asset is its

FIGURE 12.7   Assigning Priorities to the Arena

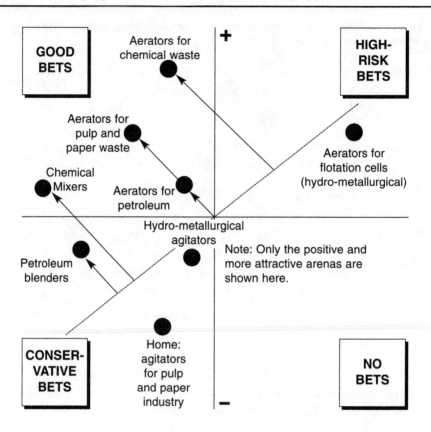

Note: Only the positive and more attractive arenas are shown here.

ability to design and engineer rotary hydraulic equipment. Embarking on new and expensive technologies, such as magneto-hydrodynamics or bio-oxidation, is deemed out-of-bounds. Moreover, having identified its current technology as a field of particular strength, and recognizing that there are many opportunities that can build on this strength, senior management elects to stay with its current technology. Management chooses to *attack from a position of strength*, and so the third dimension, alternative technologies, is deleted. The result is the two-dimensional grid in Figure 12.5.

Next, the twelve new arenas plus the home base are rated on the two key dimensions of market attractiveness and business position. A list of questions is employed similar to those in Table 12.2, with each arena rated on each question. The questions are weighted, and a business strength and arena opportunity index are computed for each of the thirteen possible arenas. The results for Chempro are shown in Figure 12.6.

Selecting the Arenas at Chempro

The choice of arenas depends on the risk/return values of management. Selecting only those arenas in the top half of the arena assessment diagram—the good bets and the high-risk bets—emphasizes the attractiveness of the external opportunity and places no weight at all on the business-strength dimension: a high return, but a higher-risk choice. The other extreme—selecting only those arenas on the left of the vertical, the good bets and conservative bets—boils down to a low-risk, low-return strategy: selection of only those arenas in which the company possesses a good business position. Ideally, one looks for a combination of the two: arenas in which the market attractiveness and the business strength both are rated high—the good bets in the northwest sector of Figure 12.6, or perhaps some balance of arenas—some attractive but riskier arenas, some lower-risk but less attractive ones.

For Chempro, six arenas were rated positively on both dimensions. In order to quantify or rank-order these opportunities, a cutoff or 45-degree line was drawn (see Figure 12.7). Arenas to the left of and above this line are positive; those to the right and below are negative. The distance of each arena from that line was measured; the greater the distance, the more desirable the arena. Based on this exercise, three good bets and one conservative bet were defined as new arenas for Chempro:

- ✓ aerators for the chemical industry (waste treatment)
- ✓ blenders for the petroleum industry
- ✓ agitators and mixers for the chemical industry
- ✓ surface aerators for the pulp and paper industry

The decision was made to continue seeking new products in the home-base arena as well. Several other arenas were put on hold for future action.

☞ **Suggestion:** The place to begin is with the *strategy of your business* and, flowing from it, your *product innovation and technology strategy.* Strategy development is the job of the senior management of the business; the senior people must lead here. Indeed, this is how senior people first become engaged in the project selection and portfolio management processes—by charting the business's strategy.

After defining the overall goals for your business, spell out your *new product goals:* for example, the percentage of sales or profit or growth that new products will contribute. Use gap analysis as Guinness does.

Then move to mapping your battlefields; that is, identify arenas of strategic focus. Undertake a strategic analysis—first on your marketplace or your customer's industry (see Chapter 6), next on your business—the search for strengths and core competencies. Identify the opportunities.

Next draw an arena diagram for your business. Use two dimensions (products and markets, as Telenor does) or perhaps three dimensions (customer groups, applications, and technologies, like Chempro). Locate your home base, and then move out on each of the three axes, identifying other customer groups, applications, and technologies. This exercise should help you uncover a number of new but related product arenas.

Now that you've identified a list of possible arenas, try to rate each on the two key dimensions of *arena opportunity* and *business strength*. Develop a list of questions for each dimension (use Table 12.2 as a guide), and score each arena on the questions. Draw an arena assessment map (similar to Figure 12.6) to see where your arenas lie.

Prioritizing: Defining the Spending Splits

Decisions on spending splits must be made in order to translate strategy into reality. Strategic priority decisions should be considered on a variety of dimensions beyond the arena assessment shown in Figure 12.6. Defining and prioritizing arenas provides a good foundation for senior management to begin the debate on spending splits. Here are some dimensions to consider when developing your business's product innovation strategy:

- *Across arenas:* The first and most obvious spending split is across the strategic arenas defined and prioritized above. Having assessed the attractiveness and defined the priority of each arena, move to deployment; that is, decide how much spending each arena should receive.
- *Types of projects:* Decisions or splits can be made in terms of the *types of projects.* For example: "Given our aggressive strategic stance, we target 30 percent of R&D spending to genuine new products and another 20 percent to fundamental research and platform development (technology development for the future); 30 percent will go to product modifications and improvements, only 10 percent to cost reductions, with another 10 percent to product maintenance and fixes." (There are various ways to define "project types"—recall the Strategic Buckets method in Figure 8.6 in Chapter 8).
- *Project newness:* Decisions or splits can be made in terms of project newness, using the a typical "newness matrix."[34] Projects might be classed as "defend and/or penetrate" projects to "new businesses/new ventures."
- *Technologies or technology platforms:* Spending splits can be made across technology types (for example, base, key, pacing, and embryonic technologies) or across specific technology platforms: Platforms X, Y, and Z.

FIGURE 12.8   Spending Splits at Chempro

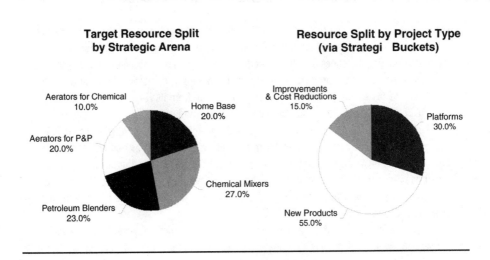

- *Stage or phase of development:* Some businesses distinguish between early-stage projects and projects in the Development Stage and beyond. Two buckets are created, one for development projects, the other for early-stage projects. One division at GTE allocates "seed" money to a separate bucket for early-stage projects.

Returning to our Chempro illustration, management prioritizes the four newly defined arenas along with the existing arena, home base. The arena map in Figure 12.6 provides a good guide for this prioritization exercise. Also considered are new product opportunities or possible projects that are proposed within each arena. After much discussion and analysis, spending levels are established for each arena (see Figure 12.8).

Additionally, Chempro's management develops Strategic Buckets for project types: genuine new products; product improvements and modifications; and cost reductions (Figure 12.8). A small percentage of resources is devoted to fundamental research. Here, the arenas chosen and the nature of the developments required in each arena help to decide the resource split by project types.

Developing Attack Plans

The goals have been decided, and the strategic arenas mapped out and prioritized. Now it's time to determine the *new product attack plan* for each arena. These attack plans tend to be fairly industry and company specific. However, there exist a number of frameworks that help guide this effort.

PLATFORMS: A BASE FROM WHICH TO OPERATE

Many businesses now look to platforms as a way to think about strategic thrusts in product development. The original notion of a platform was very much *product based*. For example, the PDMA handbook defines a platform product as "design and components that are shared by a set of products in a product family. From this platform, numerous derivatives can be designed."[35] For example, Chrysler's engine transmission from its K-car was a platform that spawned other vehicles, including the famous Chrysler minivan.

The notion of platforms has since been broadened to include *technological capabilities*. For example, Exxon's metallocene platform is a catalyst that has spawned an entirely new generation of polymers. A platform is like an oil drilling platform in the ocean, which you invest heavily in. From this platform, you can drill many holes relatively quickly and at low cost. Thus, the platform leads to many related new product projects in a timely and cost-effective manner.

The definition of platforms has also been broadened to include *marketing or branding concepts* as well as technological capabilities. For example, some consider 3M's *Post-It Notes*™ to be a platform that has created many individual products; Nabisco's *Snack Well*™ products—indulgent but low-fat dessert food items—is another example of a marketing platform.

Innovation Scenarios

The strategy typology offered earlier in this chapter provides a useful way to visualize your attack approach. Recall these strategy types:

- *Prospector*—you are the industry innovator, the first in with new products, and the first to adopt new technologies;
- *Analyzer*—you are the fast follower, monitoring competitor entries, and bringing superior or more cost-effective products to market;
- *Defender*—you maintain a secure position in a niche or stable market, and protect your position through better service, higher quality, or lower prices;
- *Reactor*—you respond only when forced to.

There are pros and cons to each approach above. You must weigh your own situation—your marketplace's dynamics, your competition, and your own capabilities and competencies—and decide. But do make a choice—don't just let it happen by default!

Strategy Types

In deciding your attack plan, also consider the five strategy types I uncovered in my strategy-performance investigation. In particular, take a close look at strate-

FIGURE 12.9   The Product Road Map

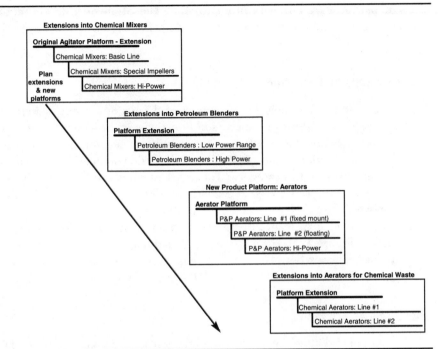

BASED ON: M. H. Meyer and A. P. Lehnerd, *The Power of Platforms* (New York: Free Press, 1997).

gy Types A and B—the differentiated strategy and the low-budget conservative strategy.

A Focus on Platforms

Instead of innovation scenarios or strategy types (above), your attack plan could focus on the *types of platforms* your business will invest in. For example, having identified certain markets as strategic arenas, certain new technology platforms may be envisioned in order to win in these market arenas (see page 388, "Platforms: A Base from Which to Operate.") In Chapter 5, I suggested that platform developments can also be stage-gated, but the criteria for selection are necessarily more visionary and strategic than those outlined in Chapter 8 for new product projects.

Split in Resources

The attack plan may also deal with the *split in resources across project types*, as in Chempro's case. For example, having agreed that certain market segments are top priority ones, what types of developments are needed to win in each arena? Do you need new products, or merely extensions, fixes, and updates? Or are new platforms required in order to win? The Strategic Buckets method (Figures 8.6 and 12.8) helps to translate strategy into resource splits by project types.

Major Assaults and the Product Road Map

Finally, your attack plan may simply consist of the major assaults or initiatives that are needed in order to be successful in a given arena—*specific new products and projects and their timing*. For example, once a product category is agreed to as a top priority one, what new products do you need in order to succeed in a major way in this category? The attack plan may boil down to the *portfolio of proposed projects* aimed at that arena—in effect, a cluster of assaults or tactical moves.

A product road map is an effective way to chart this series of assaults. An example is in Figure 12.9. Here the product road map not only defines the various product releases but also specifies what features or functionality will be built into each new release and, finally, indicates timing (launch date).

Chempro's Attack Plan

Chempro's general attack plan was the same across all arenas: a differentiated approach focusing on delivering superior products with unique features and benefits to customers. This strategy requires a marriage of Chempro's core technology competency (prowess in the field of rotary hydraulic equipment design) with a customer-orientated, market-driven approach to defining product requirements. Thus, the strategy is really a combination of the analyzer strategy and Type A differentiated strategy.

At the same time, a product road map was developed. This outlined the major new product projects and their timing in order to successfully attack the designated strategic arenas.[36] For example, top priority was given to extension of the current platform—agitators and mixers—to both the chemical and petroleum industries, and priority was given to the development of a family of high-efficiency surface aerators targeted initially at the pulp and paper industry. Next, the extension of this product line into chemical waste treatment was charted on the road map (see Figure 12.9).

Key Points for Management

Reflect on Chempro's strategic exercise for a moment. There are several positive points to note:

1. First, senior management leads the way. It is the senior people of the business who took up the challenge and mapped out the business's new

product strategy. This task was not left to a marketing or R&D group to do. This is not the time or place for "hands-off" management!

2. The new product strategy goes beyond vision and mission and nice-sounding words. It consists of goals and prioritized arenas (defined by application and customer groups), which are translated into decisions on resource deployment and major initiatives.

3. The split in resources across arenas, although top-down and strategically driven, considers opportunities within each arena. This was not a sterile strategic exercise, but rather an iterative one between a top-down strategic approach and a bottom-up approach that took into account active and proposed projects and opportunities.

4. Finally, attack plans were developed for each arena—how management intends for Chempro to win on each battlefield. In Chempro's case, this attack plan went as far as charting major new product initiatives on a product road map.

☞ **Suggestion:** *Identify your top priority arenas.* Start with your arena assessment as illustrated in Figure 12.6, which identifies possible battlefields. Prioritize your arenas, looking for those in the desirable northwest sector (upper-left), perhaps seeking a balance by including a few projects from the high-risk bets.

Next, *focus on deployment of resources.* Develop spending splits across key dimensions (for example, splits by arenas or splits on other dimensions such as project types; or pick dimensions that represent strategic thrusts). Define Strategic Buckets across dimensions (as in Figure 8.6 or Figure 12.8).

Finally, *define attack plans* for each arena . . . how you plan to win on each battlefield or in each arena. This could be a general attack plan coupled with a road map of specific major assaults or initiatives (as in Chempro's case) or an attack plan based on other dimensions, including strategic scenarios, strategy types, platforms, or splits in resources by project types.

Putting Your Product Innovation Strategy to Work

The goals and the top priority arenas for the business's new product strategy have been defined. Let's look at how this new product strategy guides the management of the enterprise's development efforts.

Discovery: Searching for Product Ideas

The Discovery Stage and the development of a product innovation and technology strategy overlap considerably—and so they should! Indeed, progressive companies build in a heavy dose of strategy development into their Discovery Stage. The search for major new product ideas begins with a strategic analysis of your marketplace (or your customer's industry) coupled with a core competencies assessment of your own business. The goal is to find opportunities in the form of gaps, discontinuities, emerging arenas, new technologies, new platforms, and unarticulated needs.

Your product innovation strategy helps to shape the entire Discovery Stage. For example, identifying and assessing your new product arenas (Figure 12.7) provide guidance to the idea search effort. Armed with a knowledge of the arenas the business wishes to target, those charged with seeking new product ideas now have a clear definition of where to search; the hunting grounds are defined. Moreover, it becomes feasible to implement formal search programs—seeking unmet customer needs and undertaking voice-of-customer research; initiating fundamental scientific research; implementing suggestion schemes, sales force programs, and creativity sessions; and all the other methods outlined in Chapter 6—to generate new product ideas. The search for ideas is more efficient, generating product ideas that are consistent with the business's focus.

In Chempro's case, all personnel, from the president to sales trainees, gained a clear view of which new product arenas the company wished to concentrate on. First, the strategic exercise identified some "must-do" projects, which are outlined in the product road map (Figure 12.9). But the new insights also made it possible for good new product ideas in the designated arenas to pour in from everyone in the company.

More Effective Project Selection

One of the most critical project selection criteria highlighted in Chapter 8 is whether the new product project is aligned with the business's strategy. All too often the question is answered with blank stares and shrugs. A clear delineation of your business's new product arenas provides the criterion essential to answer the "strategic alignment" question. Either the new product proposal under consideration fits into one of the designated arenas, or it does not. The result is a more effective and efficient screening: Precious management time and resources are not wasted on new product proposals that may seem attractive on their own merits, but simply do not mesh with the long-term strategy of the business.

A Guide to Portfolio Management

Effective portfolio management is almost impossible without a well-defined new product strategy in place for the business, complete with goals and prioritized arenas. Strategic Buckets are essential for effective portfolio management—ideal resource splits by market, by product line or category, or by project type—and flow directly from the business's new product strategy.

Additionally, the ideal balance of projects and the identification of strategic imperative projects—must-do-now projects—are similarly driven by the business's product innovation and technology strategy.

Personnel and Resource Planning

Resources essential to new products—R&D, engineering, marketing, operations—cannot be acquired overnight. Without a definition of which arenas the business intends to target, planning for the acquisition of these resources is like asking a blindfolded person to throw darts.

At Chempro, aerators for the pulp and paper industry were defined as one top priority arena. R&D management hired researchers in the field of biochemistry and waste treatment; the engineering department acquired new people in the field of aeration equipment design and aeration application engineering; and plans were made to add aeration experts to the sales force. Finally, several small exploratory technical and market research programs were initiated in aeration and bio-oxidation.

Some Final Thoughts on New Product Strategy

With the increasing importance of new product warfare comes a desire to more effectively manage innovation, hence the wish to develop product innovation strategies. Developing a product innovation strategy for your business is not easy. Nevertheless, a product innovation and technology strategy is a must for all businesses that are serious about building new products into their long-range plans. Many businesses operate without such a strategy, and the senior managements know the problems only too well. There is no direction to the Discovery Stage or to idea search, or there is no discovery at all. Much time is wasted in screening proposed projects and agonizing over the question, Should we be in this business? Portfolio management is almost impossible, and there are difficulties in making a long-term, sustained budget commitment for new products. And personnel, resource, and technology acquisition planning is hit-and-miss.

Methods for defining the new product strategic direction have been outlined in this chapter. I began with a recognition of the need for and rewards of having such a strategy. Goals are defined that tie the business's new product effort firmly to the business's overall objectives. Strategic arenas—the target battle-fields or arenas of strategic thrust—are identified and pared down to a set of top-priority fields for exploitation. These arenas give the new product effort direction and focus—ingredients that are critical to a successful innovation strategy. These arenas are prioritized, and from these priorities, spending splits are decided, as the business's new product strategy begins to drive portfolio management. Finally, attack plans are developed for each arena. And so the new product strategy evolves to guide your business's new product war effort.

Appendix A: *ProBE* Benchmarking Tool

How well are you doing at new product development? And how do your methods and approaches compare with industry best practices? *ProBE* is a diagnostic tool that helps provide answers to these vital questions. (*ProBE* stands for Product Benchmarking and Evaluation.)

ProBE was originally developed in response to repeated requests by companies whose managements wanted to compare their businesses to those scores of companies in our database. Recall the benchmarking study we undertook, where we looked at hundreds of businesses in an attempt to learn what the drivers of new product performance are.[1] In this study, almost one hundred drivers of performance were considered. The result was that we amassed a huge database—many companies rated on the numerous drivers of performance.

ProBE enables your business to compare its new product performance and practices with those of the companies in the database. This is a questionnaire-based method, where a number of people in your organization answer a detailed, tested questionnaire. The questions are relatively simple ones—using zero-to-ten scales with anchor phrases—that seek subjective opinion from these knowledgeable people.

Topics covered in *ProBE* include those practices that our benchmarking studies revealed are critical to high performance, specifically

- ✓ your business's culture and climate
- ✓ adequacy of resources committed
- ✓ effective resource allocation
- ✓ your new product process
- ✓ quality of execution of key tasks in a typical project
- ✓ degree of market orientation
- ✓ your business's new product strategy
- ✓ top management involvement and its role
- ✓ competitive advantage of your new products
- ✓ your portfolio management approaches

FIGURE A.1: Sample ProBE Output—Organizational Design (Project Teams)

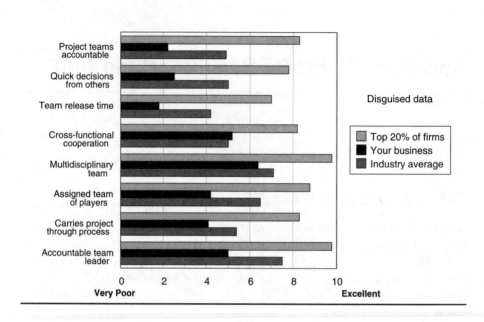

The *ProBE* software analyzes your questionnaire data and produces an initial report. This report—a set of bar charts and pie charts—pinpoints your areas of strengths and weaknesses and helps identify areas needing fixing. Figure A.1 shows a sample output page (there are fourteen such pages of output). *ProBE* benchmarks your practices and performance against industry averages and also against the 20 percent best-practice firms.

Next, the *ProBE* consultants conduct a diagnostic session with the management of your company. They review the results and identify the causes of substandard performance. Finally, they develop a plan of action for your company to improve its performance.

ProBE is an ideal way to begin your new product internal audit. Before you embark on a major overhaul or redesign of your new product process or rethink your entire approach to product innovation, consider using *ProBE* or a similar structured technique to pinpoint what needs fixing. Remember: The beginning of a solution is understanding the problem!

ProBE is commercially available from a number of sources. For more information, see the outline at the Product Development Institute's web page: www.prod-dev.com.[2]

Appendix B: The *NewProd*™ Model

NewProd™ is a scoring model with a difference. It's based on the profiles and outcomes of hundreds of past new product projects. And it serves as both a diagnostic tool and predictive model.[1]

NewProd is a computer-based scoring model that helps the project team understand their project much better—its strengths, weaknesses, risks, critical areas of ignorance, and what needs fixing. Thus it leads to a common understanding of the project, and it helps the project team develop an action plan for the project.

NewProd also predicts the likelihood of commercial success and therefore is valuable as an input to the go/kill and portfolio management decision. For example, Procter & Gamble uses the NewProd score—likelihood of commercial success—as one axis in their three-dimensional portfolio bubble diagram (see Figure 8.5).[2]

NewProd™ is premised on the fact that the profile of a new product project is a reasonable predictor of success. The model was developed from the experiences and outcomes of hundreds of past new product launches.[3] Profile characteristics include measures of competitive and product advantage, leveraging core competencies, market attractiveness and competitive situation, project innovativeness, and so on.

In use, up to twelve evaluators assess the project on each of thirty key questions, which are proven discriminators between winners and losers. The profile of the project, based on these ratings, is analyzed by computer and, in effect, compared with the profiles of hundreds of projects in the database that have known commercial outcomes. In this way, a likelihood of success and the project's strengths and weaknesses are determined.

Although originally developed for DuPont and Procter & Gamble, *NewProd*™ is now commercially available and has been adopted as a selection and diagnostic tool in about 150 companies in Europe and North America. Additionally, there are industry-specific versions, for example, for the chemical industry, the pharmaceutical industry, the service sector, and consumer goods industries. It has been successfully validated in Holland, Scandinavia, and North America and yields predictive abilities in the 73 to 84 percent range—not perfect, but considerably better than the typical manager's ability to pick winners![4] See www.prod-dev.com.

Notes

Chapter 1

1. R. N. Foster, "Managing technological innovation for the next 25 years," *Research-Technology Management* 43, 1 (January-February 2000): 29.

2. A. Griffin, *Drivers of NPD Success: The 1997 PDMA Report* (Chicago: Product Development & Management Association, 1997).

3. Ibid.

4. R. G. Cooper and E. J. Kleinschmidt, "Performance topologies of new product projects," *Industrial Marketing Management* 24 (1995): 439–456; see also NewProd studies in R. G. Cooper and E. J. Kleinschmidt, "Major new products: What distinguishes the winners in the chemical industry?" *Journal of Product Innovation Management* 2, 10 (March 1993): 90–111; R. G. Cooper and E. J. Kleinschmidt, "New product success in the chemical industry," *Industrial Marketing Management* 22, 2 (1993): 85–99.

5. "Strong U.S. economy drives continued R&D growth," *Barrington*, January 1999, 17–26.

6. R. G. Cooper, "Stage-Gate systems: A new tool for managing new products," *Business Horizons* 33, 3 (May-June 1990): 44–54.

7. "America's most admired companies," *Fortune* (available at Fortune.com), 1999.

8. B. O'Reilly, "Secrets of America's most admired corporations: New ideas, new products," *Fortune*, March 3, 1997, 60–66.

9. Cited in C. F. von Braun, *The Innovation War* (Upper Saddle River, N.J.: Prentice Hall PTR, 1997).

10. Griffin, *Drivers of NPD Success.*

11. Booz-Allen & Hamilton, *New Product Management for the 1980s* (New York: Booz-Allen & Hamilton, Inc., 1982).

12. A. L. Page, "PDMA new product development survey: Performance and best practices," paper presented at PDMA Conference, Chicago, Nov. 13, 1991.

13. Griffin, *Drivers of NPD Success.*

14. Booz-Allen & Hamilton, *New Product Management.*

15. The original typology of new products was developed by Booz-Allen & Hamilton; the "all industry" data in Figure 1.5 is from the PDMA best practices study in Griffin, *Drivers of NPD Success.*

16. Booz-Allen & Hamilton, *New Product Management.*

17. E. J. Kleinschmidt and R. G. Cooper, "The impact of product innovativeness on performance," *Journal of Product Innovation Management* 8 (1991): 240–251; and Griffin, *Drivers of NPD Success*.

18. Booz-Allen & Hamilton, *New Product Management*.

19. Kleinschmidt and Cooper, "The impact of product innovativeness on performance."

20. These NewProd studies began in 1975. More recent publications include R. G. Cooper, "The invisible success factors in product innovation," *Journal of Product Innovation Management* 16, 2 (April 1999): 115–133; R. G. Cooper, "New product leadership: Building in the success factors," *New Product Development and Innovation Management* 1, 2 (1999): 125–140; R. G. Cooper, "New Product Development," in *International Encyclopedia of Business and Management: Encyclopedia of Marketing*, ed. Michael J. Baker (London: International Thomson Business Press, 1999): 342–355; R. G. Cooper, "New products: What separates the winners from the losers?" in *PDMA Handbook for New Product Development*, ed. Milton D Rosenau Jr. (New York: John Wiley & Sons, 1996); R. G. Cooper, "Overhauling the new product process," *Industrial Marketing Management* 25, 6 (November 1996): 465–482; R. G. Cooper, "Debunking the myths of new product development," *Research and Technology Management* 37, 4 (July-August 1994): 40–50; R. G. Cooper and E. J. Kleinschmidt, "Major new products: What distinguishes the winners in the chemical industry?" *Journal of Product Innovation Management* 2, 10 (March 1993): 90–111; R. G. Cooper and E. J. Kleinschmidt, "New product success in the chemical industry," *Industrial Marketing Management* 22, 2 (1993): 85–99; R. G. Cooper and E. J. Kleinschmidt, "Uncovering the keys to new product success," *Engineering Management Review* 21, 4 (Winter 1993): 5–18; R. G. Cooper and E. J. Kleinschmidt, *New Products: The Key Factors in Success* (Chicago: American Marketing Assoc., 1990); R. G. Cooper, "Pre-development activities determine new product success," *Industrial Marketing Management* 17, 3 (1988): 237–247; R. G. Cooper and E. J. Kleinschmidt, "An investigation into the new product process: Steps, deficiencies, and impact," *Journal of Product Innovation Management* 3, 2 (1986): 71–85; R. G. Cooper and E. J. Kleinschmidt, "New products: What separates winners from losers," *Journal of Product Innovation Management* 4, 3 (1987): 169–184.

21. These benchmarking studies were undertaken by the author and his colleague, Professor Elko Kleinschmidt, and are reported in R. G. Cooper and E. J. Kleinschmidt, "Winning businesses in product development: Critical success factors," *Research-Technology Management* 39, 4 (July-August 1996): 18–29; R. G. Cooper and E. J. Kleinschmidt, "Benchmarking the firm's critical success factors in new product development," *Journal of Product Innovation Management* 12, 5 (November 1995): 374–391; R. G. Cooper and E. J. Kleinschmidt, Benchmarking firms' new product performance and practices," *Engineering Management Review* 23, 3 (Fall 1995): 112–120; R. G. Cooper, "New product leadership: Building in the success factors," *New Product Development and Innovation Management* 1, 2 (1999): 125–140; and R. G. Cooper, "Benchmarking new product performance: Results of the best practices study," *European Management Journal* 16, 1 (1998): 1–7.

22. Just in case you get too enamored with these high ROI figures, remember that these highly positive returns must also cover the costs of the many new product projects that were killed prior to launch, as well as the misfires after launch.

Chapter 2

1. A number of studies have focused on resources spent on winners and losers and on the success, fail, and kill rates of new products. One of the most comprehensive was an early study: Booz-Allen & Hamilton, *New Product Management for the 1980s* (New York: Booz-

Allen & Hamilton, Inc., 1982). See also A. Griffith, *Drivers of NPD Success: The 1997 PDMA Report* (Chicago: Product Development & Management Association, 1997).

2. D. S. Hopkins, *New Product Winners and Losers,* Conference Board Report #773, 1980; and D. S. Hopkins and E. L. Bailey, "New product pressures," *Conference Board Record* 8 (1971): 16–24.

3. Our recent benchmarking studies that looked at quality of execution of key tasks include the following: R. G. Cooper and E. J. Kleinschmidt, "Winning businesses in product development: Critical success factors," *Research-Technology Management* 39, 4 (July-August 1996): 18–29. Also by the same authors: "Benchmarking the firm's critical success factors in new product development," *Journal of Product Innovation Management* 12, 5 (November 1995): 374–391; and "Benchmarking firms' new product performance and practices," *Engineering Management Review* 23, 3 (Fall 1995): 112–120. Our first study of failures goes back to the 1970s: R. G. Cooper, "Why new industrial products fail," *Industrial Marketing Management* 4 (1975): 315–26. But the reasons remain much the same!

4. R. G. Cooper and E. J. Kleinschmidt, "Resource allocation in the new product process," *Industrial Marketing Management* 17, 3 (1988): 249–262.

5. R. G. Cooper and E. J. Kleinschmidt, *New Products: The Key Factors in Success* (Chicago: American Marketing Assoc., 1990), monograph.

6. Booz-Allen & Hamilton, *New Product Management for the 1980s* (New York: Booz-Allen & Hamilton, Inc., 1982).

7. Ibid.

Chapter 3

1. See R. G. Cooper, "The invisible success factors in product innovation," *Journal of Product Innovation Management* 16, 2 (April 1999): 115–133.

2. Reports of studies of success/failure include R. G. Cooper, "New products: What separates the winners from the losers?" in *PDMA Handbook for New Product Development,* ed. Milton D Rosenau Jr. (New York: John Wiley & Sons, 1996); R. G. Cooper, "Developing new products on time, in time," *Research and Technology Management* 38, 5 (September-October 1995), 49–57; R. G. Cooper, "Debunking the myths of new product development," *Research and Technology Management* 37, 4 (July-August 1994): 40–50; and M. M. Montoya-Weiss and R. J. Calantone, "Determinants of new product performance: A review and meta analysis," *Journal of Product Innovation Management* 11, 5 (November 1994): 397–417.

3. A. Griffin, *Drivers of NPD Success: The 1997 PDMA Report* (Chicago: Product Development and Management Association, 1997).

4. R. G. Cooper, "Introducing successful new products," *MCB Monographs, European Journal of Marketing* 10, 1976.

5. NewProd is a registered trademark of the author in the United States and Canada.

6. The first NewProd study paved the way for a succession of success/failure investigations. It appeared in R. G. Cooper, "The dimensions of industrial new product success and failure," *Journal of Marketing* 43 (Summer 1979): 93–103; and R. G. Cooper, "Identifying industrial new product success: Project NewProd," *Industrial Marketing Management* 8 (May 1979): 124–135.

7. M. A. Maidique and B. J. Zirger, "A study of success and failure in product innovation: The case of the U.S. electronics industry," *IEEE Transactions in Engineering Management* 31 (November 1984): 192–203; M. A. Maidique and B. J. Zirger, "The new product learning cycle," *Research Policy* 14, 6 (1985): 299–313; and B. J. Zirger and M. A. Maidique, "A model of new product development: An empirical test," *Management Science* 36, 7 (1990): 867–883.

8. Booz-Allen & Hamilton, *New Product Management for the 1980s* (New York: Booz-Allen & Hamilton, Inc., 1982).

9. E. Wilson, *Product Development Process, Product Definition Guide, Release 1.0*, internal Hewlett-Packard document, Palo Alto, Calif., 1991.

10. M. X. Song, M. M. Montoya-Weiss, and J. B. Schmidt, "Antecedents and consequences of cross-functional cooperation: A comparison of R&D, manufacturing, and marketing perspectives," *Journal of Product Innovation Management* 14 (1997): 34–47.

11. E. W. Larson and D. H. Gobeli, "Organizing for product development projects," *Journal of Product Innovation Management* 5 (1988): 180–190.

12. More recent NewProd studies have been undertaken by Cooper and Kleinschmidt and are summarized in references in notes 1 and 2 above. Parts of this section are taken from R. G. Cooper and E. J. Kleinschmidt, *New Products: The Key Factors in Success* (Chicago: American Marketing Assoc., 1990), monograph.

13. For NewProd in the chemical industry, see R. G. Cooper and Kleinschmidt, "Major new products: What distinguishes the winners in the chemical industry?" *Journal of Product Innovation Management* 2, 10 (March 1993): 90–111; and R. G. Cooper and E. J. Kleinschmidt, "New product success in the chemical industry," *Industrial Marketing Management* 22, 2 (1993): 85–99.

14. R. G. Cooper and E. J. Kleinschmidt, "Winning businesses in product development: Critical success factors," *Research-Technology Management* 39, 4 (July-August 1996): 18–29.

15. R. G. Cooper, "Benchmarking new product performance: Results of the best practices study," *European Management Journal* 16, 1 (1998): 1–7.

16. A. Griffin, "PDMA research on new product development: Updating trends and benchmarking best practices," *Journal of Product Innovation Management* 14, 6 (1998): 429–458.

17. Mercer Management Consulting, Inc., in conjunction with *R&D Magazine* conducted a survey of 193 R&D managers. See *High Performance New Product Development Practices That Set Leaders Apart* (Boston: Mercer Management Consulting, November 1994).

18. Product Development Consulting Inc. developed a list of best practices in product definition from 129 responses. See S. Mello and D. Vermette, "Developing breakthrough products: How the best in class do it," *Proceedings, Management Roundtable Conference on Product Development Best Practices for Defining Customer Needs*, New Orleans, La., January 1995.

19. Based on a survey of more than 200 organizations from six industry groups: *Product Development Leadership for Technology-Based Companies: Measurement and Management—A Prelude to Action* (Weston, Mass.: Pittiglio Rabin Todd and McGrath, 1995).

20. Based on 134 responses from seven industries: *Southwestern Bell Telephone Product Development Benchmarking Study* (Fact Finders, Inc., September 1996).

21. A. Griffin, *Drivers of NPD Success: The 1997 PDMA Report* (Chicago: Product Development and Management Association, 1997).

22. Ibid.

23. ProBE: Product Benchmarking and Evaluation. Respondents in your company rate the business in terms of eighty characteristics—both performance and practices. Results are tabulated and, through bar charts, are compared to other companies: the top 20 percent (best) performers and the average business. This evaluation enables you to immediately spot critical areas of weakness that need fixing in your business. See: www.prod-dev.com; also see Appendix A for more details.

Chapter 4

1. Some of these success factors are reported in various publications. See for example, R. G. Cooper, "New product development," in *International Encyclopedia of Business and Management: Encyclopedia of Marketing,* ed. M. J. Baker (London: International Thomson Business Press, 1999), pp. 342–355; R. G. Cooper, "New product leadership: Building in the success factors," *New Product Development and Innovation Management* 1, 2 (1999): 125–140; and R. G. Cooper, "The invisible success factors in product innovation," *Journal of Product Innovation Management* 16, 2 (April 1999): 115–133.

2. Havelock and Elder as cited in E. M. Rogers, "The R&D/Marketing Interface in the Technological Innovation Process," in *Managing the R&D/Marketing Interface for Process Success: The Telecommunications Focus,* vol. 1, *Advances in Telecommunications Management,* ed. Massoud M. Saghafi and Ashok K. Gupta (Greenwich, Conn.: JAI Press, 1990).

3. R. G. Cooper, "Stage-gate systems: A new tool for managing new products," *Business Horizons* 33, 3 (May-June 1990):44–54.

4. Ibid.

5. R. G. Cooper, "The new product process: A decision guide for managers," *Journal of Marketing Management* 3, 3 (1988): 238–255.

6. Cooper, "The invisible success factors in product innovation"; Cooper, "New product leadership"; and R. G. Cooper, "Developing new products on time, in time," *Research and Technology Management* 38, 5 (September-October 1995): 49–57.

7. C. M. Crawford, "Protocol: New tool for product innovation," *Journal of Product Innovation Management* 2 (1984): 85–91.

8. E. Wilson, *Product Development Process, Product Definition Guide, Release 1.0,* internal Hewlett-Packard document, Palo Alto, Calif., 1991.

9. R. G. Cooper, "Winning at new products and services," *Ivy Business Journal* 64, 4 (July 2000): 52–58.

10. Ibid.

11. E. J. Kleinschmidt, unpublished research results, McMaster University, School of Business, Hamilton, Ontario, Canada, 1999. The study cited is J. King, "Poor planning kills projects, pushes costs up," *Computerworld,* September 22, 1997.

12. Cited in "Doubts linger over clearing solution," *Risk,* October 1999, p. 44.

13. T. Peters, *Thriving on Chaos* (New York: Harper & Row, 1988), p. 261.

14. A. Griffin, *Drivers of NPD Success: The 1997 PDMA Report* (Chicago: Product Development and Management Association, 1997).

15. Peters, *Thriving on Chaos.*

16. Ibid., p. 302.

17. These very close-to-home projects most often were incremental products, modifications, and tweaks; they leverage the firm's competencies very well but provide little opportunity for product differentiation.

18. A. J. Campbell and R. G. Cooper, "Do customer partnerships improve success rates?" *Industrial Marketing Management* 28, 5 (1999): 507–519.

19. M. E. Porter, *Competitive Advantage: Creating and Sustaining Superior Performance* (New York: Free Press, 1985).

20. G. Day, *Analysis for Strategic Marketing Decisions* (St. Paul, Minn.: West Publishing, 1986); and La Rue Hosmer, *Strategic Management: Concepts and Cases* (Englewood Cliffs, N.J.: Prentice-Hall).

21. R. G. Cooper and E. J. Kleinschmidt, "Winning businesses in product development: Critical success factors," *Research-Technology Management* 39, 4 (July-August 1996): 18–29.

22. R. G. Cooper, "The NewProd system: The industry experience," *Journal of Product Innovation Management* 9 (1992): 113–127.

23. Parts of this section are taken from Cooper, "The invisible success factors in product innovation."

24. R. G. Cooper and E. J. Kleinschmidt, "Resource allocation in the new product process," *Industrial Marketing Management* 17, 3 (1988): 249–262.

25. R. G. Cooper, S. J. Edgett, and E. J. Kleinschmidt, "New problems, new solutions: Making portfolio management more effective," *Research-Technology Management* 43, 2 (2000): 18–33.

26. This resource capacity analysis is taken from Cooper, "The invisible success factors in product innovation."

27. This section is taken from R. G. Cooper, *Product Leadership: Creating and Launching Superior New Products* (Reading, Mass.: Perseus Books, 1998).

28. PDMA best practices study; see Griffin, *Drivers of NPD Success.*

29. C. M. Crawford, "The hidden costs of accelerated product development," *Journal of Product Innovation Management* 9, 3 (September 1992): 188–199.

30. Peters, *Thriving on Chaos*, p. 257.

31. First-generation new product processes are described in Booz-Allen & Hamilton, *New Product Management for the 1980s* (New York: Booz-Allen & Hamilton, Inc., 1982).

32. See Griffin, *Drivers of NPD Success.*

Chapter 5

1. This chapter is taken from many sources: R. G. Cooper, "Overhauling the new product process," *Industrial Marketing Management* 25, 6 (November 1996), 465–482; R. G. Cooper and E. J. Kleinschmidt, "Stage gate systems for new product success," *Marketing Management* 1, 4 (1993): 20–29; R. G. Cooper, "The new product process: A decision guide for managers," *Journal of Marketing Management* 3, 3 (1988): 238–255; R. G. Cooper, "Stage-gate systems: A new tool for managing new products," *Business Horizons* 33, 3 (May-June): 1990; and R. G. Cooper, "A process model for industrial new product development," *IEEE Transactions in Engineering Management* EM 30 (February 1983): 2–11.

2. A. Griffin, *Drivers of NPD Success: The 1997 PDMA Report* (Chicago: Product Development and Management Association, 1997).

3. Bro Uttal, "Speeding new ideas to market," *Fortune* (March 1987): 62–66.

4. A test market or trial sell is both expensive and time consuming, yields information that can be sometimes obtained through other methods, and hence is not always appropriate for every project.

5. "Stage-gate" is a term coined by the author; see R. G. Cooper, "The new product process: A decision guide for managers," *Journal of Marketing Management* 3, 3 (1988): 238–255. Second-generation processes are what many companies began to implement toward the end of the 1980s; the third-generation processes of the late 1990s have improved time efficiencies. See R. G. Cooper, "Third-generation new product processes," *Journal of Product Innovation Management* 11 (1994): 3–14.

6. The first-generation development process was a technical process, designed largely for use by technical or R&D people only.

7. "Camping out" is the term that Hewlett-Packard uses to describe this immersion research, whereby the project team or designers spend time with customers learning about the customers' operation, needs, problems, and so on.

8. Concept tests can be done globally on the Internet. See, for example, Global Market Insite, Inc., at: www.GMI-MR.com

9. See PDMA study in Griffin, *Drivers of NPD Success*. For a thorough description of third-generation new product processes, see Cooper, "Third-generation new product processes."

10. See PDMA study in Griffin, *Drivers of NPD Success*.

11. Parts of this section are taken from Cooper, "Third-generation new-product processes"; and R. G. Cooper, *Product Leadership: Creating and Launching Superior New Products* (Reading, Mass: Perseus Books, 1998).

12. L. Yapps Cohen, P. W. Kamienski, and R. L. Espino, "Gate system focuses industrial basic research," *Research-Technology Management* 41, 5 (July-August 1998): 34–37.

Chapter 6

1. Ro Pavlick and Dodge Bingham modified the typical stage-gate process by adding their Discovery Stage. Questions above are taken from the *Thomson Solutions Process* (internal company document).

2. M. E. Porter, *Competitive Advantage: Creating and Sustaining Superior Performance* (New York: Free Press, 1985).

3. O. Gadiesh and J. L. Gilbert, "How to map your industry's profit pool," *Harvard Business Review* (May-June 1998): 3–11.

4. Parts of this section on scenarios is taken from P. Schwartz, "The official future, self delusion, and value of scenarios," *Financial Times*, May 2, 2000, Mastering Risk section, pp. 6–7. He is also author of *The Art of the Long View* and is former head of scenario-planning at Royal Dutch Shell.

5. R. Sears and M. Barry, "Product Value Analysis™: Product interaction predicts profits," *Innovation* (Winter 1993): 13–18.

6. Viactiv™ is a trademark of Mead Johnson Nutritionals.

7. Source of information on Viactiv™ is internal company documents and *Viactiv™ "Energy Crisis" Summit White Paper*; web-page: www.viactiv.com

8. For more information on the use of lead users in idea generation see E. A. Von Hippel, M. Sonnack, and J. Churchill, *Developing Breakthrough Products and Services: The Lead User Method* (Minneapolis: St. Lucie Press). See also C. Herstatt and E. A. Von Hippel, "From experience: Developing new product concepts via the lead user method—A case study in a 'low tech' field," *Journal of Product Innovation Management* 9 (1992): 213–221; G. L. Urban and E. A. Von Hippel, "Lead user analyses for the development of new industrial products," *Management Science* 34, 5 (May 1988): 569–582; E. A. Von Hippel, *The Sources of Innovation* (New York: Oxford University Press, 1988).

9. Adapted from E. A. Von Hippel, S. Thomke, and M. Sonnack, "Creating breakthroughs at 3M," *Harvard Business Review* (September-October 1999): 47–57.

10. L. Yapps Cohen, P. W. Kamienski, and R. L. Espino, "Gate system focuses industrial basic research," *Research-Technology Management* 41, 6 (July- August 1998): 34–37.

11. Von Hippel, *The Sources of Innovation*.

Chapter 7

1. A. J. Campbell and R. G. Cooper, "Do customer partnerships improve success rates?" *Industrial Marketing Management* 28, 5 (1999): 507–519.

2. J. Terninko, *Step-by-Step Product Design*, 2nd ed. (Minneapolis: St. Lucie Press, 1997).

3. Much of this section is taken from an excellent summary of QFD: A. Griffin and J. R. Hauser, "The Marketing and R&D Interface," in *Handbook: MS/OR in Marketing*, ed. G. L. Lillien and J. Eliasberg (Amsterdam: Elsevier Scientific, 1992). See also: A. Griffin, "Evaluating QFD's use in firms as a process for developing products," *Journal of Product Innovation Management* 9, 3 (1992): 17–28.

4. J. R. Hauser and D. Clausing, "The House of Quality," *Harvard Business Review* (May-June 1988): 33–56.

5. Griffin and Hauser, "The Marketing and R&D Interface."

6. Ibid.

7. Ibid.

Chapter 8

1. The first part of this chapter is based on Chapter 5 in R. G. Cooper, *Product Leadership: Creating and Launching Superior New Products* (Reading, Mass.: Perseus Books, 1998), which in turn is based on the second edition of this book.

2. R. G. Cooper, "The NewProd system: The industry experience," *Journal of Product Innovation Management* 9 (1992): 113–127.

3. See R. G. Cooper and E. J. Kleinschmidt, "Winning businesses in product development: Critical success factors," *Research-Technology Management* 39, 4 (July-August 1996): 18–29; R. G. Cooper and E. J. Kleinschmidt, "Benchmarking the firm's critical success factors in new product development," *Journal of Product Innovation Management* 12, 5 (November 1995): 374–391; R. G. Cooper and E. J. Kleinschmidt, "Benchmarking firms' new product performance and practices," *Engineering Management Review* 23, 3 (Fall 1995): 112–120; R. G. Cooper, "New product leadership: Building in the success factors," *New Product Development and Innovation Management* 1, 2 (1999): 125–140; and R. G. Cooper, "Benchmarking new product performance: Results of the best practices study," *European Management Journal* 16, 1 (1998): 1–7.

4. R. G. Cooper and E. J. Kleinschmidt, "An investigation into the new product process: Steps, deficiencies, and impact," *Journal of Product Innovation Management* 3, 2 (1986): 71–85.

5. See A. Griffin, *Drivers of NPD Success: The 1997 PDMA Report* (Chicago: Product Development and Management Association, 1997); also Booz-Allen & Hamilton, *New Product Management for the 1980s* (New York: Booz-Allen & Hamilton, Inc., 1982).

6. M. R. Baker, "R&D project selection models: An assessment," *IEEE Transactions on Engineering Management* EM–21 (November 1974): 165–171; see also M. R. Baker and J. Freeland, "Recent advances in R&D benefit measurement and project selection methods," *Management Science* 21 (1975): 1164–1175.

7. Baker, "R&D project selection models.".

8. A good summary article on such methods is B. Jackson, "Decision methods for selecting a portfolio of R&D projects," *Research Management* (September-October 1983): 21–26.

9. P. Roussel, K. N. Saad, and T. J. Erickson, *Third Generation R&D: Managing the Link to Corporate Strategy* (Cambridge: Harvard Business School Press and Arthur D. Little, 1991).

10. R. G. Cooper, S. J. Edgett, and E. J. Kleinschmidt, *R&D Portfolio Management Best Practices Study* (Washington, D.C.: Industrial Research Institute, 1997); R. G. Cooper, S. J. Edgett, and E. J. Kleinschmidt, "Best practices for managing R&D portfolios," *Research-Technology Management* 41, 4 (July-August 1998): 20–33; and R. G. Cooper, S. J. Edgett, and E. J. Kleinschmidt, "New product portfolio management: Practices and performance," *Journal of Product Innovation Management* 16, 4 (July 1999): 333–351.

11. See Baker, "R&D project selection models"; and Baker and Freeland, "Recent advances in R&D benefit measurement."

12. Taken from a presentation by H. Korotkin, Controller, New Product Process, Polaroid Corporation, Portfolio Planning and Management for New Product Development Conference, by the Institute of International Research and Product Development Management Association, December 1996. See also R. More and B. Little, "The application of discriminant analysis to the prediction of sales forecast uncertainty in new product situations," *Journal of Operations Research Society* 31 (1980): 71–77.

13. Cooper, Edgett, and Kleinschmidt, *R&D Portfolio Management Best Practices Study*.

14. Faulkner, "Applying 'options thinking' to R&D valuation." For more information on this issue and options pricing theory (OPT) in general, see R. Deaves and I. Krinsky, "New tools for investment decision-making: Real options analysis," McMaster University Working Paper, April 1997; T. Faulkner, "Applying 'options thinking' to R&D valuation," *Research-Technology Management* 39, 3 (May-June 1996): 50–57; T. Luehrman, "What's it worth? A general manager's guide to valuation," *Harvard Business Review* (May-June 1997): 1321–1342.

15. See Cooper, Edgett, and Kleinschmidt, *R&D Portfolio Management Best Practices Study*.

16. W. E. Souder, "A system for using R&D project evaluation methods," *Research Management* 21 (September 1978): 21–37.

17. *Aliah STP* was developed by Professor Aly Abulleil in Pittsburgh. It is a paired comparison method. Contact: SPIRC (Southern Pennsylvania Industrial Research Council, Pittsburgh), which helps firms implement the method.

18. G. L. Lillien and P. Kotler, *Marketing Decision Making: A Model-Building Approach* (New York: Harper & Row, 1983); W. E. Souder and T. Mandakovic, "R&D project selection models," *Research Management* 29, 4 (1986): 36–42; and F. Zahedi, "The analytic hierarchy process: A survey of the method and its applications," *Interfaces* 16, 4 (1986): 96–108.

19. NewProd™ is a registered trade name of R. G. Cooper and Associates Consultants, Inc., a member firm of the Product Development Institute, Inc. See: www.prod-dev.com. NewProd is also available from Sopheon-Teltech, Inc.: www.sopheon.com

20. S. B. Graves and J. L. Ringuest, "Evaluating competing R&D investments," *Research and Technology Management* (July-August 1991): 32–36.

21. In the IRR calculation, the discount rate is determined such that the NPV equals zero.

22. Faulkner, "Applying 'options thinking' to R&D valuation.".

23. A. Albala, "Stage approach for the evaluation and selection of R&D projects," *IEEE Transactions on Engineering Management* EM–22 (November 1975): 153–162.

24. R. G. Cooper, "A process model for industrial new product development," *IEEE Transactions on Engineering Management* EM–30 (February 1983): 2–11.

25. See Albala, "Stage approach for the evaluation and selection of R&D projects."

26. Ibid.

27. In third-generation *Stage-Gate*™ processes with fuzzy gates, a fifth decision is possible, namely, "conditional go" (see Chapter 5).

28. Much of this section of the chapter is taken from two articles that the author wrote with coauthors: R. G. Cooper, S. J. Edgett, and E. J. Kleinschmidt, "Portfolio management in new product development: Lessons from the leaders—Part I," *Research-Technology Management* 40, 5 (September-October 1997): 16–28; and R. G. Cooper, S. J. Edgett, and E. J. Kleinschmidt, "Portfolio management in new product development: Lessons from the leaders—Part II," *Research-Technology Management* 40, 6 (November-December 1997): 43–57. For more detail on portfolio management, see R. G. Cooper, S. J. Edgett, and E. J.

Kleinschmidt, *Portfolio Management for New Products* (Reading, Mass.: Perseus Books, 1998).

29. Cooper, Edgett, and Kleinschmidt, "Portfolio management in new product development," Part I, p. 16.

30. Cooper, Edgett, and Kleinschmidt, "Best practices for managing R&D portfolios."

31. The rest of this chapter is taken from R. G. Cooper, S. J. Edgett, and E. J. Kleinschmidt, "New problems, new solutions: Making portfolio management more effective," *Research-Technology Management* 43, 2 (2000): 18–33.

32. For a complete illustration of these various bubble diagrams and pie charts—and there are many more examples—see the book and articles on portfolio management listed in Note 28.

33. Resource capacity analysis is described in more detail in R. G. Cooper, "The invisible success factors in product innovation," *Journal of Product Innovation Management* 16, 2 (April 1999): 115–133. See also Chapter 4.

34. Kodak's portfolio management approach is described in E. Patton, "The strategic investment process: Driving corporate vision through portfolio creation," *Proceedings, Product Portfolio Management: Balancing Resources with Opportunity,* Management Roundtable, Boston, 1999.

35. Based on the results of a study of portfolio management practices.; see Cooper, Edgett, and Kleinschmidt, *R&D Portfolio Management Best Practices Study.*

Chapter 9

1. M. D. Roseanau Jr., "Phased approach speeds up new product development," *Research and Development* 30, 11 (November 1988): 52–55.

2. W. J. Vrakking, "The innovative organization," *Long Range Planning* 23 (1990): 94–102.

3. C. M. Crawford, "The hidden costs of accelerated product development," *Journal of Product Innovation Management* 9, 3 (September 1992): 188–199.

4. Some of this section is taken from our *Stage-Gate*-in-a-box model, called *RAPID*. *RAPID* is a best-in-class, best-in-world *Stage-Gate* process—a composite model based on many leading firms. It is available from the Product Development Institute Inc.: www.proddev.com

5. See NewProd studies, Chapter 1, Note 20.

Chapter 10

1. R. Piirto, "VALS the second time," *American Demographics* (July 1991): 6.

2. E. Schonfeld, "Corporations of the world unite! You have nothing to lose but your supply chains," *eCompany Now* 1, 1 (June 2000): 123–132.

3. Parts of this section on e-commerce are taken from a book coauthored by the author: R. G. Cooper and S. J. Edgett, *Product Development for the Service Sector* (Reading, Mass.: Perseus Books, 1999), ch. 6.

4. G. Hamel and J. Stampler, "The e-corporation," *Fortune*, December 7, 1998, 80–93; and E. Schonfeld, "Schwab puts it all on-line," *Fortune*, December 7, 1998, 94–100.

5. Some items in this paragraph are taken from Schonfeld, "Corporations of the world unite!"

6. See NewProd studies, Chapter 1, note 20.

7. R. D. Buzzell et al., "Market share: A key to profitability," *Harvard Business Review* (January-February 1975): 97–107. See also S. Schoeffler, "Impact of strategic planning on profit performance," *Harvard Business Review* (March-April 1974): 137–145.

8. "The Product Portfolio," pamphlet no. 66 (Boston: Boston Consulting Group, 1970).

Chapter 11

1. A. Griffin, *Drivers of NPD Success: The 1997 PDMA Report* (Chicago: Product Development Management Association, 1997).

2. R. G. Cooper and E. J. Kleinschmidt, *Formal Processes for Managing New Products: The Industry Experience* (Hamilton, Ont., Canada: McMaster University, 1991). See also R. G. Cooper and E. J. Kleinschmidt, "New product processes at leading industrial firms," *Industrial Marketing Management* 10, 2 (May 1991): 137–147.

3. Twenty-nine managers in nine business units in five leading U.S. firms that had implemented formal new product processes took part in the study.

4. A. Griffin, "Metrics for measuring product development cycle time," *Journal of Product Innovation Management* 10, 2 (March 1993): 112–125.

5. The percentage of managers noting. The total is more than 100 percent since comments are not mutually exclusive.

6. For more information on *ProBE*, see: www.prod-dev.com and Appendix A.

7. Griffin, *Drivers of NPD Success*. See also Chapter 3, notes 16–19.

8. R. G. Cooper, S. J. Edgett, and E. J. Kleinschmidt, *Portfolio Management for New Products* (Reading, Mass.: Perseus Books, 1998).

9. R. G. Cooper, *Product Leadership: Creating and Launching Superior New Products* (Reading, Mass.: Perseus Books, 1998).

10. R. G. Cooper and S. J. Edgett, *Product Development for the Service Sector* (Reading, Mass.: Perseus Books, 1999).

11. Available from Product Development Institute, Inc. (www.prod-dev.com); from Stage-Gate.Com, Inc. (www.stage-gate.com); and from Sopheon (www.sopheon.com).

Chapter 12

1. See the benchmarking studies in Chapter 1, Note 21.

2. This chapter is based, in part, on Chapter 11 of the 2nd edition of this book, and it draws heavily on Chapter 7 of my book *Product Leadership: Creating and Launching Superior New Products* (Reading, Mass.: Perseus Books, 1998), and on the recent article, R. G. Cooper, "Product innovation and technology strategy," a contribution to the series "Succeeding in technological innovation," *Research-Technology Management* 43, 1 (January-February 2000): 28–44.

3. Booz-Allen & Hamilton, *New Product Management for the 1980s* (New York: Booz-Allen & Hamilton, Inc., 1982).

4. C. M. Crawford, "Defining the charter for product innovation," *Sloan Management Review* (1980): 3–12.

5. D. J. Luck and A. E. Prell, *Market Strategy* (Englewood Cliffs, N.J.: Prentice Hall, 1968), p. 2.

6. I. H. Ansoff, *Corporate Strategy* (New York: McGraw-Hill, 1965).

7. R. E. Corey, "Key options in market selection and product planning," *Harvard Business Review* (September-October 1978): 119–128.

8. Some sections in this chapter are taken from R. G. Cooper, S. J. Edgett, and E. J. Kleinschmidt, *Portfolio Management for New Products* (Reading, Mass.: Perseus Books, 1998).

9. Crawford, "Defining the charter for product innovation."

10. J. B. Quinn, "Formulating strategy one step at a time," *Journal of Business Strategy* 1 (1981): 42–63.

11. Booz-Allen & Hamilton, *New Product Management*.

12. H. Nystrom, "Company strategies for research and development," in *Industrial Innovation*, edited by N. Baker (New York: MacMillan, 1979); H. Nystrom, *Company Strategies for Research and Development*, Report S–750 07, Institute for Economics and Statistics, Uppsala, Sweden, 1977; H. Nystrom and B. Edvardsson, *Research and Development Strategies for Swedish Companies in the Farm Machinery Industry*, Institute for Economics and Statistics, Uppsala, Sweden, 1978; and H. Nystrom and B. Edvardsson, *Research and Development Strategies for Four Swedish Farm Machine Companies*, Institute for Economics and Statistics, Uppsala, Sweden, 1980.

13. The Cooper strategy studies consist of the following: R. G. Cooper, "The performance impact of product innovation strategies," *European Journal of Marketing* 18, 5 (1984): 5–54; R. G. Cooper, "How new product strategies impact on performance," *Journal of Product Innovation Management* 1 (1984): 5–18; R. G. Cooper, "The strategy-performance link in product innovation," *R&D Management* 14 (October 1984): 151–164; R. G. Cooper, "New product strategies: What distinguishes the top performers?" *Journal of Product Innovation Management* 2 (1984): 151–164; R. G. Cooper, "Industrial firms' new product strategies," *Journal of Business Research* 13 (April 1985): 107–121; and R. G. Cooper, "Overall corporate strategies for new product programs," *Industrial Marketing Management* 14 (1985): 179–183.

14. M. M. Menke, "Essentials of R&D strategic excellence," *Research-Technology Management* 40, 5 (September-October 1997): 42–47.

15. Paragraph taken from R. G. Cooper, "Benchmarking new product performance: Results of the best practices study," *European Management Journal* 16, 1 (1998): 1–7.

16. For benchmarking studies, see Chapter 1, Note 21.

17. R. E. Miles and C. C. Snow, *Organizational Strategy: Structure and Process* (New York: McGraw-Hill, 1978).

18. These definitions are taken from an article by Griffin and Page, who provide a breakdown of project types by strategy elected. See A. Griffin and A. L. Page, "PDMA success measurement project: Recommended measures for product development success and failure," *Journal of Product Innovation Management* 13, 6 (November 1996): 478–495.

19. Ibid.

20. See strategy studies listed in Note 13.

21. Roger C. Bennett and R. G. Cooper, "The product life cycle trap," *Business Horizons* (September-October 1984): 7–16.

22. Booz-Allen & Hamilton, *New Product Management*.

23. Ibid.

24. Griffin and Page, "PDMA success measurement project."

25. G. S. Day, "A strategic perspective on product planning," *Journal of Contemporary Business* (Spring 1975): 1–34.

26. See strategy studies listed in Note 13.

27. Booz-Allen & Hamilton, *New Product Management*.

28. Day, "A strategic perspective."

29. Corey, "Key options in market selection."

30. D. F. Abell, *Defining the Business* (Englewood Cliffs, N.J.: Prentice Hall, 1980).

31. Crawford, "Defining the charter for product innovation."

32. The original concept for developing a product innovation strategy for the business is found in R. G. Cooper, "Strategic planning for successful technological innovation," *Business Quarterly* 43 (Spring 1978): 46–54. See also R. G. Cooper, "Defining the new product strategy," *IEEE Transactions on Engineering Management* EM–34, 3 (1987): 184–193; and R. G. Cooper, "Identifying and evaluating new product opportunities," in *The Interface of Marketing and Strategy*, ed. G. S. Day, B. Weitz, and R. Wensley, vol. 4 of *Strategic*

Management Policy and Planning: A Multivolume Treatise (Greenwich, Conn.: JAI Press, 1990).

33. Technological elasticity captures the slope of the technology S-curve: the curve that plots product performance versus development money spent to achieve this. Technology elasticity answers the question, Will a dollar spent on product development in this arena yield products with significant competitive advantage?

34. The usual axes are "technology newness to the company" and "market newness to the company."

35. The PDMA definition of "platform" is found in the glossary of *The PDMA Handbook of New Product Development*, ed. M. D. Rosenau Jr. (New York: John Wiley & Sons, 1996).

36. See M. H. Meyer and A. P. Lehnerd, *The Power of Platforms* (New York: Free Press, 1997).

Appendix A

1. See benchmarking studies in Chapter 1, Note 21.

2. *ProBE* was developed jointly by Jens Arleth of U3 Innovation Management (Copenhagen) and Robert Cooper and Scott Edgett of Product Development Institute, Inc.

Appendix B

1. *NewProd*™ is a registered trade name of R. G. Cooper and Associates Consultants, Inc., a member firm of the Product Development Institute, Inc. See: www.prod-dev.com. *NewProd* is also available from Sopheon-Teltech: www.sopheon.com

2. For more information on Procter & Gamble's portfolio model, see R. G. Cooper, S. J. Edgett, and E. J. Kleinschmidt, *Portfolio Management for New Products* (Reading, Mass.: Perseus Books, 1998), p. 62.

3. For more information on the *NewProd*™ model, see: www.prod-dev.com. See also R. G. Cooper, "Selecting winning new products: Using the *NewProd* system," *Journal of Product Innovation Management* 2 (1987): 34–44; and R. G. Cooper, "The *NewProd* system: The industry experience," *Journal of Product Innovation Management* 9 (1992): 113–127.

4. For example, Procter & Gamble uses the *NewProd*™ model and reports a predictive ability of about 84 percent. See R. E. Davis, "The role of market research in the development of new consumer products," *Journal of Product Innovation Management* 10, 4 (1993): 309–317; and J.J.A.M. Bronnenberg and M. L. van Engelen, "A Dutch test with the *NewProd* model," *R&D Management* 18, 4 (1988): 321–332.

Index